T0306173

HUMAN FACTORS FOR CIVIL FLIGHT DECK DESIGN

For Megan Elizabeth

Human Factors for Civil Flight Deck Design

Edited by
DON HARRIS
Cranfield University

Routledge
Taylor & Francis Group

LONDON AND NEW YORK

First published 2004 by Ashgate Publishing

2 Park Square, Milton Park, Abingdon, Oxon OX14 4RN
711 Third Avenue, New York, NY 10017, USA

Routledge is an imprint of the Taylor & Francis Group, an informa business

First issued in paperback 2016

British Library Cataloguing in Publication Data
Human factors for civil flight deck design
   1.Airplanes - Cockpits - Design and construction
   2.Airplanes - Design and construction - Human factors
   I.Harris, Don, 1961-
   629.1'3445

Library of Congress Cataloging-in-Publication Data
Human factors for civil flight deck design / [compiled] by Don Harris.
   p. cm.
  Includes index.
  ISBN 0-7546-1380-1
 1. Airplanes--Cockpits. 2. Human engineering. I. Harris, Don, 1961-

  TL681.C6H37 2004
  629.135--dc22

                                     2004015358

ISBN 978-0-7546-1380-0 (hbk)
ISBN 978-1-138-26377-2 (pbk)

Transfered to Digital Printing in 2012

Contents

Contents

Contributors

Guy A. Boy is President of the European Institute of Cognitive Sciences and Engineering (EURISCO International). He received his Ph.D. in Automation and System Design from the Ecole Nationale Supérieure de l'Aéronautique et de l'Espace (ENSAE) in 1980, his 'Habilitation à Diriger des Recherches' in 1992 (LAFORIA, Paris VI), and his Full Professorship Qualification in Computer Science and Psychology in 1994. He was a Research Scientist at the Office National d'Etudes et de Recherches Aérospatiales (ONERA) from 1980 to 1988. He was a Principal Investigator and Group Leader (Advanced Interaction Media) at NASA Ames Research from 1989 to 1991. His research is in human-centred design of safety-critical dynamic systems. He is the author of three books in the field of cognitive engineering: 'Intelligent Assistant Systems' (Academic Press, 1991), and 'Cognitive Function Analysis' (Ablex, 1998), and the coordinator of the 'French Handbook of Cognitive Engineering' (Hermes-Lavoisier, 2003). From 1995 to 1999, he served as Executive Vice-Chair of the ACM-SIGCHI Executive Committee (Association for Computing Machinery-Special Interest Group on Computer-Human Interaction). He is a member of the French Academy of Aerospace.

Hazel Courteney is Head of Research Management at the UK Civil Aviation Authority (CAA). A Chartered Psychologist and Fellow of the Royal Aeronautical Society, she holds an Honours degree in Psychology, a Masters in Ergonomics (both from Birmingham University) and a Ph.D. in Regulation of Aircraft Flight Deck Design from London University (Goldsmiths College). She has spent ten years working for Westland Helicopters in cockpit design and research, two years working on the Eurofighter Typhoon cockpit design team at BAe Warton, and a further ten years at the CAA. Her first eight years there were spent formulating and implementing new regulatory material to address the crew related aspects of flight deck design during Type Certification, and she was the first Human Factors specialist to be appointed to an international aircraft Type Certification Team. During this time she was also Chairman of the JAA Human

Factors Steering Group and the JAA representative to the transatlantic Harmonisation Working Group. She has now moved on from these responsibilities to lead the CAA Research Management team addressing all areas of safety research for civil aviation. Most recently, she has been appointed Visiting Professor to Cranfield University.

Sidney Dekker received his Ph.D. in 1996 from The Ohio State University, and is currently Associate Professor at Linköping Institute of Technology in Sweden. His specialties are human error, accident investigations and automation. Previously he worked at the British Aerospace Dependable Computing Systems Centre in the UK, the Public Transport Corporation in Melbourne, Australia, and the Massey University School of Aviation in New Zealand. He is a pilot and has completed First Officer training on the DC-9. His latest book is 'The Field Guide to Human Error Investigations'.

Steve Fadden is an Associate with the Human Centered Systems Engineering team at Booz Allen Hamilton in McLean, VA. He serves as a Human Factors and Systems Engineering consultant for multiple government clients, including the FAA, NASA, TSA, FRA, and DIA. He has worked in individual contributor and management positions in Human Factors and Usability Engineering departments with Intel Corporation, PeopleSoft, Inc., and Lockheed Martin Aeronautical Systems. Dr. Fadden is currently an adjunct faculty member in the Human Factors and Applied Cognition program with George Mason University in Virginia, and previously taught Human Computer Interaction at Brigham Young University in Utah. He received his Ph.D. at the University of Illinois in Urbana-Champaign, where his research included the evaluation of display location and conformal symbology, the application of exploratory sequential data analysis techniques, and the use of eye movement measures to assess expert scanning patterns and develop models of cognitive processes.

Daniel Ferro graduated in 1983 in Aeronautics at the Ecole Nationale Supérieure d'Ingénieurs de Constructions Aéronautiques in Toulouse. Since then, he has worked for seven years on Airbus developments (fly-by-wire systems, displays, FMS, Human Factors certification), eight years on research into general cockpit HMI functions and ADS-B applications and he has undertaken five years of research on Hermes European spacecraft operations and HMI functions. Daniel is currently the co-ordinator of the EC co-funded OPTIMAL project. His past projects have included being co-ordinator of the EC co-funded DIVA project, being the Airbus focal point for five other EC co-funded projects and he was also co-ordinator of one major national cockpit project.

Edmund Field graduated from Imperial College of Science and Technology, London with a B.Eng. in Mechanical Engineering. After a short period in industry he pursued his postgraduate education at Cranfield University, graduating with an MSc in Flight Dynamics and a Ph.D. in Flying Qualities. Following a brief period on the staff of the Empire Test Pilots School in England, he moved to McDonnell Douglas in Long Beach, California. Currently he works in the Phantom Works Division of the Boeing Company in Southern California. His research activities include conducting piloted handling qualities experiments using simulators and aircraft and the development of handling qualities criteria and flight control system design guidelines. Additionally, he has supported certification activities on the MD-11 and Boeing 717 aircraft. He also teaches aircraft performance and stability and control at the University of California, Los Angeles.

Don Harris is Reader in Human Factors Engineering in the Human Factors Group at Cranfield University. Since completing his Ph.D. in 1988 on the subject of Human Factors in road traffic accidents, his principal teaching and research interests have been in the design and evaluation of flight deck control and display systems. Until recently he was also an aircraft accident investigator (specialising in Human Factors) on call to the British Army Division of Army Aviation. He is the Chairman of the International Conferences series on Engineering Psychology and Cognitive Ergonomics. Don sits on the UK National Advisory Committee of Human Factors for Aerospace and Defence and the FAA/JAA Human Factors Harmonisation Working Group. He is also co-editor in chief of the academic journal, 'Human Factors and Aerospace Safety' (also published by Ashgate) and sits on the editorial boards of the International Journal of Cognitive Ergonomics and the International Journal of Cognition, Technology and Work.

Piet J. Hoogeboom graduated in 1986 from the Technical University of Delft after studying in the area of Avionics. He works currently works as a senior scientist in the area of Human Factors' Analysis Methods within the Training, Simulation and Human Factors department of NLR in the Netherlands. His research in the aviation domain started with the in-flight investigation of advanced runway approach procedures like the continuous descent and has included the optimisation of information presented on the flight deck. He gained substantial experience with the characteristics of avionics position determination sensors, their integration and the operational use. Working together with psychologists the emphasis of work shifted in 1990 to more objective (e.g. physiological) assessments and the optimisation of the man-machine relationships. The current focus of work is at the autonomous adaptation of working environments towards the actual needs of its users by real-time determination of their functional state based on task performance, machine observed behaviour and physiology, for example EEG, heart rate and eye movements.

Peter G.A.M. Jorna is an Experimental Psychologist who graduated from Groningen University specialising in physiological measurements. His research interests focus on the determinants of potentially unsafe variations in human performance, especially for demanding jobs such as aviation, air traffic control and military and security functions. The necessity for objective measurement techniques for the advance of insights in human performance is a central theme for the research on selection, training and equipment design. Peter held various positions in the field of Human Factors such as research co-ordinator special personnel selection in the Royal Netherlands Navy and research scientist for training as well as deputy department leader of human performance research at the TNO Human Factors Institute, Soesterberg. Peter founded the well-known aviation Human Factors department of the Netherlands Aerospace Laboratory (NLR) and was head of its former Flight Division comprising departments on military flight operations, helicopters, flight mechanics, Human Factors and training and simulation. In that period a great deal of experience was gained with the technological management of effective human-machine integration. Peter participated in a multitude of working groups and projects, such as the FAA/EASA Harmonisation working group on Human Factors for flight decks and project leader of the Eurocontrol Ground Human Machine interface project. Presently, he is the NLR business manager for Training, Human Factors and Cockpit operations and works enthusiastically at Cranfield University as a Professor in Aviation Psychology.

Mandana L.N. Kazem graduated from the University of Bristol with a first class Master of Engineering in Avionic Systems in 1999. After the second year of her degree she completed a year's industrial placement with British Airways Engineering at Heathrow where she worked within the Logistics and Avionics departments of the company. During the final year of her degree she designed and completed a final year project, which laid the foundation for a Ph.D.. The project involved investigation of information display within the cockpit and tackled the issue of pilot task 'involvement'. She presented a paper detailing this research work at the international 'People In Control' conference in Bath, 1999. The Ph.D. in progress is based within both the Aerospace and Psychology departments of the University of Bristol and is currently focusing upon novel information displays.

Brian D. Kelly received a Bachelor of Science in Aerospace Engineering from the University of Southern California in 1978 and a Master of Science in Aeronautics and Astronautics from Stanford University in 1979. He then joined Boeing at the beginning of the 757 and 767 programs in Flight Deck Integration assisting in the development and certification of the crew interfaces for EICAS (Engine Indication and Crew Alerting System) and other airplane systems. Subsequent assignments involved development of guidance, alerting systems, and displays in support of the Boeing-led Windshear Task Force, development and testing of primary flight control interfaces and displays concepts on the 7J7 program, and participation on RTCA and ATA industry committees associated with the definition of crew interfaces and procedures for TCAS. As a manager in Flight Crew Operations Integration from 1991 to 1998, Brian oversaw several aspects of the development and certification of the 777 flight deck including autoflight and primary flight control interfaces and introduction of predictive windshear and terrain awareness and warning systems. He is now a Boeing Technical Fellow and represented Boeing on the ARAC Harmonization Working Group for Flight Crew Error/Flight Crew Performance Considerations in the Flight Deck Certification Process. For the past three years he has been involved in development leading up to the 7E7 flight deck, including certification and validation plans.

Ted Lovesey began a career in Aeronautical Engineering as an apprentice at the Royal Aircraft Establishment at Farnborough. He went on to Cranfield and A & AEE Boscombe Down where he became increasingly involved in ergonomics. He returned to RAE Farnborough to develop techniques to investigate pilot activity patterns. This work led to the Ergonomics Society's prestigious award of the Bartlett Medal. Further work involved the use of flight simulators, trials from Timbuktu to the Arctic, and learning to fly hovercraft and helicopters. His involvement in early simulations of Concorde was followed by Helmet Sight air combat weapons studies. These demonstrated the importance of getting the ergonomics right before the full weapons potential could be achieved. Although much of his activities have been to do with the development and evaluation of military systems, there has been considerable 'spin off' into the civil and health areas. This has taken the form of organising Health Ergonomics courses at the University of Surrey and, more recently, providing basic ergonomics expertise to the UK's primary opto-electronics manufacturer.

René Nibbelke has worked for eight years on Human Factors Research in the Aerospace and Defence industry, contributing to air safety through research and as a member of industry working groups (e.g. the Propulsion Malfunction and Inappropriate Crew Response Working Group and the Human Factors Working Group on Flight Deck Certification). René helped to set-up various European research projects on flight deck design (e.g. DIVA) and aircraft maintenance (ADAMS-2) and initiated an Airbus working group on human error prevention in aircraft maintenance. In 2000, Rene was part of the Airbus Human Factors Operations Group (representing the UK). Rene worked at NLR in Amsterdam and BAE SYSTEMS in Bristol. He is currently a Programme Manager in BAE SYSTEMS.

Jan M. Noyes is a Reader at the University of Bristol. She has published extensively in the area of Human Factors of interface design including work on keyboards, automatic speech recognition, pen-based technologies, and warning systems within an avionics application. She is a Fellow of the Ergonomics Society and an Associate Member of the IEE and the British Psychological Society. In 1999, she was awarded the Otto Edholm medal for her contribution to ergonomics application and research. She has produced over 120 publications including six books, and in 1998 was awarded the IEE Informatics Premium Award for her paper on 'engineering psychology and system safety'. She was also Chair of the 1999 and 2001 IEE People In Control (PIC) conferences, and is on the Editorial Board of the journal *Ergonomics*.

Florence Reuzeau is an Aviation Engineer with a Ph.D. in ergonomics. She has been employed by Airbus since 1988, and has worked for five years as safety assessment specialist (on autopilot, navigation systems). Since 1995, she has organised the Human Factors activity in Airbus France and developed the Human Factors Plan to support aircraft design. The first full-scale applications of this plan are the A380 and the A400M cockpit design to comply with to the new Human Factors regulations. She also participated in setting up the HFOG (Human Factors Operational Group) in 1997 whose objective was to define Human Factors policy for all Airbus domains. She has been the executive secretary of the HFOG since 2000. She is involved in many regulatory activities and participates in several Human Factors research projects in Europe. In particular, during her Ph.D., she studied the different contributions of Test and Airline pilots during the cockpit development cycle in order to understand and rationalise the involvement of users during design and certification.

Gideon Singer is a Senior Test Pilot at Saab Aircraft. Prior to returning to Saab Gideon was at Fairchild-Dornier, Germany, engaged in the development and certification of the new 70-seater Do728. His aviation background started in 1975 as military pilot in the Israeli Air force. In 1989, after completing a M.Sc. in Aeronautics at the Royal Institute of Technology (KTH) Stockholm, Sweden, he was employed by Saab Aircraft in Linköping, as a test pilot and participated in several development and certification projects of commercial aircraft such as the S2000 and S340. Between 1996 and 2000 he was involved in Human Factors research addressing cockpit design including national and European projects. During resent years he published several papers on the subject and completed his doctoral thesis concerning methods for validating cockpit design in April 2002 (KTH). Since 1999 Gideon has been an active member in the FAA/JAA Human Factors Harmonisation Working Group developing a new approach to Human Factors for aircraft certification

Alison F. Starr is the Head of Crew Support Systems in the Advanced Technology Department of Electronic Systems, Smiths Aerospace. Since graduating from the University of Wales College Cardiff, she has worked on Human Factors research and design aspects of systems for aviation and defence systems at Westland Helicopters and Smiths Industries. She has published extensively in the area of Human Factors of interface design including work on automatic speech recognition, warning systems and new concepts of crew support systems. She is currently Chair of the National Advisory Committee of Human Factors for Aerospace and Defence, and sits on the MoD/Industrial liaison committee for Human Factors and on the FAA/JAA Human Factors Harmonisation Working Group. She has had experience of project management in the DTI AFDT II and AFDT III programmes and the European DIVA programme, and also holds a Diploma in Effective Management.

Patricia May Ververs is a Principal Research Scientist in the Human Centered Systems group at Honeywell Laboratories. She completed a BA degree in Psychology in 1991 from Villanova University, a MA in Human Factors in 1993 from the Catholic University of America and a Ph.D. in Engineering Psychology in 1998 from the University of Illinois at Urbana-Champaign, where she received the 1999 Stanley N. Roscoe award for the best doctoral dissertation in the area of Aerospace Human Factors. Since joining Honeywell in 1998, she has worked on such programs as High Speed Research, Flight Critical Systems Research, Aviation Safety Program's System Wide Accident Prevention, Advanced Primary Flight Displays, and Augmented Cognition. Currently, Dr. Ververs is the program manager for the DARPA Augmented Cognition program aimed at developing a wireless, wearable system that uses neurophysiological data to determine the attentional state of a mobile warfighter to optimise cognitive throughput. She is also the program manager and principal investigator on Alerting and Notification of Conditions Outside the Aircraft (ANCOA), a NASA sponsored program that is developing an alerting system that integrates the traffic, terrain, weather, and communications systems for aviation flight decks.

Christopher D. Wickens is currently a Professor of Psychology, Head of the Aviation Human Factors Division and Associate Director of the Institute of Aviation at the University of Illinois at Urbana-Champaign. He also holds an appointment in the Department of Mechanical and Industrial Engineering and the Beckman Institute of Science and Technology. He received his A.B. degree from Harvard College in 1967 and his Ph.D. from the University of Michigan in 1974 and served as a commissioned officer in the U.S. Navy from 1969 to 1972. His research interests involve the application of the principles of human attention, perception and cognition to modelling operator performance in complex environments, and to designing displays to support that performance. Particular interest has focussed on aviation, air traffic control and data visualizations. He has published textbooks in Human Factors, Engineering Psychology and Air Traffic Control. He is an avid mountain climber.

Acknowledgements

Firstly I must express my deepest thanks to all those people who have contributed their work to this volume. These people are representatives at the very forefront of the vast range of knowledge and skills required to design, develop and test a modern airliner flight deck. It goes without saying that without them this book would not have been possible.

I need to thank John Hindley of Ashgate, whose help and advice in the preparation and marketing of this book was most welcome, and Pauline Beavers also of Ashgate, for her help in turning the manuscript into a book worthy of publishing.

Finally, I also must thank my wife, Fiona, for her help and support over the years.

If I have omitted anyone from this list, may I apologise now, however, they can rest assured that their efforts were most appreciated.

Don Harris
Cranfield University
April 2004

Section One
Flight Deck Design

1 Flight deck design and integration for commercial air transports

Brian D. Kelly

Introduction

About 35 years ago, the world had discovered how to fly efficiently anywhere in the world at high subsonic speeds without benefit of advanced flight deck technology and crew interfaces. Since that time, safety has improved so dramatically that the industry now has the luxury of concentrating its efforts for improving safety on a relatively few agendas. Robust technological solutions are in sight for major causes for accidents involving the flight crew, especially controlled flight into terrain, loss of control, and approach and landing. So one might legitimately question whether much more advancement in the state of this art is justified.

Nowhere other than a commercial aircraft flight deck can one find a system involving extensive interactions with human beings which is as complex and critical to public safety and yet so commonplace. Furthermore, the interactions and complexities do not end on the flight deck, but extend into many other infrastructures such as air traffic control. Flight deck (cockpit) design, and operational practices in commercial aviation have experienced significant evolution since the introduction of the jet age in the early 1960s. During the last four decades the industry has accomplished a revolution in digital avionics enabling new kinds of flight deck displays and controls, communication, navigation, surveillance, and aircraft system management. The role of the flight crew has shifted, and new methods and standards for training of flight crews have also emerged. During this time, safety has improved dramatically, and commercial aviation remains the safest mode of transportation, not withstanding the fact that deregulation has simultaneously increased pressure to improve efficiency and reduce costs while the business has grown exponentially. The challenge now is to increase efficiency and reduce costs while continuing to maintain safety margins.

Flight decks have evolved from a place where the pilots sit amidst numerous independent and disparate indications and controls toward integrated designs where the pilots and all of the aircraft systems come together and operate as an integrated whole.

This chapter examines the problem from a manufacturer's perspective. It begins with an outline of an aircraft programme, showing the kinds of tasks and deliverables expected of Human Factors and flight deck integration organisations, followed by a discussion of design considerations to provide a practical sense of the depth and breadth of design challenges. Further discussions cover integration and proper application of Human Factors disciplines including the philosophies, tools, methods, and areas of expertise required to meet the needs. Emphasis is placed on the necessity of achieving balance and appropriate compromises between dissimilar requirements (the essence of practical integration), and of the need to bring multiple dissimilar areas of talent to bear on this complex and crucial part of the aircraft design. The chapter concludes with a discussion of future challenges and opportunities in the hope that the reader will conclude that much interesting work lies in the decades ahead.

The major sections are:

- Crew interface development in the context of an engineering programme.
- Some specific flight deck design considerations.
- Human-centred design philosophies and design strategies.
- Assuring integration.
- Test and evaluation strategies for programme phases.
- Organisational considerations.
- Challenge and opportunity.

Crew interface development in the context of an engineering programme

The life cycle of an engineering programme has many phases and milestones, and usually follows or has elements of the following:

- Research and development, concept development.
- Product development, design integration, market assessment, high-level design requirements.
- Initial configuration and performance definition.
- Authorisation to offer a product.
- Programme kick-off, and announcements of orders.
- Initial detailed design requirements.
- Validation of design requirements, emphasis on integration.
- Certification plans, and their concurrence from authorities.
- Preliminary Design Review (PDR).
- Final design requirements, Design freeze.

- Design specification and drawing releases.
- Critical Design Review (CDR).
- Component build.
- Verification testing of flight hardware and software.
- Final integration.
- Flight Test.
- Certification and delivery.
- Fleet experience, support, lessons learned.

This pattern is shown in figure 1, with typical flight deck and crew interface design activities shown in the lower half, (Jacobsen, Kelly, Mumaw and Hilby, 2002).

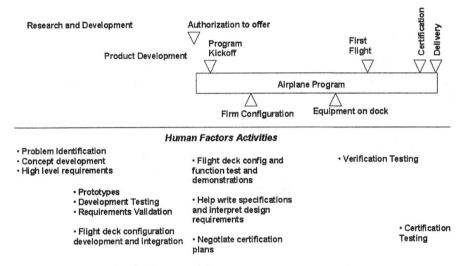

Figure 1 Engineering programme phases and related human interface development activities

Configuration control is typically imposed early in the programme to allow time for detailed design, build, delivery, integration, and test. Therefore, the critical pilot interface design decisions should be finalised as part of the initial design process, to support detail design specification and drawing releases. This underscores the necessity of the involvement of Human Factors and operational specialists early in the design.

The flight deck controls and displays are part of the design of virtually every other aircraft system. So, it is critical that the design decisions for the flight deck and crew interfaces be made in concert with those for other parts of the aeroplane.

Brian D. Kelly

Because the value of effective flight deck design is often difficult to quantify, these aspects are particularly vulnerable to deletion or simplification if their design and validation is not completed before design of aeroplane systems is frozen.

New designs

Design of an all-new vehicle (as opposed to a derivative of an existing design) requires greater resources and expertise early in the programme, especially if significant advances in technology, configuration, or processes are being applied. Testing of concepts and validation of the design requirements characterise the front end of the programme, with particular emphasis on any novel interfaces or design features.

Derivative designs

So called 'derivative programmes', where the design is based on improvements to an existing product, are driven by economic necessity to require fewer resources and usually require a high degree of commonality in training and operations with the existing product. This shifts the emphasis in crew interface design to one of sufficient involvement in changes to the systems to ensure that commonality with existing operations stays within limits. In a more complete treatment of this aspect, Boyd and Harper (1997) show how Human Factors and operational considerations are critical to the design of a derivative flight deck, where judicious and creative compromises should be struck between innovation and the need for commonality with past versions of the design.

Retrofit

With an installed fleet of over 10,000 commercial transports in service with useful product lives measured in decades, it is no surprise that business opportunities for servicing and upgrading the world fleet are substantial. Retrofits have enabled significant safety improvements such as predictive windshear systems, Terrain Awareness and Warning Systems (TAWS), and head-up displays. Retrofits of such systems have high safety leverage because a larger fraction of the world fleet can benefit in a comparatively shorter time.

Retrofits in the near future are likely to involve new communications systems and means of sharing data between the aeroplane and ground as air traffic infrastructures and operations change to accommodate increasing traffic. Retrofit of modern flight deck technology to older aeroplanes can be driven by maintenance costs associated with obsolete technology, consolidation of functions into fewer units, or in some cases by enabling a two-crew flight deck.

Some specific design considerations

Requirements for the design of commercial flight decks cover the full range of ergonomic, environmental, perceptual and cognitive considerations. To progress beyond current practice, a clear understanding of the sciences involved is needed to ensure that errors in new design concepts are caught. But the problem is sufficiently complex that awareness of the history and rationale behind current practice and requirements should also be kept in mind. Therefore, the traditional, but important, issues of ergonomics, geometry, and environment are discussed before proceeding to the more popular design considerations associated with cognitive tasks.

Basic ergonomics, geometry and arrangement

Spatial arrangement and the physical ergonomics of a flight deck begin at the eye reference point, or ERP. From this 'design eye' position, internal and external vision, reach, strength, and accessibility are addressed. The general arrangement of a 777 flight deck is shown in figures 2 and 3.

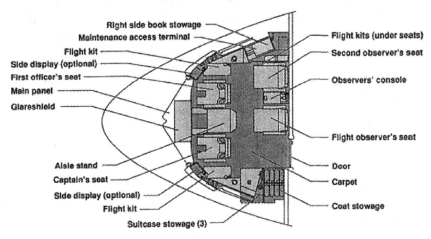

Figure 2   Boeing 777 flight deck arrangement

Brian D. Kelly

Figure 3   Boeing 777 flight deck

The exterior shape of the aeroplane is of course strongly influenced by aerodynamic concerns. But the best aerodynamic shape for the nose of an aeroplane is one with minimum volume and disruption of flow, and therefore at cross purposes with flight deck equipment volume and external vision requirements. FAR/JAR 25.773 regulates external vision for the pilots. Advisory circular AC 25.773 documents acceptable means of compliance. The primary considerations are the vision 'polar', a plot of the window edges from the ERP in spherical coordinates, and the 'three-second rule, depicted in figure 4.

The polar establishes a minimum standard for view of the outside world for safe accomplishment of any procedure or manoeuvre and collision avoidance. The three-second rule ensures sufficient vision over the nose in poor weather to assess the runway environment at low altitude on final approach. The viewable segment of ground must not be covered in less than three seconds. Therefore this criterion influences the required approach speed and attitude of the aeroplane. The vision cut-off line in turn affects the amount of available front panel and glare shield panel areas. Other sections of the AC address optical properties of the transparencies, post width, and other blockages.

Reach and accessibility of controls are also addressed from the ERP, and include devices such as flight controls, aircraft systems controls, landing gear, thrust levers, reversers, rudder pedals, tiller, window opening, oxygen masks, flight bags, charts, etc. Also, FAR 25.1523 and Appendix D establish criteria for determining the minimum flight crew and require that either flight crew member be able to reach and operate all controls necessary if the other pilot is incapacitated.

- Vision Polar

- 3-Second "Rule"

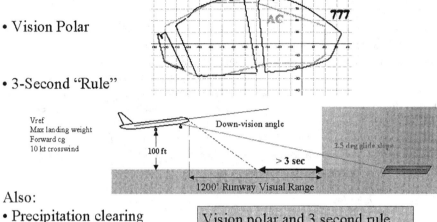

Also:
- Precipitation clearing
- Post widths
- Other details

Vision polar and 3 second rule drive airplane configuration (approach attitude and speed)

Figure 4   External vision guidelines from FAA AC 25.773-1

Seats must be designed to withstand 16g crash loads, subject to a head impact criterion (HIC). Strength and flexibility of the seat, restraints, and cushions are obvious considerations, but a windshield that is too close to the path that the head follows or glare shield and panel structures which do not absorb enough energy can also lead to failure of this test.

Seat cushions firm enough to comply with HIC, may present challenges in designing for comfort. Comfort testing, particularly for long-range aircraft should employ a variety of statures, and evaluations after being seated for at least two hours. Seat and rudder pedal adjustments are usually employed to provide appropriate accessibility to controls for pilots ranging in stature from 5'2' (153 cm) to 6'3' (183.5 cm) (FAR/JAR 25.777). Beyond that, the seats should also be sufficiently adjustable to accommodate ingress and egress without interference with the flight controls, and napping if operational approval of that practice is anticipated.

The length of the flight deck behind the ERP is driven by considerations such as space for observer seats (required under operating rules, e.g. FAR Part 121) stowage and accommodations, and space for emergency equipment. The flight deck must also provide an alternate means of escape for the flight crew, which is usually accomplished by openable windows or a hatch.

Internal vision requirements include readability of instruments and displays in all lighting conditions, and avoidance of obscuration from flight or thrust controls. Readability of displays and lighting of instruments are strongly influenced by the wide range of ambient lighting conditions. Reflections pose a particular challenge due to the complex geometry and arrangement of reflective surfaces like windows and instrument and display faces. The challenge is further compounded by the fact that light from the outside can come from any direction allowed by windows, and reflect off many surfaces including the pilot's white shirt. For large glass displays, anti-reflective coatings are likely required to ensure readability under bright lighting conditions. At night, the flight deck is filled with emissive displays, lighted panels (light plates), and other light sources which can reflect in displays or windows. The designer is wise to thoroughly address reflections early in the design cycle with mockups. Analytical or computer-based tools that can address this problem are scarce at present.

Noise and sound levels

Noise level in the flight deck should be controlled to facilitate communication between crew members and to avoid fatigue. Numerous sources of noise can contribute, adding noise energy in different parts of the sound spectrum. Aerodynamic noise may correlate best with either Mach number or indicated airspeed and is affected by the shape of the nose, intersections with windshields or other discontinuities in the shape, local Mach number and location of shock waves, and the quality of gaps and seals in hatches or openable windows. Engine noise in the flight deck for jet commercial transports is not usually a significant contributor. Noise level on the flight deck can be dramatically affected when the nose gear is lowered, depending on its proximity to the flight deck. The character and level of noise can also change dramatically when the nose gear contacts the ground, especially on rough runways. Air conditioning noise can play a prominent role, being especially sensitive to the detail design of the ducts and nozzles and the speed and volume of air needed. Even windshield wipers contribute.

These background noise sources are also of interest relative to the design of crew alerting sounds and voice alerts, which must always be audible and have attention-getting properties. The sound level for the alerts can usually be adjusted to accommodate varying background noise according to a schedule based on airspeed or Mach, aircraft configuration, and sensed air/ground state. Also, the sound level for each sound or voice must be individually established, depending on the background noise level in the same frequencies. For this reason, as well as to guard against hearing loss in individuals at certain frequencies, alerting sounds are usually multi-spectral in nature and composed of at least two dominant frequencies.

'Aviate' tasks

Up to this point, the discussion has centred on classical ergonomic and geometry considerations, not complex cognitive tasks. The following sections discuss parts of the design that have a major impact in this area. As the discussion moves to subjects associated with pilot tasks, it is useful to consider the flight-training axiom that the priority of pilot tasks is 'aviate', 'navigate', and 'communicate'.

The 'aviate' task involves manual control of the vehicle attitude, direction, and energy state. So, in addition to the obvious controls for pitch, roll, and yaw, controls for thrust, reverse thrust, speed brakes and ground spoilers, flaps, landing gear extension/retraction, and steering and braking on the ground should also be considered.

This adds up to a fair number of controls that must be easily operable by either pilot. All anticipated tasks should be supported, the most challenging of which involve transitions from one operational phase to another. One example is accomplishment of a rejected takeoff involving maintenance of directional control while braking, reducing thrust to idle, ensuring that the ground spoilers have deployed and deploying and modulating reverse thrust, all in the space of a few seconds. In such scenarios, reach, travel, and relative locations of controls all come into play.

See the later chapter by Edmund Field for a thorough treatment of the subject of flight controls, handling qualities, and the benefits and choices that the designer has available when using modern fly-by-wire control systems.

Communication, navigation, surveillance, and air traffic management

In the early days of aviation, the pilot's communication task was trivial (there was nobody to talk to and no radio) and the navigation task was difficult, imprecise, and prone to error. Today, it is somewhat the opposite. Numerous ways have evolved to communicate inside and outside the aircraft using either data or voice, while navigation has become much more reliable and precise.

The crew of the modern airliner now has the ability to communicate using voice or data, using a variety of bands and protocols. Voice communication can be accomplished using VHF or HF bands, and via satellite using SATCOM systems. Data link communications are used for maintenance, airline operational communications, and air traffic control. But, data link communications will not completely replace the need for rapid access to voice communication. Sometimes seen by flight deck engineers (and even pilots and Human Factors experts) as merely a problem of installation of the radios, the management of different voice communication tasks is complex and must accommodate a wide variety of tasks under occasionally unpredictable conditions.

Technology has made navigation easier in some respects and more difficult in others. The technical problem of establishing the location of the aircraft on the earth to high accuracy has been made almost trivial by the advent of global positioning satellites, enabling higher confidence in navigation display accuracy and new kinds of approaches. However, programming of routes and complex paths has added a significant training burden, and complex GPS-based paths have added new kinds of navigation system accuracy requirements.

Current flight management systems fill the need to program the intended path on moving map or horizontal situation displays which, along with routes and other information, provide graphical feedback and intuitive awareness of the position and the planned route of the aircraft. Use of these systems has become a virtual standard for modern flight decks. Providing equivalent awareness of vertical navigation, climbs and descents, has been much more of a challenge because flight path angle, rate of climb, thrust, drag, speed, and acceleration are inextricably linked by the laws of physics. Autoflight and thrust management modes for vertical navigation are therefore inherently more complex to design and more difficult for pilots to understand than those for lateral navigation.

Figure 5 Navigation display formats with vertical situation displays on lower part. Left image shows an encounter with terrain. Right image shows normal approach to landing

Vertical situation displays (VSD, or profile map view, figure 5) can help pilots understand and anticipate the energy situation. This information is especially important during non-precision approaches, or 'slam dunk' approaches when the glide slope is being approached from above due to a late descent (Chen, Jacobsen, Hofer, Turner and Wiedemann, 2000). VSDs also provide hope for clarifying the vertical navigation path in the flight management system. However they present some fundamental design choices and training issues of their own in terms of which view of the route should be portrayed (a lateral projection, or a projection of an 'unwound' route) and what should be portrayed when the aircraft is not on the depicted lateral route.

Vertical and horizontal situation displays have become natural homes for a wealth of external hazard information including terrain, traffic, and weather. In addition to integrating navigation information with hazards, they have become integral parts of ground proximity warning, traffic alert, weather radar and predictive windshear alerting systems. Turbulence detection systems will likely add to this list. All of these systems provide improved awareness to the crew but complicate management of information on the displays. For example, the designer may choose automatic or manual control of display mode and range when threat alerts occur. Horizontal displays are also being used for ground manoeuvring situation awareness, and perhaps someday guidance, to improve airport throughput and enhance the safety of ground operations. They can be expected to be an integral part of future ground collision and runway incursion alerting systems.

Following the introduction of flight management systems with map displays in the early 1980s there has been a steady evolution of added functions, but also progress in the usability of the interface. Improvements have been developed in particular to simplify tactical tasks such as inserting or deleting intermediate altitude constraints, or dealing with late runway changes on approach. The flexible interface offered by the CDU (Control Display Unit for flight management systems) has also lent itself to many other functions such as radio tuning, backup display management controls, satellite communication and flight interphone functions.

Recent efforts in the industry are focusing on further streamlining of such tasks through the use of graphical user interfaces. At this point it remains to be seen whether these interfaces can dramatically simplify the tasks. Regardless of the interface design, it is unlikely that training time can be reduced due to the inherent complexity of the functions required of flight management systems. The mode structures and operation of the flight management system itself will have to be streamlined in order to realise large benefits.

Navigation has long been inseparable from the tasks of communication and air traffic management. Future air traffic environments will place greater emphasis on traffic awareness, time-based navigation, and datalink communication, including clearances. Four-D, or time-based navigation, will add the need to portray the 4th dimension to the horizontal and vertical display suite mentioned above. Air traffic management techniques will make greater use of traffic awareness in the flight deck as an integral part of new procedures including closely spaced parallel approaches and control of in-trail position. Many challenges for integration and design of flight deck interfaces lie ahead for existing, as well as new aircraft.

Surveillance, the ability to provide data about other aircraft in the air traffic system, is a critical element. Traditionally, aircraft position and altitude in continental and terminal area airspace are provided to air traffic controllers on the ground using ground based surveillance radar and aircraft based transponders. In oceanic environments, beyond reach of radar, this is done using voice radio to provide position and altitude reports, although the FANS (Future Air Navigation System) controller to pilot data link communication (CPDLC) has been adopted in the Pacific and is gaining acceptance in the north Atlantic.

TCAS (Traffic Alert and Collision Avoidance System) has provided traffic information in the flight deck for about the last 15 years, sensing azimuth and altitude of other aircraft from Mode S transponder broadcasts. Thus, pilots and air traffic controllers today see different data. The ability of aircraft to broadcast own-ship GPS position and other data such as altitude, current speed or intended flight path (as programmed in the FMS) offer the possibility that all participants in the system will have access to the same data. Pilots will have more data on surrounding traffic, including tail number designation, enabling positive identification and more efficient methods of moving traffic in cooperation with ground controllers.

The development of communication, navigation, and surveillance systems is not limited by technology at this point. To move ahead, the primary need is to develop industry consensus on operational concepts, procedures, and data protocols in parallel with development of functional requirements of the systems and the intended use by pilots. This is underway in a large number of industry committees in the U.S. and Europe, and will offer no shortage of challenges on how best to retrofit this information into existing aircraft or integrate it into new flight deck designs.

Systems management

The flight deck is where operation of the aircraft systems comes together. Crew knowledge requirements for aircraft systems (e.g. electrical, hydraulic and pneumatic power systems, pressurisation, flight controls, landing gear, brakes, and steering) today typically account for about a third of the training associated with transition to a new aircraft type. Major advancements in the technology and reliability of airframe systems have enabled the change from three-crew to two-crew flight decks for jetliners beginning in the mid 1960s with the Boeing 737, Douglas DC-9, and becoming the industry standard in the early 1980s with the introduction of the Boeing 757 and 767, followed by the Airbus A-310 and A-320. Reductions in flight crew workload for operation, monitoring, and coping with system failures were made possible by improved crew interfaces, simplified system architectures, and greater reliance on the systems to accomplish monitoring tasks.

During development of the Boeing 737, 757, and 767 a design strategy of applying 'simplicity, redundancy, and automation', in that order, to the design of aircraft systems architecture and control was responsible for reducing crew tasks and knowledge for safe, efficient operation. Simplification of system architectures has the greatest leverage on simplifying crew knowledge requirements and procedures. Adding redundancy to systems is sometimes necessary to manage crew tasks following failures, for example an additional automatic cabin pressurisation system so that after a single failure of the primary system, one crew member is not completely occupied with manual control of cabin pressure. Automation of crew tasks following failures can be beneficial if it is sufficiently reliable that the crew does not have to be trained for both automatic and manual modes.

Due to the number of different systems, consistency of indications and controls is important to minimise errors and simplify training. Coding of colours, switch position and state, system behaviour and feedback are all important elements. Physical controls should provide tactile feedback. The choice of employing a knob, toggle switch, or pushbutton switch should be directed according to a philosophy applied across all of the indications and controls. Controls and indications should be arranged or be accessible in a way which permits efficient normal operation, particularly when starting up or shutting down the aircraft, and they should enable the flight crew to cope with failures that affect multiple systems.

However, consistency should be balanced with the need for distinguish-ability between similar controls and similar indications. Arrangement of controls, use of flow diagrams on control panels and physical separation between controls that appear or feel similar are some techniques used to avoid inadvertent selection of the incorrect controls. But, even with ideal crew interface designs errors occur, and are in fact likely. So, indications, switch position, or in many cases crew alerts are used to provide feedback to the flight crew so that errors can be detected. For switch actions that have irreversible effects (e.g. discharging a fire bottle, or disconnecting a generator drive on many aircraft), switch guards are used to further discourage inadvertent or unintended operation.

Display formats showing more detailed states of aircraft systems have become popular on more recent commercial flight decks. The intended use of these indications varies between manufacturers from being supplemental information only and not required for accomplishment of any procedure, to automatic appearance of the information during normal and non-normal operations, to use of the synoptic displays themselves for control as well as indication of system state.

Brian D. Kelly

Crew alerting and electronic checklists

The need to alert the flight crew to non-normal or hazardous conditions arises from aircraft or propulsion system faults, threats external to the aircraft such as terrain, weather, and other aircraft, or operational conditions such as deviation from assigned altitude. Each of these has some unique needs and constraints, presenting a challenge to the flight deck and Human Factors engineers in developing consistent and understandable means to alert the crew.

In the late 1970s a series of studies done under contract from the FAA evaluated trends and practices in alerting systems typified at that time by the Boeing 747-200, Lockheed L-1011, and Concorde (Boucek et al, 1977, and Berson et al, 1981). The studies documented the rapid increase in number of alerts, and inconsistency in their presentation, and lack of any centralised way of dealing with multiple alerts. They also found excessive numbers of alerting sounds, many without visual indications of the condition, thus requiring the flight crew to memorise the meaning of the sounds. The studies proposed methods of categorising and centralising alerts, use of alerting sounds primarily for attention-getting purposes, and use of visual means to convey detailed information. In addition, the concept of a 'quiet/dark' philosophy was developed wherein the number of indications for system that are operating normally (e.g. green lights) were drastically reduced in favour of alerts that indicated when a problem existed.

Since the early 1980s with the introduction of the Boeing 757 and 767, modern flight decks employ crew alerting systems which centralise crew alerts in one location visually and categorise alerts according to required timeliness of crew action or awareness. There has also been a reduction in the dependence on alerting sounds to convey information, instead relying primarily on sounds to gain the attention of the crew and emphasising visual indications for the purpose of providing information. The 'quiet/dark' philosophy in combination with simplification, redundancy, and automation of aircraft systems reduced flight crew workload to the extent that two-crew flight decks became the industry standard. The Engine Indication and Crew Alerting System (EICAS) introduced with the Boeing 757 and 767 in 1981 accomplished centralisation and prioritisation of most alerts on the flight deck into Warnings, Cautions, and Advisories. The system also combined the alert message list, engine indications, and pre-flight and maintenance indications in one information system (figure 6).

The alert level definitions now under development for a revised FAR/JAR 25.1322 are:

Warning For conditions that require immediate flight crew awareness and immediate flight crew response. If warnings are time critical to maintain the immediate safe operation of the aircraft, they must be prioritised higher than other warnings.

16

Caution   For conditions that require immediate flight crew awareness and subsequent flight crew response.

Advisory   For conditions that require flight crew awareness and may require subsequent flight crew response.

Note that the definitions are human-centred; they are based on the urgency that the flight crew be aware of the alert condition and the timeliness of action required. The purpose of the definitions is not to add another learning point for pilots to be quizzed about, but rather for use by designers to ensure that failure conditions are categorised appropriately and to ensure that the alert visual and aural indications acquire the attention of the flight crew and convey the needed information in an appropriate manner.

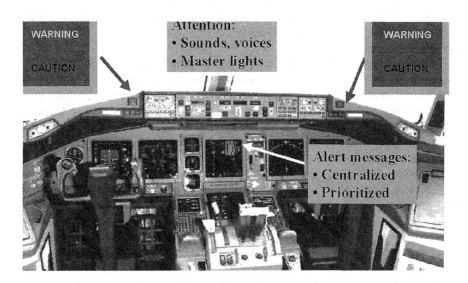

Figure 6   Boeing 777 crew alerting system

External threat alerting systems were introduced as soon as the technology became feasible because weather and controlled flight into terrain caused the largest number of accidents. Introduction of such systems cannot wait for the next new aircraft design, and so are designed to facilitate retrofit, resulting in maximum penetration into the large existing and diverse fleet of air transports. With these systems came some new flight deck integration and Human Factors issues, due to a natural conflict between the desire for consistency within the flight deck design of an aircraft model versus the desire for consistency across all models and manufacturers. The latter consideration has won the day because of the need for maximum deployment of systems with such high safety value.

In the late 1970s, the only 'time critical' warning system on commercial aircraft was the Ground Proximity Warning System. It was unique in its use of voice, and the alerts did not match the philosophies for categorisation of alerts or use of sounds used by the new centralised crew alerting systems. In the two decades since, the industry has seen the introduction of four more systems of this type, the reactive windshear warning system, Traffic alert and Collision Avoidance System (TCAS), Terrain Awareness and Warning Systems (TAWS), and predictive windshear warning systems. These systems introduced a large number of different time critical alerts, some not-so-critical alerts, and some use of voice under normal conditions, such as radar altitude callouts used during landing and decision speed callouts used on takeoff. In order to facilitate retrofit, and ensure that safety benefits of such systems could be enjoyed by as many aircraft in the fleet as possible, voice alerts were a natural choice, requiring a minimum of new wiring and visual indications. But introducing so many systems also resulted in the need to prioritise voice warnings, and made consistent categorisation with aircraft systems alerts difficult.

TCAS, predictive windshear, and TAWS all introduced the need to indicate external threat conditions on the moving map, or navigation display in order to enhance the credibility of the alerts and provide the flight crew with improved awareness of the alert as well as normal conditions for weather, traffic, and terrain. A number of issues arose including whether alert conditions should cause the navigation display to automatically reconfigure mode and range or de-clutter by removing other information.

Electronic checklists (figure 7) are becoming more common on commercial flight decks, posing some key implementation questions that highlight automation philosophy of a given flight deck. Some designs cause checklists to be displayed automatically under normal and non-normal situations, and others (Boeing 777) are selected manually, sacrificing a small amount of workload in order to encourage a deliberate approach to accomplishing procedures and ensure the flight crew is aware of any reason for displays changing. Electronic checklists may contain 'open loop' items that must be checked off manually or 'closed loop' items that sense system state and check themselves off. The major safety benefit of these systems is that they indicate what has or has not been accomplished thus aiding in correct completion of checklists, especially when the flight crew is interrupted during execution. Also, automation is used to facilitate rapid and correct selection of the appropriate checklist under non-normal conditions. The benefits of electronic checklists are difficult to realise unless airlines have the ability to customise and update the content of the checklists in order to maintain consistency within their operation and accommodate changes that occur with some regularity. Without a customisable and updateable checklist, flight crews are generally forced to use the paper system. McKenzie and Hartel (1995) provide development history, operational philosophy and explanation of the functions of the electronic checklist for the 777. Boorman (2000 and 2001) further describes error reduction and means to assess the safety benefits of the ECL.

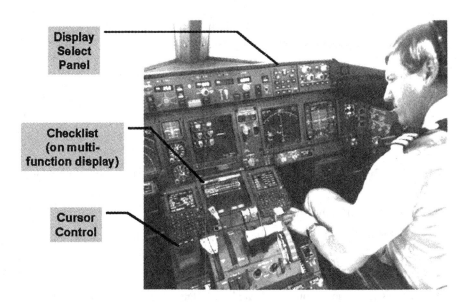

Figure 7   Boeing 777 electronic checklist

Human-centred design philosophies and design strategies

Simultaneously achieving consistency in the way displays and controls operate, while giving appropriate consideration to task and information requirements are just a few criteria for successful design and integration of a flight deck. To ensure that these kinds of attributes are considered in each part of the design requires that top-level human-centred design philosophies are established and applied to all of the interfaces on the flight deck. Doing so will reduce the time, effort, and uncertainty associated with defining more detailed design requirements, and result in a design which better addresses human error and training. As an example, Boeing's flight deck design philosophies are shown in table 1.

Design philosophies are needed to guide every aspect of the design, but perhaps most for automated systems. Billings (1996, 1997) provides an applied treatment of this subject. Philosophies only go so far toward establishing a detailed design specification, so a hierarchical approach is generally used. One step down from philosophy might be referred to as 'design strategies' (Kelly, Graeber, Fadden, 1992; and Bresley, 1995) or high level design requirements, where the statements now apply directly to the design itself, but still focus on the interface with the pilot. After a design is established and validated through prototype and testing, design requirements can then be expressed in enough detail that a design specification can be written.

Table 1
Example of human-centred design philosophies

- The pilot is the final authority for the operation of the aircraft.

- Both crew members are ultimately responsible for the safe conduct of the flight.

- Flight crew tasks, in order of priority, are: safety, passenger comfort, and efficiency.

- Design for crew operations based on pilots' past training and operational experience.

- Design systems to be error-tolerant.

- The hierarchy of design alternatives is: simplicity, redundancy, and automation.

- Apply automation as a tool to aid, not replace, the pilot.

- Address fundamental human strengths, limitations, and individual differences for both normal and non-normal operations.

- Use new technologies and functional capabilities only when:
    o They result in clear and distinct operational or efficiency advantages, and
    o There is no adverse effect to the human-machine interface.

Assuring integration

The flight deck is where the aircraft, its flying characteristics, all of the aircraft systems, aviation system infrastructure, and the flight crew come together. Engineering is the art of making the appropriate compromises to achieve a goal. This is certainly true of the design and integration of aircraft, where traditional and quantifiable metrics such as weight, cost, and performance are traded against each other. Flight deck design is no stranger to compromise, but the challenge is somewhat unique because of the need to balance among myriad, dissimilar requirements, that are difficult to measure and for which clear criteria do not exist. For example, how many 'units' of workload would one trade for one 'unit' of situation awareness?

Beginning with the eye reference point, external vision is affected by such considerations as crash-worthy glare shield design, forward panel space, down-vision requirements, aerodynamic shape of the nose, and structural considerations such as bird strike. The displays themselves, limited by panel space, should display information to a level of detail appropriate to the pilots' tasks. Novel designs, even if superior, should be balanced against the benefits of common operations and training for the crews of existing fleets. More information might be better in some circumstances, but could be an additional training burden or interfere with tasks in others. Workload can be reduced by automation, but possibly at the expense of situation awareness (figure 8). The pilots' tasks are dissimilar as well. They must 'aviate, navigate, and communicate' as well as manage aircraft systems. They must make appropriate choices when these tasks compete, divide tasks between themselves and the aircraft systems, and they must do it in a coordinated manner. None of the attributes above have common metrics or criteria, but they must be balanced according to the needs of the flight crew.

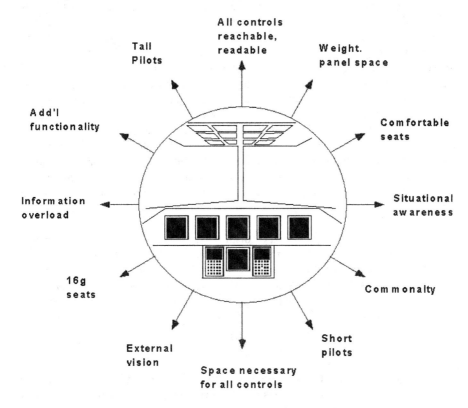

Figure 8 Compromises are required between dissimilar goals

Brian D. Kelly

Integration in the usual engineering context means that all of the parts of the design should work as originally intended when the final product comes together. The goal of 'integration' in this context is that the flight deck design ensures efficient and safe operations. Diverse considerations go into meeting these two goals, so it is not surprising that the designers should employ multiple dissimilar methods.

Common philosophies As noted earlier, the critical human interface design decisions should be finalised early in the programme to support design specification and drawing releases. The ability to validate these requirements is in turn dependent upon early establishment and agreement of the philosophies and guidelines that describe the key properties and objectives of the pilot interface designs. This practice supports integration by helping to ensure that all participants in the design abide by the same principles and objectives, and the resulting designs will operate in a consistent manner.

Prototyping There is no substitute for 'hands-on' tests and evaluations of designs when validating concepts for crew interfaces, so the ability to prototype and evaluate candidate designs is crucial. This does not mean that a full-mission simulation should always be employed, as this would be a waste of critical resources for a design that is still in the formative stages, or represents few unknowns in terms of novelty or potential for interaction with other systems. Development of new concepts should use methods that allow rapid design revisions to allow consideration of many possibilities and iterations. The most effective tools in this regard can be as simple as paper sketches, and design reviews or storyboards to walk through sequences of events. Once the concepts are understood to the extent that simple techniques allow, it is appropriate to expend more resources on higher fidelity methods such as desktop computing prototypes and engineering simulators. For physical concepts focusing on ergonomics, combined use of mockups and human modelling is called for.

Common user interfaces (CUI) For display based applications, where so many different user interface designs are possible, a common user interface description should be established defining the look, feel, and behaviour of graphic elements such as text boxes, selector buttons, and menu navigation. During the early stages of development, this specification should not constrain the design excessively, so as not to inhibit innovation or the discovery of difficulties or issues that might not have been foreseen. Crane, Bang and Hartel (1994) offer a complete discussion of CUI and the development of display based applications for the Boeing 777.

Flight crew procedures, training and operations Often considered last, these are far better considered early in the design. Normal and non-normal pilot procedures for each system should be developed in parallel with the crew interface and system definition to ensure that controls and information are available for the flight crew to accomplish their tasks and so that a common understanding exists throughout the design organisations of the functions expected of the system and the tasks expected of the flight crew. Flight crew procedures are the first step in task analyses that occur in the early development of training programmes. The activities associated with development of crew procedures will tend to force integration because poor compromises or inappropriate interactions between systems tend to manifest themselves in non-sensible or onerously complex crew procedures.

Test and evaluation strategies for programme phases

The preceding sections have discussed design issues in the context of an engineering programme and the broad range of tools and methods that can be employed. However, practitioners cannot employ all of these techniques all of the time. An evaluation strategy should be established that is consistent with the goals of a programme, the degree to which it advances the state of the art, and the inevitable limitations on time and resources (Jacobsen, Kelly, Hilby and Mumaw, 2002).

Evaluation methods should be consistent with a clearly stated *purpose* and set of *objectives* for each evaluation. The *purpose* should address the reason why the evaluation is being done at this time in the programme, what the results will be used for, and by whom. The *objectives* of the evaluation are more specific, and describe the facts and/or data that are sought. Naturally, these facts and data should be useful in meeting the purpose of the evaluation, and they will also drive the test design. While this may seem self evident, in practice it is difficult to do, as insufficiently detailed or competing objectives cause the test design to grow exponentially. To ensure that the results of the evaluation are accepted (not questioned after the fact), the test plan, including the purpose and objectives, should be reviewed with all stakeholders prior to beginning.

The following discussion may help flight deck developers clarify their purpose, and thus move forward toward common goals and a plan that will make best use of the available time and resources. The purpose of an evaluation is closely related to the phase of development. For illustration, the phases are referred to as *research, concept development, requirement validation, verification,* and *certification.*

Research in its purest form is the undirected process of generating new knowledge. In industry settings it is highly directed, and may be thought of as the R in Research and Development. In the context of flight deck development and design, this may be research into the identification or characterisation of a problem or technical challenge, or the imaginative creation of new, high level concepts. Research establishes the high level goals, and the initial direction of concept development. Since the purpose of most research evaluations is to gain new knowledge, the tests are exploratory in nature. Clearly this is activity that occurs well prior to the launch of an engineering programme.

Concept development usually thought of as the D in Research and Development, should also occur before the launch of a development programme. The purpose of evaluations in this context is to establish the ability of several competing designs to accomplish some set of goals. If this stage is done with only one design candidate, the developers risk meeting a dead end if it does not work well, and may even have difficulty understanding why. If success criteria are absolute, e.g. 'completing the mission objectives', then pilots representative of the user population should be used, and objective performance data figure more prominently. If, perhaps in the later stages of development, the emphasis is on the relative merits of several competing designs, the emphasis may shift toward observations made by the evaluating pilots. In this case, performance data is still important, but the reasons for pilot observations or preferences should be carefully understood. In order to be keen evaluators, and provide relevant observations, the pilots should be well briefed on the purpose and objectives of the evaluation, and should fully understand the design goals and philosophy of the flight deck as a whole in order to be competent to evaluate candidate designs.

Requirement validation Having chosen a design from several competing possibilities, it may be advisable to conduct validation testing to show that the design is 'valid' in that it meets all of the needs of the programme. Development testing may have been robust enough that this step can be reduced or eliminated, if sufficient data and confidence exist to write the design specifications and requirements. To reduce the risk of late changes in design as a result of 'surprises' later in the programme, this step should be completed before the requirements for implementing a system are established. The process at this stage should involve the customers, and may take the form of structured demonstrations of a variety of scenarios and conditions, as well as more formal tests. Involvement of pilots from certifying authorities is appropriate and highly recommended, because their expertise and input can be inexpensively accommodated at this point in the programme (not so once in flight test). Certification plans are also being negotiated at this point, and this process is vastly improved if the certification pilots are aware of the qualities of the design.

Verification testing is the term applied to the business of verifying that delivered equipment performs to the requirements and performance that were specified. In theory, with avionic systems this could be done on a bench, but in reality this is the first time many components are brought together in an integrated fashion or operational environment (e.g. an engineering simulator). This is likely to reveal system integration issues which may not have been realised earlier in the programme when individual functions were specified. It is often true that integration oversights manifest themselves in inconsistent flight deck indications or crew procedures. This stage of the programme is characterised by the need to iteratively and rapidly evaluate new software loads, which have hopefully corrected previously identified deficiencies. Testing with pilots in the loop (or at least operationally experienced engineers and Human Factors specialists) is essential to capture subtle effects in context, and identify them with operational consequences. Follow-up is required to ensure that fixes are justified and correctly designed.

Certification As a final examination of appropriate Human Factors properties, the aircraft and the flight deck designs are subjected to testing with certification authority pilots as members of the flight crew. It is essential at this point in the programme that these pilots fully understand the rationale, development history, and flight deck design and automation philosophies, etc. to appropriately judge and certify the human interface. Moreover, it is in the interest of the manufacturer that these authorities are not surprised or asked to evaluate a system they are not familiar with. In the press of time and resources on all parties at this point, misunderstandings can result in costly delays and design changes.

Organisational considerations

Engineers in traditional fields can validate their designs through processes that are quantifiable. In the field of human engineering, validation is not as conceptually simple as testing a component to its structural limit. Variability in the user population (pilots), and the high probability that line operations, procedures, standard practices, air traffic control, and other environmental issues will change over time and may invalidate design assumptions. Precise and certain measurement of success is not possible when designing for a large user population over the significant life span of the design.

In the face of such uncertainties, diversity of expertise is a key strategy to ensure that correct integration takes place. Diverse points of view, experience, technical background, and techniques provide a kind of dissimilar redundancy in the design process. Another can catch what may be missed by one point of view. Dissimilar approaches can be either competitive or cooperative. Efficiency and effectiveness clearly favour a cooperative teaming approach. Human Factors cannot and should not be a separate expertise or process in design of a flight deck. To be effective, the various Human Factors disciplines should contribute from within the team responsible for designing and integrating the flight deck. The team's expertise is composed of at least three major elements; Human Factors, engineering, and operational experience. In addition, individuals with abilities spanning two or even all three areas can be particularly valuable, (figure 9).

Human Factors

Ergonomics
* *Anthropometry*
* *Visual Perception*
* *Physiology*
Cognitive
* *Display Format Design*
* *Automation*
* *Test and Evaluation*

Engineering

* *Aeronautical*
* *Electrical*
* *Mechanical*
* *Systems*
* *Simulation*

Flight Operations

* *Flight Test Pilots*
* *Flight Training*
* *Military pilots*
* *Airline Experience*
* *Air Traffic Controller*
* *Dispatchers*

Figure 9   Diversity of disciplines and individuals for integrating flight crew operations with the design

The potential weak link in the practice of Human Factors engineering is the lack of ability to involve the right players at the earliest stages of design. Effective crew interface design should not be done in isolation, or applied as a fix late in the design. Organisational structure and corporate culture are critical to success:

* Effective crew interface should be established as a high-level programme objective, with clear, specific objectives for the flight deck design.
* A crew interface design philosophy should be established.
* Persons or groups tasked with defining operational and functional aspects of the crew interface should be given the responsibility and means to do so.
* These persons or groups should be involved at the earliest possible opportunity.
* These persons or groups should have the ability to evaluate and express in tangible terms the value of effective human interfaces (e.g. training, safety, operational capability).
* A strong 'user advocate' (e.g. individual or team of project pilots) should be part of the team.
* The organisation should be able to balance the engineering, Human Factors, and operational requirements and practitioners of these three critical areas should understand the others.

- Appropriate time in the schedule early in the programme should be planned to evaluate competing designs and validate the robustness of the selected design, while changes can be made without adding cost.
- Evaluations are essential for any novel concepts or techniques, and less important in areas where there is much operational experience. However, integration with the new and old concepts should not be overlooked.
- These persons or groups should have responsibility to test and evaluate production designs and participate in the overall test programmes to facilitate lessons learned for the next programme.

Challenge and opportunity

Safety

Increased safety, improved economy, and airspace system capacity have been and continue to be the dominant drivers for change. Increases in the number of flights worldwide each day will drive us to an even higher standard of safety. Regardless of how low the number of accidents per million flights, the flying public will not accept news reports of accidents on a too-frequent basis (Weener and Russell, 1993). The flight crew has been identified as the primary cause in approximately 67% of the hull loss accidents that occurred between 1990 and 1999 (Boeing Commercial Airplane Group Airplane Safety, 'Statistical Summary of Commercial Jet Airplane Accidents – Worldwide Operations – 1959-1999, Rev A', June 2000). Another study has shown that failure of the flight crew to follow established procedures is relevant in over 50% of commercial transport hull loss accidents occurring between 1982 and 1991 (Boeing Commercial Airplane Group Airplane Safety, 'Accident Prevention Strategies – Removing Links in the Accident Chain – Worldwide Operations, 1982-1991', October 1993).

Improved awareness and intuitive indication of threats from terrain, weather and traffic have been aggressively dealt with through the introduction of alerting systems such as ground proximity warning systems, traffic alert and collision avoidance systems, and windshear warning systems. Most recently the Global Position Satellites (GPS), and weather radar technology have enabled predictive terrain and windshear alerts, which are expected to offer further substantial reductions in those segments of the accident record. New trends in providing graphic display of the vertical situation and standardisation of constant angle approaches at virtually all airports will also provide improvements.

Accident data shows that the level of safety is not evenly distributed worldwide. Logically then, many initiatives for further improvements in commercial air safety have focussed on further improvement in areas such as infrastructure and safety culture, flight crew selection and training and special emphasis training modules focussed on key safety issues. (US Commercial Aviation Safety Team, 'Results and Analysis – Joint Safety Implementation Team (JSIT) – Controlled Flight into Terrain (CFIT)', June 1, 2000, and US Commercial Aviation Safety Team, 'Results and Analysis – Joint Safety Implementation Team (JSIT) – Approach and Landing – January 2001). These activities are of key importance, but issues have also arisen with respect to new types of flight crew errors in which the design of modern displays, controls, and system logic play a role as described in the FAA Human Factors Team report on The Interfaces Between Flight crews and Modern Flight Deck Systems (Abbott, Slotte, Stimson, et al, 1996). To achieve higher standards in safety, continuous improvements will be required in the systems that the flight crews interact with on a daily basis, the structure and operation of the air traffic control system, and the design of the flight deck and displays and controls in it.

Safety improvements are not necessarily at odds with improvements in efficiency or cost where the design of flight decks is concerned. While a flight deck with superior flight crew interfaces will have greater initial design costs, this investment has the potential of greater value to the operator in reduced training requirements. The flight deck with reduced training requirements is also likely to be a design that embodies intuitive and standard operation with correspondingly lower rate of errors on the part of the flight crew.

Capacity

The apparent dominance of safety and economic considerations does not mean that technical challenges have ended. Computing and display technology used in flight avionics continue to advance quickly, with greater memory and speed allowing functions that have been dreamed of for decades to become practical reality. At the same time, airspace system capacity limitations continue to drive new methods of managing air traffic, which will require or encourage development of new functions in the flight deck and present new challenges in information management.

Increases in the capacity of the air transportation system will require changes in the airspace infrastructures of communications, navigation, and surveillance (CNS) and air traffic management (ATM). Sweeping changes are hoped for in the next two decades involving changes in operations and the way information is used and managed by flight crew in every phase of a flight. Negotiation of a pushback clearance may be enabled by collaborative decision making procedures and information. After engine start the flight crew will have access to taxi situation information, their taxi clearance, guidance for low visibility conditions and alerts and indications to prevent runway incursion accidents. Head-up displays today can provide improved takeoff guidance. Once in flight, pilots are likely to take on a greater degree of responsibility for separation from other aircraft enabled by new GPS-based surveillance systems. These same systems will enable a higher level of organisation of airspace and datalinked communications anywhere in the world. Virtually all approaches will have precision guidance with a minimum of step down procedures, and awareness of external threats (terrain, weather, and traffic) will be achieved intuitively through use of enhanced and synthetic vision techniques.

Experience versus novelty

Design and integration of an all-new flight deck, particularly on a new aircraft design, is a large task and is historically underestimated because details often do not become apparent until the design is well underway. In the face of the uncertainties mentioned above, overall risk to a programme should be carefully weighed. Reliance on past practices, proven in service, will reduce schedule and certification risk, and leave critical resources to focus on areas of highest novelty. Novel features or crew interfaces should be well validated before the beginning of a programme.

Standardisation versus flexibility and innovation

Aviation is a business, and will become increasingly so as deregulation spreads. So, the flight deck designer should take into account both cost and value to the customer. Value is much more difficult to assess. But with the unpredictable growth of capabilities in the near future, particularly in CNS/ATM, it is clear that there will be value in the ability to easily update designs. Without this, new standards in operations will be much more difficult and expensive to achieve. Clearly, flight deck designs for the future should be designed to accommodate new functions, even if they cannot be known in advance.

The future flight crew?

The world evolves inexorably not only in technological capability but also in public understanding and expectations of its use. The flight crew of two pilots is expected to be the norm until technology can replace them entirely. The military applications of unpiloted aircraft are being aggressively explored, but decades will elapse before public expectations, a consistent worldwide infrastructure for operation of such vehicles, and replacement of the massive existing commercial fleet will come to pass. Even with the eventual advent of unpiloted commercial aircraft, system integration and validation of the system end to end, including the inevitable interfaces with human operators will take on a role of even greater criticality than that ascribed to the flight crews of today.

Brian D. Kelly

References

Abbott, K., Slotte, S., Stimson, D. et al. (1996). *Federal Aviation Administration Human Factors Team Report on: The Interfaces Between Flightcrews and Modern Flight Deck Systems.* Washington DC: Federal Aviation Administration. June 18, 1996.

Berson, B.L., Po-Chedley, D.A., Boucek, G.P., Hanson, DC., Leffler, M.F. and Wasson, R.L. (1981). *Aircraft Alerting Systems Standardization Study Vol. II – Aircraft Alerting System Design Guidelines.* (FAA Report, DOT/FAA/RD-81/38/II). Washington, DC: Federal Aviation Administration.

Billings, C.E. (1996). *Human-Centered Automation: Principles and Guidelines.* (NASA Technical Memorandum 110381). Moffett Field, CA: NASA-Ames Research Center.

Billings, C.E. (1997). *Aviation Automation – The Search for a Human Centered Approach.* Mahwah, NJ: Lawrence Erlbaum Associates.

Boeing Commercial Airplane Group Airplane Safety (1993). *Accident Prevention Strategies – Removing Links in the Accident Chain – Worldwide Operations, 1982-1991.* Seattle, WA: Author.

Boeing Commercial Airplane Group Airplane Safety (2000). *Statistical Summary of Commercial Jet Airplane Accidents – Worldwide Operations – 1959-1999,* Rev A. Seattle, WA: Author.

Boorman, D.J. (2000). Reducing flight crew errors and minimizing new error modes with electronic checklists. In, *Proceedings of the International Conference on Human-Computer Interaction in Aeronautics* (pp. 57-63). Toulouse: Cepadues-Editions.

Boorman, D.J. (2001). Safety Benefits of Electronic Checklists: An Analysis of Commercial Transport Accidents. *Proceedings of the 11th International Symposium on Aviation Psychology*, University of Ohio. Columbus, OH. (revised after proceedings came out)

Boucek, G.P., Veitengruber, J.E., and Smith, W.D. (1977). *Aircraft Alerting Systems Criteria Study, Volume II: Human Factors Guidelines and Aircraft Alerting Systems* (FAA Report, FAA-RD-76-222). Washington, DC: Federal Aviation Administration.

Boyd, S.P. and Harper, P.M. (1997). Human Factors Implications for Mixed Fleet Operations. In, *Ninth International Symposium on Aviation Psychology*, Ohio State University, (pp. 831-836). Columbus, OH: Ohio State University.

Bresley, W.M. (1995). 777 Flight Deck Design. *Airliner.* Seattle, WA: The Boeing Company, Apr-Jun, 1995.

Chen, S.S., Jacobsen, A.R., Hofer, E., Turner, B.L. and Wiedemann, J. (2000). *Vertical Profile Display Development* (Paper 2000-01-5613). SAE World Aviation Congress, San Diego, CA, 2000.

30

Crane, J.M., Bang, E.S. and Hartel, M.C. (1994). *Standardizing Interactive Display Functions on the 777 Flight Deck.* SAE Aerotech '94, Los Angeles, California, 1994.

Jacobsen, A.R., Kelly, B.D., Hilby, D.L. and Mumaw, R.J. (2002). Human Factors Testing and Evaluation in Commercial Airplane Flight Deck Development. In, S.G. Charlton, and T.G. O'Brien (Eds) *Handbook of Human Factors Testing and Evaluation.* Mahwah, NJ: Lawrence Erlbaum Associates, Publishers.

Kelly, B.D., Graeber, R.C., and Fadden, D.M. (1992). *Applying Crew-centered Concepts to Flight Deck Technology: The Boeing 777.* Flight Safety Foundation 45th IASS and IFA 22nd International Conference, 1992.

McKenzie, William A. and Hartel, Martin C., *Design of the Electronic Checklist on the Boeing 777 Flight Deck.* SAE Aerotech '95, Los Angeles, California, 1995.

US Commercial Aviation Safety Team (2000). *Results and Analysis – Joint Safety Implementation Team (JSIT) – Controlled Flight into Terrain (CFIT).* June 1, 2000.

US Commercial Aviation Safety Team (2001). *Results and Analysis – Joint Safety Implementation Team (JSIT) – Approach and Landing.* – January 2001.

Weener, E.F. and Russell, P.D. (1993). *Aviation Safety Overview.* Proceedings of the Flight Safety Foundation 46th International Air Safety Seminar, November 8-11, 1993.

2   Flight deck design process

Florence Reuzeau and René Nibbelke

Introduction

The integration of knowledge about Human Factors into the system engineering process is an important issue, due to its potential impact on the cost effectiveness of the design process, the quality of the product and safety. Recent studies have suggested several ways to facilitate this integration. Perhaps the most significant is to promote the idea of including the entire organisation from the very outset of the design process. The US Army, through MANPRINT (Booher, 1990), has proposed an approach that helps organisations to consider Human Factors requirements such as manpower, personnel, training, the design process, safety risk management and health hazards. MANPRINT describes *what* should be considered, but each design organisation is free to adapt the general principles. For example, Ward and Harmer (1999) have proposed enhancements to the approach to cover specific issues such as cultural changes, design process improvement and organisational changes (i.e. *how* organisationally Human Factors should be considered in the design process). AIRBUS has a multi-disciplinary Human Factors group, including all relevant parts of the organisation: design, certification, operations, maintenance and training (for both crew and maintenance operators). Each discipline has developed a Human Factors manual, describing the way Human Factors is integrated into their organisation and processes.

This chapter will present an overview of the role of Human Factors in the design process of a civil flight deck from a manufacturer's perspective. It will take into account current academic research and the commercial and certification constraints of a design organisation. The aim is to describe the process for considering design requirements, how the requirements can be captured and how the design can be evaluated against these requirements. An example of the design and evaluation of the Future Air Navigation System (FANS) Human-Machine interface is presented to illustrate the process.

Human Factors methods can be used in several contexts:

- Determining design improvement.
- The social acceptability of the product.
- To obtain certification.
- To gain a deeper understanding of crew behaviour.

As well as internal feedback and data from customers, our Human Factors approach benefits from current knowledge and best Human Factors practice recommended by academic organisations. From these sources we are able to generate the elements to build scenarios in order to test design solutions.

We have been able to develop a *product approach (on **what** the design requirements are)* combined with a *process approach (**how** the organisations should work to meet these requirements).*

The evolution of aviation systems

Technological advances and changes in the operational context for civil aircraft have resulted in the constant evolution of flight decks. Designs have had to change to adapt to the new technologies, operational requirements, and the more restrictive requirements (safety, availability, maintainability, etc). Traditional Human Factors methods such as anthropometry, biomechanics and medical sciences were adequate for older, low-tech flight decks. Workload assessment, for example, has always had an important place alongside engineering (Speyer et al, 1993). In these disciplines, scientific knowledge is relatively mature and there is a movement towards the development of formalisation and measurement tools. The use of simulation and virtual reality (based on digital mock-ups and mannequins), for example, is standard practice (Goutal, 1999).

With respect to cognition, however, the Human Factors methods are relatively immature. Technological evolution (cf. cockpit picture) has had an important impact on the way the crew flies the aircraft. Today, the commercial task (passengers and freight management) is quite demanding in term of cognitive resources. Three different forms of difficulties can be highlighted:

- The *'distance'* between the systems and the human is growing.
- The systems are coupled.
- The human is an integrated multifaceted system.

The distance between the systems and the human is growing

Guillevic (1991) has illustrated (figure 1) that the difficulty in using a system is related to the *'distance'* that separates the work object from the human in terms of the required direct actions to achieve the task's goal. He proposes to represent these difficulties with a four levels scale. A tool that is supposed to help the human operator is adding some secondary or 'parasitic' tasks (Valot, 1988), relating to the tool handling and management, in addition to the primary task at hand. ICAO has used the same idea in discussing the Flight Management System (FMS). The operator has to have a clear vision of the final objective of the work but also of the intermediary objectives relating to the tool. The problem for the designer is to provide timely, context sensitive information. Obviously, the information needed to use a landing gear (level II) is not the same as the information needed to manage an automatic system that could have its own internal control logic. The problem of providing adequate and timely information is not easily solved because one cannot convey all possible strategies and conditions to the pilots if they are to react in the appropriate way, quickly and in a co-ordinated manner. It is essential that pilots can choose the appropriate aid, which corresponds to their own current capabilities. For example, Nordwall (1996) recalled that 'one major difficulty in the cockpit, is re-establishing automatic flight after a computer upset, not just the autopilot but the full automation'.

In summary, current Human Factors methods are not well suited to the modern aircraft, where pilot and machine (automated systems) are engaged in a co-operative activity for which it is essential that pilots and machine share flying strategies all along the flight.

The systems are coupled

The previous model masks a part of the reality. Technical systems are coupled and exchange many types of information. The technical coupling can also be extended to the wider environment and human agents (e.g. crews, Air Traffic Controllers). If the early prototype evaluations (at a specific interface level) show that the new system is very efficient in a conceptual design phase, it is necessary to go from these traditional local evaluation methods towards integrated system evaluations, which include coupled functions. This is essential because the systems coupling can result in large cognitive demands for the pilots. For Amalberti (1996), the pilots have to navigate between the different abstraction levels of the systems to understand a situation. The more the systems are coupled the more complicated the representation of the reality (conceptual or physical), to the point at which it can become incomprehensible and unusable. Therefore, the evaluation has to account for these different levels in order to test the information that is actually useful to the pilots. But as the complexity is growing, the cost of performing the adequate testing effort becomes prohibitive (Abbott, 1999).

The human is an integrated multifaceted system

There are a great number of Human Factors issues being investigated, which has resulted in a large body of knowledge. However, when a designer is thinking of a design solution one can appreciate the difficulty of integrating all the available data on such a multi-facetted discipline as Human Factors.

Two problems can be identified for the manufacturer, when designing and evaluating a solution:

1. What are the relevant, necessary and adequate Human Factors topics, which have to be studied to make a good design?
2. How can the different Human Factors topics be gathered in a set of requirements that can be reasonably evaluated? One should understand that it is not possible to perform different evaluations for each Human Factors topics. Manufacturers have to take strategic decisions on how to adequately address the Human Factors in the design process?

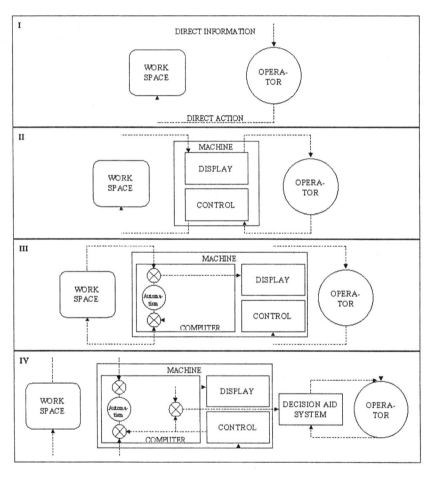

I	INSTRUMENTATION – Handling	**II**	MECANISATION – Control
III	AUTOMATISATION – Supervision	**IV**	INTERCONNECTION – Diagnostic

Figure 1   The complexity scale (translated from Guillevic 1991)

36

An important issue encountered by an aircraft manufacturer, is the wide variety of Human Factors characteristics that must be taken into account. During the design cycle, different topics may be studied independently or in an integrated manner. From the pilot's points of view, one specific sub-system is not the main focus. He or she has to work in a situation where the constraints are interlinked. Consequently, the methods used by the manufacturer have to scale-up to the whole flight deck system and (to keep it manageable) the methods should be filtered in order to concentrate on the most relevant and most significant ones.

The complexity of the human-human machine interaction must be tackled by a systems approach. Simulation plays an important role, although it should be noted that it also has its limitations in terms of ecological validity.

In conclusion, the designers are more focussed on the product and practical solutions in the bigger picture of an overall flight deck. Traditionally, academics are more judged by the approaches, the hypotheses (including the theoretical models) and the way to put the evidence, but increasingly the academic research is addressing the system integration issues.

The manufacturer's constraints

The intention of this chapter is to highlight constraints and room for manoeuvre that the manufacturer has during the design process. The best the manufacturer can do to preserve design robustness is to anticipate the consequences of the evolution/revolution induced by some changes inside the aircraft due to the introduction of new technologies, or in the environment due to the ATC changes, or in the pilot's capabilities. However, before discussing the details of the manufacturers' constraints, it can be useful to review the main functions of a manufacturer.

Designing and manufacturing the product

Developing a new aircraft today takes significantly less time than it did 10-20 years ago. Today, it takes five years from the program launch to entry into service. During this period, it is only possible to test new and different design concepts during the first two years. These constraints are not unique to the aviation domain. Middler (1993) has suggested that the same principle applies in the car industry. Whatever the product being designed, there is an inverse relationship between the ability to change the product and the stage of the design process (i.e. further in the design process, there are fewer opportunities to modify the product). It means that all the novel design components (as regards to Human-Machine interface) cannot be reinforced by large-scale research studies during the design process. Either they must have been validated before the start of the design process or – at a minimum – research has significantly reduced the risk associated with the novelty being

Florence Reuzeau and René Nibbelke

introduced. This constraint also applies to the design of other safety critical systems in which mature solutions are preferred over innovative but unproven ones. Time and cost effectiveness are two other very important constraints for the manufacturer.

Certifying the product: obtaining and maintaining the certification

In order to achieve a timely and cost-effective design process, risk management is a key factor. Unidentified risks (for example in the area of Human Factors) can result in large delays and overspends. One of the risks is legal liability. Even if all the available knowledge and best practice is considered, it is acknowledged that flight deck design is too complicated, to anticipate all the potential causes of future accidents.

Because too many different fields of H-HMI causes are interlinked, there is a real danger that too much emphasis on research and psychological literature will mean that Human Factors recommendations will be too late to influence the design. It is recognised that the technology evolves more quickly than the Human Factors techniques can be developed. This implies that the basis for validation of the tools may not exist in time for the design evaluation. Manufacturers have to create evaluation criteria adapted to new devices. Even if an old system is renewed, if the operational conditions have changed, some new Human Factors issues can arise. For example, the advantage of a human on the flight deck is the ability to adapt to the environment. However, this can also be seen as an inconvenience. The adaptation strategies are unlimited and can be unpredictable. There is no reliable reference for human performance in complex situation with highly automated systems. This baseline is essential, but currently none exists. Academics, regulatory authorities, and industry have to jointly develop such a baseline.

For the manufacturer, there are also problems resulting from conflicting recommendations in the Human Factors research literature. For example, whereas Wise (1994) advocates minimising human error, Amalberti (1997) defend that human error is a positive factor for pilots training and an efficient way to keep the pilots in the loop. These two viewpoints have repercussions for cockpit design. On the one hand designs can be made to prevent human error (by eliminating human interaction) on the other hand the design can be made to improve the detectability of errors, ease of 'undoing' the error or minimise the consequences of the human errors. If one recognises the benefits of human error, the manufacturer and the authorities have to revisit certification and safety analysis methods, which are currently more orientated towards error limitation.

Commercialising the product

In the aviation community, the manufacturer is also the vendor, whose aim is to maintain and develop its market share. Given that the product has to be developed, tested and delivered on time to the customer, the question is how to decide the

38

focus of Human Factors efforts. The design process tends to be driven by what is considered useful for the program and demanded by the authorities. For research activities, on the other hand, it is possible to modify the study depending on criteria such as cost, time, available tools and available human resources and their competencies.

Although academic knowledge may not be easily transferable, data associated with a specific interface (e.g. a specific FMS, head-up display) in specific experimental conditions may provide valuable results for the designers. In addition, a few models are available for criteria like 'understanding', 'easily amendable', 'modifiable' and 'adjustable' exist, as do some guidelines (Billings, 1997), general criteria (norms ISO, military handbook) and usability criteria (Nielsen, 1993). Nevertheless, the quality of cockpits cannot be guaranteed by the application of good design principles. The complexity of the product and the variety of possible solutions make simple – and often general – design principles inadequate. EADS Airbus SA has developed its own grid of criteria (Robert and Buratto, 1998). It contains twenty Human Factors criteria to consider when designing an interface in the cockpit.

The final design decision depends on many factors and compromises made throughout the design process. The design process itself is complex, due to the number of people involved, the number of components, the number of decisions and its reliance on the experiences and expertise of different individuals. A solution to cope with these difficulties is to define:

- A Human Factors process in term of the major design stages, and
- A methodology,
- A Human Factors team able to support the designers in application to the design process, and
- A way to improve the tracability of the various actions made through this process.

In the literature several theoretical models of the design process are presented. It should be noted that in a commercial design organisation the design process is only a guide and it has to be flexible and compatible with the aircraft or the system being developed.

The Human Factors process: systemic, iterative and participative

To understand how the industry sets up its own design methods, it is necessary to briefly describe the basic principle of design. Design can be seen as a problem solving activity in which three main activities can be distinguished: problem setting, solution generation and solution evaluation.

The Human Factors experts can help the designers in two of these activities, the problem setting and the solution evaluation. The solution generation is a designers' specific activity for which they use their expertise and experiences.

In fact, several authors have shown that the problem and the solution definition are very closely linked (Hoc, 1987; Hayes-Roth, 1979). The problem representation guides the designers towards the solution. The two activities can even be combined, but this is to the detriment of a good requirements analysis because solutions may be overlooked if the problem is not defined separately. The integration of Human Factors experts and users at the early stages of design enhances the actual problem setting.

Design models have changed in several aspects over recent decades. In the 1970s, the Cascade model (a deterministic step-by-step design process without interactions) was held up as an accurate description of the design process. Engineers themselves carried out the user requirements analysis, without the direct involvement of the users (De Marco, 1978). Design models that became more requirements-oriented followed this. In the 'V-design cycle' as well as in the 'Spiral model' of design (Bohem, 1988), the needs analysis is formalised as a separate task to be accomplished. These later models emphasise the role of rapid prototyping, which facilitate the integration of the users in the design activities. Several tools and methods have been proposed to support the user requirements analysis (Caroll, 1995).

As an illustration of this more recent model of the design process and how Human Factors can play a role in it, the V-model is presented in figure 2. This V-model describes:

- A systematic process.
- An iterative process.
- A human-centred design process, involving the user as necessary.
- A process fully integrated in the general design process, integrating knowledge and expertise from the different design disciplines. The results of the Human Factors studies have to serve the specifications.

Figure 2 indicates that the different design specialities are developed in the spirit of concurrent engineering in order to (1) take into account the perspectives of other disciplines, (2) to facilitate explicit trade-offs and (3) to improve the design quality at each stages of the design (the design stages are described below).

The Human Factors design process (Reuzeau, 1997) is based on:

- The involvement of a Human Factors practitioner in the design team in order to guarantee consideration of the users' needs and ensure an optimal degree of usability.
- User participation.
- Modelling of crew tasks as a core activity and as a basis for analyses (design/evaluation).

The crew task can be defined as the crew goals (and sub-goals) and the means to realise the goals. The crew task modelling reveals what the designers expect the pilots to do with the existing or future device. In fact many studies have shown that the task analysis is not sufficient when the users' activity is very context-dependent.

That is why we have combined the task analysis with a scenario based similar to that of Caroll (1995). The scenarios are used in all the phases of the design cycle.

The three main phases of the design process are presented below:

- Concept exploration and definition (stage A).
- Concept demonstration and validation (stage B).
- Solution verification and validation (stage C).

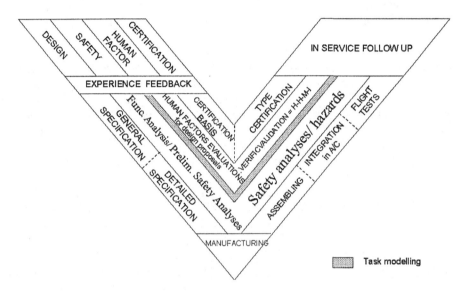

Figure 2   The 'V' development cycle

Stage A: concept exploration and definition

This phase is related to the identification and analysis of pilots' needs and the research on the concepts of a design solution. This phase is essential because the designers have to try to predict the future environment in which the aircraft or the system will be used (type of mission, critical operations, crew concept, physical or sensory skills, any factors that may result in frequent or critical human performance errors) in order to begin the crew task modelling and to look for the technical solution available. At this stage the relevant information about the human, the environment and the tasks is gathered. Vicente (1999) has defined five models necessary to help to build the design, which are used at this first stage:

1. The domain (technical feasibility, certification rules, etc.).
2. The system users, their experience, their expertise, their cultural specificities, their motivation, etc.

3. The operators' tasks, the difficulties, the strategies employed by operators to perform the work.
4. The artefact: informational and functional contents, dialogue mode.
5. The environmental constraints (physical environment in terms of temperature, humidity, vibrations, cultural constraints, organisation, etc.).

This phase is very reliant on experience, experience feedback, general rules, norms and standards and lessons learned. It results in a contribution to the user requirements document (including functionality, information requirements and usability requirements). The issue of user requirements is detailed below.

The requirements definition   'Requirements are descriptions of *how* a system (which can be a Human-Human-Machine Interface) should behave, a system property or attribute or may be a constraint on the development process of the system' (Sommerville and Saywer, 1997). It can also include requirements for the systems' functionality or the desired effect of the system on, for example, workload. They can be considered as a common reference between the engineers, the pilots and the Human Factors specialists. These requirements are defined at various levels, from a high-level design philosophy to a details requirements and constraints.

The requirements analysis   As the requirements are conceptualised elements, they change throughout all along the development cycle. The requirements analysis is a useful exercise if the requirements are formalised and become a living component of the design process by using Requirements Engineering techniques. To meet the traceabilty objective, EADS AIRBUS SA has developed a method and associated tool supporting the requirements process: CARE (Common Airbus Requirements Engineering). In addition, EADS AIRBUS SA and BAE SYSTEMS have both been involved in a large scale European Human Factors Research (the DIVA project), investigating new approaches to requirements analysis in multi-disciplinary, multi-national teams (Nibbelke et al, 1998).

In this design phase, alternative product solutions can be generated and compared. At the end of this process the final document will also include an analysis of the main Human Factors issues for the system or the aircraft.

The inputs are based on general guidelines, cockpit philosophy and experience feedback. During this phase, several specific actions have to be achieved in close co-operation between the Human Factors specialists, the engineers and the pilots: the Mission analysis, the Pilots needs and preliminary task modelling, the preliminary interface design, the analysis of the operational concept (system functions, use of the system in normal and abnormal situations). The first work on defining pilots' knowledge requirements can begin in this phase. For example, even during the first interface evaluation, an analysis of the knowledge necessary for the pilots to use the systems can be carried out.

The allocation of functions (functional flows, functional allocated humans and machines) is also part of this phase.

(Hopkin, 1994) quoted several kinds of data that can contribute to the evaluation of a new process:

- Theory and constructs that provide a basis and rationale for generalisation.
- Data representative of the original data, but that may be at different levels (e.g. theories vs. laboratories studies).
- Similar data from another application, domain, context or disciplines. These situations are called 'reference situations' by Daniellou and Garrigou (1993).
- Operational experience relevant to expectations and predictions.
- Expert opinions compared to the preceding items.
- Users' comments based on their experience and knowledge.
- Case histories, incidents, and experience with the operational system.

At the end of the exploration phase, some design solutions are ready to be thoroughly evaluated. They are accompanied by the operational requirements analysis and the list of the main Human Factors issues to study in the next stage.

Stage B: concept demonstration and validation

The second stage is the system and interface definition, with the refinement of the pilot's needs, taking into account the specificities of the technical solution. Among the major products of this phase are the specifications and the design baseline for the control and display definition and for the geometrical implementation.

The allocation of functions is a critical step in the design and includes analysis of performance, reliability and costs. The major Human Factors issues at this level are the levels of automation desired, analysis of tasks and skills required for operation, usability considerations and training requirements. These solutions are tested with pilots on tools representing the system and often the entire aircraft. The result of this stage is a system (and interface) definition.

Because of the complexity of the system, this stage can include several iterations in order to make different refinements of the product or of its use.

The main contributions from the Human Factors points of view are:

- Analysis of users tasks and interfaces.
- Definition of information content, languages/vocabulary, form of dialogue, help and errors messages.
- Definition of geometry implementation.
- Definition of documentation (users procedure, etc).

Stage C: solution verification and validation

The last stage includes the verification of the product and the final validation (corresponding to the climbing branch on the V representation).

Human performance is considered throughout this stage, from rigorous tasks and time line analyses to full operational tests. The objectives of the tests are to check if the system is correctly addressing the users needs, capabilities and limitations and secondly to check that the system meets the requirements defined in the specifications. The design stages described previously are all supported by different tests and evaluation methods and tools. The list of the methods and tools (experimental, analytical, ecological) is too long to be presented here but is widely reported in the literature.

The role of pilots in the design and evaluation

Involvement of pilots in the design and evaluation is not a recent issue. Pilots have always taken an active role. Several authors have tried to build models of pilot behaviour for certain tasks and for various sub-systems. Amalberti and Valot (1990) modelled the decision making of an expert pilot in a dynamic and risky flight phases in order to design an electronic co-pilot. Javaux (1997) is interested in the pilot model to study the pilots' behaviour face to the automation. Nibbelke and Emmerson modelled the management of decision-making in icing conditions and navigation decision-making during sub-system failure conditions (Emmerson and Nibbelke, 1998 and Nibbelke et al, 2000). A comprehensive universal pilot model – asked for by some – is however not a realistic ideal.

It is important to consider the role of test pilots and airline pilots (Reuzeau, 2000) for different design and evaluation tasks in the design process. Test pilots have been involved in the design from the early days of aviation. They have several roles (tester in simulator and in flight, designer, etc) and they play an important role in the demonstration of the compliance to the safety objectives. They are also most familiar with abnormal and potentially dangerous situations. Airline pilots also participate in the design and evaluation of the cockpit. They bring to the design and evaluation process operational feedback (especially in normal situations) and they are involved in the solution evaluation when a design solution is proposed. Manufacturers' experience shows that the involvement of pilots in the design process is not straightforward. Data collected with the pilots have to be consolidated. Where opinions between pilots differ, it is important to analyse the contexts in which judgement and arguments are being made. Moreover methods adapted to solve differences between users' arguments have to be defined. They cannot be based only on quantitative assessments. Qualitative ones are very relevant.

In conclusion, many categories have been proposed for methods and measurements in Human Factors. They rely on the subjective or objectives characteristics, the ecological value (laboratories or field methods), and are characterised by many criteria (their validity, reliability, acceptance, quantitative data). In addition to using these parameters as decision criteria in the design and evaluation plans, manufacturers can add some others to take into account the industrial constraints, for example:

- The repercussions of the Human Factors issues on safety.
- The main Human Factors issues.

- The moment of the design cycle.
- The effective cost and delay due to the methods.
- The choice of the testers/users (test pilots or airline pilots) and,
- The available tools (the type of prototyping tool has a large influence on the methods).

The next part describes an example of a Future Air Navigation System (FANS) interface study, in its exploration phase.

Application of the methodology to a FANS study

The introduction of FANS (Future Air Navigation System) is considered an important change in the aeronautical world. It provides part of a solution to coping with air traffic increases. It will have an impact on both a cockpit design and the pilots' tasks (including its operational context). The controllers' tasks and the pilots' tasks are changed.

In particular, the possibility to use written 'datalink' messages instead of voice communications will significantly affect the dynamics of the communication task and probably the tasks sharing between the pilots because the messages are available to both pilots (through shared audio on the headphones).

Practically, the major changes to be considered are:

- The new human-machine interfaces.
- The new tasks to be achieved.
- The new environment: the high density of the traffic, the lower aircraft separation and the new navigation rules.

The method

The Human Factor methodology set up to develop the new data link interface complies with the Human Factors process presented earlier in this chapter. The approach is complex due to the strong constraints induced by the introduction of the FANS. The study presented here below takes place at the start of the design cycle, in phase A. Initially based on a PC-based early prototype, it is eventually integrated into a simulator later on for a more global evaluation. Inside the *conceptual exploration phase* (phase A), the several tasks were undertaken which are described below.

The context and requirements analysis   FANS has to be introduced on existing aircraft as well as on new aircraft programs. For the aircraft in line service, one has to respect the cockpit philosophy, the basic principles (the colour coding, the dark cockpit principle) but also the existing equipment in the cockpit. The design of a common solution for A310, A320, A330 and 340 is a requirement. This makes it difficult to add a new device in the panels. The FANS device has some

45

specific new requirements: it has to be shared by both pilots, it has to be accessible to both pilots, it has to have a certain level of redundancy for safety, etc. In addition these new requirements issues with current communication systems have to be taken into account so that the new system is able to address some of these shortcomings. These requirements are all set in the overall context of an industrial project with its technical and commercial planning.

The manufacturer has to develop the Human Factors criteria to design and evaluate the new interface. Even if the traditional ones are usable (about the presentation of the information, SAE ARP 4791, RTCA, Human Factors requirements for Data link, ICAO DO-219, etc), it is not sufficient. FANS introduced a change in the dynamics of the exchanges between the ground controllers and the pilots. For example, a controller can send a message, the aircraft receives it, the pilot can read it immediately or he can wait to respond. This is different from the voice communication because the pilots now has a reminder of the message in a form of an 'external memory' with the FANS interface and doesn't have to memorise it. The pilots now have the possibility to prioritise which message to respond to first and how to mix the communication task with the priorities of other cockpit tasks.

This illustrates the importance of designing a new way of using the aircraft (procedures) when designing a new device. In the same way that the design has to follow the previous design philosophy, the procedures also have to be fully integrated and compatible with the skills acquired by the pilots in their years as an airline pilot.

A set of basic rules was formulated to design and evaluate the human machine interface:

- Dedicated interfaces for ATC communication exchange (for all up and downlink messages).
- Reduced interference on the existing systems operations.
- Minimised crew training requirements.
- Manual operation for the first phase of development of FANS.
- Immediate access to the standard message answers (WILCO, STANDBY, UNABLE).
- Adequate growth capability for future enhancement.

These rules can be interpreted as being Human Factors oriented as well as illustrating industrial constraints (the last one). Experience shows that it is very important to anticipate the future design solutions to keep continuity in the cockpit. All discontinuity can lead to an increase workload for the pilot, during the training or during the daily work.

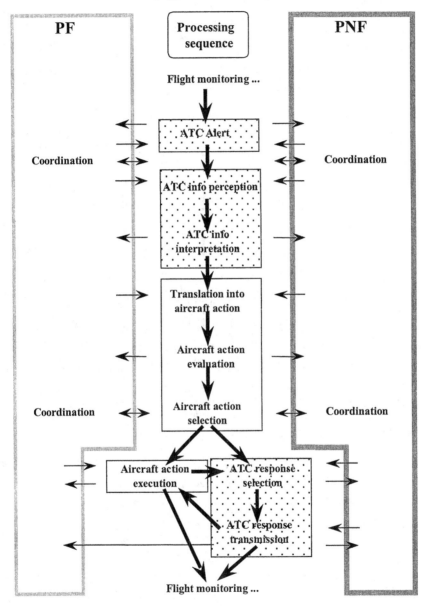

Figure 3a   The flight crew tasks model – reactive model

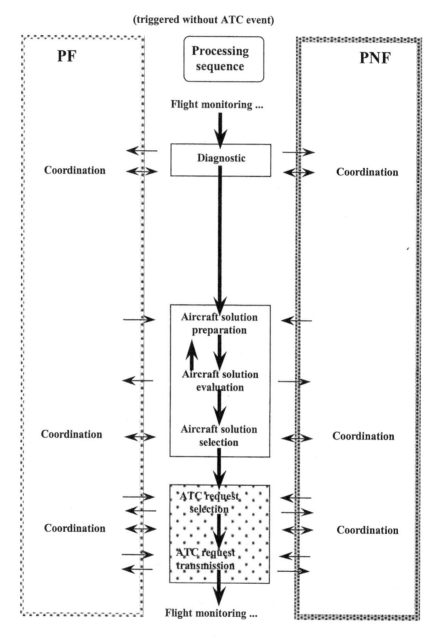

Figure 3b   The flight crew tasks model – scheduled model

During this period, a flight crew task model has been developed with the support of airline pilots. This model aims at providing a common framework for the design team (engineers, pilots and Human Factors) to understand the new communication tasks, to define the information needs, the critical phase of the pilots' activities and then to define the first main operational requirements.

The model is divided in two parts corresponding to two different attentional patterns (figures 3a and 3b).

In the 'reactive model' (figure 3a), a message is received on board while the pilots' attention is engaged in another task, which is different from today's ATC message management. He/she is then interrupted in his/her activity to take into account the incoming information. Anticipation is not possible and the pilots have to reconfigure their attentional resources. These conditions impose some requirements to the design. For example the alert (indicating the arrival of an ATC message) has to be unmissable (e.g. a visual and an aural alert), visible from both pilots, but it has not to be a nuisance because ATC messages are frequently received during the flight duration.

The pilots also have to send a reply to the ATC controller after having examined the situation and some flight crew co-ordination. To facilitate the diagnostic of the situation, it was suggested to provide easy access to the useful information (flight plan, etc). This implies that the FANS interface is well integrated in the rest of the flight deck interfaces.

In the 'scheduled model' (figure 3b), the pilot has planned to send a message to the ATC controller in accordance to the flight management and flight conditions. The HMI has to facilitate the ATC request preparation and transmission.

Three solutions   After a paper study, three possible solutions were identified which were both promising from a Human Factors point of view and technically feasible. We decided to keep and evaluate the three solutions, as they seemed to cover the requirements but with a different mix of compromises.

The first solution is based on the MCDUs: the FANS interface is integrated in the current MCDUs with an additional mode key for the ATC function. The second solution uses two additional Dedicated Control Display Units: the DCDUs. They are equipped with dedicated keys and reconfigurable soft keys. The installation constraints determined the size of the display. The third one uses the ECAM System Display.

Figure 4 gives the structure of the methodology and the specialists involved in it at the different stages of the design and evaluation activities.

At the first stage of the design, the most appropriate prototyping tool was the mock up station as it easily allowed modifying the solutions. The medium cost of prototyping is a key factor to design and evaluate different solutions. An evaluation questionnaire was defined and used by the Human Factors specialists during the evaluations sessions.

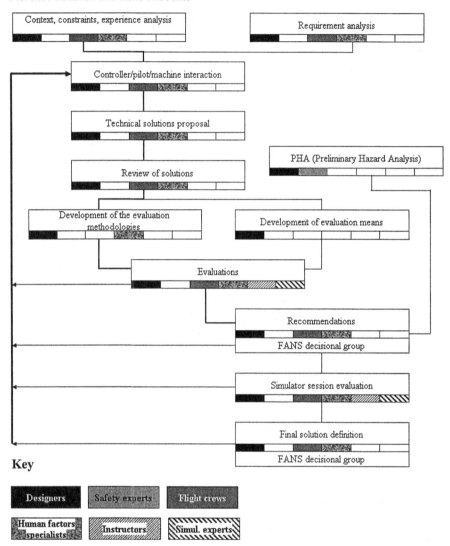

Figure 4   Organisation of the study

It is based on various usability criteria, ranging from the utility of the information (for the situation awareness), crew co-ordination, information presentation (character size, shape, colour coding, etc.) and the handling of the interface (number of action to do, guidance, number of items to memorise, type of errors and error management, etc.). During the evaluation session, the Human

Factors specialist observed the pilot's behaviour, the operative strategy and the types of errors.

At the beginning the audience was limited to a panel of experts pilots with various backgrounds (flight test, flight training, airline operation) because the concept was very novel, the mock-up limited and the solution not mature enough to allow the standard airline pilots to efficiently participate. The HMI was revisited to take into account the pilots comments and arguments. The requirements were also refined.

Simulator sessions were necessary in a second stage. The solutions were presented to a wider group of pilots. Several airline representatives from around the world (from different cultures) and Authorities expert pilots were involved in the evaluation.

Results of the study

As a result, the comparative evaluation allowed the design team to choose one solution among the three solutions: the Dedicated Control Display Unit. This device is located on the main instrument panel, just above the two MCDU. To capture the attention of the pilots, an aural alert (specific sound) and two visual data link ATC communication alerts (push button located in the glare shield, in front of the pilots' view) were provided.

The operational and technical requirements were refined in terms of information (type of information and presentation of information), in terms of control and the levels of automation.

The difficulties encountered in this study were focussed on the cost and the delay introduced in the design program (the evaluation sessions lasted 3 hours, there were 20 pilots, and a debriefing followed each evaluation). Three people, engineers and Human Factors specialists, were engaged in the preparation, the evaluation sessions and the data processing.

Even during the simulator sessions, the environment was not sufficiently realistic to attach a high level of confidence to the results. Some of the Human Factors issues have been unresolved and will require more investigation. The scenarios covered only a few normal and downgraded conditions. More difficult environments are also required to test the robustness of the solutions.

Despite these shortcomings, the study was very interesting for the manufacturer. It has brought a vast amount of information on FANS use and allowed to pose the basic requirements for the human-machine system design.

Conclusion

It is now commonly recognised that a solution for improving safety is to develop the Human Factors approach at every stage of the design process. This has to be

Florence Reuzeau and René Nibbelke

done through a multidisciplinary approach, including engineers, pilots, and Human Factors specialists. Industry, authorities and academic bodies have to reinforce their partnership. EADS Airbus SA is providing Human Factors training courses to designers and people with a technical background to make them aware of Human Factors issues and to improve co-operation with the Human Factors specialists. Several research issues are still to be investigated further (Reuzeau, 2001): the scenario development, the choice of users to be involved as well as the validity of data collected with the pilots. From a methodological point of view, there is a lack of formalised evaluation tools and tools which assist the Human Factors activities in the design process. This requires more attention in the future.

References

Abbott, D.W. (1999). Underpinnings of System Evaluation. In, D.J. Garland, J.A. Wise and V.D. Hopkin (Eds), *Handbook of Aviation Human Factors* (pp. 33-49). Mahwah NJ: Lawrence Erlbaum Associates.

Amalberti, R. (1996). La conduite des systèmes à risques. Puf (pub). Le travail humain (Coll).

Amalberti, R. and Wioland, L. (1997). Human error in aviation. *Aviation Safety Conference*. Rotterdam, August 1997.

Billings, C.E. (1997). *Aviation automation: the search for a human-centered approach*. Mahwah, NJ: Lawrence Erlbaum Associates.

Boehm, B.W. (1988). A spiral model of software development and enhancement. *IEEE Computer, 21*, 61-72.

Booher, H.R. (Ed.) (1990). MANPRINT: an approach to systems integration. New York: Van Nostrand Reinhold.

Caroll, J.M. (1995). Scenario-Based Design. Envisioning Work and Technology in System Development. New York, NY: J. Wiley and Sons, Inc.

Daniellou, F and Garrigou, A. (1993). La mise en œuvre des représentations des situations passées et des situations futures dans la participation des opérateurs à la conception. In, A. Weill-Fassina, P. Rabardel and D. Dubois (Eds). *Représentations pour l'action*. Toulouse: Octares.

De Marco, T. (1978). *Structured analysis and system specification*. New York, NY: Yourdon Press.

Emmerson, P.G. and Nibbelke, R.J. (1998). Worked Example of Cognitive Task Analysis: Aircraft Icing Management. UK Advanced Flight Deck Technologies II Project, Workpackage 10, Deliverable 10.2/2.

Goutal, L. (2000). Ergonomics assessment for aircraft cockpit using the virtual mock-up. In, K. Landau (Ed.) *Ergonomic Software Tools in Product and Workplace Design* (pp. 173-182). Stuttgart Germany: Ergon.

Guillevic, C. (1991). *Psychologie du travail*. Paris: Nathan.

Hayes-Roth, B. and Hayes-Roth, F. (1979). A cognitive model of planning. *Cognitive science, 3*, 275-270.

Hoc, J.M. (1987). *Psychologie cognitive de la planification.* Grenoble: Pug.

Javaux, D. (1997). Explaining Sarter and Woods' classical Results. The cognitive complexity of pilot-Autopilots Interaction on the Boeing 737-EFIS. In, N. Leveson and C. Johnson (Eds.) Proceedings of *Second Workshop on Human Error, Safety, and Software Design. Seattle, WA :* University of Washington.

Javaux, D. and De Keyser, V. (1998). Complexité et conscience de la situation dans les glass-cockpits. *Rapport final de la convention SFACT-Univerité de Liège.* (1995-1998). SFACT.

Meister, D. (1999). Measurement in Aviation Systems. In, D.J. Garland, J.A. Wise and V.D. Hopkin (Eds). *Handbook of Aviation Human Factors*, (pp. 33-49). Mahwah, NJ : Lawrence Erlbaum Associates.

Midler, C. (1996). Modèles gestionnaires et régulations économiques de la conception. In, G. De Terssac and E. Friedberg (Eds) *Coopération et conception,* (pp. 63-86). Toulouse: Octares.

Nibbelke, R.J., Pritchard, C., Emmerson, P.G., Leggatt, A.P. and Davies, K. (2000). Where do we go from here? Navigation decision aiding in the case of sub-system failure. In, D.Harris (Ed) *Engineering Psychology and Cognitive Ergonomics, Volume 5* (pp. 135-142). Aldershot: Ashgate.

Nibbelke R.J., Tomoszek, A. and Emmerson, P.E. and Fox, J. (1998). The use of Quality Function Deployment to analyse Human Factors Requirements in Civil Flight Deck Design. In, D.Harris (Ed) *Engineering Psychology and Cognitive Ergonomics, Volume 3* (pp. 85-92). Aldershot: Ashgate.

Nielsen, J. (1993a). *Usability Engineering.* New York, NY: Academic Press.

Nielsen, J. and Mack, R.L. (1994). *Usability inspection méthodes.* New York, NY: J. Wiley and sons Inc.

Reuzeau, F. (1997). Current methods and measures used by aircraft manufacturers for assessing the p ilot-machine interface. In. D. Harris (Ed.) *Human Factors for Flight Deck Certification* (pp. 9-20). Cranfield: Cranfield University Press.

Reuzeau, F. (1999). The pilot's participation in cockpit design: what can the manufacturer expect from them ? In, R.S. Jensen (Ed.) *Proceedings of the 10th International Symposium on Aviation psychology.* May 3-6. Colombus. USA. Columbus, OH: Ohio State University.

Reuzeau, F. (2001). Finding the best users to involve in cockpit design: a rational approach. *Le travail Humain 64(3)* 223-245.

Robert, J.M. and Buratto, F. (1998). Towards a grid for integrating ergonomic requirements into cockpit interface design. *Proceedings of HCI-Aero'98.* International Conference on Human Computer interaction. May 98.Canada.

RTCA (1992). *Human Factors Requirements for Data link.* RTCA paper 754-92/Sc 169-194-10/1992.

SAE (1994). ARP 4791 – *Human Engineering Recommendations for Data Link Systems*- Issued 1994-02.

Sommerville, I. and Sawyer, P. (1997). *Requirements Engineering: A Good Practice Guide.* New York: John Wiley.

Speyer, J.J, et al (1993). Assessing Crew Workload: from Flight Test Measurement to Airline Monitoring and Management. In, *Proceedings of the 2 day Conference on Workload Assessment and Aviation Safety* (April 27th to 28th 1993). London, UK: Royal Aeronautical Society.

Valot, C. (1988). Paradoxes de la confiance dans les systèmes d'aide. *Actes du colloque ERGO-IA'88.* Biarritz, 4-6 October, 1988.

Vicente, K.J. (1999). *Cognitive work analysis: towards safe, productive, and healthy computer-based work.* London: Lawrence Erlbaum Associates.

Ward, G. and Harmer, S. (1999). Integrating Human Factors within Systems Engineering. In, *Proceeding of the Ninth Annual International Symposium of the International Council on Systems Engineering*-Volume II). 6-11 June 1999.

Wise, J.A., Abbott, D.W., Tilden, D.S., Guide, P.C., and Dyck, J.L. (1994). Automation and the corporate aviation environment. In, N. MacDonald, N. Johnston and R. Fuller (Eds.) *Applications of Psychology to Aviation System.* Aldershot: Avebury Aviation.

3 Using cognitive function analysis to prevent controlled flight into terrain

Guy A. Boy and Daniel Ferro

Abstract

The DIVA project, launched in 1998, aimed at building and evaluating improved methods for Human-Machine Interface (HMI) design and evaluation. Its main goal is to improve crew situation awareness, one of the key safety factors in civil aviation. Controlled Flight Into Terrain (CFIT), one of the two design cases of the DIVA project, focuses on the prevention of a specific category of ground collisions. Such collisions are usually due to inappropriate terrain awareness. The Cognitive Function Analysis (CFA) method was used to support this design case. CFA is a cognitive engineering method that aims at describing the cognitive functions used by human agents interacting with automated systems, in order to help the design team optimise the human-centred design of those systems, for example. Appropriate Aerospatiale-Matra Airbus personnel were trained on and applied CFA to the CFIT design case in the industrial context of the design office. This chapter describes some of this work and the main lessons learned.

Introduction

Today, most civil aviation accidents are attributed to Human Factors. The aerospace industry needs to develop and evaluate new methodologies for human-centred design, i.e. that incorporate Human Factors (HF) in the design and evaluation process. The DIVA project is a European Collaborative three-year project (1998-2000). It involves 14 Aerospace companies and Research Centres[1] from seven different countries and is

---

Aerospatiale Matra Airbus, BAE SYSTEMS, SAAB, Sextant, Smiths Industries, Alitalia, NLR, DERA, RISO, EURISCO, CASA, Alenia, GKN Westland Helicopters, DQS.

partly funded by the European Commission under the program Brite-Euram III. The aim of the project is to develop, apply and evaluate in an *industrial* context a *methodology* that systematically uses up-to-date HF techniques for HMI design and evaluation. This methodology aims at minimising aircrew errors and maximising effectiveness by improving situation awareness (SA). It includes:

- A new HF-driven design process based on new methods for analysing the improvements which have to be made;
- Cognitive engineering methods and tools based on Cognitive Function Analysi (CFA) (Boy, 1998) and COGNET to develop the new HMIs;
- A new process of HMI evaluation on simulator based on objective and subjective measures of crew effectiveness.

Two other important outputs of this project are: the experimental human-machine interfaces developed to enable the evaluation of the methodology and recommendations on possible Human Factors certification requirements.

Design methodology

Two case studies have been used to evaluate the three phases of the methodology, i.e definition, design and evaluation on simulator. In the design phase, based on requirements produced during the definition phase, the new HMI solutions were designed and prototyped to allow a first Human Factors review. One case study aimed at improving terrain awareness (external situation). The second aimed at improving situation awareness with respect to understanding aircraft system failure (internal situation). During a workshop an expert group reviewed the resulting design Following this design review, design modifications were done. This chapter presents how CFA was adapted by EURISCO to DIVA needs, and used in an industrial setting (Aerospatiale-Matra Airbus) for one of the design cases (i.e. improving terrain awareness).

The aviation context: controlled flight into terrain issues

Controlled flight into terrain (CFIT) constitutes by far the most important category of fatal accidents in civil aviation. Moreover, in almost all the CFIT accidents, aircraf were totally destroyed and the number of fatalities is extremely high. CFIT i consequently the first issues to attack in order to significantly improve safety in civi aviation. It is widely accepted that CFITs are accidents related to collision with the ground or with fixed obstacles where crews were not aware enough of the relativ position and/or trajectory of the aircraft with respect to the ground. Crews wer therefore not aware of the imminence of the collision. We can see from this definitio that the most important characteristic of the CFITs is the lack of situation awarenes that the crew has with respect to the terrain. Obviously, those accidents happen whe the aircraft is close to the ground: take-off and initial climb account for roughly 25%

f the accidents; approach and landing account for about 55% of the accidents. In fact, 0% of the CFITs occur at less than 15 NM from the runway threshold. Main factors f risk (but not causes) are non-precision approaches (especially with multiple step-iowns), adverse weather conditions, night conditions, and mountainous zones.

The importance of CFITs motivated the development of the Ground Proximity Varning System (GPWS, in the 80s) and more recently that of EGPWS (Enhanced iPWS, in the 90s). Both systems are based on a detection of ground proximity from ensor information. EGPWS, in addition, provide the crew with cartographic iformation of terrain, centred on the aircraft's position. Statistics clearly show that rom the introduction of GPWS in 1985, the probability of CFITs decreased Iramatically, but that they still remain high. Current thoughts about CFIT prevention re based on the improvement of crew awareness in order to better anticipate possible onflicts, improvement of procedures and means for navigation (e.g. RNP[2], DGNSS[3], onstant slope approaches, crew surveillance procedures such as altitude/height erifications, consistency in the identification of all geographical waypoints among the iifferent systems that refer to them, such as paper and electronic data).

Cognitive function analysis (CFA)

CFA is a methodology that strongly encourages event-driven human-centred design hat can be seen as cognitive function allocation. Event-driven human-centred design s essentially based on the use of scenarios. Conventional ways of doing design is ased on goal-driven methods, i.e. designers start with an overall goal in mind and ttempt to decompose this goal into sub-goals until basic actions can be derived and ffectively performed. Goal-driven approaches to design are strongly anchored in idustry since they lead to manageable and explainable products. Resulting products re usually technology-centred. In many cases, they are easy to maintain also. The rawback in goal-driven design approaches is their failure to handle end-users equirements well. At the other end of the spectrum, event-driven design approaches end to foster participatory design (Muller, 1991) and use of experience feedback data. ince design is intrinsically iterative, event-driven approaches to design can be very me-consuming and unstable. CFA proposes to handle these issues in two necessary nd complementary ways:

- Categorisation of experience feedback cases into cognitive functions and scenarios that may be re-used in design
- Use of an integrated methodology based on the use of active design documents (ADDs) that enable design teams to implement participatory design (Boy, 1997).

RNP = Required Navigation Precision.
DGNSS = Differential Global Navigation Satellite System.

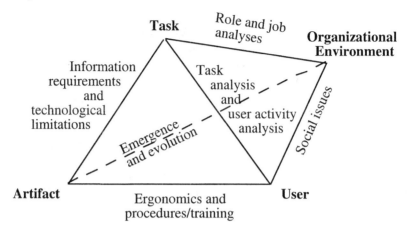

Figure 1   The AUTO pyramid

The categorisation of cognitive functions in a domain such as aeronautics is carried out using the paradigm of the AUTO pyramid (figure 1). Experience feedback cases are analysed and synthesised into four general categories related the *Artefacts* (e.g. aeronautical systems), *Users* (e.g. pilots or other relevant actors of the aeronautical community), *Tasks* (e.g. flying, maintenance), and *Organisational environment* (e.g. other actors who are likely to influence or participate in the performance of the task, environmental disturbances). Categorisation should be conducted within a group of experts that includes operational personnel.

Active design documents are mediating tools that provide both inputs and outputs of a human-centred design process. This process is human-centred because it systematically encourages the participation of various actors in the design process. The use of ADDs has two main goals:

- Associate a goal-driven approach (analytical description of design rationale and derivation of design solutions) and an event-driven approach (evaluations of incrementally generated solutions) to design; and
- Document the various steps of the design process and its solutions.

Step-by-step CFA

Categorisation of cognitive functions for the problem to be solved

Step 1: Use available relevant experience feedback databases   There are various sources of experience feedback data that includes ASRS, CHIRP or AIRS databases as well as various accident databases. Experience feedback is also available from discussions with experts, e.g. commercial pilots. In the DIVA context, we tried to use various sources including pilot experience, Flight Safety experience feedback data on CFIT and Airbus Industrie knowledge on the topic. There are various techniques that can be used to analyse experience feedback data such as Root Cause Analysis, Tree of Causes (Variation Diagram), and MORT (Management Oversight and Risk Tree). In the scope of the DIVA project, we have conducted very simple analyses of CFIT accidents. We use the interaction block representation to capture Human Factors data. This step provides synthetic cases. Another source of Human Factors data is scenario construction and exploitation. Flight scenarios involve the use of interface prototypes, as well as engineering and operational expertise.

Step 2: Elicit cognitive functions for the problem to be solved   Cases determined in Step 2 are used to elicit relevant cognitive functions for the problem to be solved. In order to conduct this elicitation process, concept graphs are generated that link experience feedback cases to cognitive functions (figure 2). Concept graphs and the AUTO pyramid help to categorise cognitive functions in a systematic way.

Step 3: Deduce usefulness and usability principles   Elicited cognitive functions are then used to derive usefulness and usability principles for subsequent evaluation. Basically these cognitive functions are likely to lead to usefulness or usability principles.

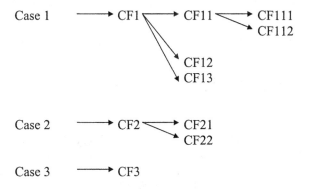

Figure 2   **Concept graph of cases and cognitive functions**

Incremental use of active design documents

Step 1: Generate a design rationale   Designers generate the requirements from creative ideas, experience feedback and directives from the management. Design rationale must include the requirements that lead to the design of a prototype (interface objects: IOs), and a description of the way to use it (interaction descriptions: IDs).

Step 2: Design an active design document   An active design document includes IOs, IDs and a design rationale for these IOs and IDs.

Step 3: Evaluate the current active design document   Usability and usefulnes
principles are used to define evaluation criteria. Tests are performed and the results are
stored in the contextual links (CLs) of the ADD. Depending on the difficulty of the
test, the evaluation can be done either directly by test-users themselves or by an
observer who scores test-users performance.

Step 4: Collect and analyse current evaluations   Once the current version of an ADD
is evaluated by several test-users, the results are collected and analysed. A single
analyst or a group of experts in aeronautics performs the analysis. This analysi
usually leads to the modification of the initial cognitive function concept graph
Consequently, usefulness and usability principles and criteria may be modified.

*Step 5: Decide that the human-centred design process is finished, if the current
solution is satisfactory for production.*

Step 6: Define a new design rationale   The design team then meets and discusses the
evaluation-synthesised results. This step usually takes place in a conventional meeting
room where the participants interact using mediating tools such as PowerPoint
presentations or directly active design document presentations. Synthetic design
rationale is derived from the discussions and explicitly expressed for subsequent use in
the next version of an ADD.

Step 7: Go to Step 2.

Application of CFA to CFIT issues

Constructing a cognitive engineering model

The following high-level requirements are related to DIVA objectives: obtain a natural
and accurate representation of the situation of the aircraft with respect to terrain as in
visual conditions; obtain awareness of the implications of aircraft performance on
terrain separation; detect terrain conflicts before an alert is triggered; provide early
alerts to crew of ground proximity; determine appropriate trajectory following terrain
separation violation.

Situation awareness is certainly one of the major issues in CFIT problems. If we
refer to Rasmussen's model of human behaviour (Rasmussen, 1986), the knowledge
based level includes three cognitive functions: situation identification that may be
recalled situation awareness at the knowledge-based level; decision-making; and
planning. The situation needs to be identified first. A decision is then made according
to goals, and finally a plan of tasks is constructed to implement the decision. Situation
awareness is a function of several quasi-independent situation types: *available
situation* in the cockpit from either the airplane, the environment (including the ATC
or the other crew member; *perceived situation* by the crew that can be disturbed by

arious personal or environmental parameters such as workload, performance, noise, interruptions and so on; *expected situation* by the crew from the requirements of ecision making or planning; *inferred situation* by the crew from incomplete or incertain data.

These four types of situations are useful in the analysis of the cognitive functions involved in CFIT issues. In particular, crew monitoring with respect to terrain is related to navigation, and thus situation identification, decision-making and planning that involve the four types of situations already described. Cognitive function analysis is then carried out by investigating two main types of variables:

- *Independent variables* that the crew can control directly such as altitude, horizontal position, airspeed and descent rate, characterise the actual situation.
- *Dependent variables* that are usually constructed from regulations or from the actual flight plan, include minimum safety altitudes, proximity positions, air speed limits, and descent rate limits.

The concept of independence (and its opposite concept dependence) is defined here o denote variables on which the crew can act (the other variables depend on various onstraints, and the crew cannot act on them). The level of freedom that the crew has s directly connected to the scope and range of independent variables. In other words, the more dependent variables are constraining the control of independent variables the ess the crew is in charge of the flight. Of course, there is no link between this istinction (dependent vs. independent variables) in the context of CFA, and the other istinction that was made in various control theories. Dependent variables can be reated as independent variables according to the level of detail in the analysis. For xample, when performance variables are considered as independent variables, e.g. hrust or engine power, altitude may be considered as a dependent variable. The nvestigation of these two types of variables leads to the elicitation of relevant ognitive functions by considering four types of situation already described.

liciting a first set of CFIT-related cognitive functions

he above high level requirements, a first cognitive function analysis leads to the ollowing set of cognitive functions:

- *Check aircraft position and trajectory versus minimum safety altitudes (MSA)* that can be decomposed into the following cognitive functions (MSA include altitudes relevant to terrain and traffic separation and VHF reception): Check actual, predicted, intended, and planned trajectory.
- *Understand minimum altitudes* through awareness of surrounding terrain and obstacles.
- *Understand type of relief* around the aircraft with respect to predicted trajectory.
- *Anticipate any conflicting situation* on intended trajectory through awareness of minimum altitudes, surrounding terrain and obstacles.
- *Detect any conflicting situation* on intended trajectory through awareness of minimum altitudes, surrounding terrain and obstacles.

- *Modify trajectory* to prevent conflicting situation and resume nominal situation.

Using scenarios to perform a CFA

CFA scenario framework   A flight scenario can be analysed using the interaction block representation. This involves the analysis of five types of attributes for each relevant agent at each relevant time:

- *Context* requirements that involve high-level cognitive functions such as mode awareness.
- *Goal* requirements that involve high-level cognitive functions such as goal identification, setting and maintenance.
- *Triggering preconditions* monitoring requirements that involve high-level cognitive functions such as situation awareness and anticipation.
- *Actions* (do-list) requirements that involve high-level cognitive functions such as crew recovery actions that need guidance and general information, e.g. in the case of alert provide safe avoidance guidance.
- *Abnormal conditions* (alert) requirements that involve high-level cognitive functions such as conflict resolution, i.e. comparison between actual or predicted altitude and safety altitude, e.g. if actual or predicted altitude is below safety altitude then an action must be undertaken; comparison between predicted altitude and the ground.

We propose to use the CFA situation analysis grid, and a time-line decomposition of the interaction blocks that are relevant for the proposed scenarios. The time-line will take the form presented in table 2.

Table 2
Time-line representation for CFA

Elapsed Time	Agent (PF, PNF, CM1, CM2, A/C, ATC)	Context	Triggering Preconditions	Goal	Actions (do-list)	Abnormal Conditions (alerts)

Example of CFA scenario analysis

To fill in the context attribute, a few definitions are needed. In particular, flight modes need to be better understood from Human Factors and cognitive perspectives. To simplify, there are two main high-level (horizontal) flying modes in usual current practice: *NAV mode*: flying by delegating various functions to the flight management system (FMS) where the pilot provides flight plan requirements to the aircraft; *HDG mode*: flying by using the autopilot (AP) where the pilot provides heading requirements to the aircraft.

HMI functions

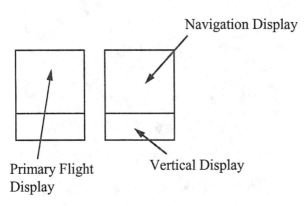

Navigation Display

Primary Flight Display

Vertical Display

Figure 3   New DIVA HMI

There are two main functions represented on the navigation display where sea is represented in blue, and altitude values are provided for some peaks:

- The *Map* function that includes the lateral representation of the aircraft position, predicted trajectory, planned trajectory, and terrain. The Map function is colour-coded (green). It is a function of terrain altitude, and is independent from aircraft altitude (figure 4).
- The *Peaks* function is similar to the EGPWS function. It provides a lateral representation of the aircraft position, predicted trajectory, planned trajectory, and terrain. The Peaks function provides the terrain below the aircraft (similar to 'Map'), and the terrain altitudes above the aircraft (colour ranges from yellow to red).

In addition to previous cockpit interfaces, there is now a vertical display for CFIT purposes. The vertical function includes the aircraft position, the predicted trajectory in the 'unrolled' vertical plan that contains the lateral predicted trajectory, the terrain shape without colour coding, the safety altitude profile, the advisory function when

63

predicted trajectory intercepts the safety altitude (or altitude constraints in NAV mode), and an alert function.

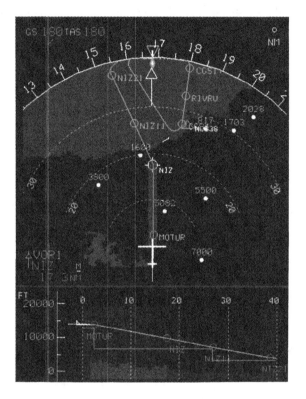

Figure 4   New DIVA display

Decomposition into interaction blocks

Let us take the example of the following context: ALT/NAV/AP1; ND-40; Non precision approach (Nice); no wind; no failures. The Goal of the crew is to fly toward MOTUR waypoint. The crew monitors the trajectory. They check terrain information (dependent variable) against current trajectory (independent variable). In conventional cockpits, the *check* cognitive function can be decomposed into three cognitive functions:

1. *Retrieve* the relevant minimum altitude value according to the current position and trajectory.
2. *Remember* the minimum altitude value and *Read* the current altitude value.
3. *Compare* both.

In the DIVA HMI, the three cognitive sub-functions for the *check* cognitive function are:

1. *Read* the minimum altitude value.
2. *Read* the current altitude value on the same display.
3. *Compare* both.

Note that the first cognitive function is very different in conventional cockpits and CFIT-based cockpits. In the first case, it involves an intensive use of the short-term memory. The cognitive load is then greater than in the case of DIVA HMI where the comparison of vertical profiles is almost instantaneous. We will say that the affordance is much better. In addition, when the pilot needs to anticipate what will happen in a few minutes, in the conventional cockpits, he or she needs to *infer* the predicted trajectory, whereas in CFIT-based cockpits, he or she directly does *see* the predicted trajectory. Again the cognitive load is much lower.

We have found that such cognitive function elicitation is a key contribution of the CFA approach. By decomposing cognitive functions into smaller grain cognitive functions, we are able to examine the complexity of the cognitive processes involved in the interaction. For example, in the current example, the *check* cognitive function is different in the two kinds of cockpits. The main difference is on the *retrieve* cognitive function compared to the *read cognitive* function. Retrieving information in the Long Term Memory is much harder than reading a colour or a value on the screen. This is basic knowledge in cognitive science, i.e. it is much better to involve recognition than recall. This kind of evaluation is rather qualitative but it is very important to orient human-centred design.

Defining usefulness and usability criteria

The cognitive functions that were elicited lead to the following usefulness and usability criteria: cognitive load from the use of the short-term memory; information retrieval load (from cockpit information); information retrieval load (human remembering and recall); understanding independent variables (minimum altitudes, terrain, and type of relief); comparison of independent and dependent variables; anticipation ease; conflict detection and resolution ease; trajectory modification ease.

This list of criteria is not exhaustive. It provides a first set of criteria that can be used to evaluate current interfaces developed by Aerospatiale-Matra Airbus. The crucial point here is to figure out how pilots will use the new artefacts such as vertical displays for example. Is the recognition cognitive function well supported? A subsequent analysis is required. We need to test which pilots anticipate using this new kind of artefact. It is not only an issue of colour coding of safety zones, even if it may end up with the fact that colour coding is an important aspect of the user interface. It is an issue of analysing the use of the new artefact in the overall context, i.e. taking into account other factors such as the organisational environment in the cockpit, the effect of the ATC in the new set-up, the adaptation of the task to this new device, and of course the co-adaptation of pilots to the artefact. If we find out that we need crosschecking from the other pilot, for example, to support the task, then this is a result. The consequences are then twofold, either we increase the display with a sound signal, or we request the change of procedure. Again, the usefulness and usability of this needs to be tested.

Lessons learned

CFA was evaluated as one of the most important tasks on the DIVA project. CFA was deliberately instructed to HMI designers within AM Airbus with the aim at applying it in the industrial context of the design office. The following feedback was used to weigh pros and cons of CFA and prepare a possible follow-up of the method:

1. *Learning effort*. Due to time and constraints, the CFA method was taught to DIVA partners during a one-day course. This short training was useful to explain the aim, content and steps of the methods. Designers had to continue to train themselves in the design office. We have progressively understood that CFA needs hands-on experience. EURISCO experts offered additional training and collaboration. Expertise is actually necessary in cognitive function definition and allocation.

2. *Description of pilots' prescribed tasks*. The first activity of a designer is always to start from the requirements. A requirement engineering method, the Quality Function Deployment (QFD), was used in the DIVA project to improve the formalisation of crew tasks in both design cases. In addition to this requirement gathering process, pilots' expertise was required. For example, DIVA members recognised that the first basic task of a pilot is to check aircraft position or trajectory with respect not to terrain, but to *the applicable minimum altitude*.

3. *Cognitive function elicitation and usability criteria derivation*. Task allocation is by far the most difficult step in the process. It requires time and experience. The difficulty is not the same with respect to the four dimensions of the AUTO pyramid, i.e. Artefact, User, Task, and Organisational environment. We are interested in the elicitation of cognitive functions involved in the use of an artefact. The elicitation of such cognitive functions provides very useful directives for the design of artefacts. The derivation of usability criteria is guided by the interpretation of elicited cognitive functions. Usability criteria help designers in HMI refinement and task allocation. The difficulty here is choosing among many usability criteria. Dealing with too many criteria entails waste of time by both designers and evaluators. It was therefore recognised that the list should preferably evolve with design maturity. For example, this first list of criteria includes mental workload that influences the original-task allocation among pilot(s) and artefact(s). Once the HMI has become more mature and its functions stabilised, the criteria should concentrate on sensorial aspects such as readability.

4. *Tools used.* CFA may be performed using paper and pencil. Nevertheless, as CFA's main purpose is to support interactive and participatory design through description of events, pilot tasks and evolving interfaces, some kind of software support is needed. In practice and within the scope of the DIVA Project, Word-based active documents were sufficient to describe the elements, i.e. interface objects (e.g. new displays), interaction descriptions (e.g. prescribed and effective pilot tasks), contextual links (e.g. usability criteria), and design rationale. Each scenario (e.g. an approach on a specific airport) was described through 10 to 20 snapshots; each of them included in one page including displays.

As this process developed, it became quite clear that CFA is a very good support for the design team. In addition to supporting traceability of various decisions, it helped drive the design process itself. Evaluation criteria may be iteratively reused to refine various design options, e.g. a display option or checklist. A subjective scale from 1 to was used to score the various evaluation criteria. Finally, the concept of active design documents is potentially powerful since it will support evaluation documentation, design rationale and decision traceability. The extra time spent filling in the design rationale and choices is the responsibility of the project leader according to the current design activity in the project or programme.

Conclusion and perspectives

Experience when using the CFA method inside Aerospatiale-Matra Airbus for HMI design shows that this method is worth pursuing on a larger scale, to show more of its advantages and weaknesses. It was recognised that CFA introduced a systematic way to take into account Human Factors and more specifically cognitive factors within the design process. In addition, it provides a way of documenting the design process and its solution. A major issue is cost. How much does it cost to carry out a cognitive function analysis? How much will we gain by carrying out a CFA? Economic issues will need to be carefully investigated.

CFA could be advantageously extended in using the AUTO pyramid as a reference analytical framework for many problems that arise during the life cycle of a product. 'What cognitive functions are involved in such a problem?'; 'What resources are poorly used or what resources should be created and allocated to which agent to improve solutions to this problem?' CFA has been developed for human-centred design, but is likely to be useful in other sectors such as training, maintenance and operations for example. CFA is currently adapted in maintenance training in three application domains: air force, car industry and road traffic management (IMAT Esprit project).

Aerospatiale-Matra Airbus decided to implement a Human-Centred Design Workshop within the Human Factors department that includes a database of scenarios describing events. HMI functions and usability criteria will be incrementally built for use by all HMI designers both in aircraft programs and research groups. EURISCO is currently using the CFA method to analyse incidents and day-to-day use of operationa procedures in aviation. A first classification of issues that arise in the use of flight dec checklists has been produced by EURISCO based on the AUTO pyramid. Thi classification is likely to be useful to generate more usability principles for appropriat design of specific interfaces, and a structure for a reusable scenario database.

References

Boy, G.A. (1997). Active design documents. *Proceedings of ACM DIS'97 Conference* New York: ACM Press.

Boy, G.A. (1998). *Cognitive Function Analysis*. Greenwich, CT: Ablex Publishing Corporation.

Muller, M. (1991). Participatory design in Britain and North America: Responding t the 'Scandinavian Challenge'. In, S.P. Robertson, G.M. Ohlson and J.S. Ohlso (Eds.) *Reading Through Technology, CHI'91 Conference Proceedings*. (pp. 389 392). New York: ACM Press.

Rasmussen, J. (1986). *Information processing and human-machine interaction. A approach to cognitive engineering*. Amsterdam: North Holland.

Acknowledgments

Hubert L'Ebraly, Thierry Broignez, Meriem Chater, Mark Hicks and Krishnakuma greatly contributed to the current state of the CFA methodology at EURISCO, AN Airbus and BAE SYSTEMS. Benoît Morizet participated in the team that applied CF in AM Airbus. Thank you all. Helen Wilson and anonymous reviewers provided astut advice towards improving the quality of this chapter.

4 Head-down flight deck display design

Don Harris

Introduction

If the eyes are the windows on the soul, then the displays on the flight deck are the pilot's windows on the world. Displays have much in common with windows; indeed it can be argued that the most important display on the flight deck is the windscreen! Pilots and flight deck designers frequently refer to making aircraft automation 'transparent', however it will only be 'transparent' if the windows onto the operation of the system are big, clear and free from distortion. Only in one way do displays differ from windows. A good display system should also help the pilot see into the future. Perhaps a crystal ball would be a better analogy.

Reising, Ligget and Munns (1998) suggest that flight deck displays have progressed through three eras: the 'mechanical' era; the 'electro-mechanical' era; and most recently, the 'electro-optical' (E-O) era. The advent of the display of flight information using cathode ray tubes (CRTs) is often described as the 'glass cockpit' revolution. However, the true revolution in glass cockpit aircraft has not been in the type of displays used, it is in the level of automation introduced onto the flight deck concomitantly with the introduction of these display systems (for example, see Billings, 1997). The 'new' CRT displays have exactly the same basic functions as the old electro-mechanical and mechanical displays; they merely have a different 'face' on them that allows different formats to be used for conveying flight-related information to the crew. CRTs are now being replaced by active matrix liquid crystal displays (LCDs) that are thinner, generate less heat and consume less power. However, both types of display system offer the display designer new opportunities. They are essentially 'blackboards' onto which can be drawn and animated almost any display format of the designer's choosing. This chapter concentrates primarily on the display formats that are currently used on these E-O displays. The object of this chapter *is not* to provide a historical overview of the development of flight deck display formats. The object is to examine current thinking about display formats. For the reader looking for a

69

historical perspective on cockpit design, Coombs (1990) is an excellent place to start. This book offers some interesting insights behind some of the design solutions found on the flight decks of modern aircraft.

There is little guidance in the airworthiness regulations (for example Federal Aviation Regulations/Joint Airworthiness Requirements – part 25) for the display designer about the manner in which information should be displayed. These regulations merely contain requirements for what should be displayed. Even then these requirements are difficult to find as the regulations are arranged on a 'system-by-system' basis, as these documents still do not treat the modern flight deck as an integrated system. The US Federal Aviation Administration did, however, produce an Advisory Circular in 1987 (AC 25-11 – Transport Category Airplane Electronic Display Systems) that contains the FAA's preferred options for the display of flight deck instrumentation on electro-optical displays. It needs to be stressed right from the start that this is an important document for the modern display designer. Although its contents are not mandatory, the display designer ignores its contents at their peril!

A further objective of this treatise is also to offer some suggestions about *why* some display formats are better than others. Put another way, some of the underlying psychological mechanisms describing why a particular display format works (or doesn't) are described. A great many of these explanations are drawn (unashamedly) from the work of Chris Wickens. However, there are many more psychological principles underlying display design than can be described in one short chapter. For those who want to find out even more about the underlying cognitive mechanisms of display design and interpretation, read Wickens (1992).

The basics

The ultimate objective of the display designer is to enhance the flight crews' situation awareness (SA), be it of their flight path, aircraft configuration or the functioning of their aircraft's systems. Situation awareness is a difficult construct to define precisely but in the context of display design Endsley's (1988) definition serves quite well. SA is '... the perception of elements in the environment within a volume of time and space, the comprehension of their meaning, and the projection of their status in the near future'. Endsley describes three levels of situation awareness. Level one (the lowest level) is based on the perception of an information element (or elements), in this case information conveyed by a single display element. If you have not got the basic building blocks (information) you cannot become situationally aware. Level two SA requires these elements to be combined to provide a 'bigger picture' of the situation. The pilot is required to form a holistic picture of the situation and understand the significance of all the elements in it. This involves the correct design and layout of the display elements into a larger whole. Level three SA is achieved when the pilot fully understands his/her current situation and can project ahead as to what is likely to happen in the future. The display designer should always be striving to help pilots achieve level three SA, hence the analogy with a crystal ball.

Endsley lists 12 principles that may be used to enhance SA. Several are particularly applicable to the display designer, for example:

- Minimise divided attention requirements – group information in terms of spatial proximity and avoid having many disparate display sources.
- Encourage holistic, 'top down' processing – present the pilot with the 'bigger picture'. Do not give them disparate components of information and expect them to assemble the 'big picture' in their heads.
- Filter information when required – in times of high workload give the pilots only the most relevant, task-related information.
- Display rate and/or trend information – all human beings are particularly poor at predicting future outcomes of events, especially in systems with either a high control order and/or a great deal of inertia.
- Spatial information should relate to the situation – for example, provide the pilot with track-up navigational information when it is important to know what is on the left or right.

The advent of the E-O display technology has enhanced the designer's chances of achieving level two and level three SA. It is now possible to present information in context, i.e. in its relative position in the 'bigger picture', rather than as piecemeal, seemingly standalone, disparate nuggets of information.

However, it is all too easy in a chapter of this type to launch into a lengthy discussion of issues such as the relative merits of tape versus dial formats for altimeters or the benefits of synoptic displays for problem solving, without first including a section on 'the basics'. 'The basics' are a set of fundamental principles and considerations that should be applied to *any* display. They include issues such as the size of characters; font types; scale increments; the use of colour and basic display formats. These may seem to be somewhat mundane, unexciting issues, however they are very necessary.

This section per force is quite brief. For more detailed guidelines the enthusiastic reader is referred to sources such as the UK DEF-STANs (Defence Standards), specifically DEF-STAN 00-25 (part 7) and the FAA 'Human Factors Design Guide', both of which are available in electronic format. These documents contain a wealth of information on these topics, are well indexed and easily searchable.

Character size and font

The character size required on a display is dependent upon the distance from the viewer. Many authors suggest that the same character sizes for the written word are applicable for the display of information on CRT displays, however, other authors have suggested that legibility and readability can be improved on these media by making the characters slightly larger, subtending an angle of 17-25 minutes of arc at the eye, (e.g. Hemingway and Erickson, 1969; Pastoor, Schwarz and Beldie, 1983). The FAA Human Factors Design Guide suggests that the height of characters should subscribe a minimum angle of 21 minutes of arc at the eye on colour E-O displays. At normal viewing distances on the flight deck, this corresponds to a character height of approximately 5mm (the size required at a viewing distance of just over 1m). Vibrating the viewer has a considerable effect on the legibility of text. While this is not a major concern in fixed-wing aircraft, vibration can pose problems for the crew of helicopters. As a result, consideration should be given to the use of a larger character size in rotary wing aircraft.

Not only should character height be considered, it is also important to consider their width. Fortunately, character width can be defined as a simple ratio of height. The FAA suggests a width-to-height ratio of 0.68-0.75:1, with the exception of such characters as 'm' and 'w' for which this ratio should be at least 0.8:1 and the characters 'l', 'i' and 't' which may be made somewhat narrower. These height/width ratios are typical of most of found in the literature. It should also be noted that these width-to-height ratios exclude the ascenders and descenders on characters such as 'd' and 'p'. The spacing between adjacent characters within a word should be approximately 10% of the standard character height and spacing between words should be the width of a standard character.

One further parameter also needs to be defined for the legible display of alphanumeric information on an E-O display, the character stroke width. Typical figures propose that for black text on a white background, the stroke width should be between 12.5-16.7% of the character's height (e.g. Cushman and Rosenberg, 1991; McCormick and Sanders, 1992). However, it is more common on avionic instrumentation that light characters are displayed against a dark background. In these conditions the edges of lighter characters have a tendency to 'bleed' into the darker background, hence it is generally recommended that the stroke/height ratio be reduced to around 8-10%.

Both the UK Ministry of Defence (DEF-STAN 00-25, part 7) and the US FAA Human Factors Design Guide specify that a simple sans serif font (e.g. Arial) should be used for lettering on the flight deck. Care should be taken, though, that certain characters are reproduced in such a way as to avoid misinterpretation, for example the lower case letter 'l' and the numeral '1', and the upper case letter 'O' and the numeral '0'. It is recommended that single words should appear solely in upper case letters. Phrases or sentences should appear in mixed upper and lower case (sentence case). Faster, more error-free reading of prose has been observed when using sentence case than when reading the same text in all upper case (Poulton and Brown, 1968).

If required, emphasis can be added to characters on a display in six general ways: increasing the brightness of characters; emboldening (increasing their stroke width); underlining; italicising; using reverse video and flashing text. As a general principle, italicising is not recommended. Its effectiveness is variable depending upon the basic font type used. Underlining reduces readability, especially if it cuts the descenders of lower case characters. The FAA (1996) recommends that when using flash rate for emphasis, a frequency of 3-5Hz should be used, with a 50% duty cycle. However, it is also suggested that this approach should be used sparingly and only to draw attention to critical items requiring an immediate response.

Luminance and colour contrast

To be easily readable any component on a flight deck display must have either a significantly higher or lower luminance contrast to the display background. This contrast is defined by the contrast ratio. DEF-STAN 00-25 (part 7) suggests that for a CRT type display, the *minimum* contrast ratio should be 3:1. Display contrast ratios should be user adjustable between up to an upper bound of about 10:1. AC 25-11 acknowledges the importance of these factors for display legibility yet merely suggests that these parameters should be 'adequate' or satisfactory' without actually specifying a value. Flat panel displays (FPDs) can achieve the same contrast ratio at lower luminance. Luminance contrast should always be used in preference to colour contrast to aid readability.

To maximise legibility when using colour contrast, a complimentary colour should be used when displaying a component against its background. As a general principle, colour should only be added to a display once the display format's effectiveness has been optimised in a monochromatic format. Colour alone is not a reliable method by which to convey information. Colour should be used sparingly and only as a redundant information code. It should always be used in conjunction with other options, such as size or shape. Furthermore, the brightness and colour of ambient light can severely effect the perception of colour. Hopkin (1992) suggests that the sole use of colour coding is potentially invalidated as a display option in situations where there is the potential for very high levels of ambient light, as can often be found on a flight deck.

The major benefits of colour construe when it is used to identify and group information on dense (cluttered) displays. Design guides and design standards strongly advise against using more than six or seven colours on an electronic display, even if it is capable of producing a far greater range of colours. Six broad considerations can be applied for the use of colour on flight deck displays. These are:

- Colours should be easily discriminated in all operating conditions.
- Colours should be consistent in their use.
- There should be only one meaning per colour.
- The colours used should be consistent with conventions.
- Few colours should be used.
- Users should not be able to change the colour conventions on a display.

Care should be taken to ensure that the use of red, yellow (amber) and green (and to a lesser extent, blue) is consistent with popular stereotypes and the conventions specified in the airworthiness regulations and advisory material (e.g.

FAR/JAR 25 and AC 25-11) for the use of warning and cautionary areas on instrumentation. Despite this warning about infringing colour stereotypes, though, a more careful consideration of the common associations made with colours suggests that these meanings are far from precise. For example, red is often associated with concepts such as 'emergency, or 'danger', but can also mean 'stop' or 'fire'. Yellow (amber) is generally used only to signify 'caution' but green has several associations, for example 'operational', 'safe', 'proceed' or 'exit'. In general, green is 'good', red is 'bad' and amber is 'potentially bad'! It is also worth remembering, though, that these stereotypes are *Western* stereotypes. Some colours have very different associations in East Asia. For example, red is considered to be a lucky colour, quite the reverse of its meaning on a flight deck designed in the West. The problems really begin to emerge with less strongly held colour stereotypes, for example that associated with the colour blue. Blue may be taken to mean 'off', 'cold', 'water' or 'sky'. However, DEF STAN 00-25 (part 7) recommends that blue should represent 'mandatory'. The same document suggests that white should be used to represent the concept 'operational'. The US civil aircraft advisory circular AC 25-11 suggests some different conventions, for example current data and armed modes should be depicted in white, selected data should be green and the selected heading/active route should be in magenta.

Basically, colour alone has no implicit meaning. If colour is to be used as a method of conveying information rather than just for display structuring and separation, its use must be consistent and users must be informed of the meanings associated with the various colour codes. Discriminating between hues or shades of a colour is relatively easy when making comparative judgements but identification of a colour can be very difficult when presented in isolation. If colour alone is used in an attempt to convey meaning, it will also be prone to the vagaries of the long-term memory of the pilot, potentially resulting in confusion and error.

Symbols

The aerospace industry is an international business. The use of symbols to label display components would initially seem to be an attractive idea as they convey their meaning irrespective of the native language of the flight crew. They also have the potential to reduce production costs. Nevertheless, if symbols are being considered for use, their design requires very careful consideration. The FAA list three criteria for the design of a symbol:
- It should be an analogue of the object it represents.
- It should be in general use and well known to users.
- It should be based on established standards and conventional meanings.

Wood and Wood (1987) suggest two further criteria to the current context:
- Each symbol must be clearly distinguishable from others.

• Newly developed symbols should not conflict with existing national and international standards.

DEF-STAN 00-25 (part 7) describes an extensive checklist for the stages in design of symbology. Similar methodologies for the design and evaluation of symbols are described elsewhere (e.g. Zwaga and Easterby, 1984). Much has been written about the design and use of symbols, but before their use is contemplated on a flight deck it is a good idea to first establish the need. Given the safety critical nature of the flight deck, only if a requirement is absolutely established should a symbol be developed and utilised. It is worth bearing in mind some of the potential disadvantages for the use of symbols, described by Cushman and Rosenberg (1991):

• Symbols are abstract, hence their meanings must be learned.
• Graphic symbols are of limited value to the inexperienced user.
• Incorrect operation may be more likely during the learning period.

Confusion may result if the user is unfamiliar with the objects or actions depicted. Despite their potential advantages, in general, the use of pictographic symbols is not recommended for use on flight decks, although as we shall see, to an extent these are increasingly being used on synoptic displays.

Display of quantitative information

Even with the advent of modern electo-optical displays, there are still only three basic formats for conveying quantitative information; digital counters; fixed-index, moving-pointer displays; and fixed-pointer, moving index displays (figure 1). Each of them has strengths and weaknesses for conveying certain types of information that depends upon the situation. These are summarised in table 1. Basically, there are two general types of information that a display provides; rate information and state information. Rate information gives the user an idea of the rate of change in a certain value. State information conveys information concerning specific values at a given point in time. Occasionally it is desired to convey both rate and state information in a single display.

With the exception of counters, both fixed-index, moving-pointer and fixed-pointer, moving-index instruments come in two common formats, circular dials and vertical or horizontal tapes. Fixed-pointer, moving-index scales can also come in either a full-scale or a windowed scale format.

When designing a display system the first step is to define the information that you need to display and the relationships between the pieces of information. Certain instruments will be used in conjunction with each other, for example when comparing the relative functioning of two (or more) engines. Other pieces of information will be used in isolation (e.g. cabin altitude). For each of these pieces of information you should ascertain if the pilot will be most interested in rate information, state information or a combination of both. Are the values to be displayed likely to change slowly or rapidly? What degree of precision is required and how quickly must the pilot read them? There is always a speed/accuracy trade-off. Displays that are designed to be assimilated quickly will be less precise; displays that are designed to convey accurate information will take longer to read. Finally, are the displays going to be utilised to make a swift check reading and does each of the systems have a nominal value that can be incorporated? Once such questions have been answered the appropriate display format can be selected.

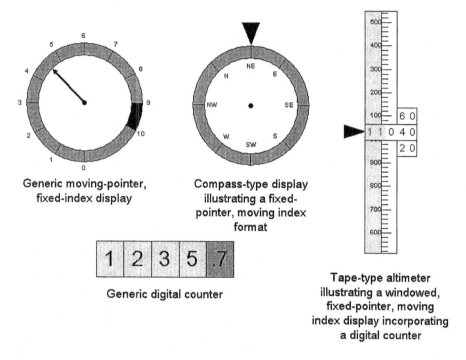

Generic moving-pointer, fixed-index display

Compass-type display illustrating a fixed-pointer, moving index format

Generic digital counter

Tape-type altimeter illustrating a windowed, fixed-pointer, moving index display incorporating a digital counter

Figure 1   The basic display types for conveying quantitative information

With modern E-O displays combined dials and counters can now be devised, giving the best of both worlds of speed and accuracy.   If the individual components on the display are arranged appropriately fast scanning 'check readings' are also possible if the nominal values are all arranged so as the pointers are all facing upward when the systems are working optimally. This is illustrated in figure 2.

It is at this point that it may be required to make some compromises in the design of the display formats.   Counters take up little space, convey precise quantitative information but are slightly slower to read that a fixed-index, moving pointer display. Many of them on the same display area will also lead to clutter and long search times to locate the appropriate piece of information. Fixed-index moving-pointer dials are the best compromise between speed and accuracy, especially if they also incorporate a digital counter, however they take up a relatively large amount of display area if they are to be readable. A circular dial format of this type of display is also good at conveying trend information, quickly. Tapes are less good in this respect as the human is more sensitive to the angular deflection of a large pointer than to the rise and fall of a tape, nevertheless they are still quite good. One advantage of tapes, however, is that they take up less display space than a dial. The FAA expresses clear preferences for the display formats and scale lengths to be used when conveying certain types of information (see AC 25-11).

Table 1
The relative merits of digital counters; fixed-index, moving-pointer displays; and fixed-pointer, moving index displays

Situation	Preferred display format		
	Analogue		*Digital*
	Fixed-index, Moving-pointer	Fixed-pointer, Moving-index	Counter
Reading accuracy is very important	✗	✗	✓
Reading speed is important	✓	✗	✓
Values change quickly or frequently	✓	✗	✗
User requires rate of change information	✓	✗	✗
User requires information about deviations from a nominal value	✓	✗	✗
Minimal space is available	✗	✓	✓
User required to set a quantitative value	✓	✗	✓

Although compliance with the material in advisory circulars is not mandatory, in most cases it is certainly wise. Perhaps somewhat unusually, AC 25-11 also describes display formats that in the past have not been deemed acceptable.

If the purpose of the display is to make a comparative check reading between several systems, then circular dials are slightly superior. Many dials on a display can all be arranged so that their nominal position is, for example, at 12 o'clock (figure 2). This allows a fast scan of the instruments as an emergent feature of the group of displays *as a whole* reveals itself, which is not apparent when each display component is considered in isolation. An abnormal value is easily and quickly spotted as the emergent feature of the vertical line formed by all the pointers when in their nominal position is broken. The processing of emergent features is automatic (i.e. not conscious) that means that monitoring displays arranged in this manner is not attentionally demanding. Tape-type instruments have a slight disadvantage in this respect. It is easy to make a swift check reading across a row of tapes but not down a column of tapes. Their emergent features are not as strong and they do not have the implicit nominal position that a dial has. Check readings can also be aided by the selective use of colour on the displays.

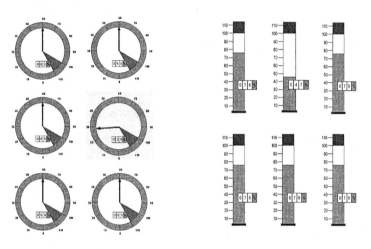

Generic fixed-index, moving pointer tapes (incorporating a counter) arranged to optimise check readings

Generic fixed-index, moving pointer dials (incorporating a counter) dials arranged to optimise check readings

Figure 2   Circular dial and tape formats of fixed-index, moving-pointer displays arranged to optimise a check reading

Barnett and Wickens (1988) described a further feature of display components grouped as illustrated in figure 2. This is the proximity compatibility principle. When information from several sources needs to be mentally integrated in some way, there is a benefit in arranging the display elements in close proximity to one another and in such a way as they form an emergent whole. However, if it is required that the user has to concentrate solely on a single display, such an arrangement can be detrimental to performance as the pre-attentively processed larger feature may interfere with the conscious, focussed attention required to interpret the single display element.

The greatest problems are associated with the 'open window' displays of moving-index, fixed-pointer design. These have all the disadvantages of both traditional dials and counters, with none of their benefits. It is impossible to make a check reading from these displays, as the operator has no idea where in the range of potential values the current value lies without actually reading the value. Additionally, they do not possess the accuracy of a counter. They do however, transmit some trend information, although not as efficiently as a fixed-index, moving-pointer displays.

Display concepts for the control of high inertia systems

So far, this discussion of the basics of display design has concentrated on the design of the instrumentation alone. However, display formats cannot be considered without reference to the nature of the control task itself. Pilots of heavy commercial aircraft face a particular problem that can be partially alleviated by good display design. The problem is that they are controlling a high inertia system with control lags (for example when hand flying the aircraft during approach and landing). This requires the pilots to anticipate the likely effect of their control inputs on the aircraft's flight path at some time in the (near) future. Unfortunately, human beings are very poor at this. However, the effect of response lags in a system may be overcome by the use of predictor or quickened displays.

Predictor displays Predictor displays are driven by a real-time computer model of the system which predicts its future state on the basis of certain assumptions, for example that the magnitude or direction of the operator's control input are not changed. The distance into the future that the computer predicts depends upon a variety of factors including such things as control lags and inertia. Predictor displays convey to the operator the current status of the system and its predicted status at some time in the near future. By displaying current and predicted state these displays also provide some idea of the error between the current state, the predicted state and the desired state.

The down side of predictor displays is that they add clutter as a result of all the elements that need to be conveyed (Stokes and Wickens, 1984). Furthermore, their predictions are only as accurate as the algorithms from which they are computed. There is also another 'Catch-22' associated with them. These displays are most useful with high inertia systems with large control lags. The further you need to look into the future the more beneficial this type of display becomes. Unfortunately, the further into the future you try and anticipate, the more inaccurate the predictions become as a result of the assumptions made in the calculations and other disturbing influences from the environment (e.g. turbulence).

Quickened displays Quickened displays are almost identical to predictor displays, however, they lack the element showing the current status of the system: they only show the predicted value. This approach is typically used in command-type displays (such as the flight director bars). However, as Stokes and Wickens (1984) note, 'the command does not represent the true zero-error flight path, but instead represents a signal which, if used as the basis for control, will produce successful guidance along the flight path' (p. 389). McCormick and Sanders (1992) suggest that this type of display can lull pilots into a false sense of security, as the true magnitude of the *current* error is not visible.

Control-display compatibility

Displays do not exist in isolation. In many instances a control input is required in response to information on a display or is needed to change a parameter setting on a display. To maximise the efficiency of a system the controls and displays must have a compatible relationship. However, some aspects of control-display compatibility are not as straightforward as they at first seem. Users have several stereotypes about the manner in which controls operate, for example in an aircraft 'up is on'; 'forward is faster' or 'clockwise to increase'. Nevertheless, some of these stereotypes may be infringed, be incompatible or be invalid in certain circumstances. However, more of this anon.

Direction of motion of scale

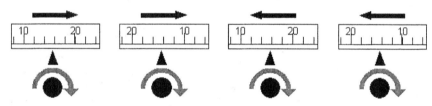

Direction of motion of knob

Direct drive	Direct drive	Reversed drive	Reversed drive
Scale numbers increase left - right	Scale numbers increase right - left	Scale numbers increase left – right	Scale numbers increase right - left
Clockwise to decrease	Clockwise to increase	Clockwise to increase	Clockwise to decrease
6% starting errors	5% starting errors	43% starting errors	52% starting errors
0% Setting errors	5% Setting errors	0% Setting errors	4% Setting errors

Attributes which do not conform to population stereotypes

Figure 3   Error rates for a setting task using a moving-scale, fixed-pointer display and a rotary control as a function of control-display relationships (from Bradley, 1954)

The three main principles for making a setting using fixed-pointer, moving-scale display using a rotary control (a task familiar to any pilot when setting the barometric pressure on a mechanical altimeter) are that the scale should move in the same direction as the control knob; the scale numbers should increase from left to right and that the control should turn clockwise to increase. However, as illustrated in figure 3, these principles are actually mutually exclusive. The question then becomes which are the most important of these principles? It would seem that the 'clockwise to increase' principle is the least important and that to avoid a setting error (which is the most important error to avoid) it is essential to retain the display of numbers increasing from left to right). However, it is again worth noting that this study was conducted on a Western population. An Arabic sample may have produced totally different results! Aircraft are sold into a worldwide market but the results of many psychological studies refer only to a Western population.

It is recommended that for a rotary control associated with a display, the control should be mounted close to and below the display. Mounting it above will cause the pilot's hand to obscure the display. Assuming the pilot is right-handed (as are approximately 90% of the population) if the control must be mounted at the side of the display it should be positioned to the right, for the same reasons.

If a rotary control is to be mounted at the side of a vertical scale, or above or below a horizontal scale, this is one of the situations in which the 'clockwise to increase' stereotype may be infringed. In this case Warrick's principle (Warrick, 1947) may be invoked. Warrick's principle is simply the expectation that the scale pointer will move in the same direction of the side of the control that is located next to the display.

Bradley's (1954) work on starting and setting errors and Warrick's principle simply look at user's expectations about the operation of a control in conjunction with a display in isolation. However controls and displays are just a way of interacting with a larger system. The user's mental model of the system as a whole can also affect the relationship between displays and their associated controls (Wickens, 1992). As an example, there is a common stereotype found in pilots about the operation of all major controls in an aircraft that can be related directly to their mental model of how an aircraft flies. In general, 'forward is faster'; push the throttles forward, speed increases; push the stick forward, nose pitches down and airspeed increases; to raise the flaps (and hence go faster) the flap lever is pushed forward. Boeing have used this mental model in the design of the autoflight mode control panel in all their newer commercial aircraft (figure 4, left) and as a result, the control/display relationship for the selection of a vertical speed at first seems counter intuitive. To increase vertical speed downwards, the speed selection thumb-wheel is rotated upwards (and vice versa). However, when this is considered from a pilot's perspective this thumb-wheel operates in exactly the same way as all the major primary flight controls; forward rotation is faster and points the aircraft's nose towards the ground. Such a control/display arrangement may not be successful with non-pilots who do not have such a mental model of an aircraft. It is also interesting to note that the 'altitude select' function on the same panel uses a simple 'clockwise to increase' logic. This would seem to imply that the mental model pilots' have of altitude relates to their position in space. However, their mental representation of vertical speed relates to the pitch attitude of their aircraft.

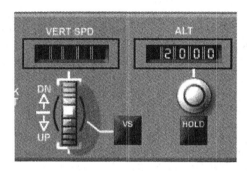

Figure 4   Sections from Boeing 777 (left) and Airbus A320 (right) autoflight mode control panels showing vertical speed and altitude select functions

In contrast, Airbus has avoided the potentially complex issues associated with control/display relationships as a product of a mental model altogether (see right-hand illustration in figure 4). On the A320 mode control panel two simple rotary knobs are used for vertical speed and altitude select that operate in an identical manner. Rotation of these knobs clockwise increases indicated vertical speed upward or the selects a higher altitude, and vice versa.

As will be discussed later in the section on system synoptics, the mental model that the user has of the arrangement of components and the operation of a system is a vital aspect of successful display design.

The primary flight display (PFD)

In many cases, the instrumentation on the modern flight deck is a product of evolution rather than optimal design. This is particularly the case with the instruments comprising the PFD. The PFD is the evolutionary manifestation of the attitude indicator (AI); air speed indicator (ASI); the altimeter and a section of the horizontal situation indicator (HSI). A typical modern PFD (in this case the one found in the Airbus A320) is shown in figure 5. The PFD is a classic example of the compromises a display designer faces. In this case the Human Factors

Engineer is not only concerned with the optimal format for the display of this information, s/he is also concerned with the technology available; the cost; but most particularly, the constraints on the format of these instruments imposed by the regulatory authorities.

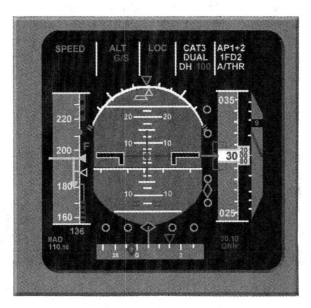

Figure 5   Primary flight display from the Airbus A320. The main instruments (from left to right) depict airspeed, attitude, altitude and vertical speed. Below of the AI is an indication track and heading. The arrow on the airspeed display is the speed trend vector

The sub-sections that follow provide a brief critique of three of the main instruments on the PFD: the AI, altimeter and the airspeed indicator (the depiction of heading and track is covered in a subsequent section). This section is concluded with a review of the PFD as a whole. Any Human Factors specialist can tell you that even if the individual components are optimised, when you put it all together the whole can be considerably *less* than the sum of its component parts!

The attitude indicator (AI)

The AI is perhaps the instrument that best exemplifies the problems posed to the display designer by history and the airworthiness regulations. In Western designed and built aircraft, the AI is an 'inside looking out' instrument; the

83

artificial horizon line always remains aligned with the natural horizon (left-hand component of figure 6). This is prescribed by the regulations of the major airworthiness authorities (e.g. FAR 25 and JAR 25). In aircraft from the old Eastern Bloc countries, the AI is of an 'outside looking in' design, where the aircraft symbol moves in relation to a fixed horizon line, (middle component of figure 6). Much research suggests that this latter design is superior, both in terms of speed of interpretation and number of errors of interpretation (e.g. Fitts and Jones, 1961). In studies during the 1950s (Bryan, Stonecipher and Aron, 1954) it was found that the 'inside looking out' horizon encouraged a loss of attitude awareness during instrument flight that subsequently resulted in a loss of control. However, with familiarity, performance with the 'inside looking out' design improves considerably. This adaptability of the human being, as we shall see, can also be problematic!

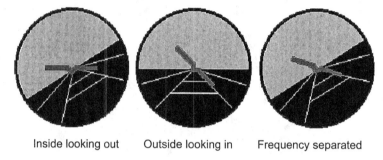

Inside looking out   Outside looking in   Frequency separated

Figure 6   Three formats for the display of attitude information (from Roscoe, 1996)

The advantage of this Eastern Bloc type of AI accrues for several reasons. The moving component of the display in this type of instrument is compatible with the movement of the primary flight control inceptor. When the pilot deflects the stick to the right to initiate a roll to the right, the aircraft symbol is seen to roll to the right (there is control-display compatibility). This display format also complies with the principle of the moving part, first described by Roscoe (1968). This principle requires that the animated portion of a display should move in accordance with the observer's mental model of the behaviour of that variable. In the conventional 'Western' AI, the horizon bar (the moving component of the display) apparently moves left when a roll to the right is initiated, that is it *appears* to deflect to the left *relative* to the pilot's immediate surroundings, i.e. the flight deck. Actually, what happens is that the horizon bar remains fixed, and in effect, the whole of the aircraft rotates around it! However, the control display relationship appears to be incompatible (Bainbridge, 1998) although one benefit is that the artificial horizon line does line up with the natural horizon, which is not true with the Eastern Bloc design. However, ask any flying instructor and they will tell you that the basic problem that trainee pilots have interpreting the AI is a tendency for their attention to be drawn to the moving part of the display (i.e. the horizon) rather that the aircraft symbol (on which their attention should primarily be fixed).

Green and Farmer (1988) suggest a further reason for the advantage conferred by the 'outside looking in' AI. The human being maintains their orientation in the environment by virtue of the mechanisms in the peripheral visual system, which utilise strong horizontal and vertical features in the environment, such as the natural horizon. The foveal (central) visual system, that the pilot uses to read the flight deck instrumentation, is not used to maintain a human beings' orientation. Nevertheless, this is the part of the visual system that the pilot is required to use to when interpreting the AI. The foveal visual system used for detailed, close up work, not as an orientation system and movement detector. It is for this reason that the horizon in Western aircraft is often interpreted as moving rather than remaining aligned with the natural horizon.

As described earlier, one problem with the 'outside looking in' display is that the artificial horizon does not line up with the natural horizon. Roscoe (1968) described a design for the AI that combines the benefits of both types of indicator (the frequency separated AI, shown on the right in figure 6). Roscoe suggested that an AI should have two components: a static and a dynamic component. In a dynamic situation, for example when the pilot deflects the control inceptor to roll the aircraft into the turn (a high frequency control input), the principle of the moving part should be applied (i.e. an 'outside looking in' display should be used). However, when maintaining a prolonged turn Roscoe argues that this is largely a static (low frequency) situation in which a one-to-one correspondence between the real and the artificial horizon is desirable (i.e. an 'inside looking out' display). Trials using this 'frequency separated' AI display (Roscoe and Willages, 1975; Roscoe, Corl and Jensen, 1981) found that this format produced fewer errors and superior flying accuracy than other formats, even when using experienced pilots.

If one were to be hyper-critical, it could be argued that this is a case of the regulations specifically mandating against a better, safer display format for attitude information. However, life is rarely that simple. The system-wide implications for a change in the design of the AI need to be considered. Every training aircraft in the Western World would require re-fitting with new AIs, as would the entire commercial fleet (much to the pleasure of avionics manufacturers but to the chagrin of the operators)! New instrument rating syllabi would need devising and implementing. The knock-on effects are endless. Every Western pilot would be required to 'un-learn' highly developed perceptual-motor skills and acquire new ones. At best, this would be frustrating and inconvenient: at worst this would be potentially dangerous. In several accidents involving Soviet-built classic aircraft being flown by American pilots in the USA, it has been suspected that mis-reading of the AI has been a significant factor contributing to their demise. These accidents exemplify the problems of re-learning highly developed skills. In short, re-specifying the manner in which the AI currently functions in neither practical nor desirable, despite the potential benefits the 'outside looking in' or the 'frequency separated' formats may offer.

The altimeter

The altimeter is probably the single instrument that has been responsible for the deaths of more pilots than any other. It has also probably attracted almost as much research attention as the AI. The basic problem faced by the display designer is balancing the demands of reading accuracy, with the scale length required (in the region of 45,000 feet) in a compact instrument that is quick to read (state information), conveys good rate information (for example, to aid pilots in such tasks as anticipating when to commence levelling off) and also results in very few reading errors being made.

While the emphasis in this chapter is firmly on E-O flight deck displays, it is traditional in a chapter of this type to include some discussion of the three-pointer altimeter! The three-pointer altimeter is slow to read and results in an unacceptable number of reading errors, even when used by experienced pilots (see Grether's 1949 seminal work on altimeter design). One of the greatest dangers posed by the three-pointer altimeter is the tendency for the smallest, 10,000 feet hand, to get lost behind the other larger hands. In times of high workload or stress, it was not uncommon for pilots to mis-read the altimeter by 10,000 feet. When descending in poor visibility this occasionally resulted in a CFIT (controlled flight into terrain) accident. Eventually, the electro-mechanical counter-pointer altimeter replaced the three-pointer altimeter. This is generally regarded to be an excellent design. The counter component is fast to read and results in few errors. The sweep of the 100s of feet hand provides the pilot with good rate of change information. The counter-pointer altimeter is fast to read and produces very low error rates (Grether, 1949).

As a slight aside, this author was passing the above opinion while lecturing on various aspects of cockpit design to a group of Test Pilots. At this point, one member of the audience (a military fast jet pilot) suggested that he begged to differ. He opined that the counter-pointer altimeter may be okay for a civil aircraft's flight deck but it was of limited use in military fast jets that were capable of climbing at 50,000 feet per minute. The numbers in the counter would be unreadable as they would be changing faster that the pilot could read them and the 100s of feet hand would be a blur providing no usable rate information. However, he suggested, the three-pointer altimeter does provide useful rate information in such circumstances from the 1,000s of feet hand. This is the principle source of anticipatory information. This pilot's observation illustrates an important point: you can only design for a specific application. Even if the task requirements appear to be very similar on the surface, there is no guarantee that the same solution will work successfully. Furthermore, just because a design solution is old does not mean to say that it is without merit. Newer is not always better.

With the advent of glass cockpit display technology, the electro-mechanical counter-pointer altimeter was replaced by the altitude tape (see figures 1 and 5). This is usually a windowed, fixed-pointer, moving index display. This use of tapes for conveying altitude information is not the best the best solution that can be applied in these circumstances (for example, see the summary of display characteristics in table 1). This format is poor for conveying rate information and is also poor for making a check reading. It is impossible to establish quickly where in the whole range of possible values the current value lies. The display must actually be read every time for it to be useful. The windowed tape-format altimeter also contravenes the principle of the moving part (Wickens, 1992). To convey an increase in altitude, the moving part of the display (the tape) actually moves downwards. Unfortunately, the alternative to contravening the principle of the moving part, which would require the tape to move upwards as altitude increases, would contradict another population stereotype. This format would require numbers to increase from bottom to top. AC 25-11 specifies that for both altitude and airspeed, for vertically orientated tape display, the larger numbers should be at the top of the display.

The window for the altitude tape is also typically only 1,000 feet 'high' (500 feet on either side of the current altitude). The crew is able to set electronic 'bugs' on the tape as reminders of such things as the next target altitude, etc., however these are often 'outside' the window (other reminders are usually included on the PFD, though). When using a high rate of climb or descent these 'bugs' may suddenly appear giving the pilots only a short time to react to them. The windowed design can be quite poor at providing the pilots with anticipatory information. On the electro-mechanical counter-pointer altimeter, the altitude 'bugs' were always visible.

Before condemning this format for the altimeter too harshly though, some words should be offered in its defence. The chief benefits of the tape-type display accrue when it is considered in the context of the PFD as a whole (discussed later). However, despite all the criticisms levelled at it above, Grether (1949) observed that it actually resulted in a slightly lower error rate (expressed in terms of the percentage of errors in excess of 1,000 feet) than the counter-pointer display format (0.3% versus 0.7%). However, it did take longer to read (a mean of 2.3 versus 1.7 seconds). A simple counter, however, also resulted in very low error rates (0.4%) and very fast reading times (less than 0.1 seconds). As a comparison, the three-pointer altimeter produced an 11.7% error rate when used by experienced pilots and took a mean time of 7.1 seconds to interpret. It is likely that the success of the altitude tapes in current use does not accrue from the fixed-pointer, moving index component of the display. Extrapolating from the work of Grether, it would appear that the critical part of the altimeter is actually the digital counter.

The airspeed indicator (ASI)

Many of the problems posed by the display of airspeed are the same as those posed by the display of altitude, although in this case the designer's task is made a little easier as the range of values is somewhat smaller. However, the precision required is somewhat greater. In a similar vein, many of the criticisms levelled at the fixed-pointer, moving-index altitude tape can equally as well be applied to the ASI on the PFD, which uses exactly the same format. The window is usually capable of only accommodating a range of 100 knots (50 knots either the side of the current speed); the speed tape format is poor for conveying rate information and check readings of airspeed are difficult and the ASI also contravenes the principle of the moving part (higher speeds are at the top of the tape).

However, the electronic instrumentation also offers many benefits. As an example of a predictor display element, the Airbus A320 aircraft contains a small addition to the airspeed tape, the speed trend vector (STV). This additional instrumentation provides an indication of the predicted speed of the aircraft in ten seconds time assuming no control inputs are made (see figure 5). This instrument was regarded as being an instrument of primary importance when flying the A320 (see Field and Harris, 1998). The importance of the STV in the A320 is probably associated with the flight control laws in its fly-by-wire system. Conventional technology aircraft, by their very nature, are speed stable (i.e. the aircraft return to a trimmed airspeed after any disturbance of flight path but do not necessarily return to the original flight path). In comparison, the A320 is flight path stable, therefore it maintains flight path in preference to speed. As a result, the prediction of future speed is a key component of the pilot's task, whereas this is a lesser problem in an aeroplane with conventional controls, hence the inclusion of the STV.

The integrated PFD

The PFD is more than just the sum of its component parts. It must be considered as a whole instrument. When this is done some of the previous criticisms of the individual components need re-evaluating. The development of the PFD also needs to be put into context.

With the advent of CRT displays, the actual area available for the display of primary flight information was reduced, hence more compact versions of the altimeter and airspeed indicator were required. The windowed, fixed pointer moving-index format for these instruments serves this requirement well (see table 1).

The format and layout of the instrumentation on the PFD is an adaptation of the US Air Force 'T-line' concept. The rationale underlying the 'T-line' concept was to display all relevant air data in a horizontal line across the central point of the AI and navigational data along a vertical line running through the centre of the same instrument (hence the inclusion of a section of the HSI, see figure 5). The 'T-line' concept was itself a development of the RAF 'basic T' developed in during World

War II. The 'T-line' arrangement of information on the PFD promotes an efficient scan of the instrumentation in instrument meteorological conditions. Although it could be argued that the section of the HSI is an unnecessary duplication of information also contained on the navigation display, it considerably reduces length of the pilot's instrument scan, especially in situations such as when performing an instrument landing system approach. Furthermore, the information on this section of the HSI can be correlated directly with the localiser and glideslope deviations displayed around the AI. The development of this format for the display of primary flight information was pursued at the behest of the airworthiness authorities during the development of the first CRT-based integrated PFDs.

In short, while all the above criticisms of the components of the PFD are valid when considered in isolation, they are perhaps less important when the PFD is considered as a whole. In the best Gestaltist tradition, whole is considerably more than the sum of its individual, component parts.

The navigation display

The navigation display (ND) is perhaps the single display the best demonstrates the advantages conferred by 'glass cockpit' technology, but again it must be emphasised that the CRT-type display is simply a display medium that allows the computing power elsewhere on the flight deck to be exploited. It is not an end in itself.

This is best demonstrated by considering the radio navigation task of a pilot flying an aircraft in the 1940s. To establish his/her position the pilot had to tune into at least two non-directional beacons (NDB). The needle on the RMI (radio magnetic indicator) would indicate the direction of the first NDB relative to the heading (*not* track) of the aircraft. This would then be plotted back on a map. This process would then be repeated for a second beacon. Where the lines crossed on the map would indicate the approximate position of the aircraft. The actual direction that the aircraft was travelling in was also not easy to establish. With any side wind component there would be a discrepancy between heading and its track. To compound the pilot's misery further, trying to calculate his/her ground speed (the crucial parameter for accurate navigation) was also far from straightforward. The reading from the ASI needed correction for altitude and barometric pressure to produce an indication of true airspeed, and depending upon any head or tailwind component, airspeed could be considerably discrepant from ground speed. As a result, answering such navigational questions as 'where am I'; 'which way am I going'; 'how fast am I going' and 'when will I get there' was not easy. The pilot was required to re-code the information from the instruments into position, track and speed, which was demanding on their working memory and Monitoring progress against the flight plan was a high workload exercise done periodically, rather than continually, and revising a route or plotting a diversion during flight was demanding prone to error. The opportunities to look ahead were minimal.

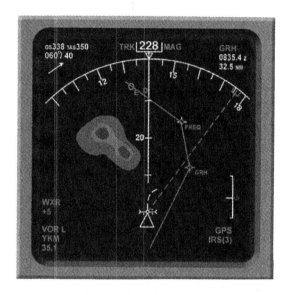

Figure 7   **Navigation display (including weather radar) from Boeing 747-400. The curved white line extending out of the triangular aircraft symbol is a track predictor based on current turn rate**

Modern navigation displays provide a 'God's eye' view of the planned and actual progress of an aircraft's flight (figure 7). The position of airports and beacons are clearly shown. Perhaps more importantly, all the corrections for side winds, altitude, etc. are now performed by the computers in the aircraft and the results are displayed on a screen in a manner compatible with the mental model the pilot has of the aircraft's progress. The information on the display does not have to be re-coded by the pilot into a format that is usable for the task at hand. As a result the pilot is now more likely to achieve level three situation awareness – the ability to assimilate the current situation and also anticipate future events.

It is also current practice to overlay the weather radar picture on the navigation display. This further aids in tactical flight planning allowing the pilots to anticipate poor weather and plan an alternative route around it. With the requirement for TCAS (traffic alert and collision avoidance systems) to be fitted in all commercial aircraft, it is also common to include the position and projected track of these conflicting aircraft on the navigation display along with a conflict resolution advisory. Displaying these critical pieces on information in such a way allows a rapid assimilation of the situation as a result of spatial information being presented in a spatial code.

Despite the advances made in the display of navigational information CFIT accidents still occur. One of the shortcomings of current displays is that while they are good at conveying lateral navigational information, they are poor at conveying vertical flight profiles and showing potential conflicts with the terrain.

Morely and Harris (1994) developed a version of the conventional map display that also contained a topographical depiction of terrain information. In the first design iteration, terrain was normally depicted in shades of green. When the predicted track of the aircraft became unacceptably close to the terrain, the terrain depiction turned yellow. When the aircraft's track was predicted to conflict with the terrain the display turned red, ultimately turning flashing red to indicate a further increase in urgency. Pilot reaction to the display proposal was very positive, however, there was an almost universal request to change the colour conventions for the display of terrain information, as the colours used were the same as the conventions used on the weather radar (as specified in AC 25-11). Pilots also requested the facility to 'switch out' the terrain information to de-clutter the display.

A different solution for the display of profile flight information was proposed for the stillborn Boeing 7J7. This used a second navigation CRT display to convey vertical navigation information. Initial objections to this solution centred on the space required for the extra display and the problems of mentally combining the individual 2-D lateral and vertical depictions of flight path information into a single composite representation. This was thought to be especially problematical when the proposed route was turning. Variations on this theme have been explored in other studies (e.g. Wickens and Prevett, 1995; Wickens, Liang, Prevett and Olmos, 1996). In these experiments, the vertical and lateral navigation displays have been presented one above each other on a single screen. These results suggested that the separate display of lateral and vertical navigation was not really a problem in maintaining pilot's terrain awareness and actually produced better navigation and tracking performance than a complex, 3-D perspective type of display. Brian Kelly describes Boeing's latest format for the display of VNAV and terrain information in chapter 1 of this volume.

However, before getting too excited about the potential for the display of all this extra information on the flight deck a look ahead is required to foresee potential developments across the whole aviation system. With full or partial implementation of 'free flight' (self-routing and self-assured separations) there will be a change in air traffic control (ATC) philosophy. Greater responsibility will be placed on the flight deck crew for flight planning, monitoring and surveillance. This will implicate the navigation and TCAS systems, which will need upgrading to handle these additional ATC-type tasks, as will the displays. As will be recalled, the TCAS advisories are integrated into the navigation display along with the weather radar. In the near future, these data are also likely to be accompanied by terrain information and/or flight profiles. In short, the flight deck crew will potentially be required to cope with more information on an 200mm x 200mm display than will an air traffic controller using a dedicated 600mm x 600mm ATC display screen.

The more 'cluttered' a display is, the longer it takes to find information and the greater the potential to not find the information (or mis-interpret it). The problem now becomes apparent if a TCAS advisory/alert needs to be displayed against a background of weather and terrain etc. The ability to 'switch out' information removes clutter and hence decreases search times. However, anything that is 'switched out' cannot be monitored.

The two main points to be made are these. Firstly, it is not possible to evaluate the usability; speed of use; accuracy of use or error potential, etc. of each of the components in an integrated display system in isolation. Major errors may result from misinterpretation, mode confusions or being in the wrong display format at the wrong time. Secondly, the net safety benefit of each function, if they are assessed and approved in isolation, may not actually be realised when they are implemented as a whole.

Display of system information

System information is mainly concerned with monitoring the performance of the aircraft's engines and other issues concerned with such things as the configuration of the high lift devices, the status of the hydraulic, DC and AC electrical systems, and the operation of the environmental conditioning system, etc. It is interesting to note that the requirements for displaying engine-related information and other systems information are quite different, which has resulted in very different display formats being developed. As a result, the following discussion is divided into two sub-sections to reflect these requirements.

Engine instrumentation

Engine instrumentation (with the exception of during start up) does not require continuous monitoring. Emphasis is placed upon periodic check readings of the various parameters to monitor health and performance. However, should the need arise, the information on the displays should be capable of conveying precise, diagnostic information.

With the advent of E-O display systems, it is now easily possible to satisfy such apparently conflicting requirements as those described above. Figure 8 shows the primary and secondary engine instrumentation from the Boeing 747-400 and Airbus A320, respectively. The engine instrumentation from the 747 uses a tape format (plus a digital counter) as a result of the need to display parameters for four engines. The simplified tapes allow for swift check readings to be made giving some idea of where the current values lie in the range of possible values, however, the digital counters are the primary source of accurate information, if required. The A320 uses the slightly superior circular dial format for its engine instrumentation (similar to the format shown on the right in figure 8) as there is the need to transmit information from only two engines (but still has roughly the same amount of display area available).

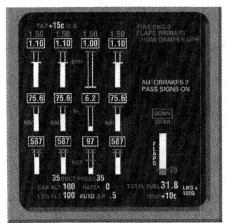

Figure 8   Primary engine instrumentation from the Boeing 747-400 (left) and secondary engine instrumentation from the Airbus A320 (right)

The greatest challenge to the display designer retrofitting new display systems into an old airframe comes not from the content and layout of the information on the engine displays but from the arrangement of the E-O display surfaces themselves. In aircraft such as the Boeing 747-400, 777 and Airbus A320, the primary and secondary engine instrumentation screens are located above each other. However, in the Boeing 737-400, they are located side-by-side. This poses the designer with an interesting problem, as was highlighted in the accident report of the Boeing 737-400 that crashed near Kegworth in 1989 (AAIB, 1990).

It was suspected that a contributory factor in shutting down the incorrect engine, which subsequently led to the accident, was the misidentification of which engine was showing a high level of vibration. A schematic of the instrumentation layout and the relative positions of the power levers is shown in figure 9. The vibration meters were the third circular instrument from the top on the secondary engine instrument display. The number 2 (right-hand) engine was throttled back and shut down instead of the malfunctioning number 1 engine. This was possibly a result of the layout of the primary and secondary engine instrumentation screens. The accident occurred at night.   All electro-luminous displays are self-illuminating, thus the bright instruments appeared against a high contrast, dark background that probably made the surrounds of the screens invisible. This may have given the illusion that the primary and secondary instruments were part of one display (i.e. a larger, emergent figure was produced). The larger emergent figure would also have hindered paying specific attention to a single display element in the middle of it (the proximity compatibility principle), especially given the higher levels of arousal of the crew as a result of the developing incident. There was also a high level of vibration in the aircraft that would have hindered reading the secondary engine instruments, which were quite small (300m in diameter). Furthermore, the power levers were also located between the two screens, thus the number 1 engine vibration gauge was directly above the number 2 engine power lever.

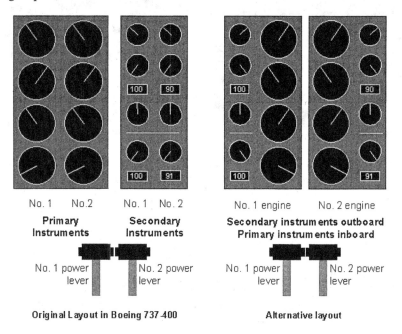

Figure 9   **Original layout of primary and secondary engine instrumentation in the Boeing 737-400 and a suggested alternative layout. (Adapted from AAIB report 4/90, 1989)**

The AAIB report on the accident describes the benefits and disbenefits of the two potential arrangements for the primary and secondary engine information depicted in figure 9. The left-hand arrangement increases the chance of an anomalous reading being detected, however control/display compatibility is sacrificed as the primary engine instrumentation is no longer aligned with the power levers. The right-hand arrangement of the instrumentation has the benefit of enhancing control/display compatibility. The down side is that making a swift check reading of the secondary engine instrumentation is now no longer possible. The larger, emergent figure has been destroyed. The advantages of mounting the primary and secondary engine instrument displays one above the other are clearly evident when the compromises necessary in using a side-by-side configuration are considered.

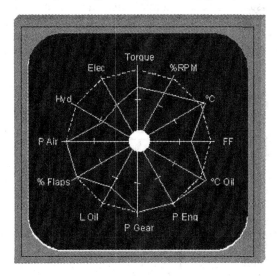

Figure 10 Emergent-feature display for No. 1 engine (adapted from Dinadis and Vincente, 1999). Normal engine operating parameters are depicted by dashed line: current parameters by solid line

Again, it is emphasised that display design is not just about individual components on a display, nor does it also just include the layout of these components. It is also about the relationship between displays and their associated controls.

Recently, there has been a move to develop emergent-feature displays for the monitoring of engine parameters (e.g. Dinadis and Vincente, 1999). These allow many more parameters per engine to be displayed simultaneously and as an integrated 'whole'. In a prototype engine display system developed for the Lockheed-Martin C-130 aircraft, Dinadis and Vincente used a 12-spoked dodecahedron (with each spoke representing an engine parameter). The spokes were scaled in such a way that when the engine was operating normally, the dodecahedron was a regular shape. Coloured tick marks on each spoke represented the allowable performance parameters (see figure 10). Initial subjective assessments of these novel display formats have been quite positive, however, the authors acknowledge (at the time of writing) empirical work is required to evaluate performance when using these displays.

System synoptics

Most secondary systems in modern aircraft are managed automatically. However, when a failure occurs in one of these systems it is necessary to display the status and the configuration of that system. Oliver (1990) argues that with the advent of systems that automatically re-configure themselves in the case of a failure there is now an even greater need for detailed feedback to the pilots to maintain their SA.

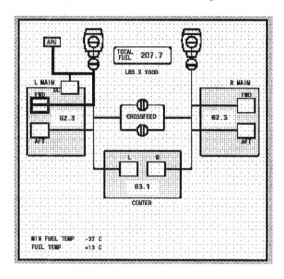

Figure 11 Diagram illustrating the Boeing 777 EICAS (engine instrument and crew alerting system) fuel synoptic

Before the advent of E-O displays quantitative information about fluid quantities, temperatures and pressures etc. were conveyed using 'traditional' electro-mechanical displays. The actual configuration of the aircraft's systems has to be deduced from switch positions and indicator lights. With modern multi-configurable displays though, other formats are now possible. One format gaining a great deal of popularity in aerospace applications is system synoptics, which are best described as schematic displays. The Oxford English Dictionary defines 'synoptic' as 'taking or affording a comprehensive mental view' which is an excellent description of the manner in which these displays function. However, this type of display can only be used to transmit status (qualitative) information to the operator. Any rapidly changing values should not be incorporated into these displays.   Typical examples where this format has been used include the configuration of fuel control systems (see figure 11). The advantage of this type of display configuration is that the information is presented in a manner that is compatible with the pilot's 'mental model' of the aircraft, (e.g. the left-hand wing fuel tank is on the left-hand side of the diagram). Not only is it possible to present fuel contents on such a display, it is also possible to simultaneously present other fuel related information, such as valve status and pump pressures, etc., thus giving the pilot all the fuel related information on one page of information. This greatly aids in the identification and diagnosis of problems if the display is properly designed. The pilot can follow through the course of the fuel from the tank to the engine. However, if the system is complex, perhaps with many pumps, lines, controls and actuators (as in the hydraulic system), it may not be possible to display all the schematic of the system in the limited display space, or it may also lead to clutter, making the display difficult and slow to read. Selective use of colour can aid in this respect.

The next generation of synoptic displays take things one step further. Using cursor-positioning devices the pilots can interact with the synoptic displays in the same manner that a user of a desktop computer navigates around a Windows™ interface. It can be seen that when taking this approach the distinction between what constitutes a control and a display becomes distinctly blurred. These interactive synoptics are the first steps toward the truly integrated flight deck. However, as we shall see, this 21st century approach to flight deck design does pose considerable challenges for certification rules conceived 50 years ago.

Looking toward the future of head-down display design

Despite the advances in aviation computing and display technology, it is likely that the scope for changes in the manner in which information is displayed will be somewhat limited, particularly in heavy civil transport aircraft. The reasons why this should be so lie in the complexity of the commercial aviation system.

Consider the design, production and in-service life of an aircraft. The design process itself may take in the region of eight years, however it is likely that the design freeze for the flight deck will be several years before the first flight. By definition, with the speed of developments in computing technology, much of the equipment will be out of date before the aircraft has ever flown! It is also likely that the aircraft will have a production life of 20-30 years, although it will be subject to several different versions and mid-life updates. Finally the in-service life of an individual airframe itself may be 30 years. As a result, design decisions taken today may still be flying in 65 years time. If this sounds absurd, just consider the Douglas DC-3! However, during this period it is certain that the arrangement of airspace and the operation of aircraft will change but will change in an unknown (and unknowable) way. For example in the moderately near future, the introduction of 'free flight' (in whatever form) is going to impose more air traffic control-type tasks onto the flight deck which will require developments in head-down display systems. The challenge faced by designers will be how to respond to these future requirements using the 'old' sensor and display technology in the aircraft.

There is also the need to consider the organisational context in which commercial aircraft operate. This needs to be remembered at all times, even when designing flight deck displays. Airlines need to manage their fleets. They are responsible for the training and rostering of their crew in such a way as not only to enhance safety but also to maximise the financial returns on their operations. Introducing a radical change in the display of information during the production life of an aircraft is going to have major implications for the operators in terms of procuring or updating of simulators, the development and approval of training programmes and may also result in a reduction in the flexibility of the rostering of crews. Half of the crews may not be type rated to fly half of the airline's fleet. The expense of developing and certificating the new displays should also not be overlooked. The costs are always ultimately borne by the end customer, be this the airline or ultimately the passenger.

As a result it is likely that the display systems on the flight deck will continue to evolve slowly. A revolution is unlikely. New displays will utilise software updates and will involve processing information from existing sensors and databases already onboard the aircraft, rather than requiring the installation of new hardware. However, advances in the display of information to enhance the pilot's situation awareness can certainly be made in this manner, for example the enhanced vertical situation/flight path display being developed as a software upgrade for most 'glass cockpit' Boeing aircraft. This system uses existing receivers and sensors (e.g. from the navigation system and the air data computers) and the terrain database from the EGPWS (enhanced ground proximity warning system) to display a slice of the aircraft's vertical flight profile under the aircraft's existing navigation display, (Jacobsen, 1999; Kelley, 2004).

Developments in display design are likely to be much more rapid in the business jet sector of the market. Without the constraints on flight deck design imposed by the complex organisational factors resulting from the nature of airline operations, the display designer can be a little more creative in the solutions that s/he produces. Integrated lateral and vertical navigation displays are already finding their way onto the flight decks of top-of-the-range business aircraft. Indeed, many customers regard it as being prestigious and desirable to equip their aircraft with the latest in flight deck technology, and the latest in display design is the most visible manifestation of this. It can perhaps be suggested that this trend was initially most noticeable with head-up displays, which began to be introduced into business jets long before commercial transport aircraft. Head-up displays are likely to be one of the major areas of development in display technology in commercial aircraft in the next decade.

However, just to finish on a slight note of caution, it must always be remembered that newer is not necessarily better. Several major avionics manufacturers are now producing optional display formats for their altimeters that utilise a circular counter-pointer format, suggesting that this approach offers benefits in enhancing altitude awareness by conveying superior rate information! What is certain is that with the initiatives being taken by the FAA and JAA to develop Human Factors certification criteria for civil flight decks, the design of instrumentation is going to be subject to much more rigorous Human Factors design and testing in the near future. The object is to ensure that design induced pilot error becomes a thing of the past. It's time to start polishing those crystal balls...

References

Air Accidents Investigation Branch (1990). *Report on the accident to Boeing 737-400 G-OBME near Kegworth, Leicestershire on 8 January 1989.* London, UK: Department of Transport, HMSO.

Bainbridge, L. (1998). Processes underlying human performance. In, D.J. Garland, J.A.Wise and V.D. Hopkin (Eds.) *Handbook of Aviation Human Factors.* Mahwah, NJ: Lawrence Erlbaum Associates. 107-172.

Barnett, B.J. and Wickens, C.D. (1988). Display proximity in multicue information integration: The benefits of boxes. *Human Factors, 30,* 15-24.

Billings, C.E. (1997). *Aviation Automation.* Mahwah, NJ: Lawrence Erlbaum Associates.

Bradley, J.V. (1954). *Desirable control-display relationships for moving scale instruments.* (Tech. Rep. No. 54-423). Washington, DC: US Air Force.

Bryan, L.A., Stonecipher, J.W., and Aron, K. (1954). 180-degree turn experiment. *University of Illinois Bulletin, 54,* 1-52.

Coombs, L.F.E. (1990). *The Aircraft Cockpit.* Wellingborough, UK: Patrick Stephens Ltd.

Cushman, W.H. and Rosenberg, D.J. (1991). *Human Factors in Product Design.* Amsterdam: Elsevier.

Dinadis, N. and Vincente, K.J. (1999). Designing functional visualisations for aircraft systems status displays. *International Journal of Aviation Psychology, 9,* 241-269.

Endsley, M.R (1988). Design and Evaluation for Situation Awareness Enhancement: *Proceedings of the Human Factors Society 32nd Annual Meeting.* Santa Monica, CA: Human Factors Society. 97-101.

Federal Aviation Administration (1996). *Human Factors Design Guide (Version 1.00).* William J. Hughes Technical Center, Arlington VA: Author.

Field, E. and Harris, D. (1998). The Implications of the Deletion of the Cross-Cockpit Control Linkage in Fly-By-Wire Aircraft: A Communication Analysis.

Ergonomics, 41, 1462-1477.

Green, R.G. and Farmer, E.W. (1988). Ergonomics. In, J. Ernsting and P. King (Eds.) *Aviation Medicine (2nd Edition)*. London: Butterworths. 445-457.

Grether, W.F. (1949). The design of long-scale indicators for speed and accuracy of quantitative reading. *Journal of Applied Psychology, 33*, 363-372.

Hemingway, J.C. and Erickson, R.A. (1969). Relative effects of raster scan lines and image subtense on symbol legibility on television. *Human Factors, 11*, 331-338.

Hopkin, V.D. (1992). Issues in color application. In, H. Widdel and D.L. Post (Eds.) *Color in Electronic Displays.* New York: Plenum. 191-207.

Joint Aviation Authorities (2000). *Joint Airworthiness Requirements (Change 15): Part 25 – Large Aeroplanes.* Hoofdorp: Joint Aviation Authorities.

Jacobson, A. (1999). The Boeing vertical navigation display. Presentation to the College of Aeronautics, Cranfield University, June 12, 1999.

Kelly, B.D. (2004). Flight deck design and integration for commercial air transports. In, D.Harris (Ed.) *Human Factors for Flight Deck Design.* Ashgate: Aldershot. 3-32.

McCormick, E.J. and Sanders, M.S. (1992) *Human Factors in Engineering and Design (7th Edition).* New York: McGraw Hill.

Ministry of Defence (1996). *Human Factors for designers of Equipment: Defence Standard 00-25 (part 7 – Issue 2): Visual Displays.* London: Author.

Morely, F.J.J. and Harris, D. (1994). Terrain and Vertical Navigation Displays to Enhance Situational Awareness: A User Centred Iterative Design Approach. In, *Proceedings of the Royal Aeronautical Society Conference on Controlled Flight Into Terrain.* 8 November 1994, London, U.K.

Oliver, J.G. (1990). *Improving situational awareness through the use of intuitive pictorial displays* (Tech. Rep. No. 901829). Warrendale, PA: SAE International.

Pastoor, S., Schwarz, E. and Beldie, I.P. (1983). The relative suitability of four dot matrix sizes for text presentation on color television screens. *Human Factors, 25*, 265-272.

Poulton, E.C. and Brown, C.H. (1968). Rate of comprehension of an existing teleprinter output and of possible alternatives. *Journal of Applied Psychology, 52*, 16-21.

Poulton, E.C. (1969). Searching lists of food ingredients printed in different sizes. *Journal of Applied Psychology, 53*, 55-58.

Reising, J.M., Ligget, K.K. and Munns, R.C. (1998). Controls, displays and workplace design. In, D.J. Garland, J.A.Wise and V.D. Hopkin (Eds.) *Handbook of Aviation Human Factors.* Mahwah, NJ: Lawrence Erlbaum Associates. 327-354.

Roscoe, S.N. (1968). Airborne displays for flight and navigation. *Human Factors, 10*, 321-332.

Roscoe, S.N., Corl, L. and Jensen, R.S. (1981). Flight display dynamics revisited. *Human Factors, 23*, 341-353.

Roscoe, S.N. and Willages, R.C. (1985). Motion relationships in aircraft attitude and guidance displays: A flight experiment. *Human Factors, 17*, 374-387.

Roscoe, S.N. (1996). *Design-Induced Errors.* http://www.aero.ca/News1_96. html#anchor113498.

Stokes, A.F. and Wickens, C.D. (1984). Aviation Displays. In, E.L. Wiener and D.C. Nagel (Eds.) *Human Factors in Aviation.* San Diego, CA: Academic Press. 387-431.

US Department of Transportation – Federal Aviation Administration (1987). *Advisory Circular AC 25-11 Transport Category Airplane Electronic Display Systems.* Washington DC: Author.

US Department of Transportation – Federal Aviation Administration (1999). *Federal Aviation Regulations: Part 25 – Airworthiness Standards: Transport Category Airplanes (Amendment 25-98).* Washington DC: Author.

Warrick, M.J. (1947). *Direction of movement in the use of control knobs to position visual indicators.* (USAF AMC Report No. 694-4C). Wright AFB: US Airforce.

Wickens, C.D. (1992). *Engineering Psychology and Human Performance (2ⁿᵈ Edition).* New York, NY: HarperCollins.

Wickens, C.D. and Prevett, T.T. (1995). Exploring the dimensions of egocentricity in aircraft navigation displays. *Journal of Experimental Psychology – Applied, 1*, 110-135.

Wickens, C.D., Liang, C.C., Prevett, T. and Olmos, O. (1996). Electronic maps for terminal area navigation: Effects of frame of reference and dimensionality. *International Journal of Aviation Psychology, 6*, 241-271.

Wood, W.T. and Wood, S.K. (1987). Icons in everyday life. In, G. Salvendy, S.L. Sauter and J.J. Hurrell (Eds.) *Social, ergonomic and stress aspects of working with computers.* Amsterdam: Elsevier. 97-104.

Zwaga, H. and Boersema, T. (1983). Evaluation of a set of graphic symbols. *Applied Ergonomics, 14*, 43-54

Zwaga, H. and Easterby, R. (1984). Developing effective symbols for public information. In, R. Easterby and H. Zwaga (Eds.) *Information Design.* Chichester: Wiley. 277-297.

Acknowledgements

The sections from the Boeing 777 and Airbus A320 autoflight mode control panels (shown in figure 4); the illustration of the primary flight display from the Airbus A320 shown in figure 5; the diagrams of the navigation display from Boeing's 747-400 (figure 7), the primary engine instrumentation from the same aircraft and secondary engine instrumentation from the Airbus A320 (figure 8), were all kindly provided by Jerome Meriweather from his excellent web site which contains detailed tours of many modern flightdecks. This can be found at www.meriweather.com.

Figure 6 is taken from the web site of AERO Innovation, Inc. of Montreal, Canada <www.aero.ca> and is reproduced with the kind permission of Dr Stan Roscoe, the author.

I would also like to thank Brian Kelly of Boeing for supplying the diagram of the Boeing 777 fuel synoptic used in figure 11.

5   Head-up displays

Christopher D. Wickens, Patricia May Ververs
and Steve Fadden

Overview

The head-up display or HUD is designed to superimpose imagery over the
forward field of view outside the cockpit, so that the pilot can simultaneously
view that imagery and the world beyond the cockpit, an information set that we
call the 'far domain' (figure 1). As such, the HUD is designed to accomplish three
valuable goals (Weintraub and Ensing, 1992; Newman, 1995).

1. Reducing the amount of visual scanning (eye movements) necessary to view
   the instrumentation and the far domain. As a consequence imagery can be
   processed while the far domain can be monitored and the fatigue of repeated
   eye movements is reduced. To the extent that the direction of gaze can be
   viewed as functionally equivalent to the allocation of visual attention, this
   feature supports the ability to better divide attention between the
   instrumentation and the far domain.
2. Reducing the need for *re-accommodating* the focus of the eyes when
   transitioning between the view of the display and the far domain. This is
   accomplished by *collimating* the visual imagery on the HUD, so that the
   light rays from that imagery travel in parallel to the eye. Thus the eye is
   'tricked' into seeing the imagery at optical infinity and so the lens is in the
   appropriate shape to view far domain imagery in focus. This will, in turn,
   increase the visibility of small traffic targets.
3. Enabling the presentation of modified imagery that directly overlays or is
   conformal with its far domain counterpart. This might include for example a
   horizon line or a runway overlay as depicted in figure 1. This feature of
   conformal imagery provides direct instrument-related guidance regarding
   where things are in the far domain, if those things cannot be directly seen
   because of darkness or poor visibility.

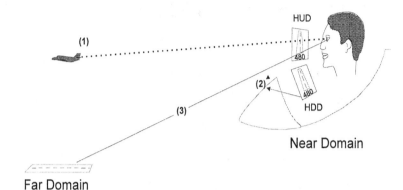

Far Domain

Figure 1   **Schematic representation of information domains (near and far) and display positions (HUD and head-down) in an aircraft. The numbers designate three generic tasks: (1) detecting information (e.g. traffic) in the far domain, (2) processing instrument information such as digital symbology in the near domain and (3) integrating information between the near and far domain, such as a runway overlay**

These valuable goals, generally met in most HUD designs have greatly increased the pilot's capabilities of performance. For example (1) HUDs in military aircraft have provided a strong combat advantage so that the pilot can keep eyes out for enemy targets while monitoring critical parameters of attitude and engine performance (energy management). Conformal imagery on military HUDs can also provide guidance regarding the location of threats and targets. (2) In civilian aircraft, for which a typical example is shown in figure 2, HUDs have allowed pilots to hand fly the aircraft to landings in much lower visibility than is authorised without HUDs (category III; Schiff, 1994). The most widely used civilian HUD supplied by Flight Dynamics Inc. is certified for Category IIIb minima. This enables pilots to land aircraft in flight conditions where no visual reference is made to the runway (no decision height) and only an alert 30 feet above the ground is required. As a consequence of the expanded flight environment, the number of flights cancelled in low visibility at airports such as Seattle and Juneau has been greatly decreased can be greatly decreased. In fact, Rockwell Collins Flight Dynamics claims equipping an aircraft with a HUD can eliminate more than 60% of the low visibility disruptions in takeoff and landings (Proctor, 1997). (3) In addition to its value in improving commercial flight productivity, HUD concepts are currently being examined to improve safety, by providing terrain and traffic warnings. Such a system for terrain warning exists in military flight in the form of the AUTOGCAS (Scott, 1999). A HUD concept known as T-NASA is designed to keep pilot's eyes head out during low visibility taxi way operations on the airport surface (Foyle, Andre, McCann, Wenzel, Begault and Battiste, 1996; McCann, Hooey, Parke, Foyle, Andre and Kanki, 1998; Proctor, 2000) and to provide them with conformal guidance cues for appropriate turn-offs and 'stop' cues for holds at runway intersections (figure 3). Such a system is intended to reduce the frequency of runway or taxiway accidents.

Figure 2   Civilian (Honeywell) HUD (Courtesy of Honeywell, Inc.)

While traditional HUDs are rigidly mounted on glass in front of the pilot's eyes (figure 2), two other variants of this procedure for overlaying images will be discussed in this chapter. First, synthetic vision displays can overlay symbolic information on computer-generated synthetic imagery in a head-down cockpit (Comstock et al., 2001), such as shown in figure 4. Such a system has many of the same properties as does a normal HUD, except that the HUD image and the synthetic imagery beyond are both positioned at precisely the same depth plane (distance from the eyes), so that issues of accommodation are irrelevant. Second, helmet mounted displays or HMDs (Melzer and Moffitt, 1997), if they are translucent, accomplish visually the same purpose as HUDs. However unlike HUDs they are mounted to the head, rather than rigidly mounted to the aircraft cockpit. As a result they have some greater advantages; but also a number of added costs and more complex design issues, which we address later in this chapter.

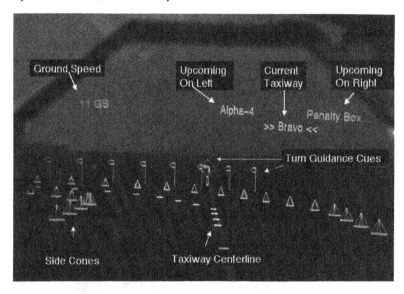

Figure 3 **T-NASA taxiway HUD display (courtesy of NASA Ames Research Center)**

Figure 4 **Synthetic imagery display**

In the following section, we will first describe a number of design related features that characterise a HUD (and distinguish it from traditional head-down instrumentation). We will then consider the empirical research that has addressed the effects of these features on pilot performance and attention allocation and hence can aide the designer in deciding which information should be better presented on a HUD and which should remain head-down. We then describe corresponding research on helmet-mounted displays finally address several issues related to HUD certification.

HUD features

Location

The head-up location is, of course, the defining feature of the HUD. In light of the advantages of this location outlined above, it might seem that this is a non-issue; that all possible information should be presented in the head-up location. However it has been argued that there may be other features of the HUD design besides location that confers its advantages (Weintraub and Ensing, 1992). One of these may be its collimation, saving the eye from the need to re-accommodate between near and far domains (and such collimation could be readily accomplished with a head-down display: Weintraub, Haines and Randall, 1984). A second may be the relatively novel symbology that can be employed on the HUD, freed from some of the design guidelines required of the standard instrument panel (FAA Advisory Circular 25-11, 1987). A third factor, related to the second, may be that the HUD can provide information that is referenced to the ground (inertial navigation) rather than to the air mass, which is the frame of reference for the standard instruments (Steenblik, 1989, 1992). This feature can make HUD information particularly valuable when navigating by reference to the ground. Any or all of these three features of difference from the conventional head-down instrumentation may be responsible for the HUD performance benefits that are observed, in addition to those differences conferred by the head-up location (and resulting reduction of scanning). Furthermore, the head-up location can impose a potential cost, related to the *clutter* of overlapping imagery, whether the pilot is trying to read HUD symbology against the distracting background of a ground scene, or is trying to see things in the far domain, through the HUD imagery. These issues will be addressed later in this chapter. Thus, one must consider the trade-off between head-up and head-down location, as one involving a 'tug-of-war' between the advantages of reduced scanning and the costs of clutter.

Collimation

As we noted above, and will discuss further below, a key feature of most HUDs is the fact that they collimate images to optical infinity. Optical infinity represents an

107

image distance of about 60 feet in front of the observer (A-4 Aircraft Instruments Committee, 1999). However, not all HUDs need do so (Sheehy and Gish, 1991). Furthermore, when HUD imagery is displayed overlaying a synthetic image display, collimation does not become an issue.

The eye box

Collimated HUDs are designed in such a manner that their imagery is legible only from a restricted set of eye positions, known as the 'eye box' (Weintraub and Ensing, 1992). Furthermore, when conformal imagery is employed, there are only certain viewpoints where that imagery can be expected to 'overlay' its far domain counterpart. A horizon line for example will rise above the true horizon if the head position is lowered from this ideal.

The HUD eye box is a three-dimensional region in which the symbology can be viewed from at least one eye. The minimum size of the eye box should be 3.0 ft (914mm) horizontal, 2.0 ft (609mm) vertical and 4.0 ft (1219mm) depth (A-4 Aircraft Instruments Committee, 1999).

Symbology

Nothing is more important than the information or symbology that is actually presented on the HUD. Such information will of course vary in its content as well as its format. For example altitude information (content) can be presented in digital form, moving tape or round dial (format). One critical symbol on most HUDs is the 'bore sight', an icon that represents the attitude of one's own aircraft and corresponds to the aircraft symbol on the conventional ADI. A key attribute of HUD information is the degree of *conformality* with far domain objects and entities, of which we can make four distinctions (Ververs and Wickens, 1998).

1. *Truly conformal information*, is that which directly overlays its far domain counterpart; and therefore the image on the HUD will move in a 1-1 fashion as the aircraft rotates or translates. This might characterise the horizon line or a runway overlay (see figure 1).
2. *Virtually conformal information* overlays entities in space, but not real objects. For example the tunnel, highway, or pathway-in-the-sky display on a HUD (figure 5) would be an example of a virtually conformal display, depicting a 3D pathway in front of the aircraft. Other examples might be a spatial cue that points in the direction of a target or of the ground, or a 'pitch ladder' that depicts angles above and below the horizon.
3. *Partially conformal information* will move in conjunction with its far domain counterpart as the aircraft rotates, but will not always overlay it in space. The best example is a reduced scale pitch ladder, such that the range of angles of far domain information exposed on the display (e.g. 45 degrees) is greater than the visual angle subtended by the HUD (e.g. 22 degrees).

Thus, as the plane pitches upward or downward, the pitch ladder will move in corresponding (opposite) fashion, the HUD horizon will overlay the true horizon when the aircraft is level, but in a 30 degrees pitch attitude, the horizon will only lie at a 15 degree angle of real space below the bore sight symbol of the aircraft, as viewed from the pilot's eye box.

4. *Non conformal information.* All other information is said to be non-conformal; e.g. digital symbology, round dial analogue instruments, etc.

Figure 5   Pathway HUD (with far domain visible beyond)

Size

The visual angle subtended by the HUD has two important implications. For non-conformal information, visual angle can affect the size and therefore acuity demands of text and symbols that may appear there. For conformal information, it determines the range of the far domain that can be represented. Small HUDs will present only a 'keyhole' view of conformal far domain information. As shown in figure 6, this constraint is critical when considering the depiction of a truly conformal runway on a landing in heavy crosswinds, when the aircraft must 'crab' into the wind. The visual angle of the HUD must be at least twice the size of the maximum crab angle in order for the runway overlay to remain visible. Conventional HUDs provide a visual angle of 30 x 24 degrees. When depicting highway in the sky symbology, Beringer recommends at least 40 degrees laterally for maximum preview in turns (Beringer and Ball, 2001).

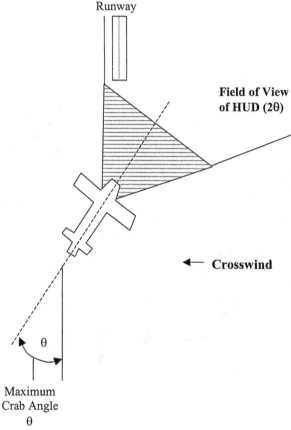

Figure 6   Field of view of the HUD shown as the shaded region = 2θ. If conformal imagery is used, the field of view should be wide enough to depict the runway at maximum crab angle θ, as shown in the figure

Image intensity

The intensity or contrast ratio of the HUD can have a great impact on its visibility. Contrast ratio is defined as:

$$\text{Contrast Ratio} = \frac{\text{display luminance} + \text{background luminance}}{\text{background luminance}}$$

The issue mirrors to some extent the same concerns for head-down imagery, but its importance is amplified because the background against which the HUD image is seen can itself vary in intensity by orders of magnitude, from a dark sky at night, to bright clouds in the day time (Weintraub and Ensing, 1992). Sufficient intensity for the symbology to be visible in the latter condition will produce overly bright symbology at night, to such an extent that it may obscure targets that need to be seen in the far domain (Ververs and Wickens, 1998). Ratios of 1.5:1 under moderately ambient illumination conditions (Weintraub and Ensign, 1992) and at least 1.20:1 under bright sunlit conditions (AS8055, Wisely, 1996) are advised. Therefore HUDs need to have a brightness control; but also guidance should be given to pilots on the appropriate settings for day and night use. Automatic brightness control, such as that found on head-down displays (Gallimore, Stouffer, Brannon and McCracken, 1997) could be of considerable value for HUDs.

Colour

HUD imagery has traditionally been presented with light green strokes because of the nature of the image generator phosphor. However with newer technology there is no technological reason to maintain a green hue nor, in general to continue with a monochrome display, should colour provide useful information (Stokes, Wickens and Kite, 1990). In fact, research indicates that using colour on a HUD can lead to faster response times and few errors when compared to monochrome displays (Hawkins, Reising, Gilmour, 1983; Dudfield, Davy, Hardiman and Smith, 1995; Baird, Dudfield, Dave and Moore, 1993). Nevertheless, as with head-down displays, it is important to keep colour coding simple, restricting the number of colours to be used and to employ standard conventions (e.g. red = warning; amber = caution; blue = sky/advisory; brown = ground).

Shared visibility

In a twin seat cockpit, unless both pilots have a HUD, then information presented on the HUD to one pilot will not be available to the other. This is different from the case with conventional instrumentation, where, if information is not repeated, the other pilot may glance across the cockpit. This limitation of HUDs results because of the constraint of the 'eye box' (which is not of course an issue with synthetic vision system HUDs). As a consequence careful consideration should be given to any circumstance in which HUD information is not available, in other formats, to the other pilot in the cockpit.

Task support

A wide range of tasks can be supported by HUD information. A useful way of representing such tasks, which will prove to have an important bearing on the best uses of HUDs, is in terms of a 2x5 representation defined by the *location* of the information necessary to support the task (near versus far domain) and the *priority* of the task, defined in terms of the standard 'aviate, navigate, communicate systems-management' hierarchy (Schutte and Trujillo, 1996). We expand these categories from 4 to 5, by discriminating navigational path following from navigational hazard (traffic, weather, terrain) avoidance. This matrix is shown in table 1. For tasks whose information is located in the far domain, such as hazard awareness, the HUD may act as guidance, directing the pilots' attention to those hazards. However, on the downside, HUD imagery may produce clutter, inhibiting the ability to see those hazard items, particularly small visual-angle traffic.

Table 1
Classification of information for task support relevant for HUD design

	Location of Information	
TASK	**Near**	**Far**
Aviate	X	X^1
Navigate (Path)	X^2	X^3
Navigate (Hazard)		X
Communications	X	
Systems Management	X	

[1]As represented by true horizon.
[2]As represented by heading indicator, altimeter and navigation instruments.
[3]As represented by position of runway.

Pilot attention

A good understanding of how the above-related design features influence pilot performance with HUDs requires consideration of the mediating role of pilot attention. Psychological research in attention has revealed four fundamental *modes* of attention that are relevant to HUD use (Wickens and Hollands, 2000; Pashler, 1998).

Selective attention

Selective attention involves the process of choosing what to look for and where to look. As such, it is often reflected by the direction of gaze. (Although this measure is not entirely diagnostic of selective attention; for example it is possible for a pilot to extract information from the peripheral visual field, away from the centre of fixation.) Particularly with regard to HUDs, there is evidence that when people view two overlapping images (i.e. with a constant fixation or direction of gaze), they can selectively attend to one of those, while ignoring the others (Neisser and

Becklen, 1975). Thus a pilot may look through the HUD, but be ignorant of important information on the HUD itself. Selective attention is also involved in visual search (Brogan, 1990), as the direction of attention (and often of gaze) systematically inspects different regions or objects in turn, until an item of interest is located. This feature of selective attention is important in HUDs because of the inhibiting role of *clutter* on visual search (Teichner and Mocharnuk, 1979; Ververs and Wickens, 1998). Anything that adds marks, objects or other visual elements to a viewing scene will be likely to increase the time required to find something within that scene.

Switching attention

While selective attention involves knowing where to look, attention switching involves the actual process (delay and effort) of redirecting attention from one location to another. The cost of switching visual attention is closely related to the cost of visual scanning, so that it is apparent that superimposing the HUD on the outside world will reduce this attention switching cost. However, it is important to realise that, while attention may co-vary with a visual scan, the two are not equivalent. For example, as we have noted above, attention may (or may not) be switched even as the eye fixation remains constant. Furthermore, one can attend to a single object (i.e. no attention switch) across more than one scan. This might describe the attention of pilots whose eyes move across the artificial horizon of the ADI, even as attention is maintained fixed upon the attitude of the aircraft (i.e. eye movement without attention switching).

Focussed attention

The concept of focussed attention relates to the success (or failure) of extracting information from a single source, while *avoiding distraction* from other nearby sources (Eriksen and Eriksen, 1974; Kramer and Jacobson, 1991). Distraction can be operationally defined as poorer performance resulting when that nearby source is present than when it is absent. For example one might observe the breakdown in focussed attention on a distant target in the far domain, resulting because of the distraction of the HUD imagery that overlays that target. Analytically such breakdowns can be attributed to two components. One is the possible *physical* masking of the far domain imagery because some or all of the HUD strokes directly hide it. The other is the *psychological* distraction, when visual attention is automatically compelled to process all information within a visual angle of around one degree (Eriksen and Eriksen, 1974; Broadbent, 1982). In many operational circumstances these two components become difficult to disentangle.

The concept of attentional tunnelling or attentional *fixation*, is a hybrid phenomenon that is related at once to selective, focussed and switching attention. It describes a circumstance when attention stays focussed on a particular object or area well past when it is advisable to switch and select another part of the environment to examine (Fadden, Ververs and Wickens, in press). It should also be noted that the effects of clutter can inhibit both selective attention (by providing more objects that need to be searched) and focussed attention, to the extent that such clutter is nearby and therefore distracting from the desired focus of attention.

Divided attention

Divided attention describes the successful endeavour of processing two entities at once (i.e. to divide attention between them). For example, a skilled pilot may in a single glance, capture both the bank and the pitch information from an ADI (i.e. divide attention between vertical and lateral guidance information). As we noted at the outset, the goal of the HUD is to allow the pilot to divide attention between *processing* HUD information and *monitoring* the far domain for traffic. Of course it is sometimes difficult to discriminate between true divided attention (parallel processing) and very rapid attention switching; and many times this distinction is one of only academic concern. It is important also to note that the conditions that may create success in dividing attention (i.e. guaranteeing that two entities will be processed at the same time) may also be the very same conditions that create a *failure* to focus attention (the inability to *not* process one of those) if it is distracting (Wickens and Hollands, 2000). Thus the spatial overlap of the HUD, facilitating divided attention between the near and far domain, may also invite the failure to focus attention on one domain to the exclusion of the other.

Divided attention is desired under two circumstances. First it may be the case that the pilot wishes to perform two tasks concurrently – such as controlling the flight path, while monitoring for traffic, reading a map or processing communications. Second it may be the case that two sources of information are relevant for a single task and the pilot needs to *integrate* information from the two sources to carry out the task (Wickens and Carswell, 1995); for example in flight path tracking the pilot will need to integrate (compare) command values with actual values of some flight parameter. In controlling altitude the pilot will need to integrate pitch, vertical speed and altimeter information.

Basic research in psychology has established two general characteristics that facilitate the division of attention: closeness in space and belonging to a common object. Indeed proponents of these two characteristics have championed what have become known as 'space-based' and 'object-based' theories of attention (LaBerge, 1995; Kahneman and Treisman, 1984; Kramer and Jacobson, 1991; Driver and Baylis, 1989). As we will see, this theoretical distinction is important for HUD design as both theories describe information processing mechanisms that help explain HUD effects. The closeness in visual space, fostered by the overlay of the near domain symbology and the far domain information will both aid divided attention and disrupt focussed attention according to space based theories;

whereas any feature that 'binds' HUD information to far domain information, through overlaying conformal imagery, or common motion as the aircraft rotates and translates, will suggest that the two domains describe a common object. Hence this feature will encourage the division of attention between the two domains (Wickens and Long, 1995).

While the four modes of attention described above are relevant for nearly all aspects of aviation performance, they have particular relevance for HUD issues because the encouragement of divided attention is one of the fundamental rationales for HUD design and because the issue of clutter, mediated by attentional mechanisms, represents one of the greatest HUD concerns. In the following section, we visit the empirical data that has examined the costs and benefits of HUDs, making references to both the features described in the previous section and to the mediating attentional mechanisms described above, as these become relevant.

Performance effects of HUDs

As we have noted above, a full conclusion on the effectiveness of HUDs needs to be based on a careful description of the display it is being compared with, as well as the tasks that pilots are performing. Much of the earliest work on HUDs which found their benefit (e.g. Naish, 1964; Fischer, Haines and Price, 1980) did not involve fully comparable baseline displays (e.g. conventional head-down instrumentation thereby differing in location, format and collimation). However some of this research did make efforts to control for some of these differences while varying others (e.g. Boucek et al., 1983; Lauber, Bray, Harrison, Hemingway and Scott, 1982; Weintraub, Haines and Randall, 1985), and the findings of these investigators were heavily responsible for the eventual certification of HUDs for use in commercial airlines (Greene, 1987). Rather than reporting the individual findings of the 20-30 studies in this area here, we instead turn to the results of a *meta analysis* of instrument location effects (HUD versus head-down) carried out by Fadden et al. (1998; 2000). The meta analysis is a statistical technique for aggregating the collective effects of multiple studies that have examined a common set of variables and have reported the statistical effects of each examination (Rosenthal, 1993). Fadden et al. examined the effect of display location across a set of 19 studies in which other aspects of the symbology were relatively carefully controlled (i.e. not confounded between the head-up and head-down location). Their meta analysis revealed an overall advantage for the head-up location (i.e. HUDs are 'good' compared to their head-down counterparts). But this advantage was seen to be modulated by a number of other factors; knowledge of which should help the designer to decide when it is more or less advantageous to display certain information on a HUD. We describe these factors below (see also Weintraub and Ensing, 1992; and Newman, 1995).

Collimation

The issue of how (and whether) the HUD image is collimated to optical infinity has implications both for its effectiveness and for the research methodology that is used to investigate HUDs. A context for understanding both of these implications is presented in figure 7, which depicts four panels, each portraying the side view of an observer, looking at HUD (dashed line) versus head-down (solid line) instrumentation and monitoring a far domain scene, represented by the black wall on the right. Figure 7a presents the typical contrast between a near domain head-down display and a collimated HUD designed to project the symbology out, but not always at the distance of the far domain viewing (optical infinity). Figure 7b presents the manner in which HUD research is often simulated, in which the 'HUD' imagery is not presented on a see-through display at all, but is projected at the same optical distance as the far domain (i.e. on a viewing screen several metres distant), figure 7c presents a corresponding contrast, except that both far domain and superimposed ('HUD') imagery are presented optically close (and at the same depth plane). This is the synthetic imagery display. Finally figure 7d presents the situation of the non-collimated HUD.

The primary issues that are raised as these different HUD viewpoints are contrasted are, (1) to what extent do the differences (real or apparent) in depth plane affect the difficulty of focusing attention on each plane and dividing attention between planes, (2) to what extent can results produced from the 'simulated HUD' in panels 7b and 7c, generalise to those of 'real HUDs' in panels 7a and 7d, (3) to what extent does the collimation of panel 7a, achieve the goals of mimicking the view in panel 7b, (4) to what extent can the non-collimated HUD in panel 7d (much less expensive technologically) maintain the performance advantages of panel 7a.

With regard to the research methodology issue (2), few studies have compared panel (a) with either (b) or (c). One study by Kaptein (1994), using automotive HUDs, found that performance (lane and speed control) was slightly better with the 'virtual HUD' in panel b, than with a non-collimated HUD in panel d, for a HUD presenting analogue speedometer information. However both conditions produced performance that was substantially better than in the head-down condition, so that the performance effects in one HUD condition could seem to generalise to those predicted in the other. An aviation study by Fadden and Wickens (1997a, 1997b) essentially compared the three instrument panels that can be represented in figure 7b: a far projected virtual HUD (containing flight path guidance information through which the far domain could be seen), a standard near head-down display and a far projected head-down display, i.e. the head-down imagery on the far screen was visible against a black background. Flight path tracking and event detection performance in both domains were assessed. The difference in contrasting the two head-down instrument panels (at the close and distant location) is in the role of visual re-accommodation between near and far domains and the authors found that the near projection of the head-down instruments (requiring more re-accommodation) inhibited the detection of far domain traffic (both slower and less accurate), but actually speeded the detection of discrete events on the near-domain instrument panel, while having no influence on flight path tracking. Thus the presence of the imagery at the close distance seems to induce a 'near focus' while its presence at the far point induces a 'far focus'. Neither condition however was directly compared with a true HUD projection (figure 7a).

From a design perspective, it does not appear that performance based studies comparing panel a (collimated HUD) with panel d (non collimated HUD) have been carried out, although such studies would appear to be of considerable import, given the lower cost of the latter display and its greater flexibility (i.e. release from the constraints of an 'eye box'). It should be noted, however, that an eye box is necessary not only to insure accommodation, but also to insure that conformal imagery roughly overlays its far domain counterpart.

An important line of research by Roscoe and his colleagues (Iavecchia, Iavecchia and Roscoe, 1988; Roscoe, 1987) has examined the extent to which the collimation of the image really does lead to effective focusing of the lens out at (or toward) optical infinity. Roscoe's findings suggest that the HUD does not accomplish this goal (although this conclusion has itself been challenged (Sheehy and Gish, 1991). Roscoe has expressed the further concern that the failure of the HUD to influence visual accommodation slightly alters the size of the HUD image on the retina, thereby influencing the judgment of true depth and distance of HUD-projected objects. While these issues also remain somewhat controversial (Newman, 1987), one clear message from Roscoe's research is to highlight the ease with which the goal of collimation of a HUD image may be defeated in its intent, by any obvious feature that signals the close proximity of the image screen. Such features might include a very prominent edge on the HUD, or scratches and dirt on the HUD surface.

Symbology, task and location

The three factors of the nature of the task, the nature of the symbology and the location of the display are integrally linked for a designer, who is to decide what information to place on a HUD. This is because the nature of such information is dictated both by the task that it must serve and the format in which it is displayed. For example, a flight path-tracking *task* dictates the display of guidance *information* that, in turn necessarily dictates analogue symbology. System monitoring tasks dictate a different kind of symbology that may have greater flexibility in its display format.

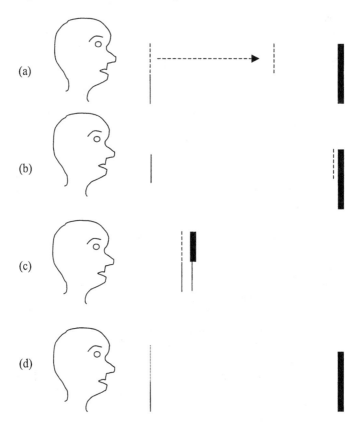

Figure 7   **Different methodologies for examining HUD location effects. The heavy vertical panel is the location of far domain imagery. The thin vertical panel is the display, either head-down (solid) or head-up (dashed). (a) collimated HUD, (b) simulated HUD, (c) synthetic imagery, (d) non-collimated HUD**

The typical simulator evaluation to answer these questions and hence advise the designer on which information is best displayed on a HUD (and how) and which information is best left head-down includes the following generic characteristics (see Lauber et al., 1982; Hofer, Braune, Boucek and Pfaff, 2000; Levy, Foyle and McCann, 1998; Martin-Emerson and Wickens, 1997; Ververs and Wickens, 1998; Fadden, Ververs and Wickens, 2001; Wickens and Long, 1995, for prototypical examples): The pilot flies a simulated flight, which may involve some combination of cruise, approach, landing and taxi phases. Any of these can be presented in clear weather or cloudy, which will dictate the degree of visibility of

118

the far domain. Displayed information is presented head-up or head-down to support (a) tasks of flight path guidance and often (b) the detection and processing of some discrete event, such as a windshear hazard alert, datalink icon, or a commanded change in a target value of heading, altitude, or airspeed. The symbology for flight path guidance is sometimes varied in its degree of conformality with the outside scene. Sometimes there are tasks imposed that require the explicit focus of attention on the far domain, typically involving traffic detection, but in some simulations requiring the identification of a signal on the runway. In some simulations these events or objects to be detected in the far domain are quite unexpected. Under the ideal experiment, the nature of the symbology and tasks will be controlled between head-up and head-down viewing conditions, so that differences in location are not confounded with those of symbology. The following general effects are supported by the research, with varying degrees of consistency and qualifications as described.

First, there are consistent and robust findings that traffic is detected better when the pilots fly with a HUD than with a head-down display (Beringer and Ball, 2001; Fadden et al., 2001, experiment 1; Fadden and Wickens, 1997b; Martin-Emerson and Wickens, 1997, experiment 1). The benefits are observed both in the speed of traffic detection (saving 2-3 seconds) and in accuracy (aircraft traffic is not missed; Ververs and Wickens, 1998, experiment 2). The only exception to this finding is the detection of very unexpected events, an issue we deal with below.

Second, there is a general, although slightly weaker trend for the detection of discrete events on the *display* to benefit from its head-up location (Fadden et al., 2001; Ververs and Wickens, 1998, Experiment 2; Martin-Emerson and Wickens, 1997, Experiment 1; Fadden and Wickens, 1997b). Collectively, both of these event detection results suggest that the benefits to divided attention (parallel monitoring) of reduced scanning, outweigh whatever costs to focussed attention are imposed by the possible 'clutter' of overlapping imagery. The reason why the benefits of HUD overlay are somewhat weaker for events on the display itself than for events in the far domain, is because this benefit depends on the source of information the pilot uses to fly the aircraft. When that information source is the outside world (e.g. sighting a true runway, or using the true horizon for attitude control), then the direction of attention to that source outside will facilitate detection of events that are along this same line-of sight; the original goal of the HUD. However, if the pilot is primarily using the instruments to fly (in particular in IMC when the true horizon is not well defined), then the detection of displayed information next to those instruments will be little effected by where all of this displayed information is located (HUD or head-down). Furthermore, it is the case that detection of discrete HUD displayed events is quite sensitive to the contrast between the instrumentation and the background behind, an issue that is not relevant when these events are represented on head-down symbology (where the contrast is uniform; Ververs and Wickens, 1998).

Third, there is, overall, a weak benefit for flight (and ground) path tracking performance in the head-up location. While more studies show this benefit than not, there are certain exceptions where a small tracking benefit for head-down displays are observed in the air (i.e. cruise or approach: Ververs and Wickens, 1998, experiment 1; Fadden et al., 2001, experiment 2). It turns out that this location effect is fairly strongly influenced by the conformality of the symbology used in flight path guidance, with fully conformal symbology generally amplifying (or creating) the head-up benefits, relative to non-conformal symbology (Wickens and Long, 1995). This as a result of the conformal symbology removing some of the clutter effects (since conformal symbology directly overlays its far domain counterpart) and 'fusing' the near and far domain as a single rigid object. As a consequence, consistent with object-based theories of divided attention, such conformality eliminates, or greatly reduces, the need for attention switching between the two domains.

A closer look at conformal symbology in a head-up and head-down location, reveals three more subtle effects, depending on how 'conformal' is defined, as discussed in the second section of this paper.

1. The greatest HUD benefits of conformal symbology appear to result when truly conformal instruments directly superimpose their far domain counterparts. These would include a horizon line, a runway overlay (figure 1) or, while taxiing on the ground, a set of pylons that mark the runway edges and a line in the centre (figure 3). This aspect of conformal guidance information serves to create a single 'scene-linked' object (Levy, Foyle and McCann, 1998), facilitating the division of attention or fusion between the instrument panel and the far domain, as predicted by object-based models of visual attention discussed above. One might predict that facilitating the division of attention between the two domains by conformal imagery would also improve the detection of discrete events described above and indeed such does appear to be the case (Fadden et al., 2001, experiment 2; Martin-Emerson and Wickens, 1997, experiment 2).

2. Virtual conformal imagery, achieved by the highway in the sky display (preview symbol) and the flight path vector (predictor symbol) does not appear to offer consistent HUD benefits relative to its head-down location (figure 5). However this lack of benefit must be considered against the backdrop of the overall tremendous advantages of such displays over more conventional guidance displays (e.g. ILS), whether presented head-up (Fadden et al., 2001, experiment 1; Martin-Emerson and Wickens, 1997, experiment 2) or head-down (Beringer and Ball, 2001; Doherty and Wickens, 2001; Haskell and Wickens, 1993; Wickens and Prevett, 1995). As Fadden et al. (2001) noted, the 5 foot (1.52m) RMS error cost of head-up compared to head-down location of a pathway display, is dwarfed in the face of the large 200 foot (61m) advantage of that pathway display over

conventional ILS symbology. This led Fadden et al. to conclude that a pathway HUD is a very acceptable flight path design.

3. The third aspect of HUD conformality concerns the distinction between truly and partially conformal HUDs, as the latter is created by compressing the pitch or azimuth (compass) scale (essentially increasing the geometric field of view, while keeping the HUD surface area constant). Three investigations have found that eliminating true conformality in a compressed scale does not disrupt flight path tracking in any way (Ververs and Wickens, 1998, experiment 1; Beringer and Ball, 2001; Geiselman and Osgood, 1992). In fact, using a pathway display, Beringer and Ball found that the compression actually improved tracking performance in that the wider field of view that resulted allowed pilots to better preview the wider range of required turns ahead along the pathway.

Finally, it is important to address the possible effects of display location on 'cognitive tunnelling,' the failure of performing the task of monitoring for and detecting very surprising events (Wickens, 2001), such as a runway incursion on the final approach (figure 8). Since the original demonstration of this phenomenon in a high fidelity HUD landing simulation (Fischer, Haines and Price, 1980), it has been replicated four times (Wickens and Long, 1995; Weintraub, Haines and Randall, 1985; Hofer, Braune, Boucek and Pfaff, 2000; Fadden et al., 2001, experiment 2), with greater experimental control and statistical power (higher n) than in the original demonstration by Fischer et al. Furthermore, while other studies have failed to find a HUD cost for unexpected event (runway incursion) detection (Martin-Emerson and Wickens, 1997, experiment 1), neither have they observed the benefits for HUD conditions that are consistently found for the detection of more expected events as described above. Two hypotheses have been offered to account for this effect (reduction or reversal of HUD detection benefits for surprising events). One is that, with a head-down display, the pilot must make constant eye movements to look outside. The brain functions in such a way so as to use the eye movement to switch attention from the near to the far domain. Without eye movements to trigger attention shifts in depth when viewing a HUD, such shifts become less frequent and have to be made with conscious effort (rather than being automatically induced as part of the pilots' heavily trained scan pattern). The other hypothesis blames the masking of the overlapping symbology for degrading the quality of a far domain traffic image. This masking (sensory or perceptual), coupled with the lack of expectancy for the surprising event (most pilots have never approached a runway upon which an aircraft suddenly pulls out), provides a double penalty to HUD detection that is not evident when the events are routine (e.g. traffic visible in the airspace), *or* in the head-down condition, when clutter masking of the far domain is not present. These two hypotheses, while involving different perceptual/cognitive mechanisms, are probably not mutually exclusive.

Figure 8   Illustrates a HUD on landing with a runway incursion present

Intensity and colour

The designer has two more considerations when deciding how to represent symbology on a HUD – intensity and colour. With regard to intensity, we have already addressed the requirement to provide an adequate contrast ratio for discriminating the imagery from the background. However, there may be cases where low-lighting certain display elements relative to others is appropriate. Ververs and Wickens (1998) suggest low-lighting less relevant display items as an alternative to de-cluttering them entirely. Low-lighting offers the opportunity to continuously present all information with less distraction to the pilot than an equally cluttered display presented at a single intensity level. The goal is to vary the intensity of a display (i.e. highlighting or low-lighting) to draw the pilot's focussed attention to the most critical elements of the display, while reducing the possibility that other elements will obscure objects in the far domain.

Due to its recent availability, the use of colour on HUDs has seen limited research regarding its application in this field and has yet to be applied to a certified HUD in the civilian market. In general, colour should be used to discriminate critical aspects of the symbology from the rest and used only as a redundant cue. However, varying the symbology colour against the continuously changing environment can also reduce the elements' overall conspicuity against some backgrounds. Green is highly discriminable in most conditions and therefore should remain the primary colour. (Inuzuka, Osumi, Shinkai, 1991; Weintraub and Ensign, 1992). Traditionally in aviation cautions and warnings have been represented in amber and red, respectively. When feasible, colour applied to HUDs should use the same conventions.

The three main areas colour has been applied to HUDs are: warnings or alerts of critical information (e.g. windshear), guidance cues (e.g. highway in the sky) and attitude awareness (e.g. pitch ladder distinctions between ground [pitch down] and sky [pitch up]). Overall, when used sparingly, colour has demonstrated positive effects on both objective and subjective measures. Baird et al. (1993) found faster response times and more accurate responses when warnings (ground proximity warning and excessive speed) were presented in colour as compared to monochrome text. Hawkins et al. (1983) found 25% fewer errors with a colour-coded pathway in the sky over monochrome symbology set. Colour-coding the pitch ladder a similar colour scheme as an ADI (blue/brown) resulted in faster initial response times to recover from an unusual attitudes as compared to a monochrome display (Dudfield et al. 1995). In all the studies reviewed, pilots preferred the multi-chromatic to monochromatic displays.

Training

Little, if any, publicly available research has focussed on training pilots to fly referencing head-up displays. One area that pilots could benefit from training is combating the effects of cognitive tunnelling. Giving pilots a general awareness of the phenomenon and techniques for combating it might reduce its negative impact on performance. One such technique is to reduce the intensity of the symbology. A common recommendation is to turn the intensity down and slowly increasing the brightness until the pilot can just see the imagery. This would reduce the chance of completely masking a far domain object with an overly bright image. Another training technique could be introduced at the yearly recurrence training. Commercial pilots who regularly hand fly approaches with HUDs might be exposed on a couple of occasions to unexpected events, such as a runway incursion. Pilots could be trained to 'expect the unexpected' (Wickens, 2001). Increasing the expectancy of these events might reverse the negative effect caused by cognitive tunnelling and possibly enable a HUD benefit similar to that seen for traffic detection. Training to expect a runway incursion in general is a good practice since their occurrence is steadily increasing with over 430 incidents reported in 2000 (Gerold, 2001). A third training technique or design implication could be to remove the HUD symbology at decision height. If the pilots are landing in category IIIa conditions (50 ft decision height, 700 ft runway visual range) or better, where visually transitioning to the runway is required, eliminating the source ensures that their attention will not be tunnelled on the HUD symbology. Training the pilots to scan the runway and announce 'all clear' as a supplement to their landing procedure could further reduce the effects of cognitive tunnelling.

HUDs in automobiles

Research on HUDs has primarily focussed on aviation. However, recently the automotive industry has begun to use the technology to display symbology (e.g. speedometer, turn signals) and night vision to drivers (Tufano, 1997). Future HUDs may include advanced technologies to support navigation guidance, hazard detection, collision avoidance and communications. There are many differences between the two environments and one must understand those differences before drawing generalisations from one domain to make design decisions in the other. We briefly review the differences between the two domains and cite some of the relevant research findings from the automotive industry.

Bossi, Ward, Parkes and Howarth (1997) notes that differences in age, selection, training, visual function and range of abilities clearly separates typical drivers from pilots. In addition, pilots are more likely to be male and possess a higher education. The pilot population tends to be more homogenous across physical and cognitive traits than the general population of drivers. Therefore in design of automotive HUDs there is a greater span of abilities and one needs to design for the lowest common denominator. For instance, there is a concern for the effect of ageing due to growing population of older drivers. Their visual performance and attentional capabilities are more likely to be impaired and their response times slower.

One must also consider the environment and the associated tasks required of the pilot or driver. Unlike the flight environment where the sky or clouds provide the primary backdrop to HUDs, drivers are confronted with rapidly changing and usually more cluttered backgrounds against which the symbology needs to be presented. The background needs to be considered since it affects luminance contrast as well as the clutter it imposes. One must also examine the task to be performed in the two domains. Aviation HUDs primarily support navigation in three dimensions (altitude, heading, airspeed) particularly when the far domain is not visually accessible through the clouds. However, HUDs for automobiles relay information about system status (telltale warnings) and speed and are used when the far domain is not only available but used as the primary source for navigation. Automobile drivers need to concern themselves with a variety of obstacles moving at varying speeds at close proximity and therefore greater attention needs to be directed to the outside world. Pilots regularly scan the environment for traffic; however, the task is secondary to controlling flight. The presence of a true obstacle is a rare event and the time horizon tends to be longer in aviation. Empirical research has generally concluded that aviation HUDs can produce cognitive capture resulting in slow responses to these unexpected events. For automotive HUDs, however, Tufano (1997) concluded that research on HUD focal distance and the likelihood of cognitive capture is still a relatively unresolved issue.

Given the different tasks of pilots and drivers, the information and display requirements vary. For instance, a contact analogue of the runway and horizon is helpful to pilots for attitude orientation and navigation. Given the fewer number and type of tasks supported (and not supported) by automobile HUDs, they tend to have a smaller field of view 15 x 10 (Bossi et al., 1997) than aviation HUDs.

With the number of differences between the two domains, one may question the relevance of information on automobile HUDs for this chapter. For one, given the longer history in aviation, automobile HUD designers reference the literature and will draw their own conclusions. But even more important is the fact that there are some key similarities. Both domains are concerned with minimising the re-accommodation when redirecting eyes from environment to projected information and vice versa. The presence of the symbology in the head-up location reduces the area that needs to be scanned and therefore is aimed at improving the drivers' and pilots' performance in detection and recognition. The goal is to maximise focussed attention on forward field of view. In this regard, the conclusion drawn by Sheey and Gish (1991) that automobile HUD symbology may be better displayed closer than optical infinity bears careful consideration for aircraft HUDs.

Contrast of the imagery against the outside environment and its overall luminance is of equal concern in both the aviation and automobile domain. Like pilots, drivers need readable instrumentation in the dark of night and on sunlit snow covered roads. Similar to aviation, guidelines need to be provided for proper display luminance. To this end, Weihrauch, Meloeny and Goesch (1989) suggest 1.5:1 as a goal and caution going less than a minimum acceptable ratio of 1.2:1. Given the many similarities, we review the literature around automotive HUDs and draw conclusions from relevant research for aviation.

General Motors introduced the first production-configured automotive HUD in the United States in 1988 (Weihrauch, et al. 1989). The display consisted of a digital speedometer and warning telltales (fuel, check gauges, high beams). In a simulator study using the GM HUD, Weihrauch et al. found obstacle detection and steering control to be superior with the head-up display than when the information was presented on a conventional instrument dashboard. Mirroring these findings, Kaptein (1994) also demonstrated an advantage of a HUD over a HDD (head-down display) in lane keeping, speed keeping and subjective workload. Sojourner and Antin (1990) also compared HUD to HDD presentation of a digital speedometer. One task required drivers to detect objects in the roadway. Drivers detected targets with greater accuracy and faster responses times when the imagery was presented HU versus HD. In another driving simulator study, Kiefer (1991) failed to find a significant performance advantage for maintaining speed with a HUD over a HDD, however drivers spent less time with their eyes off the road monitoring speed without showing a decrement in driving performance. All drivers preferred the head-up speedometer to the head-down display. Clearly, the HUD location is not only suitable but preferable for displaying vehicle status information.

The major concern with automobile HUDs is the complex background against which the symbology is presented. Unlike the typical aviation environment where the symbology is superimposed on a grey or clear sky, the driving environment offers a densely varied scene. This greater complexity in the environment can interfere with the legibility of HUD information. In fact, Ward, Parkes and Crone (1995) found that increasing the background complexity decreased the subjects' ability to correctly identify HUD targets. Performance improved only when the HUD image, consisting of a digital speed readout and three Landolt 'C' targets, was superimposed on the bare roadway rather than the scenery.

Since conformal presentation of information is not a concern for automobile HUDs, designers are faced with the question of where in the forward field of view (FFOV) to present the imagery. In a monitoring task performed in a driving simulator, Yoo, Tsimhoni, Watanabe, Green and Shah (1999) required drivers to detect events in the environment (roadway) and on a HUD. The positions of the HUD warnings were varied. The fastest response time came when the HUD warnings were displayed just to the right of the central location. The effects of eccentricity were magnified for older subjects resulting in slow RTs and missed targets. Similar effects of ageing were found for a detection task with a collimated HUD. Inuzuka, Osumi and Shinkai (1991) required subjects to read a HUD speedometer after focusing on a near target. Though the focal distance of the imagery did not affect the younger subjects' response times, slower recognition times were found with older drivers (50-70 years of age) when the imagery was presented closer than 2.5 meters. Clearly age plays a factor for presentation of HUD imagery. If the population is anticipated to include users aged 50 or older, display collimation and location must be a consideration.

We have seen many of the same advantages found with aviation HUDs in the automotive industry. One may wonder whether the same costs to unexpected surprise events would exist as well. In a study by Kiefer and Gellatly (1996) drivers were presented with surprise objects in the environment while driving with a digital speedometer HU and HD. Drivers were significantly *more* likely to report the presence of the surprise targets if they were driving with the HUD as compared to the HDD location. In another simulator study, drivers were briefly presented with unexpected telltale warnings in the near domain on either the HUD or the head-down display. Drivers detected the warning faster and with greater accuracy for identifying the warning when presented on a HUD as compared to a conventional head-down display (Grant, Kiefer, Wierwille and Beyerlein, 1995). Contrary to the two previous studies, Ward, Parkes and Lindsay (1995) found a slower response to a critical braking event by the lead car when driving with a HUD with varying degrees of information (including lateral and longitudinal position indicators and speed). However, their comparison was to a no HUD condition as opposed to a HD presentation. Without a point of comparison we cannot know the true cost to performance. Tufano (1997) notes a study in which drivers using a HUD failed to detect an unexpected baby carriage rolled onto the roadway. However, since the research study was not publicly available no further information was given with regard to a baseline comparison. Without further research, we can generally conclude that drivers are better able to detect unexpected surprise events when viewing symbology with HUD versus HDD. These findings are different from those in the aviation research. One explanation may be that with driving the primary task requires focussed attention on the outside environment rather than on the near domain instrumentation. Therefore, they may be less susceptible to cognitive tunnelling. This finding may also hold true for pilots once they have landed and taxi to their gate, explaining the strong advantage for taxi HUDs in obstacle detection (Fadden et al., 2001; Foyle et al., 1996; Hooey, Foyle, Andre and Parke, 2000).

When considering the transfer of these findings to aviation, we find that detection of expected events and position tracking benefit from the reduced scan area provided by HUDs. Designers need be concerned when presenting symbology against a complex background since the added clutter disrupts performance. This result is particularly applicable to low flying aircraft such as nap of the earth manoeuvring in helicopters and taxiway navigation. With the preponderance of the driving task requiring attention on the outside environment, drivers appear to be less susceptible to cognitive tunnelling. This finding may transfer well to ground navigation tasks in aviation where the primary task requires the pilot to access the far domain.

The helmet mounted display

The helmet mounted display or HMD is analogous in some respects to the HUD, in that the pilot can look at or through a displayed image, to view the world beyond (Melzer and Moffitt, 1997; figure 9). However, the see-through display of the HMD is rigidly attached to the head, rather than to the airframe. The HMD may be presented either monocularly (to one eye) or binocularly (to both). In aviation applications, the binocular display must of necessity be translucent, so that the far domain can be seen through the HMD imagery. However, the monocular image can either occlude the far domain entirely, or it can be displayed on a translucent surface, so that the far domain can be seen through this image. The latter design is greatly preferable since a wider range of the far domain can be seen and it avoids the costs of binocular rivalry (i.e. seeing one image or the other, but not both).

Figure 9   Helmet Mounted Displays (HMDs). The man on the left is wearing a monocular, opaque head mounted display (also known as a wearable computer). The model shown is an MA IV manufactured by Xybernaut. The soldier on the right is wearing a monocular opaque helmet mounted display coupled with a computer in his backpack. The soldier shown on the right is participating in a programme of research by Sytronics Inc. called Digitally Aided Soldier for Human Engineering Research (DASHER)

Benefits and costs

While the HUD and HMD both present images overlaid on the far domain, there are some important functional differences between the two displays. Most importantly, HUD imagery can only be viewed when the pilot is looking more or less straight ahead because the HUD is rigidly mounted to the aircraft. In contrast, HMD imagery can be viewed independently of the head's orientation. This feature has two distinct benefits. First it means that pilots can view HMD imagery when they scan the far domain beside and behind the aircraft heading vector, or even when they look down inside the cockpit. In this sense, the HMD is functionally equivalent to the now popular 'wearable computer.' This feature is particularly advantageous for 'eyes-out' viewing in the military cockpit (where the enemy can be very much of a threat behind; Geiselman and Osgood, 1995), or in low altitude rotorcraft operations (when the hovering pilot must keep eyes out of the cockpit, in order to avoid contact with ground hazards; Hart, 1988; Hamilton, 1999; Haworth and Seery, 1992). The second advantageous feature of the HMD is that it enables conformal imagery to be depicted across a much wider range of space than is possible with the narrow field of view of the cockpit-mounted HUD. This greater range then allows the pilot to look at an off-axis or 'off boresight' target in order to place an HMD-displayed reticule on the target (Brickman, Hettinger, Haas and Dennis, 1998), or to view a conformal horizon symbol, as he looks to the side. When the HMD presents synthetic imagery from a night vision sensor, it allows the pilot to look around and 'see' the terrain representation co-located at its natural location, even when that terrain is not visible. Sometimes this use of the HMD is referred to as creating an 'augmented reality' (Milgram and Colquhoun, 1999).

The benefits which the HMD provide for a greater range of superimposed viewing and conformal imagery are also offset by some competing costs. The first – the cost of clutter of overlapping imagery – is the same as that which was discussed in the HUD context: If HMD imagery is dense, it may hinder the focus of attention on far domain information and correspondingly, a busy rich-textured scene in the far domain, can disrupt the readability of the HMD imagery (Yeh, Wickens and Seagull, 1999; Yeh, Merlo, Wickens and Brandenburg, 2001). The second cost applies only to conformal HMD imagery and this is the need to update, or redraw the location of that imagery rapidly, as the head is rotated, so the imagery always overlays its far domain counterpart. Where such imagery is complex and the head movement is rapid, a lag in image updating can be quite disruptive to human perception and performance. It can lead to motion sickness,' can sometimes be disorienting and can lead to a less than natural, more constricted amount of head movement (Seagull and Gopher, 1997). A particular problem when viewing synthetic imagery results when the location of the image generating sensor is offset from the pilots head by a few meters, as will be the case if those sensors are located outside the body of a large helicopter (Hart, 1988).

Operational evaluations and comparisons between HMDs and head-down, or vehicle mounted head-up displays for similar tasks are fewer than comparisons between HUDs and their head-down counterparts discussed in the previous sections (see Yeh and Wickens, 1998). While HUDs are common features in many cockpits, HMDs are only standard equipment in some military aircraft (the Apache helicopter) and will probably be considerably slower to be implemented in the cockpit of the civil fixed wing aircraft (although the fact that they are portable, like handheld GPS receivers and therefore less governed by certification regulations, suggest that their use may grow rapidly). Those few comparisons that have been carried out (Geiselman and Osgood, 1995; Yeh et al., 1999) suggest that, as with HUDs, the helmet mounted display can provide very effective target and orientation cueing, so long as their potential costs are considered in design.

The frame of reference issue

As noted above, the HMD has two distinct benefits relative to the HUD: allowing continuous viewing of instrumentation across a wide range of head movements (in particular, when engaged in off-axis viewing) and enabling a much wider range of visual space within which conformal imagery can be displayed. These two benefits are generally associated with different 'frames of reference' of HMD imagery (Wickens, Vincow and Yeh, in press). Specific images (usually non-conformal) which are viewable independently of the orientation of the head, are said to be *screen referenced*, since the co-ordinates upon which those images are drawn, are defined exclusively by X-Y co-ordinates on the HMD surface. In contrast, conformal imagery on an HMD is said to be *world referenced*, since it overlays distinct positions in the world and its location on the screen will be contingent upon the momentary orientation of movement of the head. World referencing on a see through HMD creates what is known as 'augmented reality' (Milgram and Colquhoun, 1999). World referencing on an opaque HMD, while not discussed in detail here, can be used to create the 'virtual cockpit' (Barfield and Furness, 1995), which might be used for training purposes, or for flying remotely piloted vehicles.

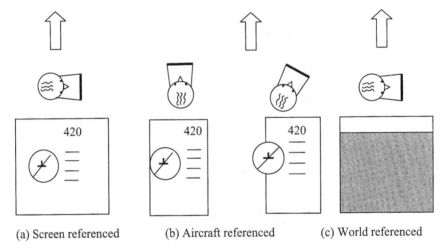

(a) Screen referenced   (b) Aircraft referenced   (c) World referenced

Figure 10   **Four views depicting three different frames of reference on a helmet mounted display. The arrow at the top shows the direction of flight and axis of the aircraft. The figures in the middle row show the orientation of the head and the HMD. The figures on the bottom show the view on the HMD screen of an aircraft banked to the right. (a) Screen referenced. (b) Aircraft referenced (two views as the head turns). (c) World referenced. The grey band represents the ground and the white band represents the air. The dividing horizon line would move downward if the pilot returned to a wings-level attitude**

A schematic representation of the view, seen by a pilot in a screen referenced and a world referenced HMD is shown in panels a and c of figure 10, for a pilot who is looking to the right and sees the indicator of his aircraft in a right bank. In addition to the world and screen-referenced frames shown in figure 10, HMDs allow depiction of a third frame of reference – the aircraft, or *aircraft referenced* symbology. Here the symbology is drawn at a fixed location relative to the axis of the aircraft. An example would be a set of flight instruments that are depicted to appear at the normal location of the HUD. This view is shown in panel b of figure 10, representing the turning head.

While the distinction between these three frames of reference for HMDs is every bit as critical as is the distinction between conformal and non-conformal imagery for HUDs, there are in fact very few studies that have contrasted them, to allow conclusions of 'which is better' to be drawn. Taylor and Kuchar (2000), compared screen-referenced to aircraft-referenced symbology for attitude recovery for fighter pilots. Their task required pilots to look off axis with the HMD while at an unusual attitude, and, upon hearing an auditory cue, immediately recover wings level flight. The investigators found that the aeroplane-referenced display imposed a delay in recovery, as the pilot needed to return the head to a forward viewing position before initiating the manoeuvre, whereas with the screen-referenced display, pilots could (and did) initiate their recovery before rotating their head forward. Herdman, Johannsdottir, Armstrong, Jarmasz, LeFevre and Lichacz (2000) also compared a screen referenced HMD with an aircraft referenced HMD and contrasted these with a mixed display containing both. Their rotorcraft pilots engaged in a forward flying manoeuvre. In the mixed display, attitude information remained aircraft referenced, so that it would be conformal with the true horizon when the pilot looked forward, but drop out of sight (like a conformal HUD) when the pilot looked off axis. The investigators found a general advantage for screen referenced information. In the mixed condition, the presence of both kinds of symbology on a single display, moving differently as the pilots' head rotated, did not appear to disrupt performance, because of the ability of pilots to cognitively separate the two domains on the basis of motion cues.

In both of the above experiments, aircraft-referenced attitude information was also configured to be partially 'conformal' with the outside world, in the sense that, when the pilot looks forward and varies attitude, the behaviour of the instrument horizon would mimic that of the true horizon, as would be the case of a partially conformal HUD. This raises the question as to whether such conformal but screen-referenced displays (like the ADI shown in figure 10a) would be disruptive to aircraft control if they are viewed off axis; that is, a contrast between panels (a) and (c) in figure 10, as these would be used for attitude control. Recall that both panels depict a plane banked to the right. However, the conformal, world-referenced horizon symbol shown in figure 10c depicts the horizon as it would look to a pilot looking outward along the right wing of a right banked aircraft. Again, there is little data to compare the efficacy of these two frames of reference. Haworth and Seery (1992) compared the two frames, across a range of typical tasks for the rotorcraft pilot in a full mission simulation, while pilots looked off-axis, as they were engaged in search for targets and maintaining awareness of terrain features. They found that neither display was terribly effective for unusual attitude recovery during off axis viewing with both showing a large number of initial control actions in the wrong direction (the world-referenced display showed more errors). However, they found that for tasks involving perception of the simulated outside world (e.g. altitude and terrain estimation, contour flight), the world referenced symbology either supported better performance or was more favourably rated than was the screen referenced symbology.

The two slightly contradictory trends (one favouring each frame) observed by Haworth and Seery are consistent with two emerging findings. First, as we described earlier in the chapter, the world referencing of the conformal symbology set may facilitate the division of attention between the instruments and the outside world, eliminating any visual conflict between the two visual sources, and, like scene linking, serve to better 'fuse' the two views (Levy, Foyle and McCann, 1998; Fadden et al., in press). This fusion would not occur as a result of the conflicting motion patterns when the screen referenced symbology is viewed off axis. Second, there is some evidence that the interpretation of displayed motion when viewed off axis, is easily and automatically mentally transformed to a forward viewing axis, just as the head itself naturally rotates to the canonical forward view relative to the trunk (Wickens, Vincow and Yeh, 2001; Worringham and Beringer, 1989; Previc, 1998). Hence, a display that presents motion that would be untransformed when viewed in a forward orientation should be more rapidly and correctly interpreted, consistent with the findings of Haworth et al. favouring the screen referenced symbology for attitude recovery.

A study by Cohen et al. (2001) is also consistent with this conclusion. Although the investigators did not employ a true HMD they positioned a standard, screen-referenced attitude indicator in either a forward view or in a 90 degree off-axis viewing plane, relative to the orientation of the pilot's trunk (and control axis). For both skilled pilots and naïve non-pilots Cohen et al. observed no cost to off-axis viewing in a standard pitch and roll tracking task. That is, even when the instrumentation was placed off axis, pilots were able to mentally rotate the frame of reference to a forward view with no cost. This equality across viewing locations was observed independently of whether an inside out (moving horizon) or outside in (moving aircraft) frame was employed. However, the investigators also examined a third attitude indicator which was a side view display somewhat analogous to the view shown in figure 10c (although presented as a moving wing/fixed horizon, rather than the moving horizon display shown in figure 10c). This depiction corresponds in some respects to the world referenced attitude indicator examined by Haworth and Seery, in that both depict *vertical* (rather than rotational) movement on the display, as the pilot views a change in bank while looking 90 degrees off axis. Consistent with Haworth and Seery's finding, Cohen et al also observed a cost to this world referencing of attitude, relative to the screen (or aircraft) referencing condition. In contrast to the experiment of Haworth et al., this study found no benefit at all for the 'world referenced' display. But, correspondingly, the pilots in Cohen et al.'s studies 'flew' entirely in an instrument environment with no outside view, so that there was no source of perceptual conflict with the outside world. Such a conflict might otherwise have been observed in a side view, screen-referenced attitude display and indeed this conflict imposed the penalties observed by Haworth and Seery.

In conclusion, the Human Factors issues of Helmet mounted displays for aviation remain complex and vastly under-investigated. The choice between displaying information on a head-down panel, a HUD and an HMD (or redundantly across any combination of the platforms) is a challenging one, involving the trade-off between many factors such as viewing conditions, symbology type and task. Yet these issues must be addressed soon by the design community because HMDs, unlike HUDs, need not be considered as part of aircraft 'equipage' (and therefore subject to certification), any more than GPS receivers or other hand held devices.

References

A-4 Aircraft Instruments Committee (1999, March). *Minimum performance standard for airborne head-up display (HUD).* SAE AS8055. Warrendale, PA: Society of Automotive Engineers.

Baird, J-A., Dudfield, H.J., Davy, E. and Moore, F. (1993). *A study to investigate the benefits of colour coding based on the results of an aircrew survey.* Defence Research Agency Technical Report DRA/AS/FS/TR 93014/1, Farnborough, United Kingdom.

Barfield, W. and Furness, T.A. (1995). *Virtual environments and advanced interface design.* Oxford: Oxford University Press.

Beringer, D.B. and Ball, J. (2001). General aviation pilot visual performance using conformal and non-conformal head-up and head-down highway-in-the-sky displays. In, R. Jensen (Ed.), *Proceedings of the International Symposium on Aviation Psychology.* Columbus, OH: The Dept. of Aerospace Engineering, Applied Mechanics and Aviation, The Ohio State University.

Bossi, L.L., Ward, N.J., Parkes, A.M. and Howarth, P.A. (1997). The effect of vision enhancement systems on driver peripheral visual performance. In, Y. Noy (Ed.), *Ergonomics and safety of intelligent driver interfaces.* Mahwah, New Jersey: Erlbaum.

Boucek, G.P., Pfaff, T.A. and Smith, W.D. (1983). The use of holographic head-up display of flight path symbology in varying weather conditions *(SAE*

Technical Paper Series 831445). Warrendale, PA: Society of Automotive Engineers, Inc.

Brickman, B.J., Hettinger, L.J., Haas, M.W. and Dennis, L.B. (1998, April). Designing the supercockpit. *Ergonomics in Design*, 15-20.

Broadbent, D.E. (1982). Task combination and selective intake of information. *Acta Psychologica, 50*, 253-290.

Brogan, D. (1990). Visual search. *Proceedings of the First International Conference on Visual Search.* London: Taylor and Francis.

Cohen, D., Otakeno, S., Previc, F.H. and Ercoline, W.R. (2001). Effect of 'inside-out' and 'outside-in' attitude displays on off-axis tracking in pilots and nonpilots. *Aviation, Space and Environmental Medicine, 72*, 170-176.

Comstock, J.R., Jr., Glaab, L.J., Prinzel, L.J. and Elliott, D.M. (2001). Can effective synthetic vision system displays be implemented on limited size display spaces? In, R. Jensen (Ed.) *Proceedings of the 11th International Conference on Aviation Psychology.* Columbus, OH: The Dept. of Aerospace Engineering, Applied Mechanics and Aviation, The Ohio State University.

Doherty, S.M. and Wickens, C.D. (2001). Effects of preview, prediction, frame of reference and display gain in tunnel-in-the-sky displays. In, R. Jensen (Ed.), *Proceedings of the 11th International Symposium on Aviation Psychology.* Columbus, OH: The Dept. of Aerospace Engineering, Applied Mechanics and Aviation, The Ohio State University.

Dornheim, M.A. (2000, July 17). Crew distractions emerge as new safety focus. *Aviation Week and Space Technology*, 58-65.

Driver, J.S. and Baylis, G.C. (1989). Movement and visual attention: The spotlight metaphor breaks down. *Journal of Experimental Psychology: Human Perception and Performance, 15*, 448-456.

Dudfield, H.J. Davy, E., Hardiman, T. and Smith, F. (1995). The effectiveness of colour coding collimated displays: An experimental evaluation of performance benefits. In, R. Jensen (Ed.), *Proceedings of the 8th International Symposium on Aviation Psychology.* Columbus, OH: The Dept. of Aerospace Engineering, Applied Mechanics and Aviation, The Ohio State University.

Eriksen, B.A. and Eriksen, C.W. (1974). Effects of noise letters upon the identification of a target letter in a non-search task. *Perception and Psychophysics, 16*, 143-149.

FAA Advisory Circular (1987). *Transport category airplane electronic display systems (AC #25-11).* U.S. Dept of Transportation, Federal Aviation Administration.

Fadden, S., Ververs, P.M. and Wickens, C.D. (1998). Costs and benefits of head-up display use: A meta-analytic approach. *Proceedings of the 42nd Annual Meeting of the Human Factors and Ergonomics Society* (pp. 16-20). Santa Monica, CA: Human Factors and Ergonomics Society.

Fadden, S., Ververs, P.M. and Wickens, C.D. (in press). Pathway HUDS: Are they viable? *Human Factors.*

Fadden, S. and Wickens, C.D. (1997a). *Maximizing traffic awareness with a head-up flight path highway display* (Technical Report ARL-97-1/FAA-97-1). Savoy, IL: University of Illinois, Aviation Research Lab.

Fadden, S. and Wickens, C.D. (1997b). Improving traffic awareness with a head-up flight path highway display. In, R. Jensen (Ed.), *Proceedings of the 9th International Symposium on Aviation Psychology*. Columbus, OH: Dept. of Aerospace Engineering, Applied Mechanics and Aviation, Ohio State University.

Fadden, S., Wickens, C.D. and Ververs, P.M. (2000). Costs and benefits of head-up displays: An attention perspective and a meta analysis (Paper # 2000-01-5542). *2000 World Aviation Congress*. Warrendale, PA: Society of Automotive Engineers.

Fischer, E., Haines, R.F. and Price, T.A. (1980). *Cognitive issues in head-up displays* (NASA Technical Paper 1711). Moffett Field, CA: NASA Ames Research Center.

Foyle, D.C., Andre, A.D., McCann, R.S., Wenzel, E.M., Begault, D.R. and Battiste, V. (1996). Taxiway navigation and situation awareness (T-NASA) System: Problem, design philosophy and description of an integrated display suite for low-visibility airport surface operations (SAE Paper 965551). In, *Proceedings of World Aviation Congress*. Warrendale, PA: Society of Automotive Engineers, Inc.

Gallimore, J.J., Stouffer, J.M., Brannon, N.G. and McCracken, J. (1997). Developing Automatic Luminance Controls for Liquid Crystal Displays in Military Cockpits. In, R. Jensen (Ed.), *Proceedings of the 9th International Symposium on Aviation Psychology*. Columbus, OH: The Dept. of Aerospace Engineering, Applied Mechanics and Aviation, The Ohio State University.

Geiselman E.E. and Osgood, R.K. (1992). A comparison of three aircraft attitude display symbology structures during an attitude maintenance task. In, *Proceedings of the 36th Annual Meeting of the Human Factors and Ergonomics Society*. Santa Monica, CA: Human Factors Society.

Geiselman, E.E. and Osgood, R.K. (1995). Head vs. aircraft oriented air-to-air target location symbology using a helmet-mounted display. In, R.J. Lewandowski, W. Stephens and L.A. Haworth (Eds.), *Proceedings of the International Society for Optical Engineers (SPIE): Helmet- and Head-mounted Displays and Symbology Design Requirements II* (pp. 214-225). Bellingham, WA: SPIE.

Gerold, A. (2001). Runway Incursions: The threat on the ground. *Avionics Magazine*, 16-19.

Grant, B.S., Kiefer, R.J., Wierwille, W.W. and Beyerlein, D.G. (1995). Exploring applications for automotive head-up displays through ergonomics research: Telltale warnings and beyond. *Proceedings of the 3rd International conference on Vehicle Comfort and Ergonomics*. Bologna, Italy: Associazione Tecnica dell'Automobile.

Greene, H.B. (1987). *Manual CAT IIIa with a HUD: Requirements and testing.* Seattle, WA: FAA.

Hamilton, B.E. (1999). Helicopter Human Factors. In, D.J. Garland, J.A. Wise and V.D. Hopkin (Eds.), *Handbook of aviation Human Factors* (pp. 405-428). Mahwah, NJ: Lawrence Erlbaum.

Hart, S.G. (1988). Helicopter Human Factors. In E.L. Wiener and D.C. Nagel (Eds.), *Human Factors in flight* (pp. 591-638). San Diego, CA: Academic Press.

Haskell, I.D. and Wickens, C.D. (1993). Two- and three-dimensional displays for aviation: A theoretical and empirical comparison. *The International Journal of Aviation Psychology, 3,* 87-109.

Hawkins, J.S., Reising, J.M. and Gilmour, J.D. (1983). Information interpretation through pictorial format. *In, Proceedings of the Aerospace Behavioral Engineering Technology Conference,* (pp. 243-248). Warrendale, PA: Society of Automotive Engineers.

Haworth, L.A. and Seery, R.E. (1992). *Rotorcraft helmet mounted display symbology research* (SAE Technical Paper Series 921977). Warrendale, PA: SAE.

Herdman, C.M., Johannsdottir, K.R., Armstrong, J., Jarmasz, J., LeFevre, J.A. and Lichacz, F. (2000). *Mixed-up but flyable: HMDs with aircraft- and head-referenced symbology.* In D. Harris (Ed.) *Engineering Psychology and Cognitive Ergonomics – Volume 5.* (pp. 73-80). Aldershot: Ashgate.

Hofer, E.F., Braune, R.J., Boucek, G.P. and Pfaff, T.A. (2000). *Attention switching between near and far domains: An exploratory study of pilots' attention switching with head-up and head-down tactical displays in simulated flight operations* (D6-36668). Seattle, WA: The Boeing Commercial Airplane Co.

Hooey, B.L., Foyle, D.C. Andre, A.D. and Parke, B. (2000). Integrating datalink and cockpit display technologies into current and future taxi operations. *Proceedings of the AIAA/IEEE/SAE 19th Digital Avionics System Conference.*

Iavecchia, J.A., Iavecchia, H.P. and Roscoe, S.N. (1988). Eye accommodation to head-up virtual images. *Human Factors, 30,* 689-702.

Inuzaka, Y. Osumi, Y. and Shinkai, H. (1991). Visibility of head-up display (HUD) for automobiles. *Proceedings of the 35th Annual Meeting of the Human Factors Society* (pp. 1574-1578). Santa Monica, CA: HFS.

Kahneman, D. and Treisman, A. (1984). Changing views of attention and automaticity. In R. Parasuraman and R. Davies (Ed.), *Varieties of attention* (pp. 29-61). New York: Academic Press.

Kaptein, N.A. (1994). *Benefits of in-car head-up displays* (TNO-TM 1994 B-20). Soesterberg, The Netherlands: TNO Human Factors Research Institute.

Kiefer, R.J. and Gellatly, A. (1996). *Quantifying the consequences of the 'eyes-on-road' benefit attributed to head-up displays* (SAE Paper 920600). Warrendale, PA: Society of Automotive Engineers.

Kramer, A.F. and Jacobson, A. (1991). Perceptual organization and focused attention: The role of objects and proximity in visual processing. *Perception and Psychophysics, 50*, 267-284.

LaBerge, D. (1995). *Attentional processing.* Cambridge, MA: Harvard University Press.

Lauber, J.K., Bray, R.S., Harrison, R.L., Hemingway, J.C. and Scott, B.C. (1982). *An operational evaluation of head-up displays for civil transport operations* (NASA Technical Paper 1815). Moffett Field, CA: NASA Ames Research Center.

Levy, J.L., Foyle, D.C. and McCann, R.S. (1998). Performance benefits with scene-linked HUD symbology: An attentional phenomenon? In, *Proceedings of the 42nd Annual Meeting of the Human Factors and Ergonomics Society.* Santa Monica, CA: Human Factors Society.

Martin-Emerson, R. and Wickens, C.D. (1997). Superimposition, symbology, visual attention and the head-up display. *Human Factors, 39*, 581-601.

McCann, R.S., Hooey, B.L., Parke, B., Foyle, D.C., Andre, A.D. and Kanki, B. (1988). An evaluation of the taxiway navigation and situation awareness (T-NASA) system in high-fidelity simulation (SAE Technical Paper #985541). *Presented at the World Aviation Congress and Exposition.* Warrendale, PA: Society of Automotive Engineers, Inc.

Melzer, J.E. and Moffitt, K. (1997). HMD design – Putting the user first. In, J.E. Melzer and K. Moffitt (Eds.), *Head mounted displays: Designing for the user.* New York, NY: McGraw-Hill.

Milgram, P. and Colquhoun, H., Jr. (1999). A taxonomy of real and virtual world display integration. In, Y. Ohta and H. Tamura (Eds.), *Mixed reality – merging real and virtual worlds.* Ohmsha (Tokyo) and Springer-Verlag (Berlin).

Naish, J.M. (1964). Combination of information in superimposed visual fields. *Nature, 202*, 641-646.

Neisser, U. and Becklen, R. (1975). Selective looking: Attention to visually specified events. *Cognitive Psychology, 7*, 480-494.

Newman, R.L. (1987). Response to Roscoe, 'The trouble with HUDs and HMDs'. *Human Factors Society Bulletin, 30*, 3-5.

Newman, R.L. (1995). *Head-up displays: Designing the way ahead.* Brookfield, VT: Avebury.

Pashler, H.E. (1998). *The psychology of attention.* Cambridge, MA: MIT Press.

Proctor, P. (1997, December 1). Economic, safety gains ignite HUD sales. *Aviation Week and Space Technology*, 54-57.

Proctor, P. (2000, August 14). New head-up tool aims to cut runway incidents. *Aviation Week and Space Technology*, 48-50.

Roscoe, S.N. (1987). The trouble with HUDs and HMDs. *Human Factors Bulletin (July)*, 1-3.

Rosenthal, R. (1993). *Meta-analytic procedures for social research* (2nd ed.). Beverly Hills: Sage Publications.

Schiff, B. (1994, May). Flight dynamics' head-up guidance system. *AOPA Pilot,* T-1-T-5.

Schutte, P.C. and Trujillo, A.C. (1996). Flight crew task management in non-normal situations. In, *Proceedings of the 40th Annual Meeting of the Human Factors and Ergonomics Society* (pp. 244-248). Santa Monica, CA: Human Factors and Ergonomics Society.

Scott, W.B. (1999, February 1). Automatic GCAS: You can't fly any lower. *Aviation Week and Space Technology,* 76-80.

Seagull, F.J. and Gopher, D. (1997). Training head movement in visual scanning: An embedded approach to the development of piloting skills with helmet-mounted displays. *Journal of Experimental Psychology: Applied, 3,* 163-180.

Sheehy, J.B. and Gish, K.W. (1991). Virtual image displays: Is redesign really necessary? *SID 91 Digest,* 308-312.

Sojourrner, R.J. and Antin, J.F. (1990). The effects of a simulated head-up display speedometer on perceptual task performance. *Human Factors, 32,* 329-339.

Steenblik, J.W. (1989, December). Alaska airlines H6S. *Airline Pilot,* 10-14.

Steenblik, J.W. (1992, December). Enhanced vision systems: Toward the autonomous airplane. *Airline Pilot,* 22-25.

Stokes, A.F., Wickens, C.D. and Kite, K. (1990). *Display technology: Human Factors concepts.* Warrendale, PA: Society of Automotive Engineers.

Taylor, J.B. and Kuchar, J.K. (2000). Helmet-mounted display symbology for terrain avoidance during low-level maneuvers. *International Journal of Aviation Psychology, 10,* 155-168.

Teichner, W.H. and Mocharnuk, J.B. (1979). Visual search for complex targets. *Human Factors, 21,* 259-275.

Tufano, D.R. (1997). Automotive HUDs: The overlooked safety issues. *Human Factors, 39,* 303-311.

Ververs, P.M. and Wickens, C.D. (1998). Head-up displays: Effects of clutter, display intensity and display location on pilot performance. *International Journal of Aviation Psychology, 8,* 377-403.

Ward, N.J., Parkes, A. and Crone, P. R. (1995). Effect of background scene complexity and field dependence on the legibility of head-up-displays for automotive applications. *Human Factors, 37,* 735-745.

Ward, N.J., Parkes, A. and Lindsay, P. (1995). The effect of automotive head-up displays on attention to critical events in traffic. In, *Proceedings of the International Conference on Experimental Analysis and Measurement of Situation Awareness* (pp. 375-382). Daytona Beach, FL: NATO.

Weihrauch, M., Meloeny, G.G. and Goesch, T.C. (1989). *The first head-up display introduced by General Motors.* SAE paper #890288 (pp. 55-62). Warrendale, PA: Society of Automotive Engineers.

Weintraub, D.J. and Ensing, M.J. (1992). *Human Factors issues in head-up display design: The book of HUD* (SOAR CSERIAC State of the Art Report

138

92-2). Dayton, OH: Crew System Ergonomics Information Analysis Center, Wright Patterson AFB.

Weintraub, D.J., Haines, R.F. and Randle, R.J. (1984). The utility of head-up displays: Eye-focus vs. decision times. In, *Proceedings of the 28th Annual Meeting of the Human Factors Society* (pp. 529-533). Santa Monica, CA: Human Factors Society.

Weintraub, D.J., Haines, R.F. and Randle, R.J. (1985). Head-up display (HUD) utility, II: Runway to HUD transitions monitoring eye focus and decision times. In, *Proceedings of the 29th Annual Meeting of the Human Factors Society* (pp. 615-619). Santa Monica, CA: Human Factors Society.

Wickens, C.D. (2001). Keynote address: Attention to safety and the psychology of surprise. In, R. Jensen (Ed.), *Proceedings of the 11th International Symposium on Aviation Psychology*. Columbus, OH: The Dept. of Aerospace Engineering, Applied Mechanics and Aviation, The Ohio State University.

Wickens, C.D. and Carswell, C.M. (1995). The proximity compatibility principle: Its psychological foundation and its relevance to display design. *Human Factors, 37*, 473-494.

Wickens, C.D. and Hollands, J. (2000). *Engineering psychology and human performance* (3rd ed.). Upper Saddle River, NJ: Prentice Hall.

Wickens, C.D. and Long, J. (1995). Object versus space-based models of visual attention: Implications for the design of head-up displays. *Journal of Experimental Psychology: Applied, 1*, 179-193.

Wickens, C.D. and Prevett, T.T. (1995). Exploring the dimensions of egocentricity in aircraft navigation displays: Influences on local guidance and global situation awareness. *Journal of Experimental Psychology: Applied, 1*, 110-135.

Wickens, C.D., Vincow, M. and Yeh, M. (in press). Design applications of visual spatial thinking: The importance of frame of reference. In, In A. Miyake and P. Shah (Eds.), *Handbook of visuospatial cognition*. New York: Cambridge University Press.

Wisely, P.L. (1996). A wide angle head-up display system for enhanced and synthetic vision applications. *SPIE*, Vol. 2736, (pp. 214-220) Bellingham, WA: The International Society for Optical Engineering.

Worringham, C.J. and Beringer, D.B. (1989). Operator orientation and compatibility in visual-motor task performance. *Ergonomics, 32*, 387-399.

Yeh, M., Merlo, J.L., Wickens, C.D. and Brandenburg, D.L. (2001). Examining the clutter-scan tradeoff with high clutter imagery: A comparison of helmet-mounted versus hand-held display presentation. In, *Proceedings of the 5th Annual Army Federated Laboratory Symposium*. College Park, MD: Army Research Federated Laboratory Consortium.

Yeh, M. and Wickens, C.D. (1998). *Visual search and target cueing: A comparison of head-mounted versus hand-held displays on the allocation of visual attention* (ARL-98-2/ARMY-FED-LAB-98-2). Savoy, IL: University of Illinois, Aviation Research Lab.

Yeh, M., Wickens, C.D. and Seagull, F.J. (1999). Target cueing in visual search: The effects of conformality and display location on the allocation of visual attention. *Human Factors, 41*, 524-542.

Yoo, H., Tsinhomi, O., Watanabe, H., Green, P. and Shah, R. (1999). *Display of HUD warning to drivers: Determining an optimal location* (Technical Report UMTRI-99-9). Ann Arbor, Michigan: University of Michigan Transportation Research Institute.

Acknowledgement

Much of the work described in this chapter was conducted under a series of grants from NASA Ames Research Center. Dr. David Foyle was the scientific/technical monitor.

6 Warning system design in civil aircraft

Jan M. Noyes, Alison F. Starr and
Mandana L.N. Kazem

Defining warning systems

Within our society warnings are commonplace, from the natural warning colours in nature, the implicit warning proffered by the jagged edge of a knife, to packaging labels and the more insistent auditory warnings (e.g. fire alarms) requiring our immediate attention. Primarily a means of attracting attention the warning often, and most beneficially, plays both an alerting and informational role, providing information about the nature and criticality of the hazard.

In many safety critical applications hazards are dynamic and may present themselves only under certain circumstances. Warning *systems* found in such applications are, therefore, driven by a 'monitoring function' which triggers when situations become critical, even life-threatening, and attention to the situation (and possibly remedial actions) are required. In summary, current operational warning systems have the following functions:

1. *Monitoring*: Assessing the situation with regard to deviations from pre-determined fixed limits or a threshold.
2. *Alerting*: Drawing the human operators' attention to the hazardous or potentially hazardous situation.
3. *Informing*: Providing information about the nature and criticality of the problem in order to facilitate a reaction in the appropriate individual(s) who is (are) assessing the situation.
4. *Advising*: Aiming to support human decision-making activities in addressing the abnormal situation through the provision of electronic and/or hardcopy documentation.

Safety-critical industries continually strive to attain operational efficiency and maximum safety, and warning systems play an important role in contributing to these goals. The design of warning systems in the civil flight deck application will be considered here from the perspective of the user, i.e. as reported by the crew. This emanates from a research programme concerned with the development of an advanced warning system in this application area. One aspect of this programme included a questionnaire survey of civil flight deck crew from an international commercial airline; the aim being to highlight the user requirements of future warning systems. Some of the findings from this work are discussed towards the end of the three sections on alerting, informing and advising in order to bring the pilots' perspective to the design of future warning systems. This is done within the context of the functions of the warning system highlighted in the definition given at the start of this chapter.

Monitoring

The monitoring function is primarily a technology-based activity as opposed to a human one. The role of the monitoring function is to 'spot' the deviation of parameters from normal operating thresholds. When these threshold conditions are crossed, a response from the warning system is triggered. The crossing of that threshold has then to be brought to the attention of the operator. On the flight deck, this is usually achieved through auditory and/or visual alerts. The earliest monitoring functions were carried out by operators watching displays of values waiting for this information to move outside of a limit. The simplest mechanical sensor is activated when a set threshold condition is met. The mechanisms by which the monitoring is now undertaken will vary from application to application, depending on aspects relating to the safety critical nature of the system, the functions being monitored, complexity of the system, and level of technology involved. However, as the focus of this chapter is on the human activities these mechanisms will not be discussed further and the three functions 'alerting', 'informing', 'advising' will provide the framework for consideration in the rest of this chapter.

Alerting

In a complex system and when the situation is particularly critical a large number of auditory and visual alerts can be activated, as in the Three Mile Island incident (Kemeny, 1979). In this particular case, over 40 auditory alarms were triggered and around 200 windows and gauges began to flash in order to draw the operators' attention to the impending problem (Smither, 1994). A number of difficulties can occur at this stage. For example:

   a. The human operator(s) may fail to be alerted to the particular problem due to overload or distraction. This can sometimes occur even with the existence of the 'attention-grabbing properties' of the alerting system. An example of this occurred on the Eastern Airlines L-1011 flight in 1972. All of the flight deck crew became fixated with a minor malfunction on the flight deck, leaving no operator flying or monitoring the rest of the aircraft. Alerts indicating the unintended descent of the aircraft and thus significant fall in altitude were unsuccessful in regaining the attention of the crew and alerting them to the hazardous situation developing. The result was that the aircraft crashed into the Everglades swamps with disastrous results (Wiener, 1977).

b. The alerting signal may also be inaccessible to the operator if sensory overload occurs. Sensory overload at this early stage is a growing problem as the number of auditory and visual alerts on the flight deck continues to increase. In their survey of alarm management in chemical and power industries, Bransby and Jenkinson (1997) found that the total number of alarms on older plants was generally less than the total number found on the modern computer-based distributed control systems. Likewise on the civil flight deck, the number of auditory and visual alerts has increased over the decades. For example, during the jet era the number of alerts rose from 172 on the DC8 to 418 on the DC10, and from 188 on the Boeing 707 to 455 on the Boeing 747 (Hawkins, 1987), and to 757 on the newer Boeing 747-400. This increase has largely been seen as a result of enhanced aircraft system functionality and therefore a more general increase in system complexity. Paradoxically, this increase in the number of alerts intended to help crew comprehend the 'dangerous' situation can lead to the reverse effect, especially in situations where several alerts appear simultaneously and are abstract, therefore requiring association with a meaning. A recent Federal Aviation Authority (FAA) report highlighted this by stating 'the more unique warnings there are, the more difficult it is for the flight crew to remember what each one signifies' (Abbott, Slotte and Stimson, 1996, p. 56). When crew are overloaded with auditory alerts and flashing visual messages, it may actually hinder appropriate response and management of the situation.

It is important in the design of alerting systems to ensure that the flight crews' attention will be drawn to a problem situation at an early stage in its development. Flight deck alerting systems all have at least two levels of alert. The caution, indicating that awareness of a problem and possible reaction is required, and the warning, indicating a more urgent need for possible action. Ideally the alerting system should enable the pilot to follow transitions between new 'critical' developments, and in conjunction with the flight deck information, as well as maintaining awareness at all times of the current state of play.

Having a system that facilitates the anticipation of problems would provide the crew with more time to consider the outcome of making various decisions. An example of this can be seen in the EGPWS (Enhanced Ground Proximity Warning System) found on some civil flight decks. In this system, dangerous areas of terrain, as relating to aircraft position, are depicted on a display. Increasing risk is depicted by a change in colour or colour saturation. Effectively this is an alert of changing urgency, which should direct crew attention to problems at an early stage (Wainwright, 2000).

143

Individuals amongst the flight crew surveyed, who flew aircraft with one of the types of CRT-based warning systems, tended to agree that their aircraft's alerting system was effective in allowing them to anticipate a problem (Noyes and Starr, 2000). This is not surprising since their alerting system was designed with a low level alert that triggered before the main caution or warning alert, thus allowing problems to be anticipated. On this aircraft, the low level alerting element of the system automatically displays the relevant system synoptics when parameters drift out of tolerance, but before they have changed sufficiently to warrant a full caution or warning level alert. The other salient feature evident from the survey was that fleets with a third crewmember were also found to be in agreement with the fact that current systems allow anticipation. These systems facilitate anticipation, but do not 'anticipate' themselves. In a three-person flight crew, part of the Flight Engineer's role is to monitor system activity and anticipate failures. In a two-person crew however, this aspect of systems' management has been replaced by increased numbers of cautions and warnings. Once these are triggered, operators must undertake prescribed set actions. A possible solution exists in developing systems, which can absorb this anticipatory role.

A truly anticipatory system has yet to be introduced to the flight deck. However, there are many design difficulties in producing an anticipatory system to be implemented in such a complex and dynamic environment. Given this fact it is prudent to remember that design should not seek to replace the decision-maker, it must support the decision-maker (Cohen, 1993); indeed, in some instances the system design may not be capable of effectively replacing the decision-maker. Results from our survey work highlighted some of the difficulties associated with the development of anticipatory facilities. For example, the following comments were made by flight deck crew in response to a question about having a warning system with an anticipatory facility:

'Most serious problems on the aircraft are virtually instantaneous – instrumentation giving anticipation would be virtually useless except on non-critical systems.'

'Workload could be increased to the detriment of flight safety.'

'Much aircraft equipment is either functioning or malfunctioning and I think it lowers workload considerably to avoid unnecessary instrumentation and advise pilots only of malfunctions.'

It could therefore be argued that perhaps it is best to leave the crew to fulfil all but the simplest anticipatory tasks. The crews are after all the only individuals with the benefit of experiencing the situation in hand; they may have information not available to the system and therefore arguably are the only decision-makers in a position to make appropriate predictions. Our survey work also indicated that flight deck crew with experience of having a flight engineer bemoaned the fact that the role of this person was gradually being phased out. This is particularly pertinent given the anticipatory function of the flight engineer. However, systems are becoming increasing complex. Interrelationships between aspects of different systems and the context in which a problem occurs are important factors in what is significant for operator attention and what is not. Thus, returning to Cohen's idea of required operator support, some assistance with the anticipatory task could, if correctly implemented, result in the better handling of problem situations.

A further consideration relating to alerting is that not all warnings may be 'true' warnings, as all warning systems can give false and nuisance warnings. False warnings might occur, for example, when a sensor fails and a warning is 'incorrectly' triggered. In contrast, nuisance warnings are by definition accurate, but unnecessary at the time they occur, e.g. warnings about open doors when the aircraft is on the ground with passengers boarding, or a GPWS (Ground Proximity Warning System) warning that occurs at 35,000 feet activated by an aircraft passing below. Nuisance warnings tend to take place because the system does not understand the context. The category of nuisance warnings may also be extended to include warnings that are correct and relevant in the current situation, but have a low level of significance under certain circumstances. For example, in some aircraft, the majority of warnings will be inhibited during take-off as the consequences of the fault(s) they report are considered to be low in contrast to their potential to interrupt the crew during what can be a difficult phase of flight.

It could be concluded from our survey work that false warnings on modern flight decks do not present a major problem, although in the words of one respondent 'One false warning is "too often".' If false or nuisance warnings occur too frequently, they can encourage crews to become complacent about warning information to the extent that they might ignore real warnings. This was summed up by two respondents as follows: '... nuisance warnings have the effect of degrading the effectiveness of genuine warnings.' and 'a small number of 'nuisance' warnings can quickly undermine the value of warnings'. Hence, there is a need to minimise false and nuisance warnings at all times. This may not be possible with existing systems, but their reduction needs to be a consideration in the design of new systems.

Another related problem of increasing concern involves the sensors on the aircraft that fail more often than the systems themselves. As already discussed, sensors failing may trigger a false warning condition, and a warning system that could differentiate and locate possible sensor failures would have operational benefits. Systems with such capability would better inform the crew and thus help prevent them from taking unnecessary remedial actions and ensure the maintenance of the full operating capability of the aircraft.

There are a number of different system solutions that could be implemented and developed to overcome these problems. More reliable sensors that fail less often comprise one mechanism for reducing false and nuisance warnings. The use of context such as phase of flight to suppress warnings in order not to interrupt a critical phase of flight with information is a feature on the new 'glass' warning systems. These aircraft suppress all but the most critical warnings from 80 knots to rotation, since at this point of the flight it will almost always be safer to leave the ground than attempt to stop since there may not be enough runway left to do this. This type of contextual support could be used to provide better information in the future. For example, sensor or warning logic that considers context such as simple logic relating to weight on wheels and no engines running in order to restrict an alert relating to a warning about the aircraft doors being open. However, for other conditions, several more complex pieces of data may be required and an 'understanding of the goal' of the warning.

Informing

Once the alert has been given, the operator(s) must use the information provided by the alerting system, their knowledge, experience, and training as well as other information displayed to them to be able to understand the nature and seriousness of the problem. However, a number of human operator failures may affect this process. Having been successfully alerted to a problem, the operator(s) may respond by acknowledging the visual and auditory alerts, but fail to take any further action, i.e. the operator(s) demonstrate a lack of compliance. On the civil flight deck, crew bombarded by several loud auditory warnings (bells, buzzers and other alarms) often initially cancel the alarms before attending to the problem. However, this action of cancellation is no guarantee that they will do anything further in terms of remedial action. This problem of initial response followed by no further action has been well documented in aviation and medical environments (see, Campbell Brown and O'Donnell, 1997; Edworthy, 1994). There are many reasons for this. The crew may be distracted by the need to complete other activities, and once having switched off the alerts may fail to turn their attention to the reasons why the alerts occurred in the first place. Edworthy and Adams (1996) studied the topic of non-compliance to alarms and suggested that operators carry out a cost-benefit analysis in order to evaluate the perceived costs and benefits of compliance and non-compliance to alarm handling. Information from the warning system (including urgency information) will be considered in this evaluation. Therefore, there is a need for the warning system to depict accurately the nature and criticality of the problem in order to provide accurate information for the pilot to aid their decision-making. At present there is much room for improvement in this respect, especially with regard to auditory warnings (Edworthy and Adams, 1996). For example, auditory alarms often activate too frequently and are disruptively and inappropriately loud (Stanton and Edworthy, 1999). They also can be relatively uninformative. To quote a respondent from our survey of civil flight deck crew 'a lot of our audio systems are so powerful they scare you half out of your skin without immediately drawing you directly to the reason for the warning' (Eyre, Noyes, Starr and Frankish, 1993).

Individuals need to assess the nature and extent of the difficulty, and to locate the primary cause in order to initiate remedial actions. They have to evaluate and consider the short-term implications of the difficulty, its criticality/urgency, any compromise to safety and immediate actions required, as well as the longer-term consequences for the aircraft, its systems and the operation/flight being undertaken. The consequences of any action taken, whether immediate or planned, must also be included in the assessment. In the development of new alerting 'supportive' systems, this is the type of information that could be of significant use to the operator. The underlying system would need to facilitate the provision of this type of information, which then has to be presented to the operator.

The situation being monitored is often complex with many components, influences and interactions, and there is a need to take into account a large number of parameters in order to assess the situation. Optimally the alerting system should assimilate relevant information from a number of sources or facilitate this task. This is difficult to realise in design as it is not always possible to predict which elements of the potential information set will be relevant to each other and to the particular situation. However, approaches are available which enable the relationships between elements, systems and context to be represented as we indicated in our work on using a model-based reasoning approach to the design of flight deck warning systems. In the past, integration of context/situation information into the design of alerting systems has not been developed to any great extent. For example, in the avionics application, warnings have been known to be given relating to the failure of de-icing equipment when the aircraft was about to land in hot climes, where there would be no need to have de-icing facilities available.

Multiple warning situations are known to be a problem for crew, since the primary failure may be masked by other less consequential cascade or concurrent failures that take the crew's attention, and maybe hinder location of the primary cause. Cascade failures are failures that occur as a result of the primary failure e.g. failure of a generator (primary failure) causing the failure of those systems powered by the generator (secondary failures). However, secondary failures may be displayed before the primary as the display of a warning in most systems is related directly to the point at which the threshold associated with a warning is crossed. To quote one crewmember 'I find it very difficult in multi-warning systems to analyse and prioritise actions'. A further problem relates to concurrent failures. The problem-solving characteristics of human operators are such that we tend to associate alerts occurring simultaneously (or within a short space of time) as having the same cause when this may not be the case (Tversky and Kahneman, 1974). Concurrent failures may also cause conflict in terms of remedial actions; i.e. one solution may resolve one problem but worsen the situation for another. It can therefore be quite difficult for crew to handle warning information in these types of situation.

Many current alerting systems present warnings/cautions in the order in which the signal reaches the method of display, and this has implications for the handling of warning information. With classic central warning panels, large cascade type failures lead to distinctive patterns of lights; recognition of these patterns can enable the crew to identify the primary cause hidden amidst the mass. With glass multifunction alerting systems, alerts are listed by criticality, e.g. all red warnings first followed by all the amber caution alerts. In general, within each of these categories temporal ordering is still used; new alerts enter at the top of the appropriate list (warning or caution list). This creates effectively a dynamic list and can result in the primary causes of multiple alert situations becoming embedded within its associated category list and possibly 'hidden' from view. The crew in our survey noted this: '… it would be helpful if the most urgent was at the top of the list'. However, some of these systems do use a limited set of rules to analyse the incoming warning information and identify a set of key primary failures which can lead to cascade effects e.g. generator failure. These systems will pull out primary failures and present them first.

The issue of handling secondary failures was addressed within the survey. Just under two-thirds of the flight deck crew (65%) surveyed felt that the alerting systems on their current aircraft were deficient in providing consequential secondary information. A closer analysis of this 65% indicated a clear disagreement between flight crew of glass flight deck aircraft and crew of other aircraft fleets. Less than 5% of the former group believed their alerting systems to be deficient in this respect, indicating that the vast majority was satisfied. Conversely between 45% and 70% of the respondents from each of the other aircraft fleet groups regarded the provision of such secondary information, on their aircraft, to be sub-optimum. Therefore, future alerting system designs should facilitate the provision of secondary information.

Advising

A further aspect of the alerting system involves the use of instructional information to support human decision-making activities, and ensure remedial actions are appropriate and successful. On current flight decks, supporting documentation can be both screen-based and in hard-copy format, whereas on classic aircraft, i.e. aircraft that have warnings based on fixed legends on lights, this information is provided in a paper Quick Reference Handbook (QRH). The way in which this information is handled will depend on the severity, complexity and frequency of the situation that activated the alert(s), as well as operator experience, skills and knowledge. However, it should be noted that designers do not always view advisory documentation as part of the alerting system. In our work with flight deck crew it was viewed as an integral part of the alerting systems, although, in certification terms, it may not be viewed as an essential component of the operating system.

All of the aircraft within the questionnaire survey had a QRH or equivalent document, e.g. the Emergency Checklist on the DC-10. For each aircraft, this document serves as the primary source of reference for the necessary remedial actions to be taken in abnormal flying situations. The documentation is originally designed by the airframe manufacturer and modified by the management of the operating company to meet their operating procedures. It would seem that there might be a trade-off between the level of completeness of the QRH information (e.g. its quantity and detail) and the ease with which the document can be used, i.e. the more information provided, the more difficult the document is to use in practise. Paper presentation of such information will inevitably lead to this problem as the information provided must be complete and therefore by nature will be difficult to present in a format that can be used quickly and effectively. Glass display presentation, on the other hand, could potentially help the pilot to locate the appropriate material quickly by tailoring the information presented to the situation.

Evolution of flight deck warning systems

This lack of assimilation is apparent throughout the evolution of flight deck alerting systems (see, Starr, Noyes, Ovenden and Rankin, 1997, for a full review). Briefly, the early warning systems were a series of lights positioned on the appropriate systems' panels, and so were located across the flight deck (Gorden-Johnson, 1991). At this stage of evolution, warning indications were predominately visual, and crew had to scan the panels continually to check for the appearance of a warning. This discrete set of annunciators was gradually replaced by the 'master/ central warning and caution' concept, which involved the addition of a master light that indicated to crew that a warning had been activated. This was further developed into a centralisation of warning lights on a single panel within the crew's forward visual field (Alder, 1991).

The next development beyond physically locating the alerts together would be to 'integrate' the alerting information for presentation to the crew, as mentioned earlier. Although modern flight deck displays are referred to as integrated, they are not truly integrated since they consist of single elements of information displayed together according to circumstances and the current phase of flight (Pischkle, 1990). A fully integrated alerting system would be capable of monitoring and interpreting data from aircraft systems and flight operational conditions in order to provide crew with a high-level interpretation of the malfunction in the event of failures and abnormal conditions.

A fully integrated warning system has yet to be realised to any great extent even in the latest civil aircraft, traditional alerting systems are generally used which conform to a 'stimulus' (e.g. valve out limits) followed by 'response' (e.g. warning light) concept. Also, monitoring to an identified risk point is traditional, and in the past there has been a lack of sophisticated display and control technology to achieve integration. This may be due to the inherent design difficulties in predicting information requirements, briefly noted earlier, and previous lack of technical ability to realise such a systems solution. However, the advent and implementation of more sophisticated software and programming techniques means that alerting systems with a greater capability to integrate information from a variety of sources can be developed, and such solutions are gradually becoming a more realistic proposition (Rouse, Geddes and Hammer, 1990). Care must be taken not to allow such systems to exceed their inherent limitations (due in part to our limited ability to predict the information requirements of unpredictable situations) or reduce data visibility. O'Leary (2000) indicates that the very task of converting data to knowledge is vital to the pilot in facilitating good pilot decision-making and therefore we must think carefully before removing this role from the crew.

A further point of contention relates to the certification requirements of alerting systems. Given the criticality of alerting information it may be that the certification requirements prevent such systems becoming feasible or economically viable. However, by functionally separating the primarily alerting processes from the more informational and supportive processes of future alerting systems it may be possible to incorporate data integration into a 'support system' whilst leaving the more critical 'alert' to follow the more easily certifiable 'stimulus-response' concept.

General discussion

During each of the alerting, informing and advising functions, operator-involved failures can occur: human operators may fail to be alerted to the warning, may fail to assess it adequately, may neglect to respond to the warning situation and/or may not make sufficient use of information available. As already stated, they may take immediate action, but fail to make follow-up actions that will lead to the restoration of normal operations, a point well documented by Campbell-Brown and O'Donnell (1997) in their work on alarms in distributed control systems. In the process control industry, as well as aviation, there are many reasons for this, from the design of the warning system per se to task considerations and the overall design philosophies of the organisation, operating policies and procedures, extending to (user) practices (Degani and Wiener, 1994; Edworthy and Adams, 1996). Analyses of specific human responses to warnings and explanations of their failures are complex and multi-faceted, and outside the remit of the current chapter.

Perhaps the very idea of having humans interact with warning systems is a problematic one. In many situations, the main part of the operator's job may be uneventful to the point of boredom with long periods of monitoring required. This state can change very quickly when an event triggers an alarm or number of alarms. Hence, the monitoring phase is interrupted by rapid activity, the occurrence of which cannot be easily predicted, and may result in information overload as the monitoring role assumed by the human operator changes to diagnostician. This latter role requires the user to comprehend and remedy what

150

may be a complicated, multi-causal, often stress-inducing situation. Further, there may be little time available to support decision-making activities. This was described by Wickens (1992, p. 508) as 'hours of intolerable boredom punctuated by a few minutes of pure hell'. Jenkinson (1997) stated that further work is clearly needed on this transition between boredom and panic.

Humans tend not to be good at either of the aforementioned task extremes – monitoring tasks or working under high stress levels. Activities under both conditions are error-prone. Evidence for this can be seen from the number of aircraft accidents (and incidents) that implicate human error as a primary cause. Figures differ according to definitions of error and methods of calculating accident and incident data, but human error has been given as a causal factor in 80% of fatal aircraft accidents in general aviation and 70% in airline operations (Jensen, 1995). Recent statistics indicate there were 1063 accidents worldwide involving commercial jet aircraft between 1959 and 1995 of which 64.4% cited flight crew error as a primary cause (Boeing, 1996). The incidence of decision-making errors in these events is estimated to be as high as 70% (Helmreich and Foushee, 1993). However, there is a need to recognise that placing the 'blame' on human error does not provide the full explanation of how and why an accident or incident occurred, neither does it take into account the multi-causal chain of events and circumstances leading up the error (Noyes and Stanton, 1997; Reason, 1990). Consequently, the concept of the 'system-induced human error' has become widely recognised (Wiener, 1987) and as a result the onus has been placed on cockpit design as a whole to alleviate this problem.

The detection and notification of problems (generally via cautions) can sometimes lead to increased workload. Information overload is certainly thought to be an issue in multiple alert situations. Although over the years, developments in alerting systems have aimed to provide the flight deck crew with the information they need, in a form they can readily understand and at an appropriate time, there are still occasions when information overload occurs (see, Starr et al., 1997). For example, multiple failure situations will trigger large numbers of lower level alerts, and can generate copious warnings. Despite this, crew agreed that additional information about the consequences of planned actions and secondary consequences of malfunctions would be an improvement on current systems, even in view of the inevitable increase in information presented. The prospect of this further increase in information is balanced by the difficulties faced currently in managing this type of failure situation.

Finally, when considering supporting documentation, the balance between the amount and level of detail given, and the ease of access to relevant information must be considered. A fundamental problem with existing checklists (as combined within the QRH), both paper and multi-function displays, is that they are designed so that each checklist is associated with one failure/abnormality. In the event of multiple failure situations, priorities are generally not adequately handled. This is a problem and it has already been highlighted that pilots would

Jan M. Noyes, Alison F. Starr and Mandana L.N. Kazem

like to see more support in this area. However, any further development of the QRH concept (paper or screen) must keep in mind that pilots literally require a *Quick* Reference Handbook.

Looking to the future, continuing technological developments mean that future alerting systems will have the capability for handling increasingly large amounts of data/information. Unless this is carefully managed, the human operator will inevitably suffer from information overload. This has already been experienced in the nuclear power industry with operators being presented with large amounts of raw data that previously would have been filtered by experienced watch keepers (Maskell, 1997). It may be that progress will depend not only on technological advances, but on making greater use of the data already available (Frankish, Ovenden, Noyes and Starr, 1991); perhaps finding new ways to display information. Furthermore, the development of 'soft displays' supported by powerful computational resources has important implications for the design of future flight deck warning systems. By providing information tailored directly to the current requirements of the users, this type of interface could not only aid the human operator, but also provide a solution in terms of enabling further information to be provided on an already crowded flight deck. The limitations of such displays however must be understood and duly considered.

The alerting system is an essential component of any safety-critical system, since it is instrumental in drawing the attention of the operator to a problem situation at a point when safety can still be maintained. To be successful in this role the system must effectively monitor, alert, inform and support the operator in order that the problem can be efficiently diagnosed and rectified/ contained. Continuing developments in advanced technologies and the use of more 'intelligent processing' in systems have increased the number of design possibilities for warning systems and may provide solutions in terms of managing information overload. However the solution to information overload may lie in information efficiency – it may be possible to combine alerting, informing and supporting functions by providing information that performs all three roles simultaneously. For example, by aiming to develop the alerting aspects of the alerting system to be more informative and striving for new ways to maintain aircraft, system and environment visibility to make the problem itself more visible and therefore naturally alerting. Indeed it has been suggested that the situation itself may provide the most important warning cues (Edworthy and Adams, 1996). Perhaps this aspect will be addressed in future work on warning systems.

References

Abbott, K., Slotte, S. and Stimson, D. (1996). *The interfaces between flightcrews and modern flight deck systems Report of the FAA Human Factors Team.* Washington DC: Department of Transportation.

Alder, M.G. (1991). *Warning systems for aircraft: A pilot's view*. In, *Proceedings of IMechE 'Philosophy of Warning Systems' Seminar S969*. London: Institution of Mechanical Engineers.

Billings, C.E. (1997). *Aviation automation: The search for a human-centred approach*. New Jersey: LEA.

Boeing Airplane Company (1996). Table of all accidents – World-wide commercial jet fleet. *Flight Deck, 21*, 57.

Bransby, M.L. and Jenkinson, J. (1997). Alarm management in the chemical and power industries: A survey for the HSE. In, *Proceedings of IEE Digest 97/136 'Stemming the Alarm Flood'*. London: Institution of Electrical Engineers.

Campbell Brown, D. and O'Donnell, M. (1997). Too much of a good thing? – Alarm management experience in BP Oil. In, *Proceedings of IEE Digest 97/136 'Stemming the Alarm Flood'*. London: Institution of Electrical Engineers.

Cohen M. (1993). The bottom line: Naturalistic decision aiding. In, G. Klein, J. Orasanu, R. Calderwood, and C. Zsambok, (Eds.), *Decision making in action: models and methods*. New Jersey: Ablex.

Degani, A. and Wiener, E.L. (1994). On the design of flight-deck procedures. *NASA Contractor Report 177642*. NASA-Ames Research Center, CA: NASA.

Edworthy, J. (1994). The design and implementation of non-verbal auditory warnings. *Applied Ergonomics, 25*, 202-210.

Edworthy, J., and Adams, A. (1996). *Warnings design: A research prospective*. London: Taylor and Francis.

Eyre, D.A., Noyes, J.M., Starr, A.F. and Frankish, C.R. (1993). *The Aircraft Warning System Questionnaire Results: Warning Information Analysis Report 23.3, MBRAWSAC Project*. Bristol: University of Bristol, Department of Psychology.

Frankish, C.R., Ovenden, C.R., Noyes, J.M. and Starr, A.F. (1991). Application of model-based reasoning to warning and diagnostic systems for civil aircraft. In, *Proceedings of the ERA Technology Conference 'Advances in Systems Engineering for Civil and Military Avionics'* (ERA Report 91-0634, pp. 7.1.1 – 7.1.7). Leatherhead: ERA Technology.

Gorden-Johnson, P. (1991). Aircraft warning systems: Help or hindrance philosophy of warning systems. In, *Proceedings of IMechE 'Philosophy of Warnings Systems' Seminar S969*. London: Institution of Mechanical Engineers.

Hawkins, F.H. (1987). *Human Factors in flight*. Aldershot: Ashgate.

Helmreich, R.L. and Foushee, H.L. (1993). Why crew resource management? Empirical and theoretical bases of Human Factors training in aviation. In, E.L. Wiener, B.G. Kanki and R.L. Helmreich (Eds.), *Cockpit resource management*, (3-45). San Diego: Academic Press.

JAR-25. *Joint Aviation Requirements for large aeroplanes*. Civil Aviation Authority, Cheltenham: Joint Aviation Authorities Committee.

Jan M. Noyes, Alison F. Starr and Mandana L.N. Kazem

Jenkinson, J. (1997). Alarm reduction in nuclear power plants: Results of an international survey. In, *Proceedings of IEE Digest 97/136 'Stemming the Alarm Flood'.* London: Institution of Electrical Engineers.

Jensen, R.S. (1995). *Pilot judgement and crew resource management.* Aldershot: Avebury Aviation.

Kemeny, J. (1979). The need for change: The legacy of TMI Report of the President's Commission on the Accident at Three Mile Island. New York: Pergamon.

Learmount, D. (1995). Lessons from the cockpit. *Flight International* 11-17th January, 24-27.

Maskell, P. (1997). Intelligent surveillance for naval nuclear submarine propulsion In *Proceedings of IEE Digest 97/136 'Stemming the Alarm Flood'.* London: Institution of Electrical Engineers.

Newman, T.P. (1991). Cephalic indications, nictitations and anopic ungulates. In, *Proceedings of ImechE 'Philosophy of Warning Systems' Seminar S969.* London: Institution of Mechanical Engineers.

Noyes, J.M. and Starr, A.F. (2000). Civil aircraft warning systems: Future directions in information management and presentation. *International Journal of Aviation Psychology, 10,* 169-188.

Noyes, J.M., Starr, A.F. and Frankish, C.R. (1996). User involvement in the early stages of the development of an aircraft warning system. *Behaviour and Information Technology, 15,* 67-75.

O'Leary, M. (2000). Situation Awareness: Has EFIS Delivered? In, *Proceedings of 'Situational Awareness On The Flight Deck: The Current And Future Contribution By Systems And Equipment' 2000.* London: Royal Aeronautical Society.

Perrow, C. (1984). *Normal accidents.* New York, NY: Basic Books.

Pischkle, K.M. (1990). Cockpit integration and automation: The avionics challenge. In, *Proceedings of 'International Federation of Airworthiness' Conference,* November 19th.

Reason, J.T. (1990). *Human error.* Cambridge: University Press.

Rouse, W.B., Geddes, N.D. and Hammer, J.M. (1990). Computer-aided fighter pilots. *IEEE Spectrum,* 38-40.

Smither, R.D. (1994). *The psychology of work and human performance.* New York: Harper Collins.

Stanton, N.A. and Edworthy, J. (Eds.) (1999). *Human Factors in auditory warnings.* Aldershot: Ashgate.

Starr, A.F., Noyes, J.M., Ovenden, C.R. and Rankin, J.A. (1997). Civil aircraft warning systems: A successful evolution? In, H.M. Soekha (Ed.) *Proceedings of IASC '97 (International Aviation Safety Conference).* Rotterdam, Netherlands: VSP BV.

Taylor, R.M., Selcon, S.J. and Swinden, A.D. (1995). Measurement of situational awareness and performance: A unitary SART index predicts performance on a simulated ATC task. In, R. Fuller, N. Johnston and N. McDonald (Eds.), *Human Factors in aviation operations*. Aldershot: Avebury Aviation.

Tversky, A. and Kahneman, D. (1974). Judgement under uncertainty: Heuristics and biases. *Science, 185,* 1124-1131.

Wainwright, W. (2000). Integration of Situational Awareness on Airbus Flight Decks. In, *Proceedings of 'Situational Awareness On The Flight Deck: The Current And Future Contribution By Systems And Equipment' 2000.* London: Royal Aeronautical Society.

Wiener, E.L. (1977). Controlled flight into terrain accidents: System-induced errors. *Human Factors, 19,* 171-181.

Acknowledgements

This work was carried out as part of a UK Department of Trade and Industry funded project, IED:4/1/2200 'A Model-Based Reasoning Approach to Warning and Diagnostic Systems for Aircraft Application'. Thanks are due to the late David Eyre for his meticulous data analyses.

7 Handling qualities and their implications for flight deck design

Edmund Field

Introduction

Since the introduction of the earliest civil airliners many new technologies have been introduced, designed to reduce the pilots' workload. This has led to the automation of many tasks that were previously performed by the pilots, or even flight engineers, navigators and radio operators. As a result, the piloting task has changed dramatically. Whereas the pilots originally flew the aircraft manually throughout the flight, today they may perform only the take-off manually, commanding the rest of the flight, including the landing, through the flight management system. Hence, most of the emphasis in Human Factors has been oriented towards pilots' interaction with the autoflight systems.

No matter how much of a flight is performed under autoflight control there are times when pilots will assume manual control. It is essential that during these periods the pilot is able to precisely control the aircraft with low workload, and for that it must possess good handling qualities. Cooper and Harper (1969) define handling qualities as:

'Those qualities and characteristics of an aircraft that govern the ease and precision with which a pilot is able to perform the task required in support of an aircraft role'.

To ensure good handling qualities it is necessary that the aircraft's responses to the pilot's inputs are appropriate and predictable and that all the information that he receives from the aircraft is clear and non-contradictory.

In Human Factors the emphasis is placed on 'human-centred design'. The term 'task tailored handling qualities' has been coined to emphasise the optimisation of an aircraft's handling qualities around particular tasks that the aircraft is required to perform. This optimisation of the handling qualities is also centred on the human operator. That is, the handling qualities of the aircraft are optimised to meet the task requirements and the capabilities of the human pilot, thus encompassing the aircraft's dynamic response, control inceptors, flight deck displays and any other sources of information available to the pilot.

This chapter addresses manual piloted control and the handling qualities of civil aircraft. Specifically, it is concerned with those aspects that affect the design of the flight deck, and discusses how the flight deck must be optimised for manual piloted control, and around the aircraft's handling qualities. The chapter is written from a handling qualities perspective, apologies are offered if its treatment of Human Factors appear somewhat basic to Human Factors specialists. The discussions are limited to the pitch axis, since this is the most critical from a handling qualities perspective, though the concepts can be easily extended to the roll axis.

The pilot information cueing model

When controlling the aircraft manually the pilot makes inputs through the primary flight control inceptor (wheel column, centrestick or sidestick) and observes the aircraft response, primarily through visual cues. In an aircraft that possesses good handling qualities the pilot should be able to predict the aircraft response, what he sees, from the control inputs he made. Through good aerodynamic, geometric and flight control system design it should be possible to design good handling qualities into the aircraft throughout the flight envelope, to ensure that the aircraft response is always predictable and appropriate for all tasks.

In making control inputs and observing the response of the aircraft the pilot utilises various information cueing channels, both to judge the appropriateness of the inputs and to observe the aircraft response. These various different cueing channels are presented in figure 1. The pilot's inputs will be judged using tactile cues through the control inceptor, both proprioceptive (force) and kinaesthetic (position). A well designed and integrated control inceptor will ensure that the proprioceptive and kinaesthetic cues are well harmonised.

The aircraft response will be determined from the visual cues, both central and peripheral visual. The central visual cues come from the aircraft displays, in modern airliners primarily the Primary Flight Display (PFD), which displays the aircraft attitude, airspeed and altitude in one display instrument. When closer to the ground the pilot will also make use of peripheral visual cues from the outside world. Predominantly these will be cues of aircraft attitude and flight path, or sink rate when in the landing flare.

Peripheral visual cues can also come from within the flight deck. The primary cues of interest here are from movement of the primary flight control inceptors and the thrust levers. Movement of both of these can come from the other pilot during manual flight, or from the autoflight systems when under autoflight control. In both cases movement of the controls can provide useful anticipatory cues to a pilot (Field and Harris, 1998). The pilot should be able to determine the aircraft response by observing the magnitude of the control input, much as he

158

would if he made the control input himself, judging the magnitude of the input using tactile cues.

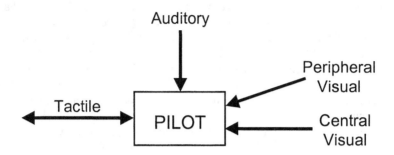

Figure 1   The various pilot information cueing channels

The final cueing channel to be considered in this chapter is the auditory channel. The auditory channel can be used to provide the pilot additional information that might otherwise overload the central visual channel. For flight path control the prime example is the call-out of height above the runway when landing. Although this information is available from the radio altimeter display, the pilot is already busy interpreting all the visual cues. These cues include both the central visual displays and the peripheral visual outside scene, as the pilot transitions his attention when in the flare. Hence, use of the auditory channel for height information makes use of an additional under-utilised cueing channel available to the pilot.

The remainder of this chapter addresses manual piloted control and handling qualities with reference to the information cueing channels available to the pilot.

Conventional aircraft handling qualities

Despite the introduction of electronic fly-by-wire flight control systems into large civil aircraft, the majority of civil aircraft flying today are essentially conventional aircraft with minimal levels of augmentation. Conventional aircraft are those where a direct mechanical link exists between the cockpit control inceptor and the control surface effector (elevator, aileron or rudder). Even with hydraulically operated actuators and limited control system augmentation, the aircraft can essentially be considered conventional from a handling qualities perspective.

159

Edmund Field

The hierarchical control of pitch attitude

Let us consider the physics of how an aircraft responds to a pilot's control inceptor inputs in the pitch axis. We will assume a stable aircraft, where the tail produces a down force, as this is representative of civil aircraft in current service. For an unaugmented aircraft with a fixed mechanical linkage between the stick and elevator, when the pilot pulls back on the stick he commands the elevator to deflect up. The change in elevator position alters the camber of the tail which reduces the lift on the tail and causes the aircraft to rotate around its centre of gravity, until it settles with the wing meeting the on-coming air at a greater angle-of-attack, which will remain constant as long as the elevator is held at its new position. (In the longer term, the increased angle-of-attack will result in increased drag and a loss of airspeed which, if sufficiently great, will result in a change in angle-of-attack. However, this phenomenon can be overcome with an increase in engine thrust to maintain airspeed constant.) Because of this direct link between stick position, elevator position and angle-of-attack a conventional aircraft is referred to as angle-of-attack command, since stick position directly commands angle-of-attack. With this new angle-of-attack the wing will start to produce more lift than at the lower angle-of-attack. This increased lift will result in an increase in normal acceleration and a concomitant increase in flight path. It is the sum of the changes in angle-of-attack and flight path that define the change in pitch attitude that the pilot sees.

This sequence of events has interesting implications for the control of the aircraft. The pilot actually commands a stick position, which in turn commands an elevator position, and so rotates the aircraft to a new angle-of-attack. Thus, the pilot has direct command of angle-of-attack. However, without special instrumentation, he cannot see angle-of-attack, nor does he wish to control angle-of-attack, except maybe when near the stall.

For most tasks, the pilot actually wants to control flight path. However, he does not have direct command of flight path, nor can he see flight path directly (he can through the altimeter or glideslope indicator, but problems determining flight path accurately from these will be discussed later). The only parameter he can observe reliably is pitch attitude. However, he cannot command pitch attitude directly, nor requires to control pitch attitude directly for most tasks.

Hence, to control flight path, the pilot commands changes in angle-of-attack, and observes the response through pitch attitude. This concept forms the basis for the series pilot model.

Conventional aircraft dynamics and control

Figure 2 shows the angle-of-attack, pitch attitude and flight path time history responses of a conventional aircraft to a step control inceptor input, that is, an immediate small application of aft stick that is held indefinitely. Clearly, after the initial dynamics settle, the angle-of-attack response remains approximately constant at the new trim angle-of-attack. To maintain this new angle-of-attack the pilot must hold the constant stick position, or trim out the forces. Once trimmed, the aircraft will hold the new angle-of-attack. It is this direct link between stick position and angle-of-attack that results in the classification of a conventional aircraft as angle-of-attack command, or an angle-of-attack response-type.

All the other responses shown in figure 2 exhibit a longer-term non steady-state response, called the phugoid mode. As long as the phugoid mode is well damped these responses will all decay to new steady state values in the long term. However, it is unlikely that this will occur before the pilot makes further inputs, possibly to damp the phugoid mode manually. Indeed, the phugoid mode is often referred to as a nuisance mode, since it results in deviations in pitch attitude, flight path and airspeed.

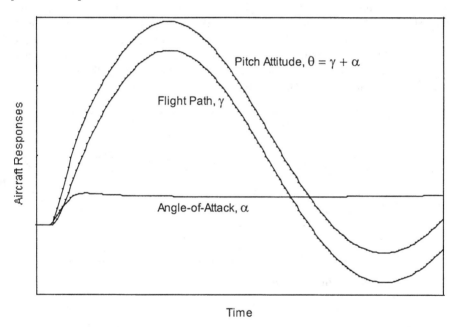

Figure 2   Time history responses for a conventional aircraft

Clearly visible in figure 2 is the similarity between the pitch attitude and flight path angle responses. Pitch attitude is the sum of angle-of-attack and flight path, and this can clearly be seen in the time history responses. Once the angle-of-attack response has settled at its new trim value, the pitch attitude and flight path responses have the same shape, but are separated vertically by the value of the angle-of-attack. It is this similarity between the pitch attitude and flight path responses that allows the pilot to judge the flight path of a conventional aircraft from observation of the pitch attitude. Also apparent in the responses is that the flight path response lags behind that of the pitch attitude, this is especially visible in the initial response. This lag is due to the finite time it takes for the wing to generate the increased lift as the aircraft is pitched to the greater angle-of-attack.

Series pilot model

The accepted pilot model for closed loop precision flight path control for a conventional aircraft is given in figure 3, taken from McRuer (1982). This consists of an inner attitude control loop and an outer flight path control loop. In attempting to change or acquire a desired flight path, or maintain a flight path in the presence of external disturbances, the pilot will perceive an error between the desired and actual flight paths. As discussed above the flight path response lags that of attitude. As a result the pilot is unable to tightly close the flight path control loop directly and so for tight closed loop control must use a surrogate feedback. Also as discussed above, for a conventional aircraft pitch attitude is a good surrogate to flight path. Therefore pitch attitude is used as the inner control loop feedback, allowing the pilot to predict the expected flight path change.

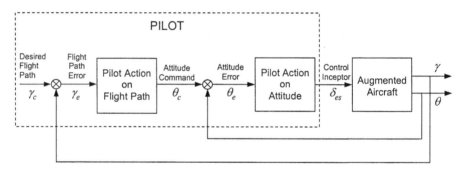

Figure 3   The series pilot model

In order to drive the flight path error to zero the pilot will pitch the aircraft to a new attitude. As the angle-of-attack changes this will result in a change of flight path. If the resultant flight path is not that which was desired then the pilot must now re-enter the inner attitude loop and repeat the procedure until the flight path is as desired. With experience of the aircraft the pilot is able to predict the magnitude of the attitude change that is required to give the desired flight path change, and so is able to select this attitude with fewer iterations until ultimately only one input is required when the pilot is now able to use an open loop, precognitive, technique. Thus by tightly closing the attitude loop and driving the attitude error to zero the pilot is controlling the flight path via the outer loop.

Handling qualities design of a conventional aircraft concerns ensuring that the pitch attitude response is precise and predictable to pilot control inputs, and that the flight path response is well tuned to that of pitch attitude. If the flight path response is lagged far behind attitude closed loop control will be impossible since the pilot is not easily able to judge the flight path. At the other extreme if the flight path response is too close to that of attitude pilots complain of an abrupt response. Only if these two responses are well behaved and well tuned will tight closed loop piloted control be possible.

The series pilot model fits well with accepted flying procedure. When flying a raw data ILS approach the pilot observes an error on the glideslope indication and therefore perceives a flight path error. Experience with the aircraft will lead him to make an attitude change that he believes to be correct to bring the aircraft back onto the glideslope after an acceptable time. He will therefore enter the inner attitude loop to make and maintain this attitude change. When the flight path starts to change the pilot will then perceive whether the rate and magnitude of change are as desired. If not he will re-enter the attitude inner loop, acquire a new attitude and thus control the outer flight path loop.

The same control strategy is used for changing and maintaining any flight path, whether it be constant altitude or a constant rate of climb or descent. The pilot cannot control the flight path directly from the altimeter or vertical speed indicator, but makes changes on the attitude indicator, and observes their consequence on the altimeter and vertical speed indicator. When a pilot does attempt to close the flight path control loop directly from observations of altitude, vertical speed or glideslope deviation he will start and sustain a flight path oscillation, deviating around the desired flight path.

It is important to appreciate that the difficulty in controlling flight path closed loop, and hence the necessity for pilots to adopt the series pilot model control strategy, is due to the lag between the pitch attitude and flight path responses, the inherent dynamics of an aircraft. It is not due to a problem with the detection of flight path, since that is available from the altimeter, vertical speed indictor and glide slope indicator.

The different flight paths

When referring to an aircraft's flight path, flight path of its centre of gravity is usually assumed. However, for large aircraft, during manoeuvring flight the flight path response at other locations on the aircraft can be appreciably different to that at the centre of gravity, which can have significant implications for handling qualities. Figure 4 shows the time history responses of flight path measured at three locations on a conventional aft tail controlled transport aircraft; the centre of gravity (solid line), the instantaneous centre of rotation (dash-dotted line), and the pilot station (dashed line).

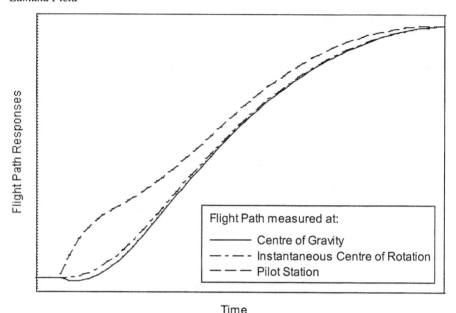

Time

Figure 4 Time history responses of flight path at three locations along an aircraft

The centre of gravity of an aircraft is usually located slightly forward of the main undercarriage, and so its flight path is usually a good indication of that at the main undercarriage. The pilot station is self evident, but the instantaneous centre of rotation does require some explanation. As described above in the hierarchical control of pitch attitude, when a pilot pulls back on the stick the elevator deflects up, altering the camber of the tail and so reducing the lift on the tail. This action causes the aircraft to rotate around its centre of gravity, thereby increasing the angle-of-attack and ultimately its lift and flight path. However, as the tail lift initially reduces, the total lift produced by the wing and tail in combination reduces, and so the centre of gravity of the aircraft actually descends, until sufficient lift is produced by the wing at the higher angle-of-attack to increase the flight path. This effect is clearly demonstrated in the initial response of the flight path at centre of gravity time history response shown in the solid line in figure 4.

Since the aircraft is rotated around its centre of gravity, the tail itself clearly descends further than does the centre of gravity, as does any point located behind the centre of gravity. Ahead of the centre of gravity is a location referred to as the instantaneous centre of rotation. At this location, there is no initial vertical movement as the aircraft is rotated in response to elevator deflections. The lack of initial flight path change at this location is clearly evident in the flight path at instantaneous centre of rotation time history response shown in the dash-dotted line in figure 4. Any point ahead of this location experiences an initial climb in response to the elevator deflection, providing a 'predictive' cue of the impending flight path change. For most conventional civil airliners the instantaneous centre of rotation is located between the centre of gravity and pilot station, closer to the centre of gravity. The pilot station is forward of the instantaneous centre of rotation, and so provides a predictive cue to the pilot of the ultimate flight path response. The magnitude of the predictive cue is dependent upon the distance between the two locations, and may become excessive if the distance is very large. This predictive effect is clearly visible in the flight path at pilot station time history response shown in the dashed line in figure 4.

For aircraft that are not configured with a conventional aft tail controller, such as a tailless delta-wing or canard configuration, the relationship between the three locations discussed above will differ. For instance, for most tailless delta-winged aircraft the instantaneous centre of rotation is close to the pilot station, in some cases even ahead of the pilot station, resulting in initial flight path cues being in the opposite sense to the longer-term aircraft response. For a canard configuration the instantaneous centre of rotation may be behind the centre of gravity. The implications of the different flight path responses to an aircraft's handling qualities will be discussed in later sections of this chapter.

Response-types

An aircraft that possesses good handling qualities exhibits desired and predictable responses to pilot inputs. Historically the aircraft responses were determined by the aircraft's geometric and aerodynamic design. With the introduction of electronic flight control systems it is possible to 'tailor' the response of an aircraft to pilot inputs. No longer must the response of the aircraft be determined purely by the geometric and aerodynamic properties of the aircraft. The flight control system can be used for two types of response augmentation, stability augmentation and control augmentation.

Limited levels of augmentation can be used to enhance the aircraft's stability to pilot inputs, improving the predictability of the response – stability augmentation. Higher levels of augmentation can be used to shape the response of the aircraft to control inputs – control augmentation. Through control augmentation it is possible to tailor the aircraft's response for particular tasks. For example, a pitch-pointing task requires accurate control of pitch attitude, while a fighter pilot performing high 'g' turns may want direct control of normal acceleration.

A number of alternative control strategies have been developed and implemented on production aircraft that allow the pilot to directly command a specific aircraft response. The term 'response-type' has been adopted to describe the response of an aircraft to pilot inputs, and is defined by the variable most closely controlled by the pilot. Examples of response-types include angle-of-attack (a conventional aircraft), pitch rate, pitch attitude and normal acceleration. Other response-types exist, but these four will be used here to demonstrate the different characteristics associated with different response-types. The response-types discussed here are all mechanised to provide long term 'hold' of the command variable. This is not a necessity of a response-type, but is common in command augmentation implementations.

Figure 5 contains time history responses of the four example response-types to a boxcar input (an instantaneous aft movement of the stick, held constant for a few seconds and then instantaneously returned to its original position). Note that the responses are not drawn to the same scale. The key characteristics of the response-types are summarised in table 1.

Different response-types require different piloting strategies, which may or may not be compatible with the series pilot model. Additionally, the control strategies may have implications for the choice of control inceptor and displays. The four response-types are discussed briefly below.

The conventional response-type was introduced earlier, and is representative of all unaugmented and limited augmentation aircraft. A constant control inceptor input produces a change in angle-of-attack. If the input is held the aircraft will hold the new angle-of-attack, and return to the original trim angle-of-attack when released. Alternatively, the control forces can be trimmed out by the pilot, in which case the aircraft will maintain the new trimmed angle-of-attack.

Conventional response-type

While figure 2 showed a conventional aircraft's responses to a step control inceptor input, figure 5 shows the responses to a boxcar input. As can be seen in figure 5, the angle-of-attack response to a boxcar input is a rapid increase to the new steady state angle-of-attack, followed by a return to the original trimmed angle-of-attack when the input is removed. The angle-of-attack then remains constant. The similarity between the pitch attitude and flight path angle responses, which allows the pilot to adopt the series pilot model control strategy as discussed before, is clearly visible. Both the pitch attitude and flight path responses exhibit the phugoid mode.

The phugoid mode is also visible in the airspeed response. Although the phugoid is often referred to as a nuisance mode, it exists because of the angle-of-attack stability to which is related the fundamental properties of speed stability in conventional aircraft (Gibson, 1999). Speed stability provides the connection between trim angle-of-attack and airspeed. When trimmed to an angle-of-attack a conventional aircraft will seek to return to the associated trim airspeed through the phugoid mode. This same speed stability feature provides speed cues to the pilot through the stick. If the pilot is holding a forward force the aircraft is at a lower angle-of-attack than trim and a higher airspeed. If the pilot is holding an aft force the aircraft is at a higher angle-of-attack than trim, and a lower airspeed.

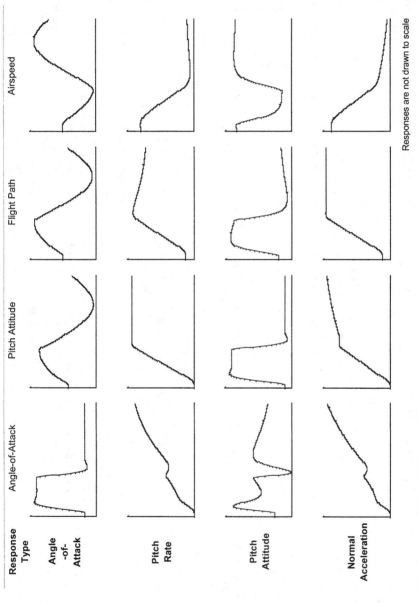

Figure 5   Time histories of four response-types

167

Table 1 Characteristics of the four response-types

	Angle-of-Attack	Pitch Rate	Pitch Attitude	Normal Acceleration
Step inceptor input results in:	New angle-of-attack	Constant pitch rate	New pitch attitude	Constant normal acceleration
Inceptor released results in:	Reverts to trim angle-of-attack	Holds pitch attitude at inceptor release	Reverts to trim pitch attitude	Holds flight path at inceptor release
Pilot trimming	Trim to new angle-of-attack	No trimming required	Trim to new pitch attitude	No trimming required
Speed stability	Yes	No	Yes	No
Pitch attitude / Flight Path Consonance	Can judge flight path from pitch attitude	Cannot judge flight path from pitch attitude	Can judge flight path from pitch attitude	Cannot judge flight path from pitch attitude
Series pilot model applies	Yes	No	Yes, in short term	No
Effect of autothrottle	Removes phugoid response from pitch attitude and flight path	Flight path follows pitch attitude	Flight path follows pitch attitude	Flight path follows pitch attitude
Flare	Hold aft stick in flare as angle-of-attack increases	May have to push forward to land	Hold aft stick in flare to maintain higher pitch attitude than trim	May have to push forward to land
Stall	Pilot must apply increasing aft stick to increase angle-of-attack	Possible in level attitude, as angle-of-attack increases at low speed	Possible in level attitude, as angle-of-attack increases at low speed	Aircraft will pitch up to increase angle-of-attack and maintain flight path
Applications	All conventional aircraft	Accurate pitch pointing and pitch attitude control tasks	Pitch attitude stability, possibly landing flare, rotary aircraft in low viz.	Flight path control, high 'g' manoeuvring

Pitch rate response-type

In the pitch rate response-type a constant control inceptor input produces a constant pitch rate. If the input is held, the aircraft will continue pitching indefinitely, provided sufficient thrust is available, resulting in continuous looping. If the control inceptor is released, the aircraft will maintain the pitch attitude at release. No pilot trimming is required to maintain this new attitude.

In figure 5 it can be seen that the pitch attitude response to a boxcar input is a constant rate of increase of attitude, followed by the new attitude being held when the input is removed. Unlike for the conventional aircraft, there is no phugoid mode apparent in the pitch attitude response. Clearly, the response of flight path does not mirror that of pitch attitude, as it did for the conventional response-type. Instead, the flight path response decays with time, as the angle-of-attack increases. This ramp-like increase in angle-of-attack is required to maintain the constant pitch attitude at the slower airspeed, and is apparent both during the initial input and after the input has been removed. Although the phugoid mode has been removed from the pitch attitude response, a residual response is now apparent in the angle-of-attack and flight path responses. The consequence is that the pilot is no longer able to use pitch attitude as an accurate surrogate of the flight path response, and so the series pilot model control strategy is not directly applicable.

Also apparent in the responses of figure 5 is the tendency for the airspeed to reduce during the control input, and then remain at the lower airspeed when the control input is removed. Since the pilot is applying no stick force at control input removal, there will be no tactile cues to the pilot that the aircraft is at a different speed than before the input was made. This lack of speed stability can cause a reduced speed awareness, requiring greater attention to be paid to the airspeed display.

Pitch rate response-types are commonly implemented in fly-by-wire fighter aircraft. When properly implemented, they provide a very stable platform with minimal pilot workload for manoeuvring. They are especially well suited to pitch control tasks, those that require gross and rapid changes in pitch attitude as well as those that require small and precise changes in pitch attitude, such as target tracking.

Pitch attitude response-type

For the pitch attitude response-type a constant control inceptor input results in a new pitch attitude. If the input is held, the pitch attitude will be held at the new value indefinitely, provided sufficient thrust is available. If the control inceptor is released, the aircraft will return to its original, trim, pitch attitude. The pitch attitude response-type is very 'attitude stable' with its trim to attitude feature. Trimming results in the aircraft maintaining the new, trimmed, pitch attitude.

Figure 5 shows that the pitch attitude response to a boxcar input is a rapid increase to the new steady state pitch attitude, followed by a return to the original trimmed pitch attitude when the input is removed. As for the pitch rate response-type, there is no phugoid mode visible in the pitch attitude response. The initial response of flight path is similar to that of pitch attitude, demonstrating better consonance between the two responses than for the pitch rate response-type. This is especially evident when comparing the angle-of-attack responses of the two response-types. While the angle-of-attack response exhibited a ramp-like increase for the pitch rate response-type, it does not for the pitch attitude response-type. In the longer-term the flight path response does decay, as the angle-of-attack increases to maintain the new pitch attitude. After the input is removed the angle-of-attack and flight path responses will eventually follow the pitch attitude to their original trim values. As with the pitch rate response-type, although the phugoid mode has been removed from the pitch attitude response, a residual response is now apparent in the angle-of-attack and flight path responses, although they are smaller than those for the pitch rate response-type. For piloted control the consonance between the attitude and flight path responses is sufficient for the pilot to use pitch attitude as an accurate surrogate of the flight path response, and so the series pilot model control strategy is applicable to the pitch attitude response-type.

The airspeed response shows that the aircraft initially goes to a new airspeed associated with the new pitch attitude, with a minimal longer-term response also apparent. Although not conventional speed stability, the airspeed response appears to the pilot to exhibit apparent, or pseudo, speed stability.

The pitch attitude response-type is suited to tasks that require a very stable pitch attitude response, with minimal deviations from that attitude. Large excursions from the trimmed pitch attitude require large control inputs, with appreciable pilot trimming to maintain the new attitude, far more trimming than is required for a conventional response-type aircraft. Therefore, in fixed wing aircraft pitch attitude response-types have been limited to applications during which minimal changes in pitch attitude are required, such as the final stages of the landing approach task.

Normal acceleration response-type

For the normal acceleration response-type a constant control inceptor input produces a constant normal acceleration, also referred to as load factor. If the input is held, the aircraft will continue pitching indefinitely, provided sufficient thrust is available, resulting in looping. However, unlike the pitch rate response-type, the continual pitching will be at a constant normal acceleration, not a constant pitch rate. If the control inceptor is released, the aircraft will maintain the flight path at which the inceptor is released. As with the pitch rate response-type, no pilot trimming is required.

Physically, normal acceleration is approximately the same as scaled flight path rate. Thus, when commanding a change in normal acceleration, a pilot is commanding a change in the flight path rate. When the control inceptor is released, the aircraft returns to the datum normal acceleration, and no further change in flight path occurs, or the aircraft stabilises at the new flight path. Thus, a normal acceleration response-type allows direct control of flight path.

As can be seen in the time histories of figure 5, the flight path angle response to a boxcar input is a constant rate of increase of flight path, followed by the new flight path being held when the input is removed. There is no phugoid response apparent in the flight path response. While there is no phugoid apparent in the flight path response, there is a longer-term response in the pitch attitude response. The increase in pitch attitude reflects the same increase in angle-of-attack that is required to maintain the flight path as the speed decays. Therefore, although the flight path response is constant, the pitch attitude response is not, and so the pilot is no longer able to use pitch attitude as an accurate surrogate of flight path, and so the series pilot model control strategy is not directly applicable.

The initial airspeed response to the control input is a reduction associated with the change in flight path. The airspeed then further reduces as the angle-of-attack increases to maintain the flight path. As with the pitch rate response-type, once the pilot releases the control inceptor he receives no tactile cues that the aircraft is at a different speed than before the control input was made. This lack of speed stability can cause reduced speed awareness, requiring greater attention to be paid to the airspeed display.

The normal acceleration response-type is especially effective for tasks that require aggressive manoeuvring and precise control of normal acceleration and flight path. For instance, a fighter aircraft performing rapid turns is ideally suited to a normal acceleration response-type, where the pilot has direct control over load factor, and so the rate of change of flight path. The normal acceleration response-type is also suited to tasks that require accurate control of flight path, just as the pitch rate response-type is suited to tasks that require accurate control of pitch attitude.

Effects of auto-throttle

As discussed earlier, when a conventional aircraft is trimmed to an angle-of-attack, it is also trimmed to a specific speed, for that aircraft configuration. An autothrottle maintains the speed of the aircraft constant, and so also maintains the angle-of-attack constant as well. Therefore, for all the unconventional response-types considered an autothrottle would maintain the angle-of-attack response constant in the long term. Any changes in the pitch attitude response would be exactly mirrored in the flight path response. Thus, with an autothrottle the ability to control flight path through observation of pitch attitude is returned.

171

However, it should be remembered that one of the most critical manual pilot control tasks that the pilot must perform is the flared landing. Once in the flare the auto-throttle is disengaged, and the natural characteristics of the response-type are returned.

Envelope protection issues

Also included in table 1 are the stall characteristics of the different response-types. While the characteristics for the angle-of-attack response-type are conventional, clearly they are not for the other response-types. It is these unconventional characteristics when near the edge of the envelope that make envelope protection a critical issue. The natural cues associated with a conventional aircraft may be absent in an aircraft that utilises alternative response-types. Thus, envelope protection or limiting may be essential for alternative response-types. However, the characteristics of the protection may appear quite different to the pilot compared to that of a conventional aircraft. Therefore, cueing of an impending envelope limit, or even being on the limit, must be clearly communicated to the pilot.

Choice of response-types and blending

Through appropriate flight control system design most response-types can be developed to produce acceptable flying qualities to the pilot. However, some response-types will require more 'tailoring' to make them acceptable throughout the flight envelope, than will others.

In most practical applications different response-types will be implemented in different parts of the envelope, with blending between the response-types depending upon flight condition. For example, response-types that exhibit speed stability are better suited to the low speed regime and the landing flare, since they provide natural tactile cues of the impending stall and the pilot preferred requirement for aft stick in the flare. Similarly, a pitch attitude response-type may be suited to tasks that require accurate control of a specific pitch attitude, but result in heavy stick forces when manoeuvring to greatly different pitch attitudes. For such tasks a pitch rate response-type is more applicable.

It is essential that the flight deck inceptors and displays are designed to be compatible with all response-types that are implemented throughout the aircraft envelope, including those that are used in the primary and back-up modes.

Inceptors

Many different primary flight control inceptors have been used since the beginnings of piloted flight. Today, the most common are the wheel column, centrestick and sidestick. While it may be felt that the choice of inceptor type should be determined from an ergonomic perspective, to ensure good handling qualities, and thereby ensure precise and predictable manual piloted control, the inceptor *must* be chosen to be consistent with the response-types employed by the aircraft.

A conventional response-type aircraft requires trimming to a new angle-of-attack as the airspeed or aircraft configuration is altered. Initially, any out of trim force will be held by the pilot during the manoeuvring portion of the task, and the trim will be used to reduce control forces in the longer term. Conventional response-type aircraft therefore require inceptors that include a reasonable inceptor displacement to allow accurate control around trim, away from trim and re-datumming of the trim position, as well as a trim control. In comparison, rate command response-types do not require trimming. The pilot uses pulse type inputs to change the state of the aircraft and then returns the inceptor to its datum neutral position. Hence, inceptor displacements for rate command response-types without trimming need not be as great as for conventional response-type aircraft. However, it is still necessary to provide sufficient displacement to allow accurate control for both small amplitude, precise, and large amplitude tasks. Attitude command response-types have strong trimmed attitude stability and so require a constant force to hold an off-trim attitude with follow up trimming required to relieve the force. While the forces may be reasonable around trim, for larger attitude changes the forces required are large and appreciable trimming is required.

Anthropometric design considerations

Regardless of response-type and its associated control strategy, the pilot will make inputs to the primary flight control inceptor through his hand. The accuracy with which he can control the aircraft will depend upon the accuracy with which he can manipulate the inceptor. That in turn depends upon the accuracy with which he can manipulate his hand, both in applying a force to the inceptor, and in physically moving the inceptor.

Critical to the accuracy of control is the design of the inceptor. An inceptor that is pivoted close to the pilot's wrist will allow only wrist movement to make inputs. An inceptor that is pivoted some way from the wrist allows the pilot to hold his wrist essentially rigid, and manipulate the force applied by his hand and the resulting inceptor position using shoulder and elbow joints and their associated muscles. The use of more joints allows more accurate control of the inceptor, and the greater variety and volume of muscles associated with the shoulder and elbow joints eases the problem of muscle fatigue that is often associated with wrist only inceptors when used for long periods of closed loop control.

With the shoulder and elbow joints immobile, the available displacement of the human wrist is limited. Therefore, an inceptor mechanised for wrist only inputs

173

will have its displacements limited to those of the human wrist. Thus, the human pilot's wrist defines the maximum displacement of the inceptor. Since such an inceptor is ideally suited to rate response-types it is likely that the pilot will be operating with pulse like inputs to change the pitch attitude and flight path, and then rely upon the flight control system to hold the new state. As a result, inadvertent control inputs are undesirable. Hence, it is likely that such an inceptor should be implemented with an appreciable deadband around trim to avoid inadvertent inputs. Given the large deadband and limited inceptor displacement the input to aircraft response gradient will have to be large to achieve large aircraft attitude and flight path changes within the displacements available. In turn, this may cause problems for precise control when operating around trim, where the pilot goes from no aircraft response to a steep response gradient once out of the deadband region.

Coupled with these characteristics of a limited displacement inceptor is the limited control that the pilot has of his wrist. Consider walking with a glass full of water. With shoulder and elbow joints available this is not difficult. Now place a stack of loose papers under your same arm, thus immobilising your shoulder and elbow. Try walking up some stairs. The task has become far harder because one is limited to controlling the glass of water with movements of the wrist only. This is akin to controlling an inceptor that only permits wrist movements as opposed to an inceptor that allows movement of the shoulder, elbow and wrist.

The problems associated with wrist only inceptors can be alleviated to some extent with an inceptor that employs greater displacements and allows shoulder and elbow movements as well as wrist. Indeed, even for longer lever inceptors the displacements are not always large, but critical is the ability to use all three joints for control.

Wheel column

The wheel column inceptor arrangement is ideally suited to all response-types. When properly designed it can be mechanised with sufficient displacement to permit precise control around the datum trim position, while also providing larger displacements for grosser control. The wheel column also allows re-datumming of the trim position for different flight conditions and aircraft configurations. It also provides the greatest peripheral visual cues of all the inceptors.

From an anthropometric perspective the wheel column arrangement is ideally suited to precise control since it allows precise control of the pilot's hands through the use of the wrist, elbow and shoulder joints, and their associated controlling muscles. Indeed, the wrist is probably the least used of these joints.

A disadvantage of the wheel column arrangement is its size, it takes up appreciable space in the flight deck and can obscure the displays. It is also the heaviest of the inceptors, which can make it unpopular with those who seek to maximise the useful payload of the aircraft.

Centrestick

The centrestick shares many of the features of the wheel column arrangement. It is suited to all response-types and can be mechanised with sufficient displacement as for the wheel column. It also allows use of the wrist, elbow and shoulder joints to provide very precise control of the inceptor. A potential advantage of the centrestick over the wheel column is that being smaller it does not obscure the displays so much, does not take up so much space and is lighter. A potential disadvantage is that being smaller it may provide lower peripheral visual cues.

Sidestick

The characteristics of sidesticks are sensitive to their mechanisation. Many sidesticks employ only a limited displacement, and are operated through wrist action only. These are best suited to rate response-types which only require occasional inputs from the pilot, but can lead to wrist fatigue if operated for long periods. Other sidesticks employ a greater displacement, allowing elbow and shoulder movement as well, although even these often use more limited displacement than wheel columns or centresticks.

The key to a successful sidestick is that it allows control through elbow and shoulder movements. Provision must also be made for trimming, even if only for a back-up mode. Re-datumming of the trim position is harder with a sidestick than a centrestick, since the pilot's seat will be optimised around the sidestick location. As a result, the trim system should be mechanised to relieve the pilot held forces, rather than move the datum trim position physically. This may at first appear unnatural to pilots, but they soon adapt to the mechanisation.

Advantages of the sidestick over the wheel column and centrestick are its smaller size and lower weight. Due to its location to the side of the pilot the problems of obscuration of the main flight deck displays that the wheel column experiences are absent. However, the outboard areas of the flight deck that are used in some aircraft for ancillary systems, or even storage, are now unavailable. Additionally, peripheral visual cues are reduced, compared to both the wheel column and centrestick.

Control inceptor crossfeeds

Another important issue for control inceptors in a multiple pilot flight deck is crossfeed between the inceptors. In addition to crossfeed between the two pilots' inceptors is feedback to the inceptors of the autoflight system commands. These linkages can provide cues to a pilot through two information channels. First are the tactile cues that a pilot may receive, and second are peripheral visual cues.

In both cases these cues inform the pilot that a change has been commanded before the change occurs. Due to aircraft dynamics the change may not occur for

175

a second or two after the command has been made, so knowing that the command has been made provides anticipatory knowledge to the pilot in determining his own control strategy. Crossfeed between the pilots inceptors was found to provide useful anticipatory information to the pilots in the survey reported by Field and Harris (1998). Comparatively, feedback from the autoflight system to the inceptor was found to be slightly less important than crossfeed between the inceptors to the pilots in the same survey. Backfeed from the autothrottle to the throttle levers was considered very important.

Knowing that a change has been commanded by a less experienced first officer may be important for the captain to be assured that the first officer has indeed taken the appropriate action, and that the captain does not need to intervene. Alternatively, when under autoflight control, feedback of an autopilot command also assures the handling pilot that the autoflight system is functioning appropriately.

The former example of the captain observing the first officer is most likely to rely upon the peripheral visual cues of the inceptor movements. However, the latter example of the handling pilot observing the autoflight system can make use of both peripheral visual cues and tactile cues, such as the handling pilot resting his hands on the inceptor prior to taking over manual control.

Displays

Display technology has advanced dramatically from the earliest instruments that were installed on aircraft. It is now possible to display virtually any parameter that a pilot may want, in many different formats. In modern civil airliners information that used to be distributed around many different displays is now concentrated on the Primary Flight Display (PFD). An increasing number of airliners are incorporating Head-up Displays (HUD), which display much of the same information as the PFD, but with the advantage that the pilot is looking out of the window as the aircraft breaks out of low cloud when in the landing flare.

While the exact format of the data displayed may be different on the PFD and the HUD, they should both contain the essential information that is required for precise and low workload manual piloted control. Consistent with the rest of this chapter, only those parameters that are of relevance to the earlier discussions will be considered here, namely angle-of-attack, pitch attitude, flight path and airspeed.

Angle-of-attack

Angle-of-attack is rarely displayed directly in civil aircraft. A pilot's main interest in angle-of-attack is to avoid exceeding the maximum angle-of-attack, and stalling the aircraft. Due to a conventional aircraft's speed stability the angle-of-attack is directly linked to airspeed, and so airspeed is used as a surrogate for the limiting angle-of-attack. Hence, the margin from stall is displayed to the pilot on the airspeed display.

Pitch attitude

Both the PFD and HUD centre on a representation of the outside world, and so are a direct representation of the aircraft's attitude with reference to the earth's surface. As discussed earlier in this chapter attitude is a very important response that the pilot tries to control, often as a surrogate for flight path. Accurate and robust sensors of attitude are readily available, and display of attitude is simple to implement.

Flight path

Some modern displays include a flight path symbol, to display where the aircraft is going. Indeed, since the pilot is actually trying to control flight path, not attitude, it would seem appropriate to include a display of flight path. However, the display of flight path is not as straightforward as attitude. As discussed earlier in this chapter flight path lags attitude by an appreciable margin, and so can be difficult for a pilot to predict. Trying to control the aircraft's flight path through a display of instantaneous flight path is extremely difficult, since the flight path will continue to change for some time after an input is made and the pitch attitude is constant. Indeed, if a pilot tries to control flight path directly he will likely drive the pilot/aircraft closed loop system unstable. An example of this is trying to control altitude from the altimeter directly.

Instead, a predicted flight path must be displayed to the pilot. The predicted flight path is effectively the current flight path with two corrections. The first is a correction for the lag between the attitude and flight path responses, as discussed throughout this chapter. The second correction is to account for the pilot being located ahead of the centre of gravity of the aircraft, as discussed earlier in this chapter. As the aircraft pitches, the pilot station will follow a different flight path than the centre of gravity. Initially the two responses will be in opposite directions, and the pilot station will always lead the centre of gravity (see figure 4). Therefore, if flight path at the centre of gravity is displayed to the pilot, it can lead to control problems since it is not synchronised with the cues at the pilot station. As a result, it is necessary to display flight path measured at a location forward of the centre of gravity, and forward of the instantaneous centre of rotation. If too far forward, such as the actual pilot station, the flight path signal can include too much lead and be over-sensitive to pilot inputs, making it difficult for the pilot to control flight path closed loop. The optimum flight path signal is usually slightly ahead of half way between the centre of gravity and the pilot station. Clearly, this correction is more important for longer aircraft.

177

Edmund Field

Airspeed

Another important parameter for piloted control is airspeed. For conventional aircraft that are speed stable the aircraft will be trimmed at a particular 'trim speed'. A backward force on the control inceptor results in a higher angle-of-attack and a lower airspeed than trim. A forward force on the control inceptor results in a lower angle-of-attack and higher airspeed than trim. Thus, for a constant flight condition and aircraft configuration a pilot is always provided a cue of airspeed relative to trim airspeed. This tactile cue can provide a useful source of airspeed information at times of high workload, without having to look directly at the airspeed display. While a constant control force is associated with a state cue of the current deviation from trim airspeed, changing control forces provides an anticipatory cue of impending changes in deviation from trim airspeed.

Aircraft that employ rate command response-types do not exhibit speed stability, and so the pilot receives no airspeed cues through the control inceptor. For these response-types the airspeed display is an even more critical display than it is in conventional aircraft, as it provides the only source of airspeed information, a cause of concern during periods of high workload as it places total dependence on the central visual cue. This is one reason why envelope protection is more common in such aircraft, not so much because it can be provided, as it is essential.

To aid manual airspeed control in such aircraft an addition to the airspeed display is the Speed Trend Vector (Field and Harris, 1998). The Speed Trend Vector is an arrow pointing from the current airspeed to that predicted in 10 seconds, if no further control inputs are made. This display provides an anticipatory cue of future airspeed, in addition to the current state cue provided by the actual airspeed display.

Envelope limits

The limits imposed by envelope protection, whether hard or soft, can easily be displayed on the PFD and HUD. With the reduction in use of alternative cueing channels leading to the increased dependence upon the PFD for all primary flight information in some aircraft, it becomes essential that all limits are clearly displayed to the pilot. The display of the limits may be the only indication the pilot has that he is at the limit of control authority.

Landing aids

Several displays have been developed, aimed at aiding the pilot in the landing task. The first is a graphical display of the runway outline, which can be displayed on either the PFD or HUD. The issue of conformity can arise when breaking out of cloud and using the HUD. The projected runway display may move relative to the actual runway as the aircraft is manoeuvred, and the two may not coincide exactly. Since at this point the pilot should be concentrating on placing the flight path marker on the touchdown point on the runway the non-conformity of the projected runway should not be a factor.

Another option is to display a flare cue on the HUD. At a pre-defined radio altitude a target flight path symbol appears and rises slightly, to position approximately at the far end of the runway. This provides flare guidance to the pilot, who should apply aft pressure on the control inceptor to raise the flight path symbol onto the target. This should ensure a smooth touchdown with a minimal dispersion from the target point.

Auditory cues

In addition to tactile and visual cues the auditory channel can also provide useful information to the pilot. Auditory cues are mostly used for warnings, often alerting the pilots to look at the displays for information. Auditory cues are also used on many larger aircraft to aid the pilot during the landing (Field, 1999).

Audio height call-out provides a flight path cue to the pilot using an additional information cueing channel. Conventionally, calls of main undercarriage height above the ground are made at fifty, forty, thirty, twenty and ten feet. Additionally, calls at five feet are available on some aircraft. The cues are used in part to alert the pilot when to make various procedural actions, such as pulling back the thrust levers and pitching the aircraft to arrest the sink rate. Additionally, they provide a cue of the change in sink rate as the aircraft is pitched. That is, the time between successive calls informs the pilot of the reduction in sink rate. However, the call-outs are only of use down to the lowest call-out, usually ten feet. Below that height the pilot is dependent upon visual and tactile cues only.

The auditory cues are especially important in large aircraft, where the pilot may be over 30 feet above the runway at touchdown. In such aircraft it can be difficult to judge sink rate visually, especially at night and in poor visibility conditions.

However, there is a potential for conflict between the various cues the pilot receives. Essentially, the pilot is trying to control the sink rate of the main undercarriage at touchdown. The most direct cue he has of this is the auditory call-outs. However, in large aircraft what he sees visually may be conflicting. In large aircraft the pilot can be located 100 feet ahead of the main undercarriage, as well as over 30 feet above the runway at touchdown. This can cause two problems with sensing sink rate at the pilot station. The first, as mentioned above, is due to the problems of determining sink rate accurately when so far above the runway. The second problem is relating the pilot station sink rate to that at the main undercarriage. Due to the long moment arm between the main undercarriage and the pilot location, if the aircraft is pitching there can be appreciably different sink rates at the two locations. Indeed, one location can be going up while the other is going down.

179

Edmund Field

The situation of conflicting cues can be compounded by poor HUD displays. Again it is essential that the correct flight path be displayed, along with appropriate flare commands.

Summary

Although modern civil airliners are flown manually for very small portions of their flights, it is essential that their handling qualities are optimised throughout the flight envelope for manual piloted control. The optimisation of an aircraft's handling qualities does not only involve the dynamic response of the aircraft, as shaped by the flight control system, but also the harmonisation of the dynamic response with the control inceptors, displays and other sources of information to the pilot.

An aircraft's handling qualities must be tailored to the specific tasks that it is designed to perform. That is, the response-type must be chosen to be consistent with the pilot performing all required tasks with maximum precision and minimum workload. Where necessary, it may be appropriate to blend from one response-type to another as flight conditions or tasks change.

The chosen response-type will determine the most appropriate primary flight control inceptor. It is essential that the inceptor be chosen to be compatible with the response-type, the required piloting tasks, and its design be optimised around the anthropometrics of the human operator – the pilot. The inceptor must be selected to ensure precise piloted control with low workload, even in aircraft where the pilot assumes manual control for very limited portions of the flight.

The displays must provide the pilot with clear and unambiguous information. The dependence upon the various displayed parameters will be dependent upon the response-type. Response-types that do not provide the pilot with speed stability, and hence tactile cues of deviation from trim airspeed, will be dependent upon the airspeed display for all airspeed-related information. Response-types that provide the pilot with more direct control of flight path may be better controlled when flight path is displayed to the pilot, although it is important that such a display is of predicted flight path, and so tuned to the aircraft's dynamics.

Finally, the use of additional cueing channels should also be considered. Sharing the information between many information cueing channels is less likely to overload any individual channel. However, care must be taken to ensure that all the channels provide complimentary, and not contradictory, information.

References

Cooper, G.E., and Harper, R.P. (1969). *The use of pilot ratings in the evaluation of aircraft handling qualities.* NASA TN D-5153.

Field, E.J. (1999). *The effect of audio height call-out on landing performance of transport aircraft.* Presented at the American Institute of Aeronautics and Astronautics Atmospheric Flight Mechanics Conference, Portland, Oregon, USA, August 1999.

Field, E.J., and Harris, D. (1998). A comparative survey of the utility of cross-cockpit linkages and autoflight systems backfeed to the control inceptors of commercial aircraft'. *Ergonomics*, 41, 1462-1477.

Gibson, J.C. (1999). *Development of a methodology for excellence in handling qualities design for fly-by-wire aircraft.* Ph.D. Thesis, Delft University Press.

McRuer, D.T. (1982). *Progress and pitfalls in advanced flight control systems.* *AGARD CP-321.*

Acknowledgements

The contributions of Dave Mitchell and Roger Hoh of Hoh Aeronautics, Inc., Lomita, California, during the preparation of this chapter are gratefully acknowledged.

8 On the other side of promise: what should we automate today?

Sidney Dekker

The natural experiment of automation in aviation

There was a time when the question of what to automate in an aircraft had a simple answer: Automate everything you technically can (Douglas, 1990). The Air Transport Association observed that 'during the 1970s and early 1980s... the concept of automating as much as possible was considered appropriate' (ATA, 1989, p. 4). The promises of automation reached wide and far, with benefits ranging from improved economics and safety to increased operator performance and comfort (Wiener and Curry, 1980). Automating everything that was technically and economically feasible was even suggested to be a systems engineer's ultimate goal – the inevitable product of the focus of that profession. As Chapanis (1970) put it: 'The nature of systems engineering... (is) such that the engineer tries to mechanise or automate every function that can be'. The introduction of automation over the past twenty years has subjected air transport to a sizeable natural experiment. Its results form a pattern that is quite different from the original promises.

Automation reduces workload

Sold as labour-saving technology, automation was expected to take work away from human operators by relieving them of certain tasks. This it has done – automation has taken over many of the more tedious tasks, from holding a heading for long stretches of time, to doing onerous fuel and weight calculations in real-time. Automation, however, has redistributed workload rather than just reducing it. The benefits of automation are most noticeable when they are of least value: during low-tempo operations when the human operator already had little to do. This while the burdens of automation (its demands on human memory, cries for more input, difficult-to-manage interfaces, etc.) accrue during high-tempo, safety-critical operations, when the operator had always been busy with other tasks and where margins for error were smaller and time pressure higher. This pattern is what Wiener (1989) called 'clumsy automation' – automation that helps chiefly when the operator did not really need its help, and getting in the way when s/he did.

Automation saves on labour costs

A powerful argument was that automation would save on labour costs. As Chapanis (1970) pointed out: '... the high cost of human labour makes it reasonable to mechanise everything that can be mechanised.' It is true that automation made particular professions redundant (from silk weavers to radio operators to flight engineers) but operators who were left had to fill part of the gap– learning to deal with often brittle, uncertain and complex technology and having to attain competencies beyond their original job mandates. As a result, automation has actually increased the need to invest in human expertise and has the aerospace industry working hard to find out how best to train operators of automated systems (Dekker and Hollnagel, 1999). Procurement of new equipment is now often driven by the trade-off between labour-intensive low-tech systems with lesser training requirements, and less labour-intensive, high-tech systems for which it will be expensive to train and retain operators.

Automation is more accurate

As another economic argument, and one with implications for safety as well, automation promised to be more accurate in the control of an aircraft than humans could be. For example, aircraft automation is able to de-rate the thrust necessary for getting an airliner off the ground based on weight, runway length and condition, ambient temperature, humidity, and so forth. This saves fuel while making exactly sure the aircraft lifts off before it is out of runway. But such accuracy comes at the price of inflexibility. The pursuit of accuracy may render automation insensitive to unanticipated changes in goals or world states. For example, higher thrust may not be available even if called for during an emergency on take-off (Billings, 1996).

Given that they are responsible for outcomes, operators will find ways to tailor highly accurate automation to suit their local ends, something that may also defeat economic gains. For example, aircraft automation calculates the optimal point, based on cost factors, to begin a descent towards an airport. Yet for many pilots, the descent that results is too steep and through experience they learn to 'trick' the automation by programming in a tailwind – causing it to descend earlier, and allowing pilots to manage a smoother, more gradual ride down (Billings, 1996).

This is a common pattern: new technology generally does not work without the expertise and creativity of people operating it, like pilots tricking flight management computers into accepting real world constraints. People who are responsible for the outcome of their work are adept at integrating quirky technology – covering its holes, making up for its shortcomings, nursing it through more difficult operational patches, feeding it knowledge where it proved clueless. This local tailoring is generally smooth. It easily goes unnoticed, certainly by engineers who look exclusively for the success of a fielded system. It is only when operational pressures get excessive or circumstances highly unusual, that leakage around the edges occurs – which then gets labelled 'human error'.

Automation reduces human errors

The reasoning went that if automation does the work, then the human cannot make any errors in doing it. But people still work with automated systems. As a result, the nature and expression of human error has changed (for example: programming errors, losing track of mode changes). Automation has also affected the manageability of error: it often moves the effect of human error further into the future. The loosened coupling between human input and machine output, where a few human inputs can lead to autonomous machine output during many hours, makes it more difficult to detect mismatches between human intentions and process behaviour (Sarter and Woods, 1997).

Automation increases system safety

Where replacement of human work was impossible or undesirable, automation promised at least to monitor and sometimes veto what the human was doing. The idea was that the human could not get the overall system outside its prescribed operating envelope. Several incidents and accidents showed, however, that automation and human inputs could together pull the system far outside safe operating boundaries (see for example NTSB, 1994). The relationship between locally rational human intentions (push the nose forward to maintain a glide path, as in NTSB, 1994) and automated countermeasures against transgressions outside the envelope proved more complex than anticipated. Systems regularly got pushed over the edge through a series of interactions between people and machines each doing what they were once taught or told to do (e.g. Aeronautica Civil, 1996). These pathways to disaster show that automation has unanticipated ways of interfering with human practice by upsetting behaviour that created safety in earlier systems. Through these unanticipated interactions between locally rational human behaviour and automated actions, new doors to system breakdown have been opened.

Out of sight, out of the loop

In efforts to sum up the issues with flight deck automation, the industry often refers to pilots being 'out-of-the-loop'. The problem is that 'as pilots perform

185

duties as system monitors, they will be lulled into complacency, lose situational awareness, and not be prepared to react in a timely manner when the system fails' (Kern, 1998, p. 240). This, however, is palpable nonsense. All the data available from accidents with computerised airliners over the past two decades indicate that an out-of-the-loop problem – in the sense that pilots are unable to intervene effectively 'when the system fails' after a stint of only monitoring – has nothing to do with why problems occur. Indeed, if this were the crux of automation problems, then we should have stopped Sperry dead in his tracks: with the three-axis autopilot he demonstrated back in 1914, pilots had already become 'out-of-the-loop' monitors. Of course, navigation was still up to the human pilot, in contrast to today's flight management systems. But the problems confronting pilots back then (boredom and limited satisfaction of looking at a machine doing the work they once did) were not qualitatively different from what their *fin-de-siècle* colleagues see as the less attractive features of their work today. Yet this is not what crashes aeroplanes.

The co-ordination irony

In fact, the opposite is true. Bainbridge wrote about the ironies of automation in 1987. She observed that automation took away the easy parts of a job, and made the difficult parts more difficult. Automation counted on human monitoring, but people are bad at monitoring for very infrequent events. Indeed, automation did not fail often, which limited people's ability to practice the kinds of breakdown scenarios that still justified their presence in the system. The pilot is painted as a passive monitor, whose greatest safety risks lie in de-skilling, complacency, vigilance decrements and the inability to intervene successfully in deteriorating circumstances. But these ironies too, are not what crash aeroplanes.

The unifying feature behind airliner crashes since the eighties is instead a 'co-ordination irony'. Automation since the eighties has not turned pilots into passive monitors. Sperry's 1914 autopilot already did that. Today, pilots have roles of active supervisors or managers who need to co-ordinate a suite of human and automated resources in order to get an aeroplane to fly. Yet pilots' ability to co-ordinate their activities with those of computers and other people on the flight deck is made difficult by silent and strong (or powerful and independent) automation (Sarter and Woods, 1997); by the fact that each human crewmember has private access to the computer systems (each pilot has his/her own flight management system CDU (control/display unit)); and because demands to co-ordinate with the automation accrue during busy times when a lot of communication and co-ordination with other human crewmembers is also needed. The same features, however, that make co-ordination difficult make it critically necessary. This is where the irony lies. Co-ordination is necessary to invest in a shared understanding of what the automated system has been told to do (yet difficult because it can be told to do things separately by any pilot and then go on its way without showing much about how it is doing). Co-ordination is also necessary to distribute work during busier, higher pressure operational episodes, but such delegation is difficult because automation is hard to direct and can shift a pilot's attention from flying the aircraft to managing the interface. The penalty for not co-ordinating can consist of a loss of mode awareness and an eventual 'automation surprise', where the automation does something unexpected or fails to do what was anticipated (Sarter and Woods, 1997).

Aircraft get managed into disaster

None of the major accidents with automated airliners over the past two decades have anything to do with pilots being passive, 'out of the loop' monitors, too complacent or too far away to intervene effectively in a failed system. Instead, almost all crashes (e.g. Strasbourg; METT, 1993: Nagoya; NTSB, 1994: Toulouse; DGA 1994: Cali; Aeronautica Civil, 1996) are linked to pilots being active managers – typing, searching, programming, planning, responding, communicating, questioning. Aircraft over the past two decades have had to be managed into disaster – into stalls, into mountainsides, into the ground. What consistently lies behind these mishaps is a co-ordination breakdown between human and automated cockpit crewmembers. A series of miscommunications and mis-assessments between humans and machines, a string of commissions and omissions, is typically necessary to push an aircraft toward and over the edge of breakdown (Sarter and Woods, 1997).

Of course, the loss of mode awareness could nominally be described as an out-of-the-loop problem. With only a few inputs, the automation is capable of carrying out long sequences of action and can change modes autonomously along the way. Pilots may be insufficiently involved in the various shifts and reconfigurations, unlike their colleagues on typical automated ship bridges who must actively approve of every heading change the autopilot wants to make. When the system goes out of sight (hiding interesting changes and events), people go out of the loop. Yet the out-of-the-loop problem does not all of a sudden explode to the fore 'when the system fails'. Indeed, what about this 'when the system fails' bit in the typical description of the out-of-the-loop problem? Which system? How so 'fails'? This characterisation could perhaps apply to Sperry's 1914 contraption, but it misses the numerous details and intricacies of both the automation and the ways in which it gets in trouble today. Very few automated systems 'fail' in the one-zero sense that they either work or go blank. Multi-layered systems, numerous redundancies and automatic reconfigurations make that pilots are virtually never required to intervene in an all-or-none way, except for the most extreme cases (e.g. running out of fuel). More importantly, automation failures are very rarely ingredients in accident sequences. From Strasbourg to Cali, the automation – as its manufacturers never hesitate to

187

Sidney Dekker

emphasise – did exactly what it was programmed to do. It behaved as designed.
No failures there.

The substitution myth

It is not necessarily so that automation has failed to fulfil its promises. In fact,
much evidence points to safety benefits and quantitative performance
improvements (Billings, 1996). Rather, automation has produced unexpected
side-effects by qualitatively shifting the way in which people do their work, and
how they interact with the actual systems they want to influence (the aircraft).
Through unanticipated and complex interplay, automation has made air
transportation vulnerable in new ways, demanding for the people left to work with
it, and sometimes more expensive for the carriers operating it.

The unifying idea behind the promises with which automation was fielded
twenty years ago is the substitution myth – the idea that machines can replace
human functions without further consequences for the larger human-machine
ensemble. Gains of such substitution were assumed to lie in increased safety,
lower operating costs, less requirements on manning and training, and so forth. In
other words, gains could be quantified, and they promised to benefit the entire
system.

MABA-MABA or Abracadabra?

Behind the substitution myth lies the illusion that people and computers have
fixed strengths and weaknesses and that the task of an engineer is to capitalise on
the strengths while eliminating the weaknesses. This is indeed the foundation for
many Function Allocation, or MABA-MABA (Men Are Better At – Machines
Are Better At) lists (e.g. Swain and Guttman, 1980). Earlier forms of MABA-
MABA lists preferred to contrast human strengths/weaknesses with machine
strengths/weaknesses, whereas latter-day counterparts typically list levels of
supervisory control, each of which makes machines and people responsible for
varying portions of the work (e.g. Sheridan, 1987; Parasuraman, Sheridan and
Wickens, 2000). Human and subordinate control over the process becomes
symmetrically apportioned as viewed from top to bottom (see table 1).

The list of levels indicates the varying degrees of possible supervisor
involvement and alludes to the nature of the human task at each of the levels.
Problematic is that neither the list nor much of the accompanying supervisory
control literature represents the cognitive work that might be involved in deciding
how and when to intervene or how to switch from level to level. The list of
supervisory control levels leaves unspecified how the human should decide when
and whether to intervene or when to back off. According to Sheridan (1987,
p. 1249), human monitoring and intervention involves activities such as observing

188

displays, looking for signals of abnormal behaviour, making minor adjustments of system parameters when necessary, and deciding when continuation of automatic control would cease to be satisfactory. These activities are all relevant of course, but their description is vague. What is 'satisfactory', for example? Such under-specification is not the only problem that leaves the list of levels with little of real relevance to add to the knowledge base. The list – like MABA-MABA lists – presume a fundamentally uncooperative system architecture: you do this, I do this. Such a division is not only counterproductive, it is inconsistent with the results of the natural experiment over the past twenty years. In reality, people and machines have to communicate, co-ordinate, play together in intricate ways to meet the challenges of their domain. The uncooperative nature of MABA-MABA lists and their latter-day counterparts makes them misguided and inapplicable to real systems.

Table 1
A list of levels of supervisory control (after Parasuraman, Sheridan and Wickens, 2000)

	Levels of Supervisory Control: *The computer*
1 (Lowest)	Offers no assistance: human supervisor must do it all.
2	Offers a complete set of action alternatives, and
3	Narrows the selection down to a few, or
4	Suggests one, or
5	Executes that suggestion if the supervisor approves, or
6	Allows the supervisor a restricted time to veto before automatic execution, or
7	Executes automatically, then necessarily informs the supervisor, or
8	Informs him after execution only if he asks, or
9	Informs him after execution if the subordinate decides to.
10 (Highest)	Decides everything and acts autonomously, ignoring the supervisor.

There are more problems. The breakdown of functions in MABA-MABA lists is always based on some model of human and machine performance. This choice of model is mostly left implicit, but it does determine the nature of the decomposition in the list. It is also completely arbitrary. If the model is about human performance, for example, it is often an information processing model, which postulates functions that are inconsistent with much of mainstream psychology today. All too often, however, the functions are derived from a machine description of functions – more algorithmic than heuristic, in other words. When the machine picks the battlefield and decides what names the various functions get, then human heuristic abilities (filtering irrelevant information, scheduling and reallocating activities to meet current constraints, anticipating events, making generalisations and inferences, learning from past experience, collaborating) easily fall by the wayside, misleading the designer who has to rely on the list (Hollnagel, 1999).

The dead-end of function allocation

History is not on the side of MABA-MABA success. What is often said to be one of the first Function Allocation lists (but was never meant to be) is half a century old (Fitts, 1951), yet Bainbridge had to conclude forty years later that automation had managed to amplify one of the best documented human weaknesses: the inability to reliably monitor for infrequent events. Either the profusion of MABA-MABA lists was not applied or simply did not work in shaping effective design decisions – or both.

The central flaw of function allocation lies in the false idea of fixed strengths and weaknesses. Capitalising on some strength of computers does not replace a human weakness. It creates new human strengths and weaknesses – often in unanticipated ways. For instance, the computer strength to carry out long sequences of action in pre-determined ways without performance degradation (because of fatigue), amplifies the human monitoring weakness. It also exacerbates the system's reliance on the human strength to deal with the parameterisation problem (having access to all relevant world parameters that the automation may not have a clue about). Yet the system's silent and strong autonomy may not give the human much opportunity to insert relevant knowledge about the world (e.g. the Warsaw runway overrun in 1993 – see Billings, 1996).

In addition, allocating a particular function does not absorb this function into the system without further consequences. It creates new functions for the other partner in the human-machine equation – functions that did not exist before, for example typing, or searching for the right display page. The quest for a-priori function allocation, in other words, is as intractable as pressing the residual air out of an inflatable mattress. Press down in one place and bubbles always bob up somewhere else.

Good to know about automation and cognition

The co-ordination of work between automated and human partners in a human-machine system is clearly more complicated than the a-priori barter trade of function allocation could ever hope to capture. In reality, automation technology brings new capabilities *and* new complexities. It creates new human strengths and weaknesses. From the natural experiment of introducing automation in aviation, designers can learn much about typical user errors, the computer features that are linked to them, and the cognitive consequences of automation that lie behind them.

Typical errors with automation

- Mode error. The user thought the computer was in one mode, and did the right thing had it been in that mode, yet the computer was actually in another mode.
- Getting lost in display architectures. Computers often have only one or a few displays, but a potentially unlimited number of things the user can see on them. It may be difficult to find the right page or data set.
- Not co-ordinating computer entries. Where people work together on one (automated) process, they have to invest in common ground by telling one another what they tell the computer, and double-checking each other's work. Under the pressure of circumstances or constant meaningless repetition, such co-ordination may not happen consistently.
- Overload. Computers are supposed to off-load people in their work. But often the demand to interact with computers accrues during those times when there is already a lot to do; when other tasks or people are also competing for the user's attention.
- Data overload. People are often forced to sort through a large amount of data, and become unable to locate the pieces that would have revealed the true nature of their situation. Computers may also spawn all manner of automated (visual and auditory) warnings that clutter a workspace and proliferate distractions.
- Not noticing changes. Despite the enormous visualisation opportunities the computer offers, many displays still rely on raw digital values (for showing rates, quantities, modes, ratios, ranges and so forth). It is very difficult to observe changes, trends, events or activities in the underlying process through one digital value clicking up or down. The user has to look at it often or continuously, and interpolate or infer what is going on.
- Automation surprises are often the end-result: the system did something that the user had not expected. Especially in high tempo, high workload scenarios, where modes change without direct user commands and computer activities are hard to observe, people may be surprised by what the automation did or did not do.

191

Automation features

What are some of the features of today's automation technology that contribute systematically to these kinds of errors?

- Automation can make things 'invisible'; it can hide interesting changes and events, or system anomalies. The presentation of digital values for critical process parameters contributes to this invisibility. The practice of showing only automated system status (what mode it is in?) instead of behaviour (what is the system actually doing, where is it going?) is another reason. The interfaces can look simple – simpler than their non-automated forebears, in fact – but they hide a lot of complexity.

- Automation, because it is often served by one or a few interfaces (this is called the 'keyhole problem'), can force people to dig through a series of display pages to look for, and integrate, data that really are required for the task in parallel. A large number of displays is not the answer to this problem of course, because navigation across displays becomes the issue (as well as limited cockpit real estate). Rather, each computer page should present aids for navigation (How did I get here? How do I get back? How do I step aside? What is the related page and how do I go there?) for standard as well as non-standard scenarios. If not, input and retrieval sequences may seem arbitrary, and people will get lost.

- Automation can force people into managing the interface (How do I get to that page? How do we get it into this mode?) rather than managing the safety-critical process (something the automation had promised to help them do). Extra interface management burdens often coincide with periods of high workload.

- Automation can change mode autonomously or in other ways that are not directly commanded by the user (for example as a result of pre-programmed logic, earlier inputs, inputs from other people or parts of the system, and so forth).

- Automation asks people typically in the most rudimentary or syntactic ways to verify their entries (Are you sure you want to go to X? We'll go to X then) without addressing the meaning of their request or whether it makes sense given the situation. And when people tell computers to proceed, it may be difficult to make them stop. All this limits people's ability to detect and recover from their own errors.

- Automation is smart, but not that smart. Automation can do a lot for people – it can almost autonomously run a safety-critical process. Yet automation typically knows little about the changing situation around it. It dutifully executes user or programmer commands even if these make no sense given the situation. It can also interrupt people's other activities without knowing it is seriously bothersome.

Cognitive consequences of automation

The characteristics of automation discussed above shape the way in which people assess, think, decide, act and co-ordinate, which in turn determines the reasons for the 'errors' that we can observe in people working with automation. Here is a basic list:

- Automation increases demands on people's memory (What was this mode again? How do we get to that page?).
- Automation asks people to add to their package of skills and knowledge for managing their processes (How to program, how to monitor, and so forth). Training may prove no match to these new skill and knowledge requirements: much of the knowledge gained in formal training may remain inert (in the head, not practically available) when operators get confronted with the kinds of complex situations that call for its application.
- Automation can complicate situation assessment (it may not show system behaviour, but rather lots of digital values) and undermine people's attention management (how you know where to look when).
- By new ways of representing data, automation can disrupt people's traditionally efficient and robust scanning patterns.
- Through the limited visibility of changes and events, the clutter of alarms and indications, extra interface management tasks and new memory burdens, automation can increase the risk of people falling behind in high tempo operations.
- Automation can increase system reliability to a point where mechanical failures are rare (as compared with older technologies). This gives people little opportunity for practicing and maintaining the skills for which they are, after all, partly still there: managing system anomalies.
- Automation can undermine people's formation of accurate mental models of how the system and underlying process works, because working the safety-critical process through computers only exposes them to a superficial and limited array of experiences.
- Automation can mislead people into thinking that they know more about the system than they really do, precisely because the full functionality is hardly ever shown to them (either in training or in practice). This is called the knowledge calibration problem.
- Automation can force people to think up strategies (programming 'tricks') that are necessary to get the task done. These tricks may work well in common situations, but can introduce new vulnerabilities under other circumstances.

Finally, the introduction of new technology can increase the operational requirements and expectations that organisations impose on people. Organisations that invest in new technologies often unknowingly exploit the advances by requiring operational personnel to do more, do it more quickly, do it in more complex ways, do it with fewer other resources, or do it in less and less favourable conditions. Improvements in the form of new technology get stretched in some way, pushing operators back to the edge of the operational envelope from which the technological innovation was supposed to buffer them. Using head-up displays for aiding non-precision approaches in bad weather is one example. Although safety may be the professed commitment, effective organisations typically exploit every technological advance to the limit.

Supporting people's co-ordination with automation

If the natural experiment of introducing automation into aviation shows one thing, it is this. 'Who does what' is not the question where designers need most guidance. Such guidance has been available for half a century, yet flight deck automation has still managed to amplify existing human weaknesses and introduce new ones. As discussed, the question is fraught with difficulties and sponsors non-co-operative system architectures where the distribution of work is translated into a trivial 'you do this, I do that' barter. In addition, the 'who does what' question will, as it always has been, continue to be determined mostly by available technological opportunities and economical considerations.

In a similar vein, the pilot who said about flying the automated MD-80 'I'm OK as long as I have this yellow button that turns it back into an old (non-automated) DC-9', is producing a red herring. The key to successful automation is not whether a pilot can switch it off altogether. The fact that pilots need to rely on this option is testimony to how uncooperative the architectures are that we have developed so far: either the automation does everything, or the human does everything. As soon as the automation gets in the way during already busy times, or does something really funny, it's good to have that yellow button. But such a distribution of labour does not work well in practice, and can leave a pilot facing difficult circumstances unaided. One ingredient of the 1989 B-737 Kegworth accident sequence in which the wrong engine was shut down was the pilot's reversal to manual flying as soon as engine trouble arose. This judgement is of course up to the pilot given the situation, but it is possible that preoccupation with hand-flying, navigating (and communicating with ATC) gobbled up human problem-solving resources that could otherwise have been directed at the engine issue.

Keys to a successful automation future

The question for successful automation is not 'who has control'. It is 'how do we get along together'. Indeed, where designers really need guidance today is how to support the co-ordination between people and automation. In complex, dynamic, non-deterministic worlds, people will continue to be involved in the operation of highly automated systems. The key to a successful future of these systems lies in how they support co-operation with their human operators – not only in foreseeable standard situations, but also during novel, unexpected circumstances. The question is how to turn automated systems into effective team players.

Christoffersen and Woods (2000) describe the characteristics of such team players. First, their activities are observable (not just physically available in the form of some digit or crude mode annunciation) The more powerful automated systems become – the more autonomous and complex, in other words – the more feedback they need to supply to make their behaviour observable. Otherwise, mis-assessments and miscommunications between humans and machines may persist and deepen, contributing to the kinds of Cali and Strasbourg accidents we have had in the past. The human operator needs to be able to understand the problem from the machine's perspective – something that would make double-checking of inputs and interpretations possible. A number of improvements can be made immediately. For example, syntactic double-checking ('you want to go to R? Which R would you like to go to?', see Aeronautica Civil, 1996) is clearly insufficient to build the kind of common ground on intentions that team players need to succeed in their joint work. Also, it could have helped in a many cases (e.g. Kegworth; Nagoya) if the automated system had given an indication of its ability to keep relevant process parameters on target. How much trouble is it having, are things becoming increasingly difficult? Which alternative options have been tried so far? How close is the system to the limits of its operating envelope? Having this kind of feedback is critical in allowing the human operator to make judgements of whether and how to intervene in (what may turn out to be) deteriorating circumstances. In order to create such feedback, representations of automation behaviour would have to be: ·

- Event-based: representations need to highlight changes and events in ways that the current generation of state-oriented displays do not.

- Future-oriented: in addition to historical information, human operators in dynamic systems need support for reasoning in advance, for anticipating changes and knowing what to expect and where to look next.

- Pattern-based: operators must be able to quickly scan displays and pick up possible abnormalities without having to engage in difficult cognitive work (calculations, integrations, extrapolations of disparate pieces of data). By relying on pattern- or form-based representations, computers have an enormous potential to convert arduous mental tasks into straightforward perceptual ones (Chistoffersen and Woods, 2000).

Second, good team players are directable – the human operator can easily and efficiently tell them what to do. The designer's focus here should be on intermediate, co-operative modes of system operation that allow human supervisors to delegate suitable sub-problems to the automation, just like they would be delegated to human crewmembers. The point is not to make automation into a passive adjunct to the human operator who then needs to micro-manage the system each step of the way. This would be a waste of resources, both human and computer. Human operators must be allowed to preserve their strategic role in managing system resources as they see fit under the circumstances (Christoffersen and Woods, 2000).

So what about the pilotless aircraft? Will automation ever be powerful enough to do it all by itself? The question itself is wrong, because it is based on the wrong assumptions, and appeals to the social unacceptability of pilotless aircraft in civil transport are just fanciful distractions. The real issue is that it re-frames the debate about the human-machine relationship in the language of a gradual marginalisation of human input – indeed in the way of Sheridan's supervisory control levels. Once again, the question is translated as one of uncooperative all-or-none control. Pilotless aircraft (e.g. military unmanned aerial vehicles) that exist today have not eliminated the human operator, but merely displaced him or her. There is still a supervisor on the ground, where the design challenges for successful co-ordination with automation – especially under unforeseen circumstances – are no less than when the supervisor sits in the cockpit.

Conclusion

Moray (1997) argues that the level of automation in many industries has reached a state of diminishing returns. In other words, greater investments in automation are leading to smaller and smaller marginal benefits in terms of efficiency and system reliability. The idea for designers to support the co-ordination between human operators and their automated systems is not a call for more automation, just as it is not a call for less automation. In fact, it is not at all a matter of automation quantity, but automation quality (Sarter and Woods, 1997). What matters is the extent to which powerful automation allows team play with its human operators. What matters is how observable the automation makes its behaviour for its human counterparts, and easily and efficiently it allows itself to be directed, even (or especially) during busy, novel episodes.

References

Aeronautica Civil de Colombia (1996). *Aircraft accident report: Controlled flight into terrain, American Airlines flight 965, Boeing 757-223, N651AA near Cali, Colombia, December 20, 1995*. Bogota, Colombia: Aeronautica Civil.

Air Transport Association of America. (1989, April). *National plan to enhance aviation safety through Human Factors improvements*. Washington, DC: ATA.

Bainbridge, L. (1987). Ironies of automation. In, J. Rasmussen, K. Duncan, J. Leplat (Eds.) *New technology and human error*, pp. 271-283. Chichester: Wiley.

What should we automate today?

Billings, C.E. (1996). *Aviation automation: The search for a human-centered approach.* Hillsdale, N.J.: Lawrence Erlbaum Associates.

Chapanis, A. (1970). Human Factors in systems engineering. In, K.B. De Greene (Ed.), *Systems psychology*, pp. 51-78. New York: McGraw-Hill.

Christoffersen, K., and Woods, D.D. (2000). *How to make automated systems team players.* Columbus, OH: Institute for Ergonomics, The Ohio State University.

Dekker, S.W.A., and Hollnagel, E. (Eds.) (1999). *Coping with computers in the cockpit.* Aldershot, UK: Ashgate.

Directorate General of Armaments (France) (1994). *Investgation committee report on A330 accident in Toulouse on 30 June 1994.* Paris: DGA.

Douglas Aircraft Co. (1990). *Functional decomposition of the commercial flight domain for function allocation* (Final report to NASA Langley Research Center, Contract No. NASI-18028). Washington, DC: NASA.

Fitts, P.M. (1951). *Human engineering for an effective air navigation and traffic control system.* Washington, DC: National Research Council.

Hollnagel, E. (1999). From function allocation to function congruence. In S.W.A. Dekker and E. Hollnagel (Eds.), *Coping with computers in the cockpit*, pp. 29-53. Aldershot, UK: Ashgate.

Ministère de l'equipment, des transports et du tourisme (1993). *Rapport de la commission d'enquete sur l'accident survenu le 20 Janvier 1992 près du Mont Saint Odile (Bas Rhin) a l'Airbus 320 immatriculé F-GGED exploité par la compagnie Air Inter.* Paris, France: METT.

Moray, N. (1997). Human Factors in process control. In G. Salvendy (Ed.), *Handbook of Human Factors and ergonomics*, pp. 1944-1971. New York: Wiley Interscience.

National Transportation Safety Board. (1994). *Safety recommendations A-94-164 through 166 concerning China Airlines Airbus A-300-600R accident at Nagoya, Japan, April 26, 1994.* Washington, DC: NTSB.

Parasuraman, R., Sheridan, T.B., and Wickens, C.D. (2000). A model for types and levels of human interaction with automation. *IEEE transactions on systems, man, and cybernetics– part A: systems and humans, 30*(3), 286-297.

Sarter, N.B., and Woods, D.D. (1987). Teamplay with a powerful and independent agent: Operational experiences and automation surprises on the Airbus A-320. *Human Factors, 39*(4), 553-569.

Sheridan, T.B. (1987). Supervisory control. In: G. Salvendy (Ed.), *Handbook of Human Factors.* New York, NY: Wiley.

Swain, A.D., and Guttman, H.F. (1980). *Handbook of human reliability analysis with the emphasis on nuclear power plant applications* (NRC NUREG-CR-1278). Albuquerque, NM: Sandia National Laboratories.

Wiener, E.L. (1989). *Human Factors of advanced technology ('glass cockpit') transport aircraft* (NASA contractor report No. 177528). Moffett Field, CA: NASA Ames Research Center.

197

Wiener, E.L., and Curry, R.E. (1980). Flightdeck automation: Promises and problems. *Ergonomics, 23*, 995-1011.

9 Anthropometrics for flight deck design

Ted Lovesey

Overview

Most populations, and especially that of aircrew, are increasing in size as time progresses. Flight deck designers need to be aware of this and, with some aircraft likely to be in service for 30 years or more, should design cockpits not just to fit the present aircrew but for the size of the aircrew expected to be using the flight deck in the future. In addition, designers must take account of ethnic differences within the aircrew. For example, although a flight deck may be designed now to fit both current and expected Western aircrew, it must also accommodate the significantly smaller aircrew from the Far East. As if this is not difficult enough, the design must also take account of gender and ensure that the smaller females are not at a disadvantage and can perform the flying task efficiently and safely.

All of these facts will require an understanding of the range of sizes to be accommodated. This will then determine the degree of adjustment to be designed into the seating and controls. This chapter will provide basic data on the size range of critical human dimensions that will influence flight deck design and an indication of how they are likely to increase with time.

Introduction

Ideally, the flight deck should be designed around the crew. This implies that account must be taken of the visual requirements, reach and movement, strength, adequate space for ingress, egress and sitting for long periods.

Starting with the design eye position and relevant anthropometric data, this will set the relative positions of windows, displays, controls and seat geometry. These will also be limited by the overall size of the flight deck that will be influenced by aerodynamic, structural and other constraints. The best result will be a compromise that incorporates all of the various requirements to an acceptable degree without over emphasising one at the expense of the other.

Visual requirements

The design eye position is where it is assumed that the pilots' eyes will be to give adequate view of the outside world, particularly when landing. Primary displays (see chapters 3 and 4) should be situated between the horizontal and 30° downwards and within 30° either side of the pilots' eyes. Head-down displays should ideally be between 50 to 70cm from the eye. Clearly this distance will depend, to some extent, upon the size of the text and symbolic information being presented.

The range of crew size

It is impractical to design a flight deck to accommodate everyone from the smallest dwarf to the largest giant. Most designs are a practical compromise intended to cover most but not all of the population. Usually this covers 90% of the population from the 5th percentile to the 95th percentile. This means that all but the smallest 5% and the largest 5% will be able to fit that particular dimension under consideration.

Unfortunately, people are not the same percentile value in every critical measurement. For example, someone who is average or 50th percentile in stature probably will not be average in leg length or arm length and there is no simple relationship between the various critical dimensions.

If six critical dimensions are used to reject people who are 5th percentile or less or 95th percentile or larger, the number excluded will be much greater than 10%. If, for example, Sitting Height is used first to select out the smallest and largest 5%, 90% will be left. If Buttock-Knee length is similarly used to select out anyone else from the remaining 90% below the 5th percentile or above the 95th percentile, the number left will be about 85% of the original number. Again, if the same selection rules are applied to Buttock-Heel length, the number left will be about 84%; applying Functional Reach, the number left will be 79% and applying the final dimension of Shoulder Width will reduce the number to 75% of the original population.

If the flight deck is to be designed to accommodate aircrew from all the developed nations it should take account of the sizes of the largest (95th percentile Western male) and the smallest (5th percentile Japanese female) aircrew. Values for the 5th and 95th percentile male and female, Western and Japanese are given in table 1. These figures have been taken from UK Defence Standard 00-25, part 2 and from Pheasant's (1996) book, *Bodyspace*.

It should be noted that the data given in table 2 are from two separate ethnic populations and both sexes with different physical characteristics. In addition, the Western aircrew population upon which the figures in table 1 are based, tend to be significantly larger than their non-aircrew counterparts.

The changing size of populations

The Boeing and Airbus flight deck designs of today are still likely to be flying two, three or even more decades from now. Already we have some designs, such as the DouglasDC3 (first flight 1935) and Nimrod (first flight as a Comet in 1949) whose in-service life spans will be more than 70 years. Both designs still essentially have the same sized flight deck that they had on their first flights, albeit now more cluttered as new equipment has been added over the years. But what of the aircrew who will fly today's designs in the future? Most will be larger than today's aircrew if current trends continue.

Stature seems to be increasing steadily in the UK male population at about 1.4mm per year, equivalent to an annual increase of 0.08% (Lovesey, 1988). Data to support female growth trends is less easy to find but has been quoted as being 0.9mm per year for Australian females since the end of World War II. Similar trends in stature have been noted by Greiner and Gordon (1990) for US Whites and Hispanics. US Army Blacks showed only a slight increase in stature while US Army Asians showed a decrease in stature.

Turner and Birch (1996) indicate that body weights of UK male aircrew have also increased steadily over the same period at a rate of about 0.2kg per year or over 0.25% annually. This is reflected in the steady increase in thigh, waist and chest circumferences. Functional reach has increased by 0.5mm annually, equivalent to 0.06%. Between 1967-1980 Swedish Air Force personnel weights have increased at a rate of 0.25% annually. A French armed forces study also accepts an increasing weight trend from a measured mean of 68.8kg in 1991 to a predicted mean of 70.2kg in 2020.

Although there is little or no precise definitive data on population growth trends, there is considerable uncorrelated information now available to indicate that populations in the developed world are increasing linearly in size and weight.

Since these increases seem to be stable over time, it is suggested that they be assumed to continue at the same rate, at least until new evidence indicates that the rates should be amended.

Critical dimensions

The 24 human dimensions that are most likely to be critical in the design of a flight deck are given in tables 1 and 2. Their definitions and reasons why they are considered to be important are also given. These are depicted in figure 1.

The effects of clothing

Because anthropometic data are generally obtained from semi-nude subjects clothing corrections must be applied to those data by designers when planning workspace layout and control positions. While these corrections may be considerable for military cockpits in cold weather environments, they will be significantly less for the 'shirt sleeve' civil flight deck environment. However, clothing can have the effects of both restricting the amount of movement and adding to some dimensions.

Footware will add about 30mm to knee height and uniform about 12mm to both abdominal depth and hip breadth. The effects of seat harness on restricting reach should also be considered.

Methods of adjustment

An adjustable seat is the primary method of adjusting crew posture to meet the control operating and viewing requirements. Also, some controls, such as the rudder pedals, are usually adjustable.

The determination of the amount of adjustment (and space) required will depend upon the following factors:

- The range of crew size to be accommodated.
- The critical dimensions for safety and comfort (see tables 1 and 2, and figure 1).
- The effects of clothing.

Control movement and force

In addition to being able to reach controls, sidestick controllers and switches from a neutral relaxed posture, aircrew should be able to 'functionally' grip controls when the control is at either extreme of its travel.

As an example of the dangers of not checking that there was adequate space to make control movements, some helicopter pilots with long forearms where unable to fully pull back on the cyclic stick due to restrictions to the rear and side of their seat and a number of accidents resulted.

Thus, on the flight deck where manual force must be exerted, it is important to provide sufficient clearance for the crew member to use their body to the greatest mechanical advantage. Cramped postures or obstacles on the flight deck lead to a reduction both in the crew's capacity to exert force and an increased level of strain. Forces to operate equipment should be low enough to be used continuously by the weakest crew member yet not so low that the controls and switches can be inadvertently operated. Indications of acceptable forces for UK military aircrew are given in part three of MoD (Ministry of Defence) Defence Standard 00-25. JAR 25.143 specifies that short term control forces, if applied with a single hand, should not exceed 50lbs (22.7kg) in pitch or 25lbs (11.4kg) in roll. Long term applications should be no greater than 10lbs (4.5kg) or 5 lbs (2.3kg), respectively.

Table 1
Critical anthropometric dimensions for designers and their limitations

No	Dimension	Measurement and Definition	Anthropometric Limitations
1	Stature	Height	Determines the minimum floor to roof clearance
2	Sitting height	Height from seat surface to top of head	Sets the minimum seat to roof clearance
3	Sitting eye height	Height from seat surface to eye level	Sets the lines of sight for displays and windows
4	Acromial height	Sitting shoulder height	A reference point for optimising control location
5	Elbow rest height	Sitting elbow height	Sets height of keyboard and other important controls
6	Thigh thickness	Height from seat surface to highest point of thigh	Sets minimum clearance between seat top and underside of equipment
7	Seat height	With thighs level and feet flat on floor	Must be adjustable to accommodate agreed range of sizes
8	Knee height	From floor to top of knee	Sets minimum clearance of underside of equipment
9	Stomach depth	From reference plane to front of abdomen	Sets clearance of equipment above thigh level
10	Buttock to knee length	From reference plane to front of knee	Sets clearance of knee height obstructions
11	Vertical functional reach	Maximum pinch grip height	Sets maximum height of controls
12	Elbow functional reach	Maximum pinch grip distance with upper arms vertical and forearm horizontal	Sets maximum forward location of controls with upper arm vertical and forearm horizontal
13	Forward functional reach	Maximum pinch grip distance from back of shoulders	Sets maximum forward reach of controls

Table 1 (continued)
Critical anthropometric dimensions for designers and their limitations

No	Dimension	Measurement and Definition	Anthropometric Limitations
14	Hand length	From wrist crease to tip of middle finger	Sets range for glove sizes
15	Hand breadth	Maximum breadth across palm	Sets sizes of handles, handgrips and aperture sizes
16	Foot length	From back of heel to tip of longest toe	Sets minimum size of foot pedals
17	Foot breadth	Maximum horizontal breadth across foot	Sets minimum size of foot pedals
18	Head breadth	Maximum breadth across the ears	Sets minimum lateral clearance for the head
19	Interpupillary distance	Distance between the pupils	Sets the range for binocular devices
20	Head height	Distance from chin to crown	Sets the range for protective headgear
21	Head length	Maximum distance from brow to rear	Sets the range for protective headgear
22	Shoulder breadth	Maximum distance across the shoulders	Sets the minimum lateral clearance in workspace
23	Hip breadth	Maximum distance across hips when seated	Sets width of seat. Minimum lateral clearance for the thighs will be up to 70mm greater than this dimension
24	Weight	Unclothed weight in kg	Influences the design of supporting structures

JAR 25.777 (Cockpit Controls) paragraphs c and f states that 'The controls must be located and arranged, with respect to the pilots' seats, so that there is full and unrestricted movement of each control without interference from the cockpit structure or the clothing of the minimum flight crew (established under JAR 25.1523) when any member of this flight crew from 5ft 2 inches (1575mm) to 6ft 3 inches (1905mm) in height, is seated with the seat belt and shoulder harness fastened ... The landing gear control must be located forward of the throttles and

must be operable by each pilot when seated with harness fastened'. The stature figures given in table 2 of this chapter for 5th percentile Western females, Japanese males and females are less than the lower specified limit. However, stature is not relevant for whether or not a seated crew member can reach controls. Sitting heights, functional reach and leg lengths are far more relevant.

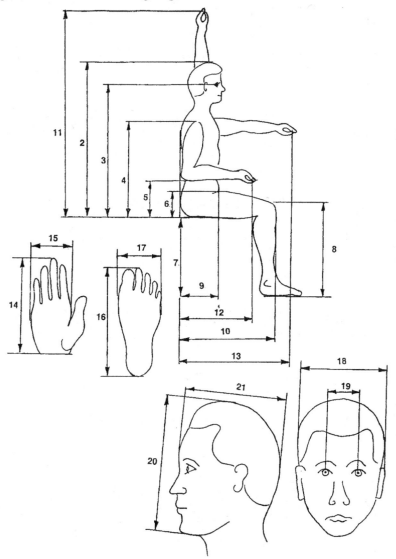

Figure 1   **Critical anthropomentric dimensions for flight deck designers (see table 1 for definitions and descriptions)**

205

Table 2
Critical anthropomentric dimensions (in mm) for flight deck designers

No.	Dimension	Western Male 5th%	95th%	Western Female 5th%	95th%	Japanese Male 5th%	95th%	Japanese Female 5th%	95th%
1	Stature	1675	1897	1543	1744	1560	1750	1450	1610
2	Sitting height	882	999	807	913	850	950	800	890
3	Sitting eye height	785	882	699	799	735	835	690	780
4	Acromial height	571	677	520	612	545	635	510	600
5	Elbow rest height	208	291	210	293	220	300	215	285
6	Thigh thickness	155	199	134	178	110	160	105	155
7	Seat height	359	443	344	430	355	435	320	385
8	Knee height	521	605	480	556	450	530	420	480
9	Stomach depth	196	291	198	288	185	255	170	240
10	Buttock to knee length	568	660	546	641	500	600	485	575
11	Vertical functional reach	1284	1481	1147	1324	1105	1265	1030	1160
12	Elbow functional reach	394	458	350	410	305	370	280	330
13	Forward functional reach	730	854	680	804	630	750	570	670
14	Hand length	181	212	170	202	165	195	150	180
15	Hand breadth	80	95	68	80	75	95	65	85
16	Foot length	248	288	222	259	230	260	210	240
17	Foot breadth	90	105	81	94	95	115	90	100
18	Head breadth	147	165	142	158	145	165	140	160
19	Interpupillary distance	58	69	54	63	59	76	57	73
20	Head height	216	297	199	230	211	261	204	237
21	Head length	189	212	179	201	170	200	160	180
22	Shoulder breadth	420	510	355	435	405	475	365	425
23	Hip breadth	310	405	300	425	280	330	270	340
24	Weight	65	103	49	82	41	74	40	63

Implementation

When the range of aircrew sizes to be accommodated, flight deck dimensional constraints, seating design, control positions and range of movements have been decided, the designer can attempt to integrate these often conflicting requirements. This is usually an iterative process that starts with dimensions that are fixed and known. This is likely to be the relative position and shape of the main structure, such as floor, windows, etc. As mentioned earlier, for the crew everything should start with the design eye position and be followed by estimating the envelope which covers the aircrew size range that is judged to be appropriate, for example the 5th percentile Japanese female to the 95th percentile Western male extrapolated to the year 2020. The designer may feel that this range is inappropriate and choose a different range of percentiles from a different population, say 10th to 90th percentile Western males. This would, of course, greatly restrict the number of aircrew who could safely use the flight deck.

If the anthropometric data given in this chapter are inappropriate, then the designer must obtain data from other sources such as AGARD surveys or books such as *Bodyspace* and apply corrections for future population growth, if this is perceived to be relevant.

When the decisions over what data should be used have been taken, the designer can map out the size range envelope. Unfortunately, the most current anthropometric data are obtained from subjects sitting or standing upright with limbs unnaturally straight. This makes the application of anthropometric data difficult to apply to 'real life' postures where the aircrew are seated in reclined adjustable seats and with limbs neither horizontal nor vertical but bent at some intermediate angle. However, the ability to bend at joints and adopt postures other than vertical or horizontal provides flexibility and allows the designer some slight ability to adapt the crew posture to fit the flight deck.

Design tools

Designers now have a number of tools at their disposal to help them 'fit' the range of aircrew into their flight deck designs. These range from pencil and paper drawings using two-dimensional mannequins (see figures 2 and 3) which now usually are computerised, to fully computerised three-dimensional dynamic man models. There are many of these man models now available. They reproduce the human body's ability to articulate and limits of joint movement can be specified. The model can even include restrictions in space and movement due to clothing. The sizes, range of postures etc. can be set to use the anthropometric and biomechanical data chosen by the designer. Use of these models will enable to designer to investigate where there may be problems with certain combinations of control movements and extremes at either end of the aircrew size range and will indicate where there may be interference between the crew and the flight deck structure or equipment.

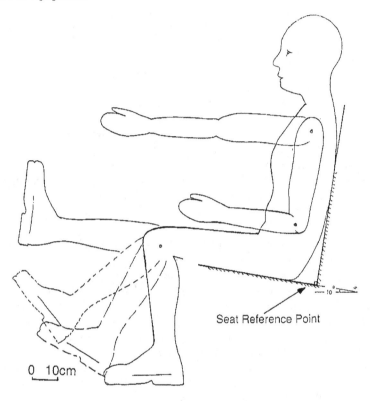

Figure 2   Mannequin for 95ᵗʰ percentile Western male

Despite the advances in computerised man models, it is essential that a full-scale space model of the flight deck, window areas and flight deck equipment is constructed for testing by a range of humans. The 'testers' should involve appropriately kitted-out aircrew who, as far as practically possible, will represent the extremes of range of the critical dimensions, e.g. sitting eye height, functional reach, etc.

It may be worth recounting a cautionary tale that demonstrates how important it is to carry out practical trials with real aircrew in appropriate clothing. Some years ago it was calculated that the use of a helmet sight would double the effectiveness of an air-to-air missile. Unfortunately, initial trials showed little advantage for the new weapon system. Upon investigation the reason was shown to be due to a lack of understanding of the effects of anthropometry and human mobility when wearing flying clothing and/or protective equipment, strapped tightly into an ejection seat and when subjected to high acceleration levels. While this example may be a little removed from the shirt sleeved environment of a civil airliner, it does demonstrate the importance of not overlooking the more mundane features than can make or break a system.

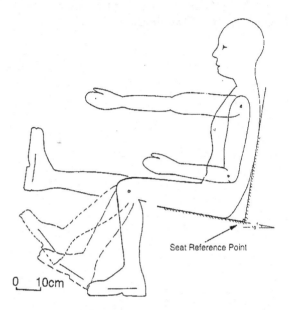

Figure 3   Mannequin for 5th percentile Western male

Concluding remarks

The successful ergonomic design of a flight deck will be a compromise between both fixed factors, due to aerodynamic and structural constraints, and variables such as the percentile range to be accommodated chosen by the designer. The flight deck designer will need to have a wide understanding of the many, often conflicting, factors that will determine if the flight deck is safe and usable.

References

Greiner, T. and Gordon, C. (1990). Secular Change of Stature of US Army Males. US Army Natick R D & C E Report TR-91/006.

Joint Aviation Authorities (1996). Joint Airworthiness Requirements (Part 25 – Large Aircraft). Hoofdorp, NL: Author.

Ted Lovesey

Lovesey, E.J. (1998). Are we getting larger? In, *Proceedings of the Global Ergonomics Conference*, Cape Town. Amsterdam: Elsevier.

Ministry of Defence (1992). *Human Factors for designers of Equipment: Defence Standard 00-25.* London: Author.

Pheasant, S.T. (1996). *Bodyspace (2nd Edition).* London: Taylor and Francis.

Turner, G.M. and Birch, C. (1996). UK Military Aircrew Anthropometric Growth Trends. DERA Report PLSD/CHS/CR96071/1.

10 Stressors in the flight deck environment

Don Harris

Introduction and overview

Not only is the flight deck the control centre of the aircraft, it also has to protect the flight crew from the hostile environment found outside the aircraft at 35,000 feet. Quite obviously, the flight deck must provide a comfortable, warm place of work in which the flight crew can work for extended periods of time but at the same time without becoming unnecessarily fatigued. The flight deck must also provide the crew with a breathable atmosphere free of toxic fumes. Perhaps less obviously, the aircraft must also offer a degree of radiological protection to the pilots. Under certain circumstances, particularly during abnormal operations, vibration by be a major concern, particularly so for the crew of helicopters (a section of the flying population that is somewhat overlooked, and I'm ashamed to say that this volume is also guilty on this count). Flight deck noise must also be kept within reasonable bounds to promote efficient communication between the crew. Finally, it almost goes without saying that it is essential to provide the pilots with sufficient illumination (when required) to perform their job safely and efficiently.

Unlike most of the other issues raised in this volume, the design parameters for these factors are actually slightly better understood and controlled than the those associated with the cognitive ergonomics of the flight deck, perhaps because they are more easily measurable and quantifiable. Unfortunately, despite this fact, for the main part they are no better described in the current airworthiness regulations. For example, part 25.771(c) of the Federal Airworthiness Regulations (FAR) simply states that 'vibration and noise characteristics of cockpit equipment may not interfere with the safe operation of the airplane'. FAR 25.773 states that 'Each pilot compartment must be free of glare and reflection that could interfere with the normal duties of flight crew ... This must be shown in day and night flight tests ...'. The physiological effects on the human body are relatively easy to describe (hence lower and upper bounds of these parameters are moderately easy to fix), however, as we shall see, their effects on the human information processing system are less easy to describe. As a result, the effects of even moderately 'abnormal' values on cognitive performance can be difficult to assess. This chapter provides a brief overview of the issues posed by temperature and humidity, atmosphere, radiological protection, noise, vibration and lighting that face the flight deck designer. The emphasis herein is firmly on a discussion of the 'recommended' operating parameters in these respects rather than the effects of grossly abnormal values on human performance.

Temperature and humidity

The crews operating on the modern flight deck are no longer faced with exposure to the elements in the same way that their counterparts flying in open cockpits in the first half of the 20th century were. As modern commercial aircraft now operate at altitudes well in excess of 30,000 feet where the temperature can be well below -50°C, perhaps this is just as well!

When it comes to a discussion of comfort and/or performance as a result of temperature and humidity it is very difficult to separate completely the effects of these two factors. Quite logically, clothing also plays an important part. As an example of how these factors interact, for a person occupied in a sedentary task (such as piloting a modern commercial aircraft), wearing light clothing, at 25°C (adjusted dry bulb temperature) they will only (generally) feel comfortable when the relative humidity is between approximately 22 and 60%. If the humidity drops below the lower figure, the person is likely to feel cool; above this figure they will generally begin to feel uncomfortably warm despite the actual air temperature remaining constant. Humidity can be expressed in several ways but is most commonly expressed as a percentage (relative humidity). There is an upper limit to the amount of water that air can hold at any given temperature. The maximum amount is when the air is fully saturated and is defined as 100% humidity. Air will hold more water at higher temperatures. Thus, air with 50% relative humidity will contain more water at higher temperatures than at lower temperatures.

Effective temperature (i.e. the thermal experience) is a product of several factors in addition to the ambient temperature, one of which is humidity. Konz and Johnson (2000) list seven factors that influence thermal comfort. Four of these are environmental components (dry bulb temperature; water vapour pressure; air velocity and radiant temperature) and two are individual factors (metabolic rate and type of clothing worn). The final factor is the length of exposure.

Comfort

The physiological effects of extreme cold are easy to quantify and need not concern us too much here in this discussion. For example, in water at a temperature of 0°C, the average human being (dressed in light, indoor clothing) is unlikely to remain conscious for more than 15 minutes and survive for more than 45 minutes. At -20°C, with a wind speed of 5 ms^{-1}, exposed skin will freeze within 30 seconds (Allan, 1988). At the other end of the scale, somewhat surprisingly, the human body can actually withstand an *air* temperature of 68°C for 15 minutes before collapsing.

Although the above figures are of some limited interest, the flight deck designer is interested in somewhat less extreme values. No flight deck designer in his or her right mind would contemplate boiling or freezing a pilot (although this is a tempting prospect on occasions ...). The flight crews need to operate within a temperature/humidity band that ensures their comfort for extended periods yet induces neither drowsiness nor fatigue. It should also be borne in mind that piloting an aircraft is now essentially a sedentary occupation which involves little physical effort, hence the pilot's physiological systems will not generate a great deal of internal heat to keep them warm in the same way that a manual labourer's will. The ambient temperature must remain high enough to ensure that the pilot's manual dexterity is not impaired but also be neither so high nor so low that their cognitive functions are adversely affected.

All discussions of optimal environmental working temperatures are of course, dependent upon the nature of the work to be performed and the clothing worn by the operator. For the purposes of this discussion it will be assumed that the flight deck crew are operating in light, indoor clothing (i.e. a shirtsleeve environment). Expressed slightly more formally, the insulation value provided by the clothing typically worn in a 'shirtsleeve' environment is approximately 0.6 clo (see Konz and Johnson, 2000).

While the airworthiness regulations (e.g. FAR 25.771) suggest that the temperature on the flight deck should remain within bounds so that the safe operation of the aircraft is not effected, this range of temperatures is not actually specified. In terms of thermal comfort, (for a sedentary person wearing clothing with an insulation value of 0.6 clo), 97% of people will be relatively comfortable between 20°C and 26°C with 50% relative humidity (ASHRAE, 1997). Parsons (1990) suggests that for a seated subject wearing indoor clothing (0.65 clo), the thermal comfort zone would be more toward the higher end of the previous values (24-28°C). As a very simple 'rule of thumb', any environment that causes an operator to develop 'goose pimples' ('goose bumps'), or makes them shiver or sweat, is not a comfortable working environment whatever they are wearing. Ramsey, Burford, Beshir and Jensen (1983) suggested that empirical evidence showed that safe working behaviour was most likely when the temperature in the working environment fell within the comfort bounds for the task.

Controlling the air temperature and humidity on the flight deck is a reasonably easy engineering problem. That is what the environmental conditioning system is for. However, the radiant heating from the sun coming through the flight deck windows is a little more difficult to control. The easiest way to control it has little

Don Harris

to do with flight deck design: simply require the crew to wear light coloured shirts! The problem with controlling the radiant heating of the pilots stems from the conflicting requirements to provide the largest flight deck windows that are possible to enhance all-round vision while simultaneously ensuring the crews' thermal comfort. FAR/JAR 25.773 requires that the 'pilots must have a sufficiently extensive, clear, and undistorted view, to enable them to safely perform any maneuvers within the operating limitations of the airplane, including taxiing takeoff, approach, and landing'. This effectively means that they must be able to see the aircraft's wing tips. However, this requires quite large windows. Tinted glass can help to reduce the transmission of radiant heat however it also distorts colours and heavy tinting is in conflict with FAR/JAR 25.773. Large, heavily-tinted sun visors, however, make a significant contribution in reducing the transmission of radiant heat to the pilot in addition to their primary purpose of reducing glare.

Physiological impairment

Some specific impairment of aspects of human performance attributable to non-optimal temperatures can be identified. For example, below 15°C (hand temperature), manual dexterity can be compromised, although the degree of impairment is also dependent upon time. Tactile sensitivity drops when hand temperature drops below 8°C. On initial exposure to a cold environment dexterity is not really impaired. However, depending upon how low the ambient temperature is, manual dexterity can deteriorate quickly (so next time that you ditch in a cold sea, make sure you do all the 'fiddly' things you need to do first and do them quickly)! While even these moderately low temperatures are not really an issue during normal operations, in the unlikely advent of a failure in the aircraft's environmental conditioning system, temperatures on the flight deck will drop. In these circumstances it is probable that the crew's ability to manipulate smaller rotary control knobs and possibly some toggle switches guarded by requiring a complex 'pull and click' action will be severely effected. Making these items larger with wider spacing will help somewhat, but not a great deal as finger strength is also compromised by the cold.

High ambient temperatures have no such effects on strength or dexterity. Indeed, unless repeated strenuous operations are required, high ambient temperatures are actually beneficial to dexterity, flexibility and strength. The biggest problem posed by high temperatures is probably associated with difficulties gripping small, high-friction controls with a smooth surface. The latest 'touch pad' cursor controls, as found on many portable computers and as an interface on some modern flight management computers, can also be compromised by sweaty fingers, as they work on the electrical conductivity of the fingertips, which is considerably reduced when they perspire. This reduces the possible control accuracy considerably.

Information processing

The effects of cold and heat (especially cold) on the human information processing system are extremely difficult to demonstrate as most psychological experiments actually require a physical response, (e.g. pressing a push button to assess a simple reaction time or manipulating a joystick in the study of psychomotor control). As a participant's responses, particularly in cold conditions, will be compromised as a result of a lack of dexterity, it is difficult to demonstrate if simply this affects performance or if there is also a performance decrement attributable to some aspect of the human information processing system.

Bensel and Santee (1997) provide a very brief overview of research investigating the effects of low ambient temperatures on cognitive performance. In general, there would seem to be little indication of any impairment even at temperatures well below 0°C. Other authors (e.g. Oborne, 1987; Sanders and McCormick, 1987) concur with this view, concluding that the results of such research into the effects of cold on the information processing system are either non-significant, ambiguous or the studies themselves are flawed in either their design or execution.

The experimental difficulties imposed by warm conditions pose far fewer difficulties to the experimenter than those posed by the cold. Grether (1973) suggested that there was some evidence to suggest that human cognitive performance and vigilance does begin to deteriorate above about 30°C. Hancock (1981), in a synthesis of studies of various different types of cognitive task found that dual tasks suffered the most in high temperatures, followed by tracking tasks. Mental tasks were least impaired, however, these analyses only demonstrated impairments above approximately 33°C (and up to 46°C). These conditions would rarely be encountered in normal conditions on a flight deck, although it needs to be noted that due to the radiant heating of the pilots, they may be significantly warmer than the ambient air temperature, so these temperatures are not totally out of the question. This is why individual air vents are valuable for local cooling as well as ventilation.

Humidity

It is also essential that the humidity on the flight deck remains relatively stable and within reasonable bounds. High levels of humidity can make a comfortable ambient temperature uncomfortable.

The FAA (1996) in their Human Factors design guide suggest that to avoid throat and nasal irritation, and dry eyes the minimum relative humidity should be at least 15%. At 21°C it is suggested that relative humidity should be approximately 45% but that this should reduce as temperature increases to maintain the effective temperature within acceptable bounds. In general, relative humidity should not exceed about 70%. High levels of humidity are often associated with stuffiness and drowsiness (Galer, 1987) and can impair the

Don Harris

evaporation of sweat (and hence bodily cooling) when ambient air temperatures become high.

Atmosphere

As noted in the introduction, it goes without saying that both passengers and crew must be provided with an atmosphere capable of supporting both their physiological requirements for survival while also simultaneously maintaining their level of alertness. Not only does this require an adequate supply of oxygen, the air provided must have suitably low levels of carbon monoxide, carbon dioxide, ozone and other toxins.

Cabin altitude

For the purposes of this section cabin air pressure will be expressed in terms of the cabin altitude (feet above mean sea level), which is the pressure altitude in the aircabin irrespective of the altitude of the aircraft itself. FAR 25 (section 25.841a) states that 'Pressurized cabins and compartments to be occupied must be equipped to provide a cabin pressure altitude of not more than 8,000 feet at the maximum operating altitude of the airplane under normal operating conditions.' Macmillan (1988) suggests that even though this is the maximum permissible cabin altitude in modern passenger carrying aircraft there is some reason to suggest that prolonged exposure may induce mild hypoxia. He suggests that there is a growing acceptance amongst manufacturers that the maximum cabin altitude that is consistent with flight safety may be in the region of 5-7,000 feet. Once cabin altitudes rise above 10,000 feet then there is a considerable impairment of the pilot's cognitive abilities to perform flight critical tasks.

Ernsting, Sharp and Harding (1988) suggest that psychomotor tasks are the most resistant to the effects of hypoxia. Performance shows little decrement until the effective cabin altitude exceeds 12-14,000 feet. Cognitive tasks involving short- or long-term memory are less resistant to the effects of altitude. In some cases a deficit may be observed at 8-10,000 feet. At altitudes as low as 5,000 feet, there is some noticeable impairment of the sensitivity of the dark-adapted eye, although as the authors note, the impairment, although detectable, is of little consequence for aviation safety. Although human performance in these various categories is impaired at the stated altitudes, it is not until somewhere between 16-24,000 feet (equivalent altitude) that unconsciousness will occur.

In the extremely rare advent of an explosive decompression the key factors are the speed of the decompression, the cabin altitude before the event and the aircraft's actual altitude at the time of the event. A rapid decompression from 8,000 feet to 40,000 feet in less than two seconds can result in the impairment of performance in 10-15 seconds and unconsciousness in 20 seconds (Macmillan,

1988). The implications for the flight deck designer from this observation are that it emphasises the speed with which the emergency oxygen supply must be available to the flight crew in such circumstances. ACJ 25.1447(c)(2), part of the interpretive material for JAR/FAR 25.1447 states that '... the design of the flight-crew masks and their stowages should be such that each mask can be placed in position and put into operation in not more than five seconds, one hand only being used, and will thereafter remain in position, both hands being free.' Less rapid losses of cabin pressure result in much longer times of usable consciousness.

Not only is it the degree of pressurisation that is important for maintaining the comfort and performance of the aircrew, it is also the pressurisation schedule (i.e. the speed at which the cabin pressure is reduced when climbing to the aircraft's cruising altitude and is increased on the descent to landing). While this schedule has no direct effect on performance, it may indirectly impair the fight crew to some extent as a result of discomfort. Macmillan (1988) notes that the cabin altitude corresponding to high rates of ascent (in the order of 5,000 to 20,000 feet per minute) are tolerated with little difficulty or discomfort. However, when descending from the cruising cabin altitude (of around 7,000 feet) to sea level, increases in cabin pressure corresponding to a 5,000 feet per minute decrease in altitude will cause discomfort in the middle ear. The rate of descent of the cabin altitude in most passenger aircraft is usually much less than this, commonly of the order of 300 feet per minute.

Carbon monoxide, carbon dioxide and ozone

In addition to the cabin altitude requirements stipulated in the airworthiness regulations, specific maximum levels for carbon monoxide, carbon dioxide and ozone are prescribed. FAR/JAR section 25.831 specifies that carbon monoxide concentrations in excess of one part in 20,000 parts of air is considered to be hazardous and that carbon dioxide concentrations during flight must not exceed 0.5 percent by volume in compartments occupied by either crewmembers or passengers. Section 25.832 of the airworthiness regulations specifies that cabin ozone concentrations must not exceed 0.25 parts per million by volume, at any time above flight level 320 or 0.1 parts per million above flight level 270.

Carbon monoxide is a major product of combustion. Low concentrations (around 20%) of carboxyhaemoglobin, the product of breathing high levels of carbon monoxide, can cause mild headaches; higher concentrations (30%) may impair vision or judgement. Ultimately high levels of carboxyhaemoglobin (around 50%) will result in severe headaches, confusion and ultimately, loss of consciousness. Such levels would only be achieved, though, after breathing carbon monoxide in air at concentrations of one part in 1,000 for over three hours.

Carbon dioxide is carried in many aircraft as either a refrigerant and/or extinguishant. At concentrations of greater than 5% (by volume) it acts as a narcotic and impairs vision and hearing. Concentrations in excess of 7% will cause unconsciousness and ultimately death (Sharp and Anton, 1988).

Ozone occurs naturally in the atmosphere, especially above 40,000 feet. At 60,000 feet (the cruising altitude of Concorde) ozone concentrations are approximately four parts per million. Ozone is an irritant to the eyes and respiratory tract at lower concentrations (in the region of one part per million) but can cause pulmonary oedema at higher concentrations (above 10 parts per million). Fortunately, ozone breaks down if heated to a reasonably high temperature (over 400°C), which is just the temperature of the bleed air from the first stages of the compressors on the engines from which the air conditioning system takes its supply. As a result, ozone concentrations in the cabin of Concorde are rarely a problem.

Many other substances may find their way into the flight deck atmosphere that are either irritants, narcotic, toxic, or a combination of all these factors! Sharp and Anton (1988) give a comprehensive list of these substances and their effects. The airworthiness regulations address these issues in their typically precise, yet generalist manner by requiring that the 'crew and passenger compartment air must be free from harmful or hazardous concentrations of gases or vapors' (FAR/JAR 25.831). Fortunately, this section of the regulations also specifies the minimum ventilation requirements for the flight deck, that under normal operating conditions, the ventilation system must provide each occupant with an airflow containing at least 0.55lbs (0.25Kg) of fresh air per minute. Such airflow helps ensure that toxic gases and vapours do not build up to significant levels on the flight deck during flight. Maintaining a steady throughput of air also helps to reduce the effective temperature on the flight deck (see previous section on temperature and humidity).

Radiological protection

Although not a major issue, the modern commercial aircraft's flight deck must offer its crew some degree of protection from naturally occurring radiation. This is of some importance to crews regularly flying trans-polar routes at high altitudes, where exposure to the naturally occurring galactic radiation is at its highest. It should be emphasised that the doses of radiation received in these circumstances are *extremely* small, however, there may be some small cumulative effects. Crew in aircraft that fly at particularly high altitudes are at the greatest danger from radiation. Concorde, which used to regularly operate at an altitude of 60,000 feet, was equipped with a radiation dose monitor in the passenger cabin that monitored both instantaneous and cumulative doses of radiation.

There are two basic types of naturally occurring ionising radiation that are of potential concern to the flight deck designer. At approximately 60,000 feet and at about 45° latitude, the background galactic radiation (emanating from the Sun and other stars) is about six milli-Sieverts/hour (mSv/h) that is about twice that encountered at 35,000 feet (Harding, 1988). To put this in context, the International Commission on Radiological Protection suggests that the maximum dose for radiological workers is 50 mSv/year. Instantaneous and cumulative doses of this type of radiation for crew of supersonic aircraft are negligible, although some airlines have a policy of re-scheduling pregnant female aircrew as a precautionary measure. The materials that the airframe is made of offer some limited shielding to higher energy radiations of this type.

The second, and potentially more dangerous form of radiation (although also fortunately a much rarer form of radiation) is that emanating from solar flares. When flying at high latitudes, a large solar flare may produce a dose of one mSv/h at 60,000 feet (Harding, 1988). It is difficult to shield the crew of an aircraft from radiation from these low-energy particles as it involves heavy and dense materials (e.g. lead) however, early warning from the radiation dose meter allows the crew to descend to a lower, safer altitude. In the whole of Concorde's operational life, though, it never activated once!

Flight deck noise

Effective and efficient communication between flight crew is essential for the safe conduct of any flight. It also goes without saying that the pilots also need to be able to hear and correctly identify any sounds generated by the aircraft warning systems. Excess background noise will interfere with both of these functions. Noise itself, especially if it is loud and/or prolonged, can also be stressful and debilitating for human performance.

Flight decks cannot be made into a silent work place. It would be almost impossible to eradicate background noise altogether. The nature of the ambient noises change with phase of flight, for example higher frequency noises generated by the window frames dominate at higher speeds: lower frequency 'rumbles' emanating from the high lift devices and the gear (especially on final approach) dominate at lower speeds. Furthermore, these noises can provide a useful source of information so perhaps should not be eliminated altogether. However, they can be controlled and their disruptive effects mitigated.

Physical properties of noise

Background noise is best described in the form of a noise spectrum, with power (loudness) plotted on 'y' axis and frequency (in bands) on the 'x' axis. Not all frequencies in noise are of the same power. In the examples given in the previous paragraph, the higher frequencies would dominate the ambient noise in the cruise whereas the lower frequencies dominate on approach. A noise spectrum analysis forms the basis for many of the noise-related remedial actions that need to be performed by the flight deck designer.

219

Perhaps the most critical frequency band that needs to be controlled is that between 600 and 4,000Hz, where the human ear is most sensitive, (the range of human hearing is about 20 to 20,000Hz). Broadly speaking, with regard to the physical characteristics of a sound there are two methods that may prevent a sound being heard by a pilot; it may be either frequency masked or amplitude masked. Frequency masking occurs when a target sound (for example some of the components of human speed or a warning sound) is masked by a component in the background noise of the same frequency. This is irrespective of the power (amplitude) of the warning sound. Amplitude masking occurs when the target sound is masked by the power of the sounds in the background noise spectrum, irrespective of their frequency.

For a sound to be heard, such as an auditory warning, it must be set at least 15dB above the corresponding frequency in the background noise spectrum. However, under no circumstances should such a sound be set at a level greater than 120dB. This is the level of pain. Warning sounds do not have to be made exceptionally loud, however, to be heard by the flight crew. Consider the simplified background noise spectrum depicted in figure 1. It can be seen that if a high frequency warning sound were used, to set it 15dB above the background noise in the higher frequency bands would require it to be set at an unacceptably high power. This would either cause physiological damage and/or increase arousal (via the startle reaction) to such a level the performance would be adversely affected. However, if a lower frequency warning signal was used it could still be set at least 15dB above the background noise (in the shaded region labelled 'auditory warning design window') but it would not be so loud as to increase arousal inappropriately or to cause physical damage. The object of a warning is to alert and orient the pilot to a problem. Increasing the pilot's stress as a product of the warning sound *is not* desirable. The following is taken from a CHIRP (confidential Human Factors incident reporting programme) report.

> *'I was flying in a Jetstream at night when my peaceful reverie was shattered by the stall audio warning, the stick shaker and several warning lights. The effect was exactly NOT what was intended: I was frightened numb for several seconds and drawn off instruments trying to work out how to cancel the audio/visual assault rather than taking what should be instinctive actions... The combined assault is so loud and bright that it impossible to talk to the other crew member and action is invariably taken to cancel the cacophony before getting on with the actual problem.'*

The latter point in this excerpt is worth reiterating. When a warning sound is triggered the pilot's instincts should be to deal with the problem that resulted in the warning sound being activated, not to deal with the problem caused by the warning sound itself!

Composing a warning tone of at least four different frequencies (in a chord-like structure) should also ensure that at least one or two frequencies are detected by a pilot even when some of the components are frequency masked by the ambient noise. This is particularly important when it is recalled that the background noise on a flight deck changes with phase of flight. Use of such a chord-like structure also aids in the discrimination of one warning sound from another.

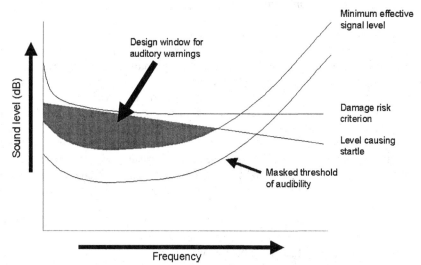

Figure 1 **The design window methodology for the definition of the appropriate location of warning tones in the noise spectrum (from Coleman, Graves, Collier, Golding, Nicholl, Simpson, Sweetland and Talbot, 1984)**

From a physical and physiological perspective it can be seen that sound deadening on the flight deck should ensure that under no circumstances should the ambient noise on a flight deck exceed 120dB at any frequency. Background frequencies in the range where human speech occurs should receive particular attention.

The effects of noise on the human are far more complex that can be described simply in terms of its physical properties. For example, the apparent 'loudness' of a noise does not equate to its power (sound pressure level) measured in decibels (dB) as the ear is more sensitive at some frequencies than at others. The 'phon' is the unit of perceived loudness. A 60dB tone at 1000Hz is defined as having a loudness of 60 phons. However, a 65dB tone at 50Hz produces a perceived loudness of only 40 phons. Unfortunately, the problem with the phon unit, is that it does not describe the relative loudness of sound. A 40 phon sound is not twice as loud as a 20 phon sound. This resulted in the development of the son. As a rough guide 40 phon = one son: every 10 extra phons doubles the number of sons (e.g. 50 phon = two son; 60 phon = four son). With this unit two sons is perceived to be twice as loud as one son. Just to confuse things a little further, though, it is sound

Don Harris

pressure that impairs hearing but perceived loudness that causes annoyance and psychologically impairs performance.

Background noise and communication

Clear communication on the flight deck is absolutely imperative for flight safety, however before the effects of noise in this context can be discussed, it is necessary to describe a further concept in the measurement of multi-frequency noise. From the discussions in the previous section centring on the use of a noise spectrum analysis, it can be seen that you cannot truly separate the power of a sound from its frequency. However, for general measurement purposes a unit is needed that can describe the level of noise in general. This led the development of the dBA (decibels on the A scale). This is now taken to be a worldwide standard. The dBA mathematically weights and combines noise measurements in several bands to produce a composite measure of noise. Greatest weight is given to sound in the 1000-4000Hz bands, and least to sounds in the very low (up to 125Hz) frequencies.

Kryter (1970) observed that speech (male or female) predominantly occurs in the 400-500Hz band, although it also includes components right up to 5,000Hz. Kryter (1985) suggested that if the background noise in an office exceeds 55 dBA, use of items such as a telephone could become slightly difficult. If noise levels exceeded 63dBA a raised voice was required to communicate with someone 1-2m away (to put this in perspective the typical distance between the centres of the seats on a commercial aircraft is in the region of 1.3m). At this distance, once the noise level exceeds 72dBA, communication in anything less than a shout becomes impossible (Peterson and Gross, 1972). Using the figures derived by these authors for speech interference levels, it can be concluded that unassisted communication on the flight deck becomes inadvisable once the background noise level exceeds about 55dBA, a figure that agrees nicely with that suggested earlier by Kryter.

Noise attenuating headsets are commonly used when the background noise levels are particularly high in the part of the frequency spectrum occupied by human speech. However, these are not a universal panacea to the problems that flight deck noise imposes on communication. Several reports of in-flight incidents have been reported to NASA ASRS (aviation safety reporting system) where pilots have failed to hear auditory warnings when wearing a noise-attenuating headset. The head set attenuated the auditory warning played over the speakers on the flight deck, hence it never reached the pilot's ears!

Annoyance effects of noise

The annoyance associated with noise is not simply just a product of its acoustic factors. It is also a product of context and the personality of the listener. Sperry (1978) separated the annoying effects of noise into two categories: acoustic and

222

non-acoustic factors (although it should be noted that these factors are associated with the environmental annoyance of noise). The acoustic factors included the sound level (and fluctuations in sound level), frequency (and fluctuations in frequency), duration, spectral complexity, and the risetime of the noise. In the context of the flight deck, the non-acoustic factors of interest included the listener's past experience with the noise, their activity, the predictability of the noise, the necessity of the noise and their personality. Basically, noises that the flight crew perceive as being a product of poor design (and hence avoidable) will be regarded as more annoying that noises regarded to be unavoidable. An example that perhaps falls into the former category is the loud, high frequency noise generated by the windscreen surrounds in some types of commercial when in high-speed cruising flight. Unfortunately, Kryter and Pearsons (1966) also observed that higher frequency noise (over 2,000Hz) was also more likely to be annoying!

Noise and human information processing

Although there is some controversy in the scientific literature, most laboratory studies would seem to suggest that high levels of noise impair human performance. The controversies tend to centre on the methodologies employed in the studies and arguments tend to be concerned with *what* caused the performance decrement rather than *if* a performance decrement was actually observed (e.g. Poulton, 1976). While these disagreements may be of scientific interest, for the purposes of flight deck design it is enough to know that high levels of ambient noise are detrimental. There are, however, some commonalties across the findings. Poulton (1977), suggests that high levels of ambient noise mask the verbal rehearsal of items in the phonological loop component of working memory (Baddeley, 1986), hence the interference often observed in these conditions in a letter and/or digit short-term recall task. Put another way, 'you can't hear yourself think'. Given the nature of such things as air traffic control clearances, this is of some concern. Indeed any impairment of the pilot's working memory, their 'central executive' responsible for all aspects of conscious thought and decision making, is not desirable. Fortunately, however impairment of this nature is only really evident above 70-80 dBA (which is about the level of moderately heavy traffic). However, this level of sound can be reached on a flight deck on occasions.

Broadbent (1976) also described the effects of high levels of noise on attention. He reported that there was a funnelling of attention onto only the most task-relevant information when performing in a noisy environment. On occasions, this may result in critical signals presented elsewhere being missed. Broadbent attributed this phenomenon to over arousal caused by this environmental stressor. Hockey (1970) also observed that in the presence of noise, certain aspects of a task that were perceived to be of higher importance were given more attention that those aspects regarded as being of lower importance.

Unfortunately, it has also been observed in some experiments that load, randomly fluctuating noises can increase vigilance in monotonous monitoring tasks and that loud noise can also counteract the effects of a lack of arousal caused by loss of sleep. These are two problems commonly encountered by pilots to which loud noises may offer a solution! It is probably best, though, to rapidly gloss over these findings and conclude that in general, there are more negative effects to high levels of noise on the flight deck that there are positive effects.

Vibration

Vibration is perhaps the most insidiously dangerous of the physical stressors on the flight deck (perhaps with the exception of a lack of a breathable atmosphere)! Fortunately, for the fixed-wing pilot, particularly those flying large turbofan powered aircraft, vibration is usually not an issue of great importance, as vibration levels in the critical frequencies, are minimal. However for smaller aircraft, (particularly those with a high wing loading) and when operating aircraft in abnormal circumstances, there still remain times when vibration should be considered in the design of the pilots' working environment. Turbulence can be considered to be a form of low, frequency, high amplitude vibration, something with which all pilots will be familiar. Initial flight trials of the (now cancelled) BAC TSR.2 strike aircraft showed that in certain flight regimes, particularly when the landing gear was lowered on final approach, the amplitude and frequency of the vibration resulting from aerodynamic buffeting, was such that the pilots could neither see ahead nor read the instrumentation in the cockpit. Vibration was also implicated in the accident involving a Boeing 737-400 at Kegworth, UK. In this accident the port engine shed a small section of fan blade from the primary stage of the turbofan. This resulted in major vibrations being transmitted through the airframe making reading the displays on the flight deck difficult.

Stott (1988) describes the major sources of the more predictable vibrations that may affect the pilot. In order of increasing (vibration) frequency, turbulence is usually of the order of one Hz, although it is usually of high amplitude (displacement). The helicopter pilot may typically be exposed to a four Hz vibration emanating from the rotational frequency of the main rotor. Associated with this there is usually a second critical frequency, the blade pass frequency. This is the main rotor RPM multiplied by the number of blades in the main rotor head. The blade pass frequency is typically in the region of 15-20 Hz. The pilot of a high performance fighter aircraft with rigid wings and wing/fuselage join (in comparison to a large commercial aircraft) may encounter vibrations in the 8-20 Hz range during high 'g' manoeuvres. The pilot of a piston-engined aircraft may be exposed to vibrations resulting from the rotational frequency of the engine's crankshaft (which is typically somewhere between 2,400 and 3,600 RPM), which corresponds to a vibration of between 40-60 Hz. The corresponding frequencies from a turbine engine are much higher, usually between 130-230 Hz. If the aircraft is a typical twin-engined turboprop, the blade pass frequency of the propellers will be approximately 100 Hz (assuming three blades on each propeller) although vibrations of much lower frequencies may be produced as a result of harmonics resulting from the two propellers turning at slightly different speeds.

Although it is the frequency of the vibration that may cause various parts of the human body to resonate, it is the acceleration associated with these vibrations that is actually damaging to the human body. All vibrations have both a frequency and an amplitude component. Assuming that the frequency remains constant, higher accelerations will be associated with larger vibrational amplitudes. Fortunately, as frequency increases, amplitude tends to decrease! For the most part, the ride in a commercial aircraft is relatively smooth. Measurements taken in a variety of aircraft show that the typical range of accelerations (expressed as the root mean square value of 'g') varies between about 0.005 and 0.055 rms 'g'. In comparison, the typical range of values for a car is 0.065-0.075 rms 'g' and for a bus, 0.035-0.10 rms 'g' (Stephens, 1979).

Vibration is transmitted through contact of the human body with a vibrating surface, most typically the pilot's seat. Most frequencies are not of great concern, however, the key frequencies are those at which the body (or parts of it) resonate, that is when the amplitude of the body *to which* the vibration is transmitted is greater than the amplitude of the vibration of the object *from which* it was transmitted. The human body as a whole has a natural resonant frequency of approximately five Hz. However, as humans are made of many different types of tissue of different densities, all of which resonate at slightly different frequencies, it is also important to consider the effects of various frequencies of vibration on specific parts of the body.

In the following, the effects of vibration will be considered under three broad headings; its effects on the limbs, and hence on the manipulation of controls; its effects on visual acuity, and hence its implications for the design of displays; and finally the effects of vibration on human information processing.

Vibration and the use of controls

When considering the use of controls, especially when seated, there are various key frequencies of concern for a variety of reasons.

The first frequency band of concern occurs between two-six Hz (although it should be noted that all the frequencies quoted are approximate; the actual resonant peaks will differ from person-to-person depending upon such things as their tissue density, the length of their limbs, etc.). In this region it is difficult to control an outstretched, unsupported arm. As a result, any manipulation of the small controls, for example those on the glareshield or overhead panel, is going to be considerably impaired. Between four-eight Hz, control inputs using a joystick, even when the forearm is supported, (as in the sidestick control inceptors in the

Don Harris

Airbus 320/330/340 series aircraft), are impaired. However, this only really becomes a problem when the acceleration associated with the vibration exceeds approximately 0.20 'g', which is not particularly common in civil aircraft (Hornick, 1973). Control using a large control-column type of control inceptor is less likely to be affected at these frequencies as a result of the damping effect of the relatively large mass that the pilot is holding. The disadvantage of this latter type of control arrangement, though, is that it is likely that the pilot's arms will be more outstretched than when using a sidestick controller, making him/her more susceptible to the negative effects of vibration in the lower frequencies. In this same four-eight Hz frequency band the muscles in the leg are also affected, which has obvious implications for inputs to the rudders (Stott, 1988).

Two further frequency bands of concern lie between approximately four-five Hz and 10-12 Hz. Both the head and the shoulder girdle resonate in these frequencies. At the lower frequency, the amplification of the vibration is greater at the head than the shoulders and vice versa in the higher frequency band (Rowlands, 1977). At approximately five Hz, the amplification ratio of any vibration at the shoulder girdle may be of the order of three times the magnitude of the input. Again, this has implications for control inputs to the primary flight controls.

Careful design of the pilot's seat to reduce the transmission of critical vibration frequencies from the airframe to the pilot and the provision of armrests (for example when using a sidestick controller) is essential to optimise control performance. However, somewhat counter-intuitively, matters may be made worse if the pilot straps in more tightly when turbulence is encountered, especially if they tighten their shoulder straps. At certain frequencies, this may actually increase the transmission of vibrations to the shoulder girdle, making control more difficult in these circumstances.

Vibration and viewing displays

Visual performance may be degraded by vibrating either the object alone, the observer alone, or both. If the object alone is vibrated, at frequencies below one Hz the eye is able to track the target without problem as long as the amplitude of the displacement of the object does not exceed 40°/second at the retina. This tracking ability begins to decrease noticeably between two-four Hz. At higher frequencies than this the eye makes no attempt to track the object and instead the eye remains stationary and the target becomes blurred on the retina. If the observer is vibrated and the object to be observed remains static, reasonable visual acuity may be maintained up to about eight Hz as a result of the vestibulo-occular reflex. At these frequencies the head tends to 'nod' (pitch) as much as resonate in the vertical plane. The vestibulo-occular reflex counteracts this pitching motion of the head and helps to keep the eye focussed on the stationary object in response to such motions. At higher frequencies than this vision begins to be compromised

226

Stressors in the flight deck environment

by the effects of resonances of the head (as described in the previous sub-section), the eye-orbit complex and the eye itself. Concerning the resonant frequencies associated with the eye, there are two different peaks that are primarily responsible for inhibiting the use of visual displays. Below approximately 20 Hz the eye-orbit socket pair resonates. This begins to become damped above 20 Hz, however commencing at about 30Hz the eyeball itself begins to resonate. This reaches a maximum somewhere in the region of 70Hz (Stott, 1980).

Unfortunately, little can be done directly to obviate the effects of vibration on vision other than make the elements on the display larger. The best option available to the designer probably lies in designing the pilot's seating to minimise the transmission of the vibrations to the pilot's body. Fortunately, objects in the distance (for example those in the visual scene external to the flight deck) are less affected by vibration than are those nearer to the observer. For objects located at optical infinity, there is no apparent motion of the image on the retina resulting from translational displacements of the head (Griffin, 1976).

Human information processing

The effects of vibration on information processing are difficult to assess as they are often confounded by the effects of experimental participants having to recognise a stimulus and then respond to it by making some sort of motor output. The vibration usually compromises the perception of the visual stimulus material and the speed and/or accuracy of any associated outputs. It is difficult to assess if any performance deficit is a product of the mechanical properties of the human body or of the human information processing system.

Several laboratory studies have shown that vibrating subjects has little effect on their reaction times while they are being vibrated but often their performance declines after the vibration has stopped. Hornick and Lefritz (1966), in a simulated military terrain-following flight task in which volunteer pilots flew a four hour mission while experiencing vibrational frequencies between 1-12 Hz and associated accelerations up to 0.2g, observed that after 2½ hours reaction times were almost four times longer compared to a control condition. Huddleston (1964) demonstrated that mental arithmetic tasks were unaffected at vibrations of up to 3.5 Hz, but performance decrements were evident between 4.8-16 Hz. However, in this study participants experienced accelerations in the region of 0.5g, much higher than would be expected in an aircraft. It has even been suggested that vibration at frequencies between 3.5-6 Hz may increase the arousal level (and hence vigilance) of participants engaged in a prolonged boring task, although it may not be a good idea to mention this to most pilots who regularly fly trans-Atlantic or trans-Pacific flights!

To summarise, it is difficult to establish if vibration at the levels or frequencies likely to be experienced by pilots of civil airliners will have any detrimental effect on their cognitive performance while flying.

227

Don Harris

Illumination

The illumination problems faced by the flight deck designer are very different to those faced by the Ergonomist working in a traditional work setting. In the traditional working environment the problem is illuminating the work piece (be it a machine tool or a piece of paper) in such a way as to ensure that the work can be accomplished to the standard required without undue discomfort or strain on the part of the operator. The problem on the flight deck is different. The modern electro-optical flight deck displays are self-illuminating. These do not pose a great problem. The main problem centres on such issues as providing local illumination for completing the mound of paperwork that accompanies every flight, reading handbooks and manuals, and inspecting maps and charts. All this must be accomplished on a darkened flight deck while simultaneously ensuring that the pilot's night vision remains unaffected. As a secondary problem, smaller advisory (or warning) lights around the flight deck should also not destroy the pilot's night vision (although this is less of a problem if the 'quiet dark' cockpit philosophy is adopted).

A treatise about the physiology and anatomy of the eye and the mechanisms of night vision are outside the bounds of this chapter. However, it is suffice to say that if a fully dark adapted eye is exposed to a moderately bright light even for a fraction of a second, it can be up to 40 minutes before the eye becomes fully dark adapted once again (Grandjean, 1969). On immediate exposure to such a bright light the eye's sensitivity (ability to detect feint objects) will decrease to approximately 20% of its fully dark-adapted level. Above 0.001 lux the eye primarily uses cone receptors in the eye that are colour sensitive and provide high visual acuity (as they are all grouped in the central, foveal region. Below 0.0001 lux the eye uses the rods, which are, more sensitive to light but do not provide colour vision. The two sets of visual receptors show peak sensitivities at different wavelengths. More importantly, the rods in the eye are insensitive to wavelengths above 650 nm while the cones remain sensitive to light up to a wavelength of approximately 760 nm. By exploiting this wavelength window between 650-760nm (at the red end of the spectrum) either by providing illuminating light with a wavelength in this region or providing goggles that filter out all other wavelengths, it is possible to maintain foveal vision using the cone receptors while simultaneously maintaining the dark adapted vision in the rods.

Many flight decks provide the pilots with small reading lamps equipped with an optional red filter, that allow pilots to complete paperwork while maintaining their dark adaptation. While this may seem desirable, the uses for such illumination are strictly limited. Red light is adequate for completing paperwork printed in dark (blue or black) inks on white paper, however such lighting makes colour discrimination almost impossible. Any pilot who has attempted to navigate at night using a red light in the cockpit and a typical low-level chart will attest to the fact that many of the map's features, especially those printed in pink or red, can become unreadable depending upon the precise wavelength of the light.

Opinions vary about the practical effectiveness of the provision of red lighting to preserve dark adaptation. The FAA (1996) Human Factors Design Guide recommends the use of red lighting or low-level white lighting to preserve night vision. In contrast to this view, Brennan (1988) suggests that 'in most instances cone acuity is imperative and the disadvantages of red cockpit lighting systems in colour discrimination, the reduction in accomodative clues and the distortion in the relative luminance of coloured objects far outweigh any theoretical advantage' (pp. 343-344). Furthermore, it is not possible to provide low-level white light of sufficient intensity to allow reading paperwork while still maintaining dark adaptation. The minimum recommended level of illumination for such work is 325 lux (or 540 lux for prolonged reading), with a recommended level of 755 lux.

Perhaps the most important design criteria for providing illumination on the flight deck is to ensure that all the self-illuminated displays on the flight deck are equipped with the ability to adjust their brightness. Furthermore the pilot's eyes should be shielded from direct sources of bright white light and care should be taken that the opportunities uncontrolled reflections are minimised.

References

American Society of Heating, Refrigeration and Air Conditioning Engineers (1997). *Handbook of Fundamentals*. Atlanta: Author.

Baddeley, A.D. (1986). *Working Memory*. Oxford: Oxford University Press.

Bensel, C.K. and Santee, W.R. (1997). Climate and clothing. In, G. Salvendy (Ed.) *Handbook of Human Factors and Ergonomics (2nd Edition)*. New York: John Wiley, pp. 909-934.

Brennan, D.H. (1988). Vision in flight. In, J. Ernsting and P. King (Eds.) *Aviation Medicine (2nd Edition)*. Butterworths: London. pp. 339-352.

Broadbent, D.E. (1976). Noise and the details of experiments: a reply to Poulton. *Applied Ergonomics, 7*, 231-235.

Coleman, G.J., Graves, R.J., Collier, S.G., Golding, D., Nicholl, A.G. McK., Simpson, G.C., Sweetland, K.F. and Talbot, C.F. (1984). *Communication in noisy environments*. Technical Memo TM/84/1. Edinburgh: Institute of Occupational Medicine.

Ernsting, J., Sharp, G.R. and Harding, R.M. (1988). Hypoxia and hyperventilation. In, J. Ernsting and P. King (Eds.) *Aviation Medicine (2nd Edition)*. London; Butterworths. pp. 45-59.

Federal Aviation Administration (1996). *Human Factors Design Guide (Version 1.0)*. William J. Hughes Technical Center, Arlington VA: Author.

Federal Aviation Administration (1999). *Federal Aviation Regulations: Part 25 – Airworthiness Standards: Transport Category Airplanes (Amendment 25-98)*. Washington DC: Author.

Galer, I.A.R. (1987). *Applied Ergonomics Handbook (2nd Edition)*. London: Butterworths.

Don Harris

Grandjean, E. (1969). *Fitting the task to the man.* London: Taylor and Francis.
Grether, W.F. (1973). Human performance at elevated environmental temperatures. *Aerospace Medicine, 44*, 747-755.
Griffin, M.J. (1976). Eye motion during whole-body vertical vibration. *Human Factors, 18*, 601-606.
Hancock, P. (1981). The limitation of human performance in extreme heat conditions. In, *Proceedings of the Human Factors Society.* Santa Monica: Human Factors Society. pp. 74-78.
Hockey, G.R.J. (1970). Effect of loud noise on attentional selectivity. *Quarterly Journal of Experimental Psychology, 22*, 28-36.
Hornick, R. (1973). Vibration. *Bioastronautics data book (second edition).* NASA Technical Report SP 3006. NASA: Washington DC.
Hornick, R.J. and Lefritz, N.M. (1966). Astudy and review of human response to prolonged random vibration. *Human Factors, 8*, 481-492.
Huddleston, J.H.F. (1964). *Human performance and behaviour in vertical sinusoidal vibration.* Institute of Aviation Medicine report 303. RAF/IAM: Farnborough.
Joint Aviation Authorities (2000). *Joint Airworthiness Requirements (Change 15): Part 25 – Large Aeroplanes.* Hoofdorp: Joint Aviation Authorities.
Konz, S. and Johnson, S. (2000). *Work Design: Industrial Ergonomics (5th Edition).* Scottsdale, AZ: Holcomb Hathaway.
Kryter, K.D (1970). *The effects of noise on man.* New York, NY: Academic Press.
Kryter, K.D. (1985). *The effects of noise on man (2nd edition).* New York: Academic Press.
Kryter, K.D. and Pearsons, K.S. (1966). Some effects of spectrum content and duration on perceived noise level. *Journal of the Acoustical Society of America, 39*, 451-464.
Macmillan, A.J.F. (1988). The pressure cabin. In, J. Ernsting and P. King (Eds.) *Aviation Medicine (2nd Edition).* London; Butterworths. pp. 112-126.
Oborne, D. (1987). *Ergonomics and Work (2nd Edition).* London: John Wiley.
Parsons, K. (1990). Human response to thermal environments. In, J.R. Wilson and E.N. Corlett (Eds.) *Evaluation of human work.* London: Taylor and Francis.
Peterson, A.P.G. and Gross, E. (1972). *Handbook of noise measurement.* Concord, MA: GenRad Inc.
Poulton, E.C. (1970). *Environment and human efficiency.* Springfield, IL: C.T. Thomas.
Poulton, E.C. (1976). Continuous noise interferes with work by masking auditory feedback and inner speech. *Applied Ergonomics, 7*, 79-44.
Poulton, E.C. (1977). Continuous intense noise masks auditory feedback and inner speech. *Psychological Bulletin, 84*, 977-1001.

Poulton, E.C. (1978). Increased vigilance with vertical vibration at 5Hz: an alerting mechanism. *Applied Ergonomics, 9*, 73-76.

Ramsey, J., Burford,C., Beshir, M. and Jensen, R. (1983). Effects of workplace thermal conditions on safe work behavior. *Journal of Safety Research, 14*, 105-114.

Rowlands, G.F. (1977). *The transmission of vertical vibration to the heads and shoulders of seated men.* Royal Aircraft Establishment Technical Report 77088: Ministry of Defence: London.

Sanders, M.S. and McCormick, E.J. (1987). *Human Factors in Engineering and Design (6th Edition).* New York: MgGraw Hill.

Sharp, G.R and Anton, D.J. (1988). Toxic gases and vapours in flight. In, J. Ernsting and P. King (Eds.) *Aviation Medicine (2nd Edition).* London; Butterworths. pp. 127-135.

Sperry, W. (1978). Aircraft and airport noise control. In, D. Lipscomb and A. Taylor (Eds.), *Noise control: Handbook of principles and practices.* New York, NY: Van Norstrand Reinhold.

Stephens, D. (1979). Developments in ride quality criteria. *Noise Control Engineering, 12*, 6-14.

Stott, J.R.R. (1980). Mechanical resonance of the eyeball. In, *Proceedings of the human response to vibration seminar.* University of Wales, Swansea. October, 1980.

Section Two
Flight Deck Evaluation

11 Evaluating the flight deck

Peter G.A.M. Jorna and Piet J. Hoogeboom

Introduction and overview

The flight deck or cockpit, depending on size and type of the aircraft, is a safety critical working area where the 'brains' of the flight crew, or the individual pilot, are connected with the sensors, controls and when applicable, the automated 'brains' of the aircraft. The designs and features of the various pieces of 'installed equipment' should all allow the human pilot or crew to perform their duties safely, efficiently and preferably with some comfort.

The majority of contemporary accidents involve a so-called 'human factor' as either a direct cause or a contributing factor. Apparently, there are problems with human performance or human behaviour that were not detected or highlighted by the evaluation and certification methods presently in use.

Human error as an example, is seen as a menace to aviation safety, but the paradox is that it is an integral and common element of normal and very often efficient human behaviour. For accidents to be attributed to human behaviour, its sufficient to know only the end state or *result* of the associated human actions. However, similar behaviour can lead to different outcomes depending on the situation or context. Therefore, safety enhancements can only be achieved by improved management or control over the production *process* i.e. the background and context of a particular action, leading to that state if not corrected. An example: typing errors in medical documents are dangerous, so one could opt to use a spelling software tool. The result can be a (more) correct spelling, but it is very likely that many more typing errors are going to be made during the process of filling the document since users are going to rely on the correction process.

Aviation is technically very safe and the evaluations and testing methods for aircraft design and construction came a long way. They are of the highest standards. If aviation is to continue its success as a prime and safe means of transportation, it is of paramount importance that the human factor oriented testing and evaluation methods are improved to similar standards. If successful, valuable

Peter G.A.M. Jorna and Piet J. Hoogeboom

information on human vulnerabilities in relation to design and working context
can be gathered before the accidents occur.

As the flight deck essentially connects the hardware with the life ware, it's
commonly referred to as 'user interface' or 'human-machine interface'. Such an
interface includes technical features to be reviewed on their impact and quality of
interaction with the non-technical part, the flight crew. In this chapter we will
focus on evaluation methods that address the latter (human) factor. Technical
evaluations naturally focus on characteristics and performance specifications of
specific pieces of equipment or 'boxes' that serve a particular 'function' aboard
the aircraft, while the human factor is on the flight deck to perform 'tasks' using
more than one piece of equipment, either in isolation or together. Evaluating the
acceptability, endurability and quality of performance of such tasks, is the topic of
this chapter.

Purpose of the evaluation

New capabilities of equipment installed on a flight deck improve the technical and
operational capabilities of the aircraft, but also change the tasks and duties to be
performed by the crew. It's a well-established fact that flying an aircraft equipped
with various forms of 'automation' requires different skills as compared with
flying more conventional aircraft. Skills are becoming more related to system
management and/or system monitoring. Automated systems can take a lot of work
out of the hands of the pilot, as long they work correctly and are used for purposes
as intended by the designer. If not, their 'handling qualities' become a matter of
concern for safety just like unpredictable handling qualities of the aircraft. Tools,
in the form of man-machine systems should be practical and 'well-designed' or fit
for their purpose, but operational experience has learned that they can be quite
cumbersome and difficult to use. Subsequently, more training is required to master
all the intricacies of the equipment involved or more complex procedures have to
be introduced that limit the operational use of some (complex) functions.
Complexity, training and detailed procedures limit performance and increase
costs. Flight deck equipment and avionics nowadays constitute a more than
significant portion of the total price to be paid for the aircraft and they should not
only be safe and effective but also practical to work with, especially under
demanding conditions.

The purpose of the various evaluations is therefore to provide data and/or
insights in support of effective decision making on the design, selection and/or
operation of such equipment during the life cycle of an aircraft. But which parties
are, or should be interested in actually performing the evaluations and do they
need similar techniques?

236

Sponsor of the evaluation

Manufacturers who want to sell aircraft and equipment need evaluations to benchmark their products against regulations and/or competitors. The latter process is quite normal in most commercial businesses i.e. automotive industry, but especially in aviation there is the complicating factor in the form of regulatory rules that require 'evidence' in order to decide if certain flight deck features can be allowed yes or no. If there is no knowledge base for such a decision of compliance, evaluations will be in need to ascertain that the selected or proposed design is in compliance with the rules.

Customers on the other side, buy or equip (second hand) aircraft and have a range of models and types to select from. An evaluation can help them in deciding which aircraft or system to buy. So, there are multiple reasons for performing some form of flight deck or cockpit evaluations:

- Intention to buy an aircraft, necessitating a comparison between aircraft.
- Intention to sell an aircraft, benchmarking it against others.
- Designing upgraded products for retrofit application in existing aircraft.
- Assessing training requirements.
- Providing evidence for certification of innovative pilot-equipment interfaces.
- Improving regulatory material.

The background and interests of these sponsors will clearly differ with respect to the types of questions that need to be answered. As a result, the focus on topics to be evaluated can also differ. As the flight deck essentially connects the hardware with the live ware, it is commonly referred to as the 'user interface' or 'man-machine interface'. So, an evaluation will most often include both a technical and a non-technical factor for review. In this chapter we will focus on the latter (human) factor.

Topics for evaluation

If one consults colleagues, experts or searches the open literature in order to get a list of all relevant Human Factors topics to consider, the result is very likely to be an overwhelming number of issues and buzz words. Examples of typical topics are display clutter, pilot workload, human error, stress, situational awareness, cognitive demands, complacency, automation issues, team work, power distance, team resource management etc. etc. Is it possible to evaluate for all such issues independently and if so, how do you know that everything critical has been covered? A most important topic for any evaluation is obviously, safety, but that intention is more easily said than exactly defined. The use of probabilities of technical failure can be established with some accuracy when physics are involved but probabilities are much more difficult to estimate reliably when humans come into play. Human performance is variable in its nature and errors are a fact of daily life. Without errors it would be difficult to learn anything at all. User related organisations such as the airlines or pilot unions, focus on the qualities of a flight deck as a working environment for humans. The regulators wants to establish at least 'minimal standards', for instance on the allowable 'workload' levels. It is well known that workload and performance variations are interrelated, although not linear as humans compensate with effort to maintain performance until their limits are reached. Ideally, one would like to have a single comprehensive index or a single measure for flight deck workload. It has often been the strategy in applied research to find or design such a 'unique measure' for topics like workload or Situational Awareness. But in most cases such container types of topics relate to wording that is known in psychology as a 'construct'. Personality is an example of a construct that is multi-facetted. In order to achieve easy communication on a very complicated multidimensional issue, a terminology is used that comfortably describes or depicts the issue of interest, i.e. it is 'constructed'.

The term 'workload' is also used to describe several things:

- It describes a certain characteristic of a task without any specific reference to the performer (i.e. it is defined as a stimulus property like task complexity).
- It is also used to index the performance efficiency of a particular individual (i.e., it is defined as some human response). Learning and practice serve to reduce individual workload, as performance is improved without an apparent change in the physical or objective appearance of the task.
- Workload is used as a composite of all imaginable aspects that contribute to the 'burden' of work. Both physical and mental factors contribute. Composite mental load has many origins like the task (responsible for 'mental task load'), or the environment (which generates 'emotional load' by being dangerous.) Other psychological factors like 'time pressure' or 'responsibility' can impose additional difficulties by their requirement to perform under emotionally taxing or stressful circumstances.

The term 'workload' therefore refers to an extensive problem area addressing the overall efficiency of human performance when working under various conditions, with different tasks and by various humans differing in capabilities, aptitude or state of fatigue etc. Were individual brain functions like human memory or perception the focus of psychological research, after introducing 'workload', it was the interplay between these systems that became crucial for understanding the complexities of humans at work (Jorna, 1991). Further specifications are required to define the relevant characteristics constructing either 'the demand' or the 'capability' side of the problem. It is therefore often helpful to use the term 'task load' for the external tasks that have to be performed and 'individual workload or effort' to denote the possible impact on a particular person in a particular working context, indicating that different levels of 'fit' can exist. The same landing task performed by either an instructor or by a student-pilot can result in quite different levels of (individual) workload. They may also respond quite differently on 'stressors' in the environment as bad weather or busy air traffic. The pilot workload topic is a good example resembling a construct look-alike in the aviation context. Finding a single best measure proved impossible and pursuing such a strategy for other constructs, i.e. 'situational awareness' is comparable with finding the Holy Grail and therefore not very realistic.

Task(s) or device based evaluation

A focus on the Human factor has clear implications for any approach for setting up an evaluation method. Technical evaluations naturally seem to focus on specific equipment or 'boxes' on the aircraft that serve a function, while humans are on board to perform certain 'tasks' operating more than one piece of equipment. It is now increasingly recognised that the flight deck serves as a working environment that should be consistent in basic ergonomic details such as similar switch operations etc. Manufacturers developed *flight deck design philosophies* such as the 'dark cockpit' where everything is ok until some light flashes up. Naturally, the crew has the 'task' to detect the lights and to check if the non-lit lights are still OK, or there should be a system doing that....

In our experience of working in a multi-disciplinary research laboratory, the human task concept led to consistent controversy between aeronautical engineers, automation researchers and various sorts of behavioural scientists. *'What do you do with a task description? What is the right format? Is there a right format? What is the use of a human anyway? Is it not sufficient for me to state that the task in question is to simply operate my piece of equipment?'*

In many cases, the design was based on technological challenges and the strive for enhancing aircraft capabilities. It was only until advents such as *human-centred design* strategies and *user oriented software* development, that task analysis was appreciated as a essential tool or a design interface to define goals, information requirements, dialogues etc.

Table 1
Design strategies and automation philosophies

Design strategies	Automation philosophies
Remove tasks	'Automatic'
Tailor tasks	'Adaptable'
Intervene with tasks	'Adaptive'
Change tasks	'Advanced'

Peter G.A.M. Jorna and Piet J. Hoogeboom

Tasks play a crucial role in various types of *automation philosophy* as illustrated in table 1.

In a task-based approach for evaluating flight decks the focus is not on particular topics in isolation but on the *process of task execution* as a whole, so including the context or working environment. If the result of that process fails in someway, the result is named pilot error. A switch on some device could be put in the (for that situation) wrong position. So, in order to prevent the same problem again, a safeguard is put over the switch under the assumption that first accidental operation will be prohibited (true) and second that the pilot will think twice before activating it (false). Clearly, such an assumption is understandable from a common sense notion, but does not respect task execution as a process of gathering data, processing it into information in relation to its context. If all data available (sound, smoke, yaw response) is perceived by the pilot as indicating a left engine problem, that engine will be switched off, what ever switch guards are present.

Installed equipment and task definition

An accurate definition of a human task is not as easy as it may seem initially.

First, there is confusion about the difference between a function and a task. A practical convention in this case is that a function assigned or allocated to a machine is a system- (or software automation) function. If the function is allocated to the human, it is designated a human task. In case of adaptive automation, functions and tasks can be exchanged.

Secondly, the level of detail for describing a task should not be so fine-grained that it is difficult to maintain an overview. When described in too much detail, making a pot of tea can even look like an impossible task. Knowing and remembering the type and location of the ingredients, knowing how to recognise tea, what to do with it, knowing how to operate the tools, lift your arm, pour water in a controlled fashion, apply safety requirements, etc. etc.

Thirdly, the timeline and sequence of events are not implicitly considered. A task can require the reading of data on one device, comparing it with data from another device and subsequently executing a response on yet another device. When considering 'devices' only, like an EFIS (Electronic Flight Instruments System), such interdependencies are easily overlooked.

Fourthly, multiple task environments are not or ill considered. If 'monitoring systems' has been named as a side task, some information should be provided on the task strategy assumed. As an example, *'monitoring of systems will occur when not occupied with other tasks'* versus *'systems will be monitored in regular intervals'*.

Last but not least, it has to be realised that training and experience serve to integrate series of sub-task into higher order competencies. Tasks should not be coded as 'easy' or 'difficult' without explicit referral to the pilot characteristics. The specification itself is completed with defining a performance parameter that allows measurement of performance on *this* task.

240

The generic human task processor

In its basic form a task is a goal oriented set of activities comprising some intake of data (Stimulus perception – S), the re-working of that data (processing – P) through memory functions into task relevant information, deciding on possible actions to take and initiating responses (action – R) while controlling and monitoring the feedback of success or failure of the process as such (Control and awareness – C). A simplified 'SPR-C' model that describes these operations is depicted in figure 1.

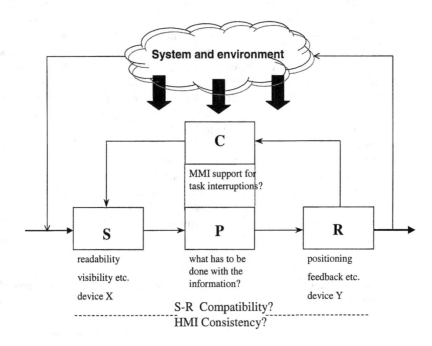

Figure 1   Simplified 'SPR-C' model for human information processing. The information is extracted through sensory systems (S), is compared with memory and decisions are made (P) and particular responses (R) or actions are executed or initiated. The net results of these actions provide feedback that is monitored by an 'upper control mechanism' (C) resulting in awareness of on going processes

Four 'boxes' have been defined that facilitate a basic understanding of the main components of the human information processing system. They can also provide a useful framework for examining potential deficiencies in cockpit design.

1. *S box (Senses and Perception) Human* task performance starts with the sensory reception of relevant external stimuli. The eyes, ears and other

241

sensory organs have unique characteristics and limitations that influence the quality and quantity of information flow. Characteristics of the retina of the eye, for example, influence the conditions under which colour can still be perceived and hence processed. Other task variables that influence readability and legibility are the intensity, size, spacing and similarity of stimuli. Environmental factors that can affect sensory processing are noise as it can mask relevant auditory signals, or visual vibration, which blurs the readability of needles and scales.

2. *P-box (Processing)* Subsequent processing of the received information depends on task variables such as the complexity of decisions, the memory load and the number of response alternatives. A choice between two alternatives (left or right-hand) is simpler and takes less processing time than a choice between more alternatives. Learning and practice serve to 'automate' the processing and reduce workload. The relationships between information and human expectations, concerning the response required (compatibility), influences the amount of recoding of the required information. The 'processing stage' is critical in determining the right sequence of information processing and can be obscured by bad cockpit design. Environmental factors like fatigue, stress, etc. influence this processing box.

3. *R-Box (Responses and Action)* To generate a response, if the decision is made, a 'motor program' is required to release the necessary muscle commands to carry out the action. Task variables affecting this box are, (1) the quality of tactile feedback, (2) adequate timing of the response and (3) forces required. Turbulence, is a well-known environmental factor that complicates data entry by switching knobs, etc.

4. *C-Box (Cognitive control and Awareness)* The 'cognitive control' mechanism finally evaluates the resulting or actual performance on basis of external feedback (i.e., monitors the consequences of the actions). It acts as supervisory 'control mechanism' that assesses time-sharing strategies for the performance of multiple tasks. The controller mechanism may generate more 'effort' to compensate for the loss of performance when a discrepancy between the actual and the desired performance is detected.

Such a model can be practically used to derive and organise Human Factors requirements for design or evaluation in a systematic and structured way. Taking the process and time line into account allows for a scenario based, more operationally compatible review and a check for closing the loop.

Human information processing principles

The task-oriented approach goes beyond the 'basic' ergonomic approach. This type of work is also described as 'arms and legs' ergonomics as it used to focus on physical dimensions. A task-based focus recognises the importance of relationships between data displayed, the type of mental operation that has to occur and the particulars of the responses that have to be performed in order to obtain the wanted result, i.e. the goal to be achieved. This side of the work is also denoted as cognitive ergonomics. Experimental psychology has provided many of the basic design principles that influence the effectiveness of particular stages of information processing with respect to time required, error probabilities and vulnerability to outside interference increasing the likelihood of errors.

A commonly known design principle is that of *consistent mapping* between information and response elements ideally also across various pieces equipment. In many multi-function display configuration this is not possible as each button will not be consistently mapped with respect to a single function and location. Additional checking and mental effort will be required. Consistent mapping facilitates learning and skill development. Human information processing for skilled operators is more efficient as compared to unskilled operators. Extensive training can result in processing that occurs nearly without mental effort, a stage which is often typified as 'automatic' processing (see the classic work of Shiffrin and Schneider 1997) in contrast with 'controlled processing'. This type of performing has the advantage that it is stress tolerant as it is not jeopardised soon by short-term memory limitations under stressful conditions. A negative side effect is a risk of negative transfer of 'habits' can occur when a frequently used association happens to be not appropriate in a particular situation that occurs relatively rare. This case occurs when pilots have to fly other types of aircraft.

A second well-known principle is that of *stimulus-response compatibility*. This design principle implies a consequent relation between the stimuli or data sources and the associated responses or type of controls. Characteristics such as location or movement direction play a role and consistency results in faster response time(s) and fewer errors. A classic type of study would include the presentation of two lights, one left and one right, with buttons located at similar left-right locations. The 'compatible' situation, left light on – press left button, is notably faster than left light on – press right button. This effect is noticeable even with such a simple task, but its implications are stronger when the operator is confronted with a more complex situation or extreme stress. Engine indicators and associated controls are an example of a design with relevance of S-R compatibility.

Many, if not all human models comply with the simplified model, but clearly differ in their level of detail. Some might add boxes or divide a box into several sub-components. An example is the so-called Multiple resource model (Wickens 1992) that sub divides the S-box in separate mental resources for auditory and visual sub-units. Another influential model distinguishes between different types of human behaviours, separating *rule-based, skilled-based* and *knowledge-based* behaviours (Rasmussen, 1983).

Peter G.A.M. Jorna and Piet J. Hoogeboom

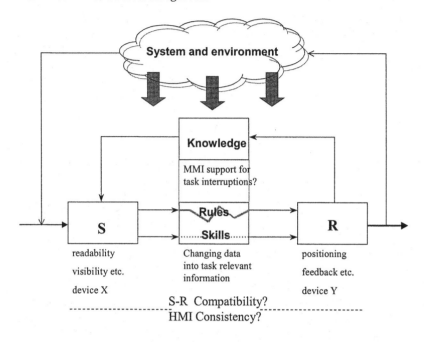

Figure 2 **Rasmussen model mapped to the simplified model for human information processing. Well practiced skills enable easy and swift processing while the mental application of rules and procedures requires controlled processing in working memory (Shiffrin and Schneider 1977)**

Working context and pilot characteristics

Performing the same task under different working circumstances can change the demands of a task imposed on the pilot. Landing an aeroplane is a task for the pilot, but it makes a difference in demand if performed in nice weather or under less favourable conditions with gusty crosswinds. The tasks can be defined and described as being identical, but they do not 'feel' the same i.e. they differ in imposed demands. Often the wording 'tasks' and 'skills' are used interchangeably in the aviation community, but there is a distinct difference. A bit extreme example from another domain illustrates the point. Performing the same task like 'hammering a nail in a piece of wood' under different circumstances can involve totally different skills. Imagine yourself hammering in the open air outside (no problem for most people) as compared to hammering 'under water' as a diver (wood suddenly floats and it is dark). In addition to such a factor interacting with task requirements, there are time restrictions that play a role in determining the

244

required level of skill. When landing a general aviation aircraft, completing a 'circuit' and performing down wind checks with a slow aeroplane requires different skills, or levels of skills, as compared to a fast(er) aeroplane. If the circuit cannot be extended for noise abatement reasons, time pressure will be imposed on all the checks and communications required. Planning and anticipation are suddenly even more critical as they are normally.

As a rule of thumb, a 'skill' can therefore only be defined if the:

- Task to be executed is known.
- Working environment and context, including other tasks, is known, and
- Timing pattern required is known.

Working with user interfaces in a laboratory is simply not the same as working with them in an aircraft under operational conditions. A flight deck tested in a laboratory can contain acceptable instruments when read in static conditions, but impossible to read under the influence of direct sun light or in-flight vibration. Environmental factors complicate task execution by making them more difficult or they compromise access to equipment such as data displays or controls.

Many tasks are performed by means of predefined procedures. Such procedures are there to assist the crew, but sometimes the procedure is so complex that it is an additional task to perform. Circumstances have occurred in which pilots saw a benefit in deviating from such procedures. Incompatibility of the procedures with that particular operational environment is a factor or the crew strives for a benefit for passengers and/or airline (for a discussion sees Karwal, Verkaik and Jansen, 2000).

Most pilots do not work 'on their own'. Even single seat fighter pilots are members of a team. Social or teaming factors on the flight deck are known to complicate task execution sometimes and a bad team can compromise performance. Safety has become increasingly dependent on adequate teamwork. Interruptions in the working environment or incompatible teaming can distract the crew and still leave tasks unattended or unfinished. The missed or incomplete data processing can evolve into a major problem when the displays (or the automation) do not indicate (provide feedback) a hint of such omissions.

The operational environment can not only make task execution more difficult, but can also influence the physical and mental condition of the crew. Environmental factors like noise levels, humidity, extreme exposures to time zones, bad teaming etc. can affect the mental fitness level of the crew. Most pilots can perform admirably, but nobody can perform admirably or perfect *all the time*. Natural variations in performance do occur. Fatigue and boredom are performance and stamina killers.

The working conditions experienced during long-haul cruise flight are generally not very loading, leading to potential vigilance and alertness problems, this in contrast with the hectic short haul terminal area operations were crews are loaded with many tasks in a short time frame. ATC procedures can change in ways not foreseen during the initial design of systems.

245

Peter G.A.M. Jorna and Piet J. Hoogeboom

A task analysis should therefore not only describe the task, its information, user interface requirements and performance levels to be attained, but also a list of critical factors depicting the assumed working context and potential interferences that exacerbate task demands. The evaluation should specify the anticipated conditions in an operational scenario, or when not available specify more generic test conditions simulating extreme working conditions (sleep loss, distractions, high task loading).

User characteristics can interact with (worsen) some of the aforementioned effects. Pilots having reading glasses will have more trouble with reading displays under severe vibration. Also pilots that are used to fly other aircraft intensively could have developed habits that unexpectedly intervene with the present design.

In summary, any evaluation dealing with pilot performance (as opposed to dealing with a design) has to address the following TEST factors: the *T*ask(s) involved, the working *E*nvironment with people to communicate with and other tasks to perform, the *S*ubject pilot characteristics that may apply and the level of *T*raining acquired (Jorna, 1993).

As illustrated above, tasks and working context needs to be addressed in concert with characteristics of the crew as they impose variable demands on variable humans, thereby causing variations in the quality of performance on the same task. These variations should not cross a certain bottom value. This is the quest for the minimal standard that has to be maintained at all safety costs.

Defining Human Factors requirements

Some variations in human performance originate as a consequence of so-called *between subject* differences. People simply differ in their aptitude for performing certain tasks. All pilots therefore pass a selection procedure. But their training levels and experience also vary. Minimal training standards should set a safe bottom value. Other variations in human performance originate from *within subject* differences. Performance shaping factors as stress and fatigue can be induced by cumbersome equipment or external factors complicate the flight and increase task demands, stress and fatigue. Also personal factors as use of drugs, sleep deprivation, stress in the family, etc. can adversely affect performance.

In summary, it has been clarified that any non-technical evaluation of a system or design involving a human–machine interface, needs to address a range of complex interrelated factors or the Human Factors topics mentioned earlier. In the end it is the goal to ensure effective and reliable human performance for airline and military operations. It is the *process* of producing that human performance that deserves most attention. Not only the design of installed equipment is important, but also the adequacy of the procedures designed to operate that equipment. The analysis should define the presence and working context of the (intended) human tasks (if any) followed by an assessment of the required

246

minimum safe standard performance levels including problems, such as error potential. It should be checked that these levels can be achieved and maintained under all circumstances that can occur operationally or with the performance and ability ranges of human pilots and crews. Data should be made available on all relevant working conditions and the intended group(s) of users. Although it is possible to specify tasks without any reference to the external world or user, it is impossible to predict performance variations without reference to the working context, procedures and pilots characteristics. The advent of the glass cockpit improved aircraft performance and safety, but also revealed vulnerabilities in human performance that were less well understood. An international team summarised the lessons learned in an extensive report on automation issues on the Flight deck (FAA Human Factors Team, 1996). As a consequence a need for new legislation and advisory material was identified.

Improving regulations

The Human Factors Harmonisation Working Group, consisting of both Authority and Industry participants, was formed in October 1999 and will complete its work in 2004. The primary aim of the Group is now to develop a new harmonised rule and advisory material relating to Human Factors on the flight deck, which will supersede the existing JAA/ EASA Interim Policy on novel flight deck features. The produced material will be considered for integration in the Part 25 of the FAA/JAA Airworthiness Requirements.

One of the first tasks of the team was to review existing regulatory material in order to identify necessary improvements with respect to now established, Human Factors requirements. A comprehensive 'double action' method was selected and implemented. First, a 'top down' task-based theoretical review was designed that employed the simplified model of human information processing described earlier for the identification and organisation of a full and harmonised list of Human Factors requirements. Second, a bottom up, accident based 'lessons to be learned' review method was designed in which experienced operational, factory and test pilots sampled and analysed accidents and incidents. Both strands were subsequently combined as a crosscheck when reviewing the regulatory material.

The task-based review methodology benefited from this work as it was closely scrutinised by this group consisting of experts from various disciplines (Test pilots, operational pilots, engineers, regulators, Human Factors specialists, psychologists, safety professionals, etc). One of the critiques was that the model was not well integrated/connected within the 'technical' aviation system. This made it more difficult to grasp its meaning from a technical or operational viewpoint. The model was subsequently extended to arrange a comprehensive overview of the role(s) of the flight crew in the overall aviation system. The results are depicted in figure 4.

Peter G.A.M. Jorna and Piet J. Hoogeboom

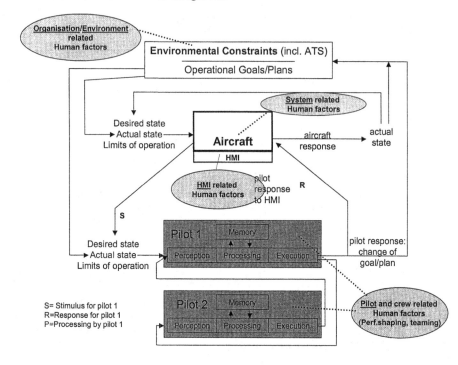

Figure 3 Conceptual model of crew-system interaction depicting role and interrelationships of flight crew in the overall aviation system (courtesy Jorna, Nibbelke and Imrich HF-HWG, 2000)

Many improvements on the regulations were deemed necessary and are now considered in draft rule making and advisory circulars.

Evaluation methods

User or customer acceptance

In most languages there are expressions that illustrate the importance of the paying customer for business. An example could be a sentence such as 'who pays, decides what stays... (in the design)'. Customer satisfaction and user acceptance are therefore high on any list of evaluation topics. But these criteria are not so simple as they seem at first hand. Suppose that the user and the paying customer are not the same? Suppose that the paying customer wants to reduce costs and the user at the same time wants to upgrade the system. These are typical

248

examples of day-to-day realities in managing business. Some form of documentation will therefore be required to allow trade off studies and provide some support for design decisions. Experiments, presentations or demonstrations can be used to compare design options and acquire data that is deemed relevant for the decisions to be made. For a detailed discussion of potential 'on the fly' techniques to be used in the design process, see Singer (2000). If there is only one deciding customer, a convincing presentation could already suffice. But if there are many users out there, a larger scale exercise will be needed.

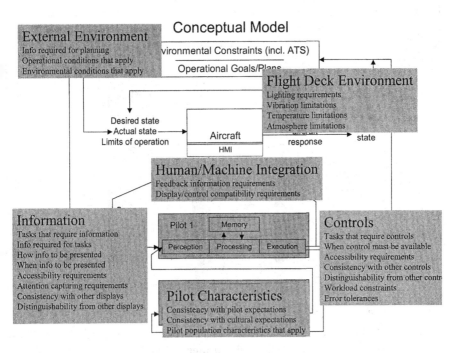

Figure 4   Examples of Human Factors requirements identified at various levels of the model including stages of task-based human information processing

An example is a full mission simulation of the flight deck application of digital data links for communication (van Gent et al., 1996). In this experiment a number of candidate user interfaces where designed and tested for potential application as communication devices enabling air-ground communication. All interfaces provided access to the various standard types of messages routinely used for communicating with Air Traffic Control (position reports, altitude changes etc). These messages were initially organised in a menu tree with groups of messages clustered together by the software designers. The organised overview served well for software design (and presentations to customer) but as a consequence, did not exactly follow a task-based design approach as was noted by operational pilots. A new design organised the possible messages in the data link device differently, taking into account when certain messages were required during the mission. This 'timing based' design was contrasted with the 'type of message' based design. The results are depicted in figure 5.

The results were in favour of the task-based design that made life a bit easier for the flight crew. Note that the redesign costs were minimal as they only involved a restructuring of already existing information. Consideration of the processes involved in task execution during an operationally relevant scenario can therefore improve user acceptance without boosting costs.

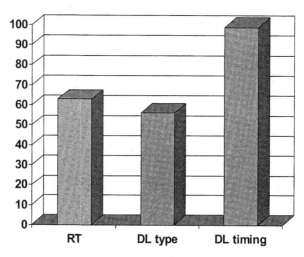

Figure 5   En-route crew acceptance levels (%) of flight deck data link communication devices with a menu based on clustering messages on type (DL type) or a task-based structure considering the timing and sequences of messages in the mission (DL timing). Radio communication (RT) in the same scenario serves as a reference

Subjective evaluation

Users do not always form a nicely homogeneous group and statistics are often needed to decide on what is noise and what is a real result. Users can also be classified in different sub-groups such as proponents or opponents with respect to technologies. In a high fidelity flight simulator experiment on the use of 'Tunnel in the sky' displays for flying complex data trajectories as up-linked in Air Traffic

Management systems, pilots were asked to rate their subjective level of experienced workload. Two display configurations were used; a tunnel in the sky display depicting a tunnel with a conflict free 'air bubble in the sky' and a modified standard primary flight display with indicators on altitude tape and heading indicator. The results indicated superior performance on flight accuracy for the tunnel display and also a trend for a reduced subjective workload rating (Huisman and Flohr, 1997). This result is positive as the tunnel in the sky display essentially contains more data in an easy to grasp format. During the debriefing of the experiment an intensive discussion between pilots was accidentally overheard. The arguments exchanged seemed to indicate the existence of a bi-modal distribution in their opinions i.e. proponents of new technologies and pilots satisfied with existing, familiar systems. Being curious, the data were sorted after coding the pilots in either a group favouring new technologies and a group favouring familiar technologies they were trained with. After re-analysing the data the results in their subjective ratings depicted in figure 6 were found.

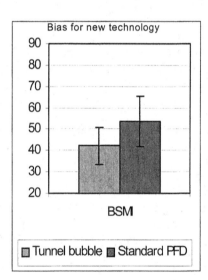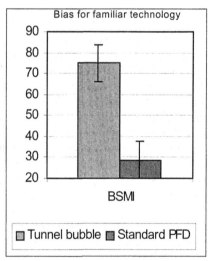

Figure 6 Ratings of Subjective Mental Effort (RSME/BSMI scale) required for operating a tunnel in the sky display versus the standard primary flight display, for two groups of pilots one favouring new technologies and the other adhering to familiar technologies. Note the different workload ratings provided

Subjective ratings are clearly prone to pre-conceptions with respect to the individual position on the issue, being it new or old technology, or high costs

Peter G.A.M. Jorna and Piet J. Hoogeboom

versus savings etc. These biases do not mean that the information gathered is useless. On the contrary; we are now pointed to the fact that at least a portion of the pilot population will have difficulties of some sort in transferring to new aircraft or retrofits. Biases such as these are simply the reality and uncovering them will allow the development of a solution. In order to select a solution, one should *never* rely on subjective evaluation as a single or sole source of information. If it is possible to find flight deck crew in favour of a design, it is almost certain that opponents can also be found.

Formalised qualitative evaluation

One way to ameliorate the vulnerabilities of assessments made subjectively, is the use of a structured method with formalised procedures for assessing Human Factors characteristics of a flight deck. Such a formalised method increases inter-rater reliability as well as test-retest reliability. The design of such a method was not easy as there are multi-disciplinary teams involved in design and evaluation activities. Cockpit effectiveness in relation with human performance vulnerabilities must be assessed in relation to the task structure, performance shaping factors and overall characteristics of its performer, that is the pilot. Many detailed models exist which attempt to explain and even predict human performance. This diversity requires a lot of academic training and complicates the transfer of knowledge within multi-disciplinary teams. In an attempt to ameliorate the situation we assembled a team of people consisting of aircraft manufacturer representatives, avionics engineers, psychologists, civil and military pilots with the assignment of coming to a mutual understandable model that could have practical utility without compromising the underlying scientific principles. The result, after being locked together for many days in a room with a cockpit simulator, was the simplified and standardised 'pilot model' discussed earlier. In that case it was used for defining and structuring the Human factor requirements to be covered by future regulations. In an earlier stage it enabled the development of a formalised tool for evaluating flight decks consistently (Bohnen et al., 1996; Bohnen and Jorna 1997). This procedure was named CODEP (Cockpit Operability and Design Evaluation Procedure).

The formalised CODEP procedure has been in practical use for flight deck evaluations for many years at the National Aerospace laboratory in Amsterdam and was applied to a series of aircraft (systems) ranging from the F-100, F-50, F-16, Bo-105, Light Attack Helicopter LAH, NFH90 to the Chinook helicopter. The basic principle of this quick reference method is to perform the evaluation one step at the time avoiding distraction by the complexities involved and following the sequence(s) or time line of human information processing required for the task at hand. So, a first step is 'can I actually see the data or read it from the instrument from my seated position?' Are the colours and symbols, irrespective of their meaning, detectable and discriminable? If so, the next question is; 'is the

252

format of that data compatible with the task at hand or is there more data sampling elsewhere required and perhaps a lot of calculation? If I am willing to initiate a response next, can I actually find the required input device and how do I know that the action was completed successfully? Last but not least, how is the system providing me feedback on what I am doing?

The method has proven particularly useful for performing 'on the spot' evaluations under high time pressure, a characteristic for most if not all, aircraft acquisition projects. For such projects the method was extended with formal procedures for determining non-changeable items, built in restrictions such as using an existing airframe etc.

The basic steps involved in the flight deck evaluation are performing a:

- *General design philosophy inventory* This inventory aims at acquiring management type of information on factors that impose 'not to change' limitations on the cockpit like using an existing aircraft hull structure, limited and fixed (lack of) display space, essential minimal equipment to be included etc. Overall design principles, if applied, will be noted to serve as inputs for checking consequent application. An example is the 'dark cockpit concept' which means 'no lights on, no problems' (but check the light bulbs!).

- *Cockpit walkthrough* This includes a first reconnaissance of the actual cockpit workspace and the basic locations of seats, panels, controls, wiring etc. The dimensions of the cockpit are determined and evaluated according to (tall Dutch) anthropometrics etc. Outside vision is verified and items like 'Eye point of regard' are checked.

- *Operational mission factors specification* The TEST (Tasks, Environment, Subject pilots, Training) approach is applied to identify the tasks pursued, the foreseen operational envelope, the flight environment and intended crew characteristics. These will be noted on a test card to be used later on as 'not to forget' items such as testing readability while actually being strapped in, using protective gloves, uniforms, breathing gear, cooling equipment etc.

- *Function(al) task-based cockpit review*
  a. *Task listing and review*: based on aircraft functions like 'navigation', 'communication' or 'system management and control', a list is produced on what specific high priority tasks have to be performed, which instruments and controls are available to perform these tasks, what is their location/organisation etc.?
  b. *'Basic ergonomics' per task* (e.g. visibility of available display elements) according to SPR-C model. Each task relevant instrument is checked for each box criteria separately. So the S-box asks questions on readability without checking immediately if the data format makes sense for the task to be performed. That is analysed by the P-box test card. The S procedure has a high resemblance with classic ergonomics checks, while the P and C procedure is more cognitive.

c. *Human information processing principles:* checks on consistency of mapping data, modes etc. as well as display-control relationships: i.e. S-R compatibility and is the presentation of other information according to pilot expectations at that time?

d. *Task and error management* (e.g. task sharing crew and automation), the C-box checks for feedback options on results including potential for error detection and handling, vulnerability for distractions and provisions to find your way back in the system when system awareness has been compromised.

- *Device based review* After having acquired insight in the task related avionics etc., it will have been noted that certain instruments, controls etc. include data that is relevant for the execution of more than one task. So next to testing 'within task' (timeline) ergonomics and cognitive properties, it is essential to test the 'in between tasks' ergonomics. During the evolutionary process of cockpit designs, supplier industries have of course noted that many tasks require similar display and/or control facilities. It was therefore technically and economically attractive to produce modules that contain such multi function options. Examples are Multi Function Displays, Command and Display Units, annunciation panels or switch panels that can be labelled according to the intended system use by the 'integrator' in most cases an airplane manufacturer. The mapping of functions to these systems is variable and could compromise integration as compared with more consistent systems.

Therefore a second part of CODEP addresses these integration issues. Within these standard procedures the cockpit is evaluated on the following Human Factors aspects:

a. *Grouping*: grouping and organisation of cockpit-and display elements according to their function(s).

b. *Consistency*: degree in which information coding and relationships between information elements are consistent.

c. *Mode error analysis*: errors that can be made because of the inability to recognise or remember the set-up ('mode') of the systems in the cockpit.

d. *Multi-operator use*: way in which both pilots can share systems, displays and controls.

- *Cockpit operability tests and aircrew ratings* Issues that are raised and prove to lead to discussions and/or require further substantiation on their impact and risks for errors are translated into 'operability tests'. An operability test takes the form of instructing a subject to perform a number of specific tasks (like changing altitude by the mode panel or FMS) and recording time to complete and type of errors made. These tests cannot replace full measured tests but serve as an aid in those cases where full testing or experiments are not possible or prohibited.

Practical value and some anecdotes

The majority of evaluations using the CODEP method were performed in the context of a competitive (military) aircraft procurement process with multiple candidate aircraft. The use of a formalised procedure is critical for a fair comparison as it helps to reduce personal biases. The available time for such reviews is always limited and the method should therefore be practical and easy to learn. Experience has learned that most evaluators tend to spontaneously opt for a device-based approach, as these devices seem to represent some form of organisation. Thinking in 'tasks' is more difficult as it relates to the operation of the flight deck as a whole. The use of the simplified model on human information processing helps to adopt the latter way of thinking.

Some parts of these reviews are based on proprietary information and cannot be released. The examples of results will therefore be limited to non-type specific (anecdotal) information.

- *Ergonomics*: anthropometric difficulties are still more the rule than the exception and long legged and/or female pilots are ill considered. It is surprising to note how often strapping in tightly with fixed gear, will result in problems to accurately read instruments.
- *Panels*: switches for on/off are often not consistently of the same type. So, a cockpit can have forward/backward switches in 99.8% of the cases, except for some particular function where the switch was perhaps out of stock and a push button was used. A detail, but more confusing than anticipated as operability tests revealed some interesting 'startle responses'.
- *Colour coding*: overall consistency was often found to be low when equipment was installed from different origin. The benefits of colour as a means for organising the human machine interfaces can be compromised. Also the number of colours can differ from the number of 'system states'. Flight Director modes as an example can have three different phases. 1) The armed phase: a mode can be engaged but can not become active immediately, because the conditions for mode operation are not yet met, 2) the transition phase: conditions are met and the mode is active to reach the desired value. When this desired value is reached, the mode switches to the final state, 3) the captured phase. Not all Flight Mode Annunciation displays use separate colour coding or an alternative as flashing for discriminating between the transition and captured phase. They are often both grouped under the captured phase.
- *Abbreviations*: as many partners are involved in the design process, it is difficult to maintain consistency. One of the results is the use of creative abbreviations. Examples are 'HOV', 'HVR' or 'HR' for 'hover' and 'LNAV' or 'LNV' for lateral navigation mode. Note that they were all observed in the same cockpit!

- *Operational environment*: An example related to the operationally environment questions, was the finding that the avionics at hand were actually NOT designed to be waterproof! Some documented consequences for civil aircraft were in flight problems due to coffee spills (did you like the manual flight over the ocean?). For military aircraft operating over sea or helicopters operating from ships, additional maintenance is due in order to prevent corrosion of delicate instruments and hardware by sea spray.

- *Design principles*: Some manufacturers refurbishing older models needed a lot of time to find the eye point used in the original design phase. Fitting the retrofit equipment into the hull was the primary target often limited to one possible solution. Reference to the crews' eye position apparently came second …

- *Comfort*: sometimes pieces of equipment are designed in such a way that they are 'asking' to be used differently as intended. Hand held mikes can be conveniently stored by hanging them on a perfectly fitting brightness control buttons on the instrument panel. They are not designed for that purpose, but they look as if that was the case. Practical, visible, easy to pick etc. But if they fall off the button, they end in the…coffee cup holder below. See the earlier discussion on waterproofing of instruments for the follow on …

The field use of a structured method such as CODEP and the suchlike proved practical for realising standardised and repeatable 'quick and ready' assessments of flight decks. Examples of related methods can be found in the documentation of the European DIVA project (Design of Human Machine Interfaces and their Validation in Aeronautics) a research project supported by the European commission (Hoogeboom et al., 2000). A positive side effect of the comprehensive method was that pilots achieved an in depth insight in potential vulnerabilities of the(ir) flight deck. The review increased their awareness of system characteristics that could represent unexpected weak spots otherwise. Pilots (private, commercial management or test) could therefore benefit from performing such a review for their own aeroplane. A short course would already provide the necessary skills.

Computer-based modelling

Structured procedures such as CODEP are useful but still operate at a qualitative level. One step towards more quantitative data is to not only describe and analyse the tasks but to integrate them in a computer simulated task network. Such fast-time simulation studies do not involve a user. Instead, the previous analysis is used to assign some sort of value to the task identified (e.g. a 'time to complete' value of 15 seconds, or a workload score of 5). Multiple tasks are specified in procedures to occur in certain combinations and frequencies in order to represent the expected activities of a real person. A scenario is described in terms of trigger events and duration, and various tasks are programmed to occur in order to achieve the aims of the scenario. By basing this scenario on task values instead of actual user data, a processing unit can calculate the resulting values almost instantaneously. Unfortunately, the results will always be the same if normal variations in human behaviour or strategies are not considered.

A combination with human modelling will allow computerised investigations into achievable response times and potential bottlenecks such as high task loading. The techniques predict how simulated operators will perform their assigned tasks and produce results that can be used to predict both performance and workload. The actual question is how the workload imposed on a (normative) operator by, for example, particular cockpit display/control configurations, procedures or environmental conditions affects pilot and hence overall system effectiveness.

Models are always an approximation of the reality but are useful for exploring new designs and the identification of problem areas that need more in depth research. Contemporary advanced modelling does not only model a generic human model, but also addresses performance shaping factors like fatigue and stress effects. Integrated performance modelling environments, such as MIDAS (Corker et al., 1993) and IPME (Dahn, Laughery and Belyavin, 1997), both incorporate a number of modules performing different tasks and relying on network analysis. They provide various opportunities to model a complete system, including the interface to the operator and the systems behind that interface, the operator and the environment in which the system operates. MIDAS provides an extensive capability to build display prototypes and to visualise and evaluate them. IPME emphasises relevant performance shaping factors that influence natural variations in human performance.

Although helpful as a tool, such models have fundamental drawbacks. First of all, all the inputs are scripted and based on assumptions with respect to task execution and strategies. The models can reveal bottlenecks in performance opportunities but they will never predict the creative ideas that the future user may have for using the design in a different way than intended or assumed by the designer originally. More empirical studies are needed to unravel and deal with possible new or even unanticipated human factor issues.

Objective evaluation(s)

Human behaviour on the flight deck will be most realistic when assessed in real world conditions. The best 'proof of the pudding' is still eating it, but the risk of losing an aeroplane by unknown problems or new error types, can be bad for the digestion. Therefore some other way of providing realism is necessary.

Simulation is by definition not the same as the real world, but serves as an acceptable approximation depending on the purpose of the evaluation. If the evaluation is only concerned with basic issues such as accessibility of display and control configurations i.e. physical dimensions, a mere mock up, avionics test rig or even a virtual cockpit may suffice. In case the real world or context contains factors that can change the behaviour of either the system or the human pilot, a discrepancy between simulated and real world will be present. The realism has to improved or the evaluation has to be performed on another simulator with high (context) fidelity in order to assure the validity of observed crew behaviour and performance measured.

A discrepancy between a simulated and a real world can be physical or psychological in nature. Turbulence, vibration and gusts will influence the quality of display (blurred text) and limit the crew in operating some controls. Motion and vibration platforms provide more realistic physical conditions for flight deck evaluations. It is quite more difficult to create a working environment that is conformal with the psychological conditions under which flight crews have to operate. Such conditions include time pressure, interaction with other traffic, confusion about ATC instructions, runway changes, taxiways under constructions, distractions, boredom, company policies and many other stressors.

Simulating a valid working context is important for evaluating new designs because of the fact that 'context' is not only influencing behaviour but also the requirements of the skills needed to perform new or modified tasks with the equipment installed. The equipment is part of a whole and will be operated by different flight crews under different circumstances.

The flight crew as instrument The observed behaviour of flight crews operating with a new system can be used as an indicator of its effectiveness as well as the workability of the associated working procedures. In case of a new design benefits can be contrasted against a certain reference. The reference could be an alternative design or existing equipment. Crews work both systems and in this way each crew forms their own control with respect to individual differences. These types of experiments are often used in research and development, but sometimes the control condition is dropped. Cost savings can be a factor, or a scenario is used where certain 'absolute' standards have to be met, such as 'acceptable workload' or no 'undue concentration'. In that case the evaluation addresses some form of minimal human performance standards. The regulator could define official standards but actual practice is often based on widely accepted methods and empirical results. In the subjective domain, ratings of handling qualities (Cooper-Harper ratings) are perhaps not perfect but widely used, the same is true for subjective ratings of workload. In the physiological domain, specialist knowledge is required for obtaining reliable objective measures based on eye tracking, heart rate, heart rate variability and brain related data, but they enjoy increasing acceptance in empirical industrial evaluations. Official standards on aviation Human Factors or pilot performance 'levels' are not yet fully developed or documented. Minimal human performance standards or descriptors of Human factor vulnerabilities of flight deck designs that can be measured with some ease are, or can be made available for the stages/resources of information processing as defined earlier in the simplified human information processing model. Most of such items are addressed in the CODEP method. Classic topics for in depth evaluations are pilot workload and situational awareness. Such, multi-dimensional constructs, can be operationalised by relating them a particular combinations of measures and minimal/maximal values of such measures.

A benefit of using the crew as an instrument for measurement is that they are able to behave 'naturally' while models are rigid. Crews are human and not all humans are alike. Training serves to reduce the impact of 'individual differences' but will not exclude them. A consequence is that flight crews under test, should be allowed some freedom in their decision-making and the strategies used to accomplish tasks. That will help to detect new error types and/or weak spots in the design. A disadvantage of 'free' interactive simulations is that the crew behaviour can influence (mess up) the complexities of their own flight. They can amend the actual route(s) flown, decide on the initiation and sort of communications etc. It will be difficult to compare results and observations across crews, when their actual flights develop differently. For a fair comparison conditions should be equal. Such an ideal situation can be approximated by organising 'mini experiments' in comparable mission segments or during system states that are comparable.

The simulator as controlled laboratory A solution to the problem of achieving high levels of realism without losing the ability to control the experiments, was the use of 'context simulation' techniques such as the controlled manipulation of 'Events' (Jorna, 1997). Events can be inserted in complex scenarios in a consistent way by linking them to pre defined crew actions, systems state or traffic conditions. The simplest example is an engine failure that can be initiated in most training flight simulators by an instructor. More complex is the linking of such an event to a particular situation such as 'now using the communication page on the CDU. Such a capability can be realised by adding instrumentation to simulators (or aircraft) that enable 'intelligent' automatic monitoring of flight and/or equipment parameters that provide a real time status of all the equipment being used. An instructor would be required to monitor and manipulate all details simultaneously and consistently for all crews.

As an example, monitoring and recording of equipment status creates the opportunity to initiate some type of an 'ATC event'. A data link up link can occur precisely at the moment that the Pilot Non-Flying is heads down at a predetermined page of the Control and Display Unit of the Flight Management System.

Events can be triggered automatically under comparable conditions or levels of imposed task loads. Particular combinations or sequence of events can be used, representing an IF this, AND that, initiate 'event', ELSE do not trigger. Such 'mini-test' conditions in dynamic scenarios can be computer arranged for all crews involved and allow fine grained assessments of actual use of equipment even under various conditions involving crew distractions, high task loading, etc.

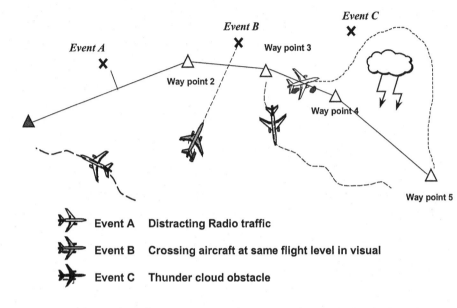

Event A   Distracting Radio traffic

Event B   Crossing aircraft at same flight level in visual

Event C   Thunder cloud obstacle

Figure 7   Scenario of a *context* experiment with cockpit data link with examples of events that can be triggered automatically and the same for all crews

Next to similar experimental conditions, quality requirements (statistics, science) necessitate sufficient numbers of repeated measurements, in order to assess the reliability of the results with statistical testing. So, conditions should not only be comparable between flight crew, but also occur in sufficient numbers to produce realistic and reliable data. This can be assured by accurate planning of the experimental scenarios.

Managing the working context   An example of a research simulation facility with advanced context control is the Air Traffic Management test bed at the Netherlands Aerospace laboratory (NLR).   In this case a flight simulator is combined with simulation facilities regarding Air Traffic Management. Both can be connected with software controlling the occurrence of events. This so-called *'Experiment Manager facility'* developed for this purpose, is a dedicated computer that contains a list of scripted events for the simulation computers to execute. These are initiated either automatically or manually when the required conditions happen to occur during that simulation.

The Air Traffic Control environment is influential on the task loads to be imposed on the flight crew.   Assistance and instructions are welcomed, but multiple and/or frequent changes in routes, altitudes or runways contribute to the task load. Experienced crews, very familiar with the route at hand will be able to cope with such events, but less experienced crews could experience high workload sometimes even close to overload. The effectiveness and ease of use of the Human interface or installed equipment will be crucial especially in such conditions. That is why such conditions have to be part of the evaluation, just as crews not too experienced.

Aviation system of systems test bed(s)

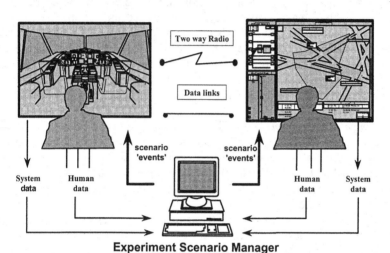

Experiment Scenario Manager

Figure 8 Simulation enabling context control for investigating all combinations of complex human-machine and teaming issues in existing and future operating environments

Air Traffic Control (ATC) is in the process of a metamorphosis into Air Traffic Management (ATM). Key elements are the increase of sustainable capacity and the provision of 'user preferred routes. More accurate navigation capabilities have come available and the exchange of aircraft and ground data through the application of digital data links has improved. This exchange of information on aircraft position and intent allows the ground system to develop a 'look or plan ahead capability'. Through the data link, some type of negotiation between aircraft and ground systems can now occur, taking into account the user preferred route and the possible interaction with other traffic in the sector or airspace. In this context, two scenarios seem to dominate ATM:

Peter G.A.M. Jorna and Piet J. Hoogeboom

- 4D Trajectory (re-) negotiation.
- Free Flight within an airspace.

Flexibility of 4D trajectories (i.e. x, y, z axis plus time) is provided by a negotiation between an ATM capable Flight Management System (FMS) and the ground systems. Conflicts with other aircraft can be resolved in advance by planned trajectory modifications where upon the route is cleared by a '4D contract'. The aircraft now has to fly the contracted trajectory accurately and within a small time window, creating the so-called 4D environment.

On the other side, the 'Free Flight' concept allows the aircraft to change its route on own initiative within a certain airspace. The ground system can act as a monitor and arbitrator in case of conflicts that cannot be resolved by the aircraft, if any. These approaches may seem to differ, but are conciliated by the option of expanding 'Trajectories' into so-called 'Tubes' of airspace of which the volume depends on the airspace available. The future system has not been defined yet, but can be built on either concept or, more likely, on a hybrid combination. The impact on the role of the flight crew and their tasks will be considerable and any new design should therefore be tested and evaluated in the right, complex traffic context.

Measurements and interpretation There is a multitude of possible measurements that can be taken from a flight crew when interacting with their systems. The data for these measurements can be acquired from sources such as the simulator, one of its many subsystems, Human Factors equipment such as eye trackers, physiological recordings, reaction time measurement devices, communication devices and many more.

As an example, a recent review (Hilburn et al., 2002) on the application of metrics to the validation of Airborne Separation Assurance Systems (ASAS) multiple metrics/measurement techniques were identified for the following areas of interest:

- Workload (Hilburn, B. et al., 1997)   66 metrics
- Situation Awareness (Alfredson, J., 2001)   9 metrics
- System Monitoring (Hilburn, B. et al., 1997)   8 metrics
- Teamwork (Kelly, C. et al., 2001)   16 metrics
- Trust (Ruitenberg, B.,1998)   11 metrics
- User Acceptance/Usability (Kirakowski, J., 1994) 20 metrics
- Human Error (EATMP 2000b)   12 metrics

It is clear that the measurement of 'workload' has attracted a great deal of attention and it is widely accepted that this concept is multi dimensional and therefore requires a combined set of measurements such as individual workload and performance both measured in concert. One aspect has no real meaning without knowing the other. The multi faceted aspect of Human Factors issues can be illustrated by using the simple human information processing model and depict the various workload aspects in that model.

262

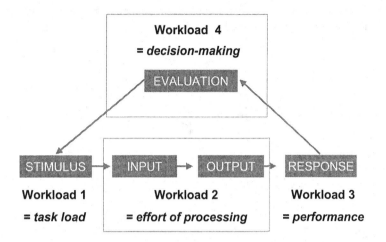

(1) task load, (2) processing, (3) performance,
(4) decision-making (excluding external stressors)

Figure 9   **Examples of where different operationalisations of workload tap into the simplified model of human operator behaviour (Hilburn et al., 2002)**

Similar to workload, situational awareness is a construct with multiple facets to consider. Following the time line of the task model, external data has to be available and accessible first in order to be able to build up a mental picture of the situation. The data has to be processed next into task relevant information and the result has to be understood correctly before a decision can be taken to seek for more information or stay with the present situational assessment. While doing all this, results have to be integrated and memorised in order to be able to project the expectations into the future. The multi-faceted nature of such a multi-dimensional construct makes it difficult to define the one best measure available. There is none.

An alternative approach is to use the structure of the task-based human information processing model for selecting generic measurements for each step or box in the model. Those dedicated measurements should provide information about what is happening, or going wrong, in the respective stages of information processing. As an example, data sampling can be measured and analysed by using eye trackers that reveal the focus of attention or momentary interest. Changes in heart rate parameters are ideal for measuring if that data is actually being processed, as some mental effort will be required for doing that. Looking at something is not a guarantee for 'seeing' something as it is well possible to dwell with your thoughts elsewhere. Monitoring the controls and displays (again) closes the task loop by the measurement of the actual actions taken as a result of all that

263

work. The measurements can be quite generic now and are not tied to a particular construct. Figure 10 provides an overview.

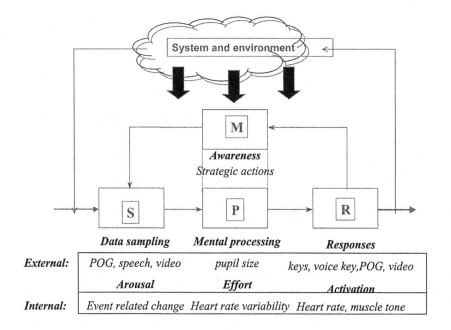

Figure 10   **Various measurements for standardised crew-based evaluations mapped to stages in task-based information processing. Measures are generic and do not depend on constructs such as workload or situational awareness**

Next to physical or behavioural measurements linked to the stages of information processing there are physiological measurements that can be tied to these stages. Several types of energetical mechanisms were found to be relevant for human performance. Pribram and McGuiness (1975) already identified three separate, although interacting energetical systems in the neurological structure of the brain. The appeal of these structures for human performance on a flight deck is their apparent functional relation with the stages in human information processing. They refer to:

1. *Arousal*, as the immediate physiological responses to input stimulation, which represents a phasic reaction;
2. *Activation* as a more preparatory and tonic readiness to respond;
3. *Effort* as a compensatory mechanism linked to reasoning and under active attentional control, which is able to compensate for sub-optimal states of either activation or arousal.

Familiar manifestations of activation are 'the butterflies' caused by anxiety or risks of failure. More concentration is required to maintain adequate performance. On the other hand, boring tasks like continuous monitoring without any action, also disturb optimal energetic patterns but now by their lack of stimulation which results in de-activation and being non-prepared. If external requirements like safety regulations do force the operator to stay alert, a conflict is created. In that case, considerable effort will be needed to adjust the level of activation and stay attentive. Humans strongly dislike such conditions and they rate boredom and fatigue consistently as being very stressful, even more stressful as those conditions that will overload the operator with information (Macky, 1987).

Training and experience serve the transition from controlled, attentive processing into more automatic processing, reducing effort. The existence of these modes is well established and can be identified in many theories about human performance. The attentional or consciously 'controlled' mode is associated with serial, time consuming, laborious analytical processing in working memory and is severely limited in capacity. It is used for problem solving in novel situations and in task conditions that are characterised by continuous variation in, or even inconsistent relations between, input and output, a condition known as 'varied S-R mapping'. The automatic mode is used to process information fast, in parallel, and with little effort. This mode can only be acquired after extensive practice in consistent and predictable conditions. The limitations of these modes are clearly different and they are associated with different error types. 'Mistakes' are made during active attentional processing, while 'slips' are representative for the execution of routine type of duties and as such are related to inattention or absentmindedness (Reason, 1987).

These theoretical considerations clearly illustrate that it is of the utmost importance to familiarise and train flight crews with the systems to be evaluated in order to assure representative behaviour and performance. Flight crew samples should include pilot's representative for the whole range of future users and adequate training as well as room for initiative is essential for the validation and safety assessments of the designs involved.

Data collection and analysis Measurements can originate from many different sources and data logging media. All such data will only be of interest if changes in the measured values can be related to changes into the operational environment or crew activities. Accurate timing of events and responses alone is necessary but not sufficient. If the data is logged on different time lines, its impossible to relate one the other reliably. Most computers, even from the same brand and type will *not* show the same time scales after the evaluation. Without a single time scale in the data sets it is still impossible to evaluate complex behavioural interactions between crew (members), their system and outside events such as ATC instructions or other traffic. Simulators use their own time scales and considerable discrepancies with real time are not unusual. Also, many simulators are limited in recording capacity and resolution possibly to prevent the copying of aircraft models etc. More add-on instrumentation may resolve that issue.

Special database techniques have been developed at the NLR to allow a combination of all data into a single data file that still can be handled on a high performance PC. The use of synchronising events and a date base technique that allows time stretching and shifting per channel of data, guarantees high quality data that is suited for time period based analysis as well as for event related techniques (Hoogeboom, 2003). The resulting software package incorporating the time synchronisation is named HEART (Human Factors Evaluations, data Analysis and Reduction Techniques).

Integrating psycho-physiological techniques

Evaluation of information scanning based on eye-data The use of eye based data is attractive as it reveals the strategies that are being used by the flight crew to access the visual data available on the flight deck. The basic technique shows the eye scan superimposed on an image taken by a head mounted camera that films the 'scene'. This technique is nice for on the spot applications, such as debrief during training, but it is to cumbersome for quality evaluations. A better technique is to combine the registration of eye movements in reference to the head, with tracking of head position as well. This will allow the use of point of gaze measurements that will directly show the position of the eye scan referenced to the actual equipment. Careful calibration is required, which needs considerable expertise. Automatic data processing is an option with this technique and that makes it the better option for validation or certification exercises. It saves both time and cost.

An example of the application of point of gaze measurements to flight display evaluation is the evaluation of a so-called 'Tunnel in the Sky' display. This classic concept can assist the pilot in flying approach profiles associated with some noise abatement procedures. The approach and landing procedures for airports can be quite complex depending on local political circumstances and/or noise abatement external safety requirements. The tunnel display is combined with representations of the speed and altitude tape displays known from modern avionics. Such as design was hypothesised to be particularly effective as it integrates various data elements etc. into one single representation. An example of the eye scanning patterns obtained is provide in figure 11.

Some critics on these displays argued that the displays are so clear or compelling that they would attract high levels of attention. If so, there could be the risk that crews miss other information on the flight deck relevant to the task at hand. Through the use of point of gaze techniques it was possible to objectively check this assumption for both normal flight and after failures such as autopilot disconnect. The results are depicted in figure 12. The number of eye fixations on the PFD are clearly reduced and not increased by the tunnel format.

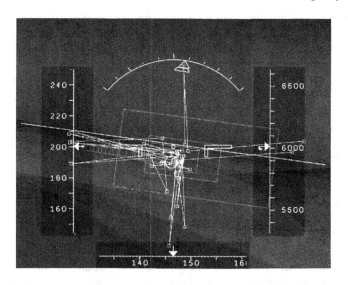

Figure 11 Eye scanning pattern (eye fixations and transitions) while flying a
noise abatement approach with a tunnel in the sky display with
integrated altitude, speed tapes and heading indicator

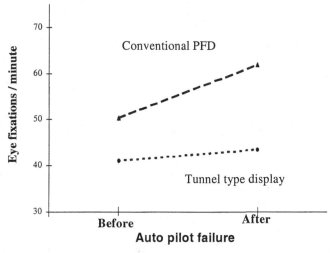

Figure 12 Evaluation of Tunnel Primary Flight Display based on eye fixation
parameters

267

Evaluation of mental effort based on heart rate parameters Heart rate, which is relatively easy to measure, has a long history as a source of information for indexing many psychological concepts like 'arousal', 'task involvement', 'anxiety' and more recently, 'mental load' and 'effort'. Heart rate frequency is influenced by the para-sympathetic nervous branch, that is quick enough in its response, to react to momentary changes in tasks. The sympathetic branch is, however, much slower in response and will therefore influence the more overall level of heart rate. As an example, if a student pilot feels intimidated by an instructor, heart rate will be raised consistently over time by the sympathetic branch and will not fluctuate clearly with on-going demands of tasks. Physical factors and psychological factors affect heart rate, and such factors must be controlled or measured independently if their separate effects are to be examined.

The observation that heart-rate variability (HRV), which is the beat-to-beat fluctuation of the heart rhythm, typically decreases under conditions that could be classified as 'mentally loading', initiated several research efforts in both laboratory and field studies (for a review see Jorna, 1992). Spectral analysis of inter-beat intervals allows an independent inspection of the influence of respiration on the heart and the blood pressure regulation. The latter component is known as the blood pressure or 0.10 Hz component and it varies with mental effort. High mental effort is associated with a reduced amplitude of the component (less vagal control) and vice versa.

The application of this measure of heart variability during simulated flight is illustrated in figure 13.

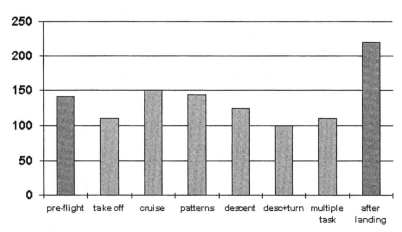

Figure 13 Heart rate variability as measured by spectral component 0.10 Hz, during simulated manual flight (gradings). Reduced values indicate higher levels of mental effort

Evaluation of human-system interaction by event heart rate parameters Spectral analysis of inter-beat intervals provided a quantification option for heart rate variability with respect to power in different frequency bands. Recording over time periods of 3-5minutes with a stable task loading are needed to allow comparisons across periods. The disadvantage is the possible impact on task realism, as 'flying turns for 5 minutes' to investigate workload of manual control, can be very relevant from a scientific point of view, but is not realistic for most operational circumstances. Pilots have many tasks of relative short duration that have to be handled in a dynamic, changing environment. An alternative technique is to record both heart rate and the actual mission 'event' timelines including pilot inputs and the occurrence of external problems and to study the direct heart rate *changes* in relation to particular mission 'events'. An accurate linking with respect to real time accuracy of heart rate with the stimulus or mission events is mandatory. The context simulation technique applied in the NLR simulators is equipped with the necessary technologies.

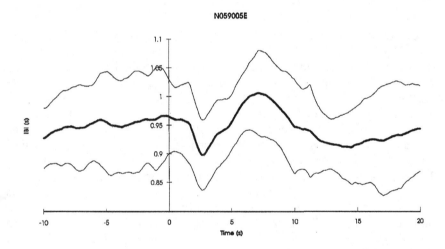

Figure 14 Event related heart rate (inter beat interval) response with side lines for standard deviation, averaged over multiple events (n=26) for a pilot not flying, handling the communications tasks with Air Traffic Control through data link. The centred event was an ATC up link (time zero) *displayed as text* **on the navigation display, which required a 'WILCO' response later on**

Segments of heart rate recorded around the events as they occurred during the flight are 'cut', inspected and *averaged* together. The reasoning is that all fluctuations that are not related to the specific event, will average out. The result

269

is a net response of that subject linked to that particular event. An event can be the display of new information, an annunciation, communications, etc.

An example is the event 'Aural alert from an ATC up link'. Normally, that data link event will initiate a number of task related activities such as: attract the attention of the pilot, followed by the task elements: process the presented information; decide on the action required in co-ordination with the fellow crew member and finish with the initiation and execution of the response by means of a down link message to ATC. In the case of data link standard replies like 'WILCO' can be selected from a display menu. The heart rate profile found for such a sequence is provided in figure 14.

In the case of reading from the display, a short period of heart rate acceleration (reduced inter beat intervals) was observed, followed by a quite more distinct increase in heart rate, apparently associated with 'working though the text'. After absorbing the information and decision making, heart rate decelerates markedly during the selection and execution of the 'WILCO' response.

Future developments

The advent of new procedures for the certification of flight decks will necessitate the further development of objective means for detecting the weak spots in the design(s) of new flight decks or updates of existing ones. From the data presented in this chapter it has become evident that no evaluation can be performed completely without using the flight crew as instruments and the simulators as a controlled laboratory. Test pilots are – and will stay critical assets for the design process but the complexities of the coming generation of flight decks can only be handled by the use of complementary methods and techniques. These techniques should provide the insight in the way that crews actually adopt and use technologies. As noted often in the experiments, it's quite common that skilled individuals are not always aware of how they perform the task. That's nothing to worry about, as it is a main characteristic of a 'skill', but it has taught us that subjective (expert) evaluations are limited by their 'wisdom of the past'. More data should become available on how and why people adopt certain task strategies. The tools and method discussed here, can help to realise that goal. In that process it is also possible to make a translation of certain certification requirements, such as: 'no undue concentration or fatigue' or 'no exceptional piloting skills' or no 'excessive workload', into well defined and measurable units of a series (or construct) of measurements.

These capabilities should become accessible before major changes in the aviation system are implemented.

References

Air Transport Association of America (1989). *National Plan to enhance aviation safety through Human Factors improvements.* Washington DC: Author.

Bohnen H.G.M., van den Bosch J.J. and. Jorna, P.G.A.M (1996). *Cockpit Operability and Design Evaluation Procedure (CODEP): Test cards.* NLR TP-97411. Amsterdam: National Aerospace Laboratory.

Bohnen H.G.M., and. Jorna, P.G.A.M (1997). *Cockpit Operability and Design Evaluation Procedure (CODEP): a systematic approach to cockpit effectiveness.* Paper presented at International Aviation Safety Conference, Rotterdam, 25-26 March 1997.

Corker, K.M and Smith, B.R. (1993). *An architecture and model for cognitive engineering simulation analysis: application to advanced aviation automation.* In, ninth AIAA Computing in Aerospace Conference, (San Diego, CA, Oct. 19-21). Technical Papers. Part 2 (A94-11401 01-62). AIAA Paper 93-4660. Washington: American Institute of Aeronautics and Astronautics.

Dahn, D.A., Laugehry, K.R. and Belyavin, A.J. (1997). *The integrated performance modeling environment: a tool for simulating human-system performance.* In, Proceedings of the 42nd Human Factors and Ergonomics Society Conference (1037-1041). San Diego: Human Factors and Ergonomics Society.

FAA Human Factors team (1996). *The interfaces between flight crews and modern flight deck systems.* Washington DC: Author.

Gebhard, A., Ketelaars, M.F.J.M., Bohnen, H.G.M. and Jorna, P.G.A.M. (1993). *Operational evaluation method for cockpit MMIs.* Report no. NLR CR 93366L. Amsterdam: National Aerospace Laboratory.

Gent, van R.N.H.W. (1996). *Human Factors issues with Airborne Data link: towards increased crew acceptance for both en-route and terminal flight operations.* NLR technical publication, TP 95666. Amsterdam: National Aerospace Laboratory.

Gent, van R.N.H.W., Bohnen, H.G.B. and Jorna, P.G.A.M. (1994). *Flight simulator evaluation of baseline crew performance with three data link interfaces.* NLR CR 94304L. Amsterdam: National Aerospace Laboratory.

Hoogeboom, P.J., (1997) *Human Factors Evaluations, data Analysis and Reduction Techniques (HEART). General Description.* NLR CR 97597. Amsterdam: National Aerospace Laboratory.

Hoogeboom, P.J. (2000). *DIVA project Evaluation methodology.* NLR Technical Report TR-2000-517. Amsterdam: National Aerospace Laboratory.

Hoogeboom, P.J. (2003). Off-line synchronization of measurements based on a common pseudorandom binary signal. *Behavior Research Methods, Instruments and Computers, 35,* 384-390.

Huisman, H. and Flohr, E. (1997). *The design and validation of a Tunnel in the sky display for aircraft operating in advanced Air Traffic Control*

271

Peter G.A.M. Jorna and Piet J. Hoogeboom

environments. NLR Technical publication TP 97 9999L. Amsterdam: National Aerospace Laboratory.

Huisman, H., and Karwal, A. (1995). *Design and initial evaluation of two 4D PFD format prototypes.* NLR CR95229L. Amsterdam: National Aerospace Laboratory.

Huisman, H. and Verhoeven, R.P.M. (1994). *Design of a 4D navigation display with interactive pilot input capabilities.* NLR CR 94094 L. Amsterdam: National Aerospace Laboratory.

Jorna, P.G.A.M. (1991). Operator workload as a limiting factor in complex systems. In, J.A. Wise, V.D. Hopkin and M. (Eds.) NATO ASI Series F, Computer And Systems Sciences: *Automation and Systems Issues in Air Traffic Control.* New York: Springer Verlag.

Jorna, P.G.A.M. (1993). *The Human component of System validation.* In, In, J.A. Wise, V.D. Hopkin (Eds.), *NATO ASI series: Verification and Validation of Complex Systems: Human Factors Issues.* New York: Springer Verlag.

Jorna, P.G.A.M. (1994). *Flight Deck Automation: Design and Safety.* European Transport Safety Council (ETSC) report on Air Transport Safety. Brussels: ETSC.

Jorna, P.G.A.M. (1997). Context simulation: an interactive methodology for user centred system design and future operator behaviour validation. In, N. Sarter and R. Amelberti (Eds.) *Cognitive Engineering in the Aviation Domain,* (pp. 181-210). Mahwah, NJ: Lawrence Erlbaum Associates.

Jorna, P.G.A.M. (1997). *The design process to optimise the Human Factors of flight decks: from theory to 'proven' human machine interfaces.* In, proceedings international workshop on Human Factors certification of cockpits. London, UK.

Jorna, P.G.A.M. (1997). Pilot performance in automated cockpits: event related heart rate responses to datalink applications. In, R.S.Jensen (Ed.) *proceedings Ninth International Symposium on Aviation Psychology.* Columbus, OH: Ohio State University Press.

Karwal, K., Verkaik, R. and Jansen, C. (2000). *Non-adherence to Procedures, Why does it happen?* NLR CR 2000. Amsterdam: National Aerospace Laboratory.

Palmer, M.T., Rogers, W.H. Hayes, N.P., Latorella, K.A., and Abbott, T.S., (1995). *A Crew-Centred Flight Deck Design Philosophy or High Speed Civil Transport Aircraft.* NASA Tech. Memorandum 109171. Langley, VA: NASA.

Rasmussen, J. (1983). Skills, Rules, and knowledge: Signals, signs, and symbols, and other distinctions in human performance models. *IEEE Trans. Syst. Man Cybern. 13,* 257-266.

Russell, M.C. and Everett, G.C. (1995). *The future flight deck.* A discussion paper by the flight operations group of the Royal Aeronautical Society and the Guild of Air Pilots and Air Navigators. London: Royal Aeronautical Society.

272

Shiffrin, R.M. and Schneider, W. (1977). Controlled and automatic human information processing II. Perceptual learning, automatic attending and a general theory. *Psychological Review, 4,* 127-190.

Singer, G. (2002). *Methods for Validating Cockpit design.* Doctoral thesis. Royal Institute of Technology Department of Aeronautics, Stockholm, Sweden.

Wickens, C.D. (1992). *Engineering Psychology and Human Performance* (2nd Edition). New York: Charles E. Merrill publishing company.

12 Human Factors in flight test and flight deck evaluation

Gideon Singer

Introduction

The problem

The basis for aircraft flight deck design is to enable the pilots to operate the aircraft in all foreseen conditions and with an exceptional safety record. In order to mitigate the risks of errors and malfunctions that originate in the flight deck, great efforts are made in the design, evaluation and validation phases of the flight deck design. There are only around a dozen manufacturers in the world today that have the capability to develop and manufacture large commercial aircraft. This is due to the complexity of the process and large investment combined with the high project risk involved. Since the design process requires qualitative evaluation by highly experienced and competent operators, a manufacturer is obliged to have a group of specialists that address flight deck design and evaluation. This group usually consists of flight test engineers, test pilots and system engineers that together evaluate the design at different stages, show that it complies with the design criteria, and that it meets all other requirements. In addition, it is the task of the group to evaluate the design in its foreseen future operational environment and make predictions as to its safety. The role of the test team, and the test pilots in particular, is to perform the task effectively and as economically as possible, producing a safe and affordable product.

Contrary to common beliefs, an aircraft prototype is usually only an intermediate step in the process of finalising a design. Much of the work done in flight deck and system design is done after the maiden flight of the prototype. It is the aim of every manufacturer to minimise the changes required at this late stage, but due to the complexity of the systems and the dynamic environment of its use, changes are always required to reach an acceptable compromise within the time and budget frames.

Gideon Singer

In order to reduce risks and costs of late changes, several methods are used during the design process to evaluate the flight deck layout, system logic and susceptibility to errors. These methods and other experimental flight deck evaluation methods will be addressed in this chapter.

Purpose

The life of an aircraft typically comprises several basic phases. They include the dynamic phase of the aircraft introduction, the improvements phase towards maturity and finally the almost endless phase of retrofit activities to keep up with new requirements and tasks. Each phase involves engineering and testing efforts in order to comply with certification and customer requirements. Each system has its own dilemmas in flight deck interface design.

This chapter reviews and evaluates the existing test methods used for flight deck issues. The purpose is to focus on the problems found in design using these methods. The emphasis is on the flight deck interfaces; whether they involve flight controls, displays, flight director guidance or the presentation of warning systems. The task is to investigate where flight test technique is an effective method for improving flight deck design and where other complementary methods would probably have identified deficiencies earlier if used correctly.

The discussion and conclusion parts include a presentation and evaluation of other methods that may result in a more user oriented approach for evaluating system integration in modern automated flight decks. These methods, when used in the right combination, should result in safer designs and lower development costs.

Methods

After looking at the problems and purpose, it is appropriate to review the methods used today to address the issue of flight deck design. The methods described here to approach the problem of flight deck design and evaluations are the ones used by the aircraft industry, being mainly flight test for development and validation. The more academically oriented one, being empirical research will not be addressed here but is mentioned in this context in previous work (Singer, 2000).

Flight test methods

The method used to achieve the goal of a safer flight deck by means of flight test is described for instance in the *Boeing Philosophy Document* (Boucek, 1996) and the *FAA Flight Test Guide* (FAA, 1995). The test team responsible for flight deck evaluation is faced with a difficult task. It is asked to complete most of the design evaluation as early as possible and make as few changes as possible after first

276

flight. This means that for the critical phases of the evaluation the group does not have a finished product to evaluate and is usually forced to use paper models, logic algorithms, and common sense combined with past experience. One of the greatest dilemmas of a design group regarding 'Past Experience' is the conflict between improving the product vs. maintaining communality with the company's previous products. This aspect affects both future crew training needs and product philosophy and profile. Another conflict in the basic process, especially noticeable in a small company, is the fact that the same people are involved in the design, evaluation and initial approval of the systems. One way of overcoming such a bias is to apply objective evaluation methods during the design and validation process.

Following is a summary of the phases of approving a new system in a flight deck to illustrate the complexity of the process:

- An application is made to the certification authorities in the form of a detailed Test Description. The test description defines new system functions, explains which specific design requirements will be complied with and lays out how compliance will be shown. Compliance may be shown by means of simulation, flight test or pilot evaluation.

- The system goes through a phase of Development Testing, which is an iterative process. Changes are made to optimise the system for its intended use. In this process, test pilots and engineers test functions, logic, display and interface with the other aircraft systems on several simulations or test flights.

- When the test team is satisfied with the results it is time to present the evaluation process to the aviation authorities for them to test and approve the system. The Certification Test Plan is the document of the agreed upon process that must be presented to the aviation authorities. The testing is then performed by either the authority or is delegated to the manufacturer.

- Several test pilots engaged in the development phase evaluate Fit, Form and Function. This includes the ergonomics of the interface units, interface with other controls in the flight deck and readability in different lighting conditions. This evaluation is very subjective and is based on the experience of the reviewing pilots. This process is completed with a report written by the Design Reviewer (a senior test pilot) stating that the system has been evaluated and found not to affect any other systems. This evaluation report does not show necessarily specific compliance with any regulatory requirements but is mainly for the internal process of quality control of flight deck changes.

- A Certification Test Report is then produced based on the previously agreed upon Test Plan. This report shows how each item has been tested successfully and forms the basis for aviation authority approval. Most system performance and reliability results must comply with objective guidelines (FAA, 1998) and are tested and reported in such a manner. The means of showing compliance can be either flight-testing the system, testing it in a flight simulator (for dangerous flight conditions) or by component lab testing. In some cases similarity with previous designs and theoretical analysis may be used as the sole means of showing compliance.

- Crew Evaluation Certification Reports are used to cover all items that the engineers do not have test or analysis results for. The reports include all the qualitative requirements that are stated in the requirements and that relate to the way the pilot communicates with the system. These Crew Evaluation statements written by a senior pilot and approved by a reviewing pilot cover issues such as ease of readability in flight, tendency to mislead and the need for excessive skill of the operator.
- When all the above-mentioned documents have been approved the system is declared Airworthy, meaning that the installation in this specific aircraft has been found safe for use.
- In order to approve the system for use in the aircraft when carrying passengers (or cargo), each operator (airline) also has to pass an Operational Approval to comply with national regulatory requirements.

Materials In an aircraft development process, the design and test teams use several vehicles for the evaluation, each vehicle has its advantages and weaknesses, and each is suitable for a different phase of the project. Each phase has a typical user involved, usually determined by the tool used for evaluation, and whether the aim is determining design options or evaluation of a specific design solution.

Participants Several test pilots participate in each review. They usually have experience from other aircraft, and with the knowledge of how the systems are going to be used by the operator. An important aspect in the test pilot background is the understanding of the detailed requirements stated in the design standards such as Federal Aviation Regulations or Joint Airworthiness Requirements (FAR/JAR) part 25. In many cases, line pilots are also used as evaluators of functions that might be used in a specific manner by the operator. These might be such functions that are closely linked with operational procedures and standards.

Test pilot qualifications should include higher education in engineering, basics of Human Factors theory, flight test technique and ability to communicate with the design engineers and managers. An important characteristic of a good test pilot is his or her ability to accept errors and difficulties they encounter as system weaknesses and not their own. In addition, it is their task to simulate all possible user misunderstandings, mistakes, slips, lapses or mode errors (Wickens, 1992).

Mockups In the initial phases of development the tools used are mockups made of wood or paper (flight deck panels), static software display concepts (EFIS display), and actual hardware controls with limited functionality (control wheel push buttons etc.) (Singer, 2000). All these features are then combined into a flight deck mockup that allows the test team to evaluate the ergonomics of the design. This includes: fit, form, function, reach and the flow logic philosophy to be followed.

Prototypes A prototype, whether as an aircraft or an avionics unit in a lab, is basically used to expose the system to the environment and check its performance and possible weaknesses. A prototype is used in the operational conditions intended for the final product but has usually only the basic functionality needed for the evaluation. The SAAB 2000 first prototype was such a tool (Singer, 1992). The flight deck included all the basic functions needed for flight though not all the communication and navigation systems intended for operational use.

A prototype is also instrumented in order to be able to document and measure behaviour and performance by an independent sensor (video cameras, pressure sensors, and data acquisition systems).

In the development of modern flight controls (Singer and Persson, 1996), prototype units are designed to be easy to modify and monitor. This might include extra modules that will then have to be removed to comply with certification requirements. Prototypes of part of a system are usually installed on an existing aircraft (test beds) in order to get initial values in the dynamic flight conditions prior to prototype first flight (flight control surfaces, new sensors, new engines etc.).

Simulators Simulation is widely used to evaluate systems, flight deck interfaces, or new flight control logic and performance. Simulators in an aircraft development phase vary from limited PC based simulators (Mårtensson and Singer, 1999), to full In-flight simulators (specialised test aircraft) of the combined aircraft and flight controls dynamics (Singer and Persson, 1996). It is essential to know the limitations of each simulation and only draw the conclusions that can be validated correctly. Flight simulators rely highly on aero data (aerodynamic modelling) and the variables of flight mechanics. Such information is usually not available prior to first flight and can only be estimated. The simulation results must therefore be treated cautiously until validation is completed.

Several methods used for testing flight deck design and evaluation

The method that will be described first is the classic 'trial-and-error' flight test approach (Singer, 1992). This method relies on the final product being flown in actual flight conditions and exposed to rigorous testing at the envelope limits. If unacceptable characteristics are found a redesign is done and the testing repeated. This is a long, expensive and time-consuming process but the results are always valid since the testing is performed on the final product.

The second method used is also a flight test method but a more refined one based on simulation in fixed-based and in-flight simulators (Singer and Persson,

1996). The same techniques as in flight test are used but utilising other vehicles, available at an earlier stage of the development process, to predict flight control characteristics prior to first flight. This method requires high fidelity simulations and experience-based test planning in order to cover the sensitive parameters. In addition, the paper describes the administrative method of decision-making and risk mitigation in the process of development and certification of a complex flight control system.

The third method addresses the issue of flight deck interface by using knowledge elicitation from the end users (Mårtensson and Singer, 1998). This included reviewing and understanding the philosophy and design features of several warning systems that exist today in modern aircraft. To get a wider picture, several military aircraft were evaluated and the differences and commonalties understood. Based on that knowledge, a detailed pilot interview was prepared covering the different types of aircraft and pilot qualifications. To get the full understanding of the limitations of design, system engineers, test pilots and instructors were interviewed. The interviews allowed us to come to several general conclusions on the subjective opinions of pilots regarding warning system features.

The last method uses the results from the interviews in an empirical experimental method to validate a hypothesis made from the subjective data gathered from the pilots and engineers (Mårtensson and Singer, 1999). By using a part task simulation, and following with a quasi-experimental method, four scenarios of multiple faults were constructed using four design philosophies based on existing modern aircraft warning systems. Several pilots were run through the same experiment using known methods of increasing workload and minimising bias. Initial results showed definite trends.

Measuring user pilot performance – A new certification method for approving Head-up displays

In order to improve the operational capability of aircraft (such as the SAAB 2000) in low visibility conditions, a Head-Up Display (HUD) has been developed for providing approach, landing and flare guidance for the pilot to follow. This HUD has been one of the recent systems that have gone through a thorough certification process that addressed the human factor issues successfully. The pilot was put in the loop both as a human servo and as a decision maker in a critical system with new and novel means of guidance. In order to prove that the reliability of such a concept was equal or better than the *Autoland systems* already in use, new requirements were set, some of which addressed the crew's ability to handle the system interface, display and guidance.

The test pilot in this development and approval process acts as an evaluator of the simulator, of the flight characteristics and system logic compared with the actual aircraft. Since the landing flare phase becomes critical for the guidance and system performance, better fidelity is required. Many aspects can only be evaluated by an experienced test pilot and might not be detected by standard automatic tests (ATG) of the simulator.

In the approval and certification phases, where the average pilot must be represented, the test pilot involved in the design should not participate, or if so, only as one of many other pilots. In this phase, performing hundreds of approaches by many different pilots produces a model of the predicted system performance. This data is then extrapolated beyond the expected lifetime of the aircraft in order to show a certain safety trend. The test pilot is involved in defining relevant failure conditions, recommended procedures and helps in debugging simulator abnormalities.

In order to address this issue, a new Advisory Circular (AC) was developed by the FAA. The FAA advisory circular AC120-28D (FAA, 1997) shows in detail how the performance of the HUD system should be evaluated with regard to workload. The circular specifies in quite a high level of detail, the evaluation method, and scope and sets success criteria. Even this level was not sufficient and was augmented by a written agreement regarding number of pilots, number of runs, airports etc. between the applicant and the authorities prior to the evaluation.

This evaluation process was found sufficient to show compliance with system performance and reliability. But more importantly, it proved that, under the test conditions, the man machine interface did not conceal any errors with hazardous effects. In addition to showing lack of errors of great consequence it also proved statistically that minor crew errors resulting in a failed approach did not exceed the 5% level (the well accepted success level of 95%).

In addition to measuring objective performance in all foreseeable conditions (weather, failures, turbulence, fatigue, unknown airports and other surprises) this method includes for the first time in flight-testing a representative population of the user pilots. Line pilots are the majority of the subjects involved in the tests and their system knowledge and training is typical of the future conditions.

Finally, the test pilot is the one that validates the simulation to the aircraft and HUD performance in the varying atmospheric conditions. It is usually only the subjective observations of test pilots that identify differences between the simulator and the aircraft and help eliminate the simulation errors.

Since the pilot, when using the HUD, is both a monitor and human servo (unlike for instance autopilot landings), great care must be taken as not to overload the pilot and to assure efficient crew co-ordination and monitoring at all times. This aspect is scrutinised thoroughly by company and authority test pilots during the development and approval phases and only then is the system certified.

Typical flight test and other experimental results

The following results are taken from four separate papers addressing flight test and other flight deck evaluation methods. They are all part of a licentiate thesis by the author on the subject (Singer, 2000). The first two papers describe flight test when used to test and when required, improve control interface and flight deck design. Flight test was in both cases the final step of a long evaluation of mockups, simulators and other development tools. In the first paper flight test uncovered problems that required major changes in aircraft controls, flight deck ergonomics and software design. In the second paper flight test validated the predictions made by other development tools and required no flight deck or other than minor software changes. This chapter reviews some of these results in order to draw general conclusions regarding flight test usefulness at improving flight deck interface, design and evaluation.

The third and fourth papers treat results from studies and experiments that can be used at an earlier stage in the development phase. Interviews are used to ensure that the assumptions in the design are understood and accepted by the end user and that the right compromise between automation and pilot involvement is kept. The fourth paper shows a method of validating such subjective customer requirements and is used to show pilot performance and understanding of new design features. These papers show results of methods that may have been used in an effective way prior to flight test to improve flight deck interface and feedback especially in the case of warning systems.

Trial and error – The SAAB 2000 initial flight test

The aileron system in the SAAB 2000 is a mechanical, aerodynamically balanced, gear tab design. In order to evaluate the SAAB 2000 aileron characteristics prior to first flight and verify computed hinge moments, an aileron with the 2000 profile and balancing was fitted to the SAAB 340 test aircraft (Singer, 1992). The aileron was test flown and the calculated data was confirmed both in sideslips and with the ailerons disconnected. A slight overbalance at high sideslip angles was encountered. A detailed aileron model was implemented in the simulator and various handling tasks and certification requirements were evaluated. The gearing-ratio for the aileron tab turned out to be a very sensitive parameter and a compromise was needed between high control forces and the non-linear response. Due to new certification requirements lowering the maximum allowed roll forces on approach to a one handed level (25 lbs instead of the 50 lbs for older aircraft), the SAAB 2000 manual aileron problem was difficult to solve.

Control wheel forces were found too high in some configurations and in order to reduce control wheel forces a SAAB 340 control wheel was installed since it was 10% wider. This gave the pilot a longer moment arm in roll manoeuvres resulting in lower roll forces.

Initial flights confirmed very high roll forces at the selected tab gearing and an airspeed limit was introduced. A higher gearing was set and test flown and the control forces were found to be satisfactory giving a good control harmony. Unfortunately sudden non-linearity was encountered at high sideslip angles and during high deflection inputs. In addition, with flaps extended, an insufficient force gradient for small deflections made precision roll control unacceptable.

Tab gearing was changed again and determined as Type Design for initial flight tests. In order to reduce the aileron forces by decreasing friction in the system, the centring springs (acting also as down-spring in case of open failure) were removed and the aileron tabs were rigged to counteract an up-float in case of an aileron failure. This change was estimated to reduce forces by up to 10 lbs but flight tests showed no apparent improvement. The Type Design was finally frozen and determined to be that with the springs removed. A temporary operational limitation was set until the high roll control forces problem could be solved in later design changes.

Flight test as a validation tool – Fly-by-Wire for the SAAB 2000

The flight controls of the SAAB 2000 initial design were of a mechanical type except for the rudder. During the initial development stages it was discovered that longitudinal stability and control were inadequate in some corners of the envelope. A decision was then taken to develop a simple but reliable Fly-by-Wire pitch control system (Singer and Persson, 1996).

The new pitch flight control system had to be simple, reliable, and easy to install and maintain. In addition it had to use existing aircraft sensors as far as possible. Since the short period stability of the aircraft was adequate, no augmentation was required for that mode, and only the long period stability modes were to be improved. The Fly-by-Wire concept was chosen to reduce weight and maintenance time, and to simplify the design. The concept was based on the powered Rudder Control System (RCS) used successfully on the original design.

In order to meet the target dates, the testing process was planned in detail allowing for one or two iterations if required by flight test results. The majority of the people involved in the design phase were also involved in the testing team allowing for an effective decision-making and risk-reduction process to be implemented as part of the development process.

The testing methodology was based on the following plan:

- Update the development simulator to the new configuration and perform an intensive development test series.
- Evaluate the critical dynamic phases of the flight using the Calspan in-flight simulator and make changes if needed.
- Perform closed-loop simulations and failure case analysis using the fixed base simulator and the hydraulic rig with the prototype hardware and software.
- Perform initial envelope opening flight tests in a safe but accelerated program.
- Collect aero-data in order to update the fixed base simulator.

Gideon Singer

- While waiting for the final software, update the simulator and repeat the simulator development testing and certification runs in order to discover potential deficiencies.
- When all simulator and software testing is completed, commence pre-certification and certification flight tests, to include also airfield performance testing, ice testing and failure case evaluation.

The major area of concern was how to achieve a system that, using simple control laws, would produce control characteristics that met the requirements, and produce good flying qualities over a wide centre of gravity (c.g.) range.

After passing the control system gains and scheduling through the usual analytical static and dynamic tests, it was essential to test the system with the pilot in the loop. For this purpose a limited task simulator is a good tool if combined with in-flight simulation testing in a realistic environment.

The development simulator is a fixed base flight deck with a three-screen, high-resolution visual system. It is equipped with partial flight deck instrumentation and full dual pilot primary and secondary flight deck controls.

Since the new elevator control system relied on a precise control feel system (springs, dampers and mechanical cams) it was decided to install the real aircraft hardware. This allowed the test team to develop an optimised feel system long before the aircraft was flown. Since lead-time in production of aircraft hardware tends to be long, this process reduced the risk for last minute changes to aircraft hardware.

A systematic matrix of flight conditions was evaluated using a few chosen sets of flight control parameters. The tests were repeated with 4-6 test pilots and a few pilots less involved in the project. The pilots rated each task of the simulated flights that included normal and extreme configurations, calm and stormy weather and a variety of failure conditions. At this stage the first flight control law configuration was frozen.

The steady state conditions showed reliable results and were a compromise between the long-term speed stability at the extreme aft c.g. and the control authority limitations at the maximum forward c.g.

Like any fly-by-wire system, the control law included delays and lags. Despite satisfactory rating in all flight phases in the simulator, and previous program experience, two areas of concern were raised. The first was the dynamics of the electronic bob-weight in quick pilot reversals and in real 'g' environment. The second was the pilot response to the non-linear gearing between the control column and the elevator movement on a high gain task like precision landings.

In order to evaluate such behaviour, manufacturers usually modify an existing aircraft with the new flight control system and evaluate it in flight prior to the first fully integrated prototype. Such was the case at Airbus, Boeing and almost all military projects. Since there was insufficient time for such a process, and the system was designed to be as simple as possible, an alternate method was required.

284

Based on previous experience with in-flight simulation the potential of such a tool was determined sufficient and flexible enough for our programme. The chosen simulation tool was the Calspan Lear 25 Variable Stability aircraft. The Calspan test aircraft was programmed to simulate the characteristics; response and control feel of the SAAB 2000. In order to make the process efficient, only two critical flight conditions were simulated and only 4-5 flights were planned. The onboard equipment allowed for real-time changes to be made and tested in order to find the optimised solution in actual high gain piloting tasks. This tool is the safest method for determining the risk for Pilot Induced Oscillations (PIO) without taking the risk of the PIO getting out of hand (the system disconnects when reaching certain limits). It allowed us to perform landings in gusty conditions and excite the system all the way down to touchdown.

Two deficiencies were identified and corrected during the in-flight simulation phase: The bob-weight lag filter time constant was found to be too long causing oscillations during 1.5-2.0g turns at cruise speeds. The non-linearity in the stick-to-elevator gain was found to have too large gradient changes within the high pilot activity band during approach and landing, resulting in risk for divergent PIO.

These problems were corrected quickly. The changes were introduced into the first prototype design and re-tested the same week. These were the only control law design changes made after the design freeze date prior to first flight.

Interviewing the end user: warning systems in commercial aircraft – an analysis of existing systems

The warning system design was chosen as an example of a complex system in commercial aircraft. A research paper addressed the issues of automation by means of a philosophy review followed by pilot interviews (Mårtensson and Singer, 1998).

In order to construct an effective interview questionnaire, the experience of test pilots is essential in order to isolate the different functions and hidden meanings of each system interface. This research was done as a combined effort between a Human Factors expert and an experienced test pilot and the result was a set of questions that managed to isolate the desired differences and weaknesses of each system feature.

The following results and conclusions could be drawn from the interviews of pilots flying DC-9, F-28, MD-80, SAAB-2000, B767, B777, and A320/340:

- All pilots admitted that they have been surprised by automation during their flying career. Since automation is a part of all aircraft systems today the answers did not reveal any specific surprises related to the warning systems. It was also evident that very few pilots have experienced actual multiple failures in flight and most of their concern was for system modeing and automation in autopilots and navigation systems.

- All pilots were pleased with the way the present warning systems handled Single Failure. Improvement was requested in checklist design.
- For Double Failures most pilots stated that the warning system does not identify the primary fault and presents too many secondary faults. This was not the case with DC-9 pilots that are presented with very little specific fault information but are required to make the diagnosis themselves.
- For Multiple Failures all pilots using electronic warning displays claimed that the system couldn't cope in a satisfactory manner. Most test pilots admitted that the systems are not designed to give a clear display in such an event. Most of these events are classified as extremely improbable but might and do happen. The only exception is the Airbus A320 family that has a pre-programmed priority system for malfunctions. This logic identifies a primary fault with the relevant checklists but might mask some other important malfunctions that are more critical at that moment.
- All pilots using the Traffic Collision Alerting System (TCAS) presentation found the function and logic satisfactory.
- Ground Proximity Warning System (GPWS) was found satisfactory by the pilots as a system. The combination of an alert, information and finally a voice command was found useful. An additional visual recovery guidance cue was recommended.
- All pilots accepted configuration, overspeed and stall warnings in the present form.
- All pilots found the ALERT function of the warning systems necessary. Inhibit functions during critical flight phases were found satisfactory. On the older generation aircraft like the DC-9 and F-28 pilots were forced to disregard alerts or give special attention to monitoring systems that had no alerts, especially during critical phases of flight.
- Some alert sounds were found too long in duration and lacking means for silencing the alert sound after pilot identification. A pilot selectable function for silencing the audio alerts was requested by most pilots. The A320 ECAM solution was found practical but should be made to affect all flight deck alerts.
- The INFORM function received different opinions from the pilots mainly depending on aircraft type. Most pilots stated that electronic displays present too much information and with no logical order.
- The pilots rejected the ADVICE function in case of malfunction. The decision for corrective action was not to be automated. This seems to be in conflict with the pilots' acceptance of automated advice in case of TCAS and GPWS high-level alerts. One explanation could be that the latter warn for trajectory conflicts and not system malfunctions and usually require immediate action.

Part-task simulation – warning systems in commercial aircraft

Some of the problem areas identified in the interviews described above were addressed by the use of a part-task simulation experiment (Mårtensson and Singer, 1999). Simulations of several scenarios of multiple failures typical of commercial aircraft were planned using several different display philosophies. This was performed as a limited simulation using a workstation with only the relevant displays visible.

The workstation was programmed to simulate a typical modern flight deck warning system using several display philosophies. The displays had various text messages at different levels of abstraction and system description. In addition, guidance was presented to the pilot in several cases. The experiment subjects were all professional pilots flying commercial aircraft and a group of military pilots flying modern fighter aircraft. The faults were presented to the pilots while engaged in a moderate workload task of flying an approach. Each subject was exposed to 16 fault scenarios. Primary fault identification, and secondary effects understanding were questioned. In addition, operator response time (RT) was evaluated. The scenarios chosen were all based on pilot interview recommendation from our earlier research (Mårtensson and Singer, 1998) and other published work (Billings, 1997; Hicks and Brito, 1998).

The initial results from 128 live runs showed that prioritised information and automated guidance on a display resulted in quicker identification times with a higher percentage of correct primary fault identification in all failure scenarios. These results, identifying the display philosophy that leads to the best pilot performance, are analysed statistically in the paper *Pilot performance during multiple failures: an empirical study of different warning systems* (Singer and Dekker, 2000).

SAAB 2000 case study – the pros and cons of flight test

The purpose of this discussion is to address the issues arising from the different methods used for improving flight deck design. Flight test will be evaluated as a method for evaluating ergonomic features, control force problems, control sensitivity and linearity and the investigation of sudden changes in aircraft characteristics (so called 'cliff effects'). Other methods, such as simulation using part-task or full-flight simulators, will be assessed in regard to flight deck improvements as a complementary to flight test or as stand-alone methods.

Ergonomic considerations – control wheel size

One of the first tasks of the test pilot is to evaluate mockups and prototypes of the flight deck and its levers. One of the most important control features in a flight deck is the primary control usually called the control-column or control-wheel. In most commercial aircraft (Airbus 320/340 family as an exception), pitch and roll are determined by the pilot by moving a control column forward and aft and rotating a control wheel left and right. The position and size of this control is central in the design of the whole flight deck and requires a thorough and systematic evaluation throughout the design and development process.

Other control features are for example the full travel of the controls when a pilot is seated in the seat, the flight deck displays obscured by the controls in any position, the ability to egress the flight deck quickly and the successful integration of subsystem buttons and switches into the controls (trim, autopilot disconnect, radio transmission button and more).

Figure 1   The SAAB 2000 flight deck

All of the above can be evaluated in a partial flight deck mockup. By selecting evaluation pilots of different sizes and percentiles (including some with some extreme combinations) the ability to use the full travel of the controls and reach the rest of the flight deck functions is evaluated. Since the pilot seat can be adjusted in several degrees of freedom, it is essential to determine that all evaluations are done using the pre-determined position that is equivalent to all pilots. One uses the 'Design Eye Point', a three dimensioned position in the flight deck where it is assumed all pilots can position themselves and perform all duties. This position is the one determining also the other display positions and the field of view available out of the flight deck windows.

Even though full travel of the controls can be determined in such a mockup, the forces required for moving the controls are not fully defined until the flight test phase. It is clear that the smaller the size of the control wheel, the less it obstructs the pilot's view. On the other hand a small wheel results in a shorter moment arm between the pivot and the pilot hands. This requires higher forces to be applied to achieve a certain control movement as explained in the example of the mechanical flight controls on the SAAB 2000 (Singer, 1992).

The SAAB 2000 control wheel was designed to give better grip and an undisturbed field of view of the primary flight display even in malfunction conditions such as an engine failure (the wheel then might be fully deflected to one side to maintain wings level). During the initial flight phase, test pilots concluded that the forces required to move the wheel in some conditions were above the allowed value, the smaller size of the controls being one of the reasons. Since changing control wheel size had unacceptable consequences on other display items, changing the gearing of the control surface itself was the preferred solution.

This was a typical case where a mockup evaluation was not sufficient and where the deficiency was discovered too late to be changed. It is also a case of relying on optimistic control force predictions during the initial design phases. One could also wonder if the introduction of a new form of control wheel as an evaluation item might have given another solution earlier on.

This case illustrates the need for good simulation aids and representative tasks when determining ergonomic features and characteristics of primary controls in the flight deck. In this project flight test did reveal the problems but due to re-design costs and complexity very little could be done at such a late stage to the controls in the flight deck. Instead the pitch flight controls were redesigned completely to become a non-reversible control system as described in Singer and Persson (1996).

Initial flights – control forces and linearity

The optimisation of flight control characteristics and control feel feedback is one of the most difficult issues in aircraft development since it involves a compromise between several opposing requirements. In addition, acceptable control characteristics must be achieved in all foreseeable conditions.

Gideon Singer

When optimising mechanical flight controls (where only the human force is applied to counter aerodynamic forces), flying the actual aircraft prototype is traditionally used. This is due to the complex interaction of airflow, inertia, control cable flexibility and aircraft elasticity with the pure control functions. Since large aircraft require large control surfaces, these become very heavy at high airspeed. To make it possible for the pilot to move the controls, they are balanced aerodynamically and the pilot then needs only to counter smaller forces. The risk of such a method is that the balance might change in dynamic situations such as high rate of change or disturbed airflow over the surface.

In the SAAB 2000 initial flight test period it was discovered that such disturbances did affect the control force feedback (in pitch and roll) and resulted in unpredictable control force feedback. It is known that the human operator reacts best to linear controls, such that change at a predictable manner or rate. If the control forces become suddenly higher or lower, the pilot control strategy does not fit anymore and erratic response can be expected. Since linear or near linear control response is also a design requirement, this feature was therefore tested thoroughly in flight and the control surface form and balancing was changed until the results were satisfactory.

The flight test technique used by the pilots was such that required precision and patience. It was the pilot's task to help define the most critical conditions for the test to cover all foreseen future flight conditions. Flight test methods functioned as expected and led to conclude that major changes must be made in order to make the control response acceptable for use in all foreseeable conditions. High fidelity simulation would have allowed an earlier fix and resulted in a better initial product.

Initial flights – engine power controls

The first SAAB 2000 prototype was unique in having new engines on a new airframe. The Alison AE2100 turboprops have never been installed on a production aircraft before and the test team had no experience with the engine characteristics. The mockup evaluations allowed the team to determine the power control lever angles and travel range but without the feedback of the engine response to each movement. The assumptions were that the engine behaved like other previous similar engine types. Based on that assumption the power lever friction was determined and set to one deemed optimal for pilot comfort. Unlike older engine control, the SAAB 2000 levers did not require a friction adjustment lever (the pilot could not change friction during flight) since the level design was such that would prevent unintentional lever movement due to vibrations or aircraft acceleration.

During the initial flight phase it was discovered that the engine was much more responsive to power lever commands than expected. This resulted in jerky response especially at low and intermediate power settings. This was only discovered in flight test when aircraft response was coupled with control inputs and pilot response. Several methods of improving power control were tested, some included lever friction, others affected the damping of power change rates and even the display of engine power was filtered to give the pilot a smoother feedback.

One indirect effect of the engine characteristics was the asymmetric effect on directional trim of the aircraft. Even small power changes resulted in aircraft trim change and increased pilot workload in order to compensate and re-trim. An intensive test program was launched to improve the yaw auto-trim function in such a way as to reduce pilot workload and improve passenger comfort. This required test pilot subjective evaluations and objective acceleration data acquired by test equipment onboard. Since such automatic augmentation systems are designed also to be able to handle failure cases, it required the design team to come to a compromise between system authority and the ability to correct for all disturbances.

It was discovered later during line introduction of the aircraft that specific training was needed to assure that the pilots did not unintentionally intervene with the augmentation system.

Also in this case the use of other methods that actual flight test by using good simulation of engine and propeller thrust models with the pilot in the loop would have allowed for a better initial design of the power controls.

Optimising Fly-by-Wire flight controls – time delays and non-linear control characteristics

The SAAB 2000 was introduced into service with mechanical flight controls in pitch and roll and an electrically controlled, hydraulic powered, rudder control system. Soon after the introduction into service it became clear that the penalties in payload and performance due to flight control characteristics were too restrictive for efficient operations. Operators required a more flexible loading capability of cargo and passengers and improved takeoff and landing performance into smaller airfields. In addition, a higher cruise speed had to be achieved at all normal operating altitudes.

The reason for the limited flight envelope and payload capability was mainly the inability of the aircraft design to meet control force and pitch stability requirements at the further forward and aft centre of gravity conditions. The most limiting system was the pitch (elevator) control system as described in the paper *Fly-by-wire for the SAAB 2000* (Singer 2000 and Persson, 1996).

After several attempts to improve the pitch flight control system by means of aerodynamic and mechanical (springs and cams) solutions, it became clear that a more drastic change was needed. This change had to improve performance, speed stability and allow for future growth of the aircraft. Since the aircraft was already in service, the new system was to be retro-fitable on the existing fleet and have a relative low project risk.

Dedicated design and test teams were formed and given responsibility for the design, development, and testing of a new flight control system. Test pilots had an important role that required a strong discipline of the participating pilots. The test pilots were involved in the design phase since they were familiar with the requirements and the present deficiencies of the aircraft. In addition they were the only members of the team that could evaluate the effect of the change on other systems and pilot actions in the flight deck, and relate to all the operational constraints. Questions such as system logic, trim feedback, warning logic and the basic characteristics of the feel system had to be answered by the test pilot.

Since the basic aerodynamic properties of the aircraft were now known, the development simulator was updated and used systematically for evaluation of the new parameters. In these evaluations it was essential to use also pilots not involved in the design decisions, as to not allow for a bias usually formed in the designers approach to their own solutions. Another method of minimising designer bias during evaluation was to delegate the evaluation process to outsiders (aerospace consultants) that were responsible for the evaluation and reporting of the simulator test results.

The standard methods used in such an evaluation are similar to any other experimental exercise (Wilson and Corlett, 1995). The aim is to minimise the number of variables, minimise the bias caused by the participants and achieve the best internal and external validity of the results (Cook and Campbell, 1979). In order to collect objective performance data, detailed tasks are defined with different levels of difficulty and with defined goals for the pilot. The achieved performance is recorded and compared with a known reference or a set of requirements.

It is usually very difficult to evaluate such data since the level of activity required for achieving a goal might not correlate with the success of goal achievement. A very active and jerky pilot could get much better final achievement than one with smooth control activity yet inconsistent final results.

In order to cover such variations, the participating pilots are asked to give their subjective opinion after each task using questionnaires and rating scales. The purpose of rating scales such as the Modified Cooper Harper, Bedford or the NASA TLX scales is to combine perceived performance with the effort involved (Wilson and Corlett, 1995). Terms such as workload, situation awareness, and effort are addressed in these scales and a rating is set for each task. Test pilots are trained to use the scales correctly and it requires a certain discipline of both the pilot and the test manager. Despite training it is known that each pilot produces biases into the results. The results are therefore used mainly as a mean of comparing several design options tested in the same conditions. Rating scales also allow the test team to set pass or fail criteria. This helps when presenting different design solutions with the appropriate rating or 'grade' to project management.

The use of simulation for finding cliff effects in flight control interfaces

Most of the control systems were developed in a fixed based part-task simulator typical for flight controls development projects. The simulator allows for a very high fidelity simulation for the flight control systems. It consists of a visual system for task feedback with minimal time delays and the correct ergonomic design of the flight deck features relevant for the task. Motion is usually not used since it's added value is considered to be minor. Unlike training simulators, in a development simulator the operator has the ability to change many variables representing different parts of the flight controls separately (gains, delays, filters, scheduling and aerodynamic characteristics) and evaluate the effect. In addition, the simulator has advanced registration capabilities for debriefing and data analysis. In order to achieve the exact initial condition repetitively, special position reset functions are available that also improve productivity during the evaluation.

The aim of the simulator evaluation is to optimise the control gains and characteristics so that they will comply with all the requirements and subjectively be judged as satisfactory by the participating pilots. Unfortunately the fixed base simulator has been known to have inherent weaknesses when testing dynamic conditions with high pilot workload. The lack of aircraft physical dynamics feedback can give an incomplete result and might hide tendencies for Pilot Induced Oscillations (PIO). The Calspan Corporation in Buffalo N.Y has explored the PIO phenomena in theory and in experiments for many years and has developed methods to minimise the risk through the use of In-flight Simulation (Singer and Persson, 1996). According to Calspan, their experience, based on many successful and unsuccessful aircraft projects, dynamic tasks close to the ground or other aircraft must be simulated in an aircraft whose capabilities can be modified in flight. The In-flight Simulator is a standard aircraft modified to have high fidelity simulation capabilities of both flight controls and aircraft characteristics. The pilot flying the simulator should have the same control and aircraft feel as in the new design and can evaluate several variations of the same design in real flight conditions.

In the SAAB 2000 modification program called the Powered Elevator Control System (PECS), the Calspan Learjet 25 In-flight Simulator was used for several highly dynamic manoeuvres in order to validate the results from the fixed based simulator. Two problems were identified during the in-flight simulation.

The first problem was the large non-linearity of the command gains between pilot control input and the elevator movement. It was apparent that when controlling within an unsymmetrical gain (different gain on both sides of neutral) the pilot had difficulties in predicting aircraft response causing tendencies to over correct. Close to the ground, during the landing flare, this resulted in pilot PIO that tended to be divergent (pilot could not control the oscillation). A

Gideon Singer

modification of the command gains to a more linear nature improved the results to an acceptable level without affecting the total control authority. The second problem was an oscillation that developed when applying a high load factor during a turn (2g – considered high for a commercial aircraft). The oscillation was due to a pure time delay feature in the control loop when reading the normal acceleration term ('g'). The time delay was initially introduced to prevent elevator movement due to turbulence or touchdown acceleration. After shortening the time delays the oscillation tendency was gone.

The background and experience of a test pilot was in both cases necessary to achieve the evaluation results and contributed to the smooth introduction of the PECS fly-by-wire system into service without the need for further changes of critical parameters. The effective and timely use of ground and in-flight simulators resulted in a very successive project where flight test was needed only for final validation purposes.

Information overload: display philosophies and pilot interviews and an experimental method for improving design

One of the most complex and time-consuming processes when developing an advanced commercial aircraft is to define the system feedback logic and display interface. With the increased complexity of aircraft systems and the reduction of the number of crewmembers that operate the aircraft in service, flight deck design philosophy has to be re-evaluated.

In the past, each system had dedicated instruments and warning lights the crew was to monitor and understand. With the limited number of systems, each having only few parameters that could give a direct feedback to the pilot, workload during malfunction was reasonable and pilot options limited.

With the introduction of advanced flight deck aircraft using highly automated engines and flight control systems, the situation changed. The systems were integrated in such a way that one failure could cascade into a multiple failure of other systems. The result was an overload of warning information from audio and visual feedback to the crew at critical stages of the flight like in the Gottröra MD80 accident in Sweden 1991 (Mårtensson, 1995).

As a method of design, the manufacturer looks at the possible failure cases for each system, the expected effects, the way the crew is expected to react and the written requirements. In addition, test pilots are involved in the determination of the system interface (displays, audio sounds and tactile feedback). Since the matrix of all combinations is endless, safety analysis is made to isolate the most probable failures and the ones with the most severe effects.

The tendency in commercial aircraft industry today is to install systems that are already fully developed ('Off-the-Shelf') and adapt them to the new aircraft design. This reduces development cost, risk and process duration. Unfortunately incidents and accidents still happen where a failure combination results in an overload of information and lack of clear guidance for the crew to follow.

In order to get a better understanding of the way current alert systems function and interface with the pilots, some of todays alert system functions were studied and the philosophy behind their design was reviewed. This was done in the report *Warning Systems in Commercial Aircraft – an Analysis of Existing Systems* (Mårtensson and Singer, 1998)

The two largest manufacturers of modern commercial aircraft are Airbus and Boeing. We chose to study the latest design from each, B777 and A340. In addition the MD-80 design was chosen as an earlier design based on the classic DC-9. The SAAB 2000 design was chosen since it was well known to the team and considered one of the most modern aircraft of its kind.

The study showed that alert systems are designed to keep the pilot informed of aircraft and system status. It has been accepted during the years that in order to make the pilot-monitoring task easier, such a system should include the following features:

- Alerting In order to attract the pilot's attention to a deviation in aircraft or system performance an attention-getting signal is required. Lights or sounds at such a level that cannot be ignored even during the most demanding of tasks achieve this.

- Informing After the alert the pilot needs to know what the problem is. Coloured lamps, text or reference to colour coded indicators does this. The pilot can either make his/her own observations and deductions or read the detailed fault description in plain text.

- Guiding In some cases the pilots require assistance as to the best action recommended. This may be done by voice, graphics or text.

- Indicating In addition to the non-normal condition, such a system is integrated into an indication system that shows full or prioritised indications of the vital system parameters.

Today's alerting systems include both aircraft system monitoring, aircraft limitation monitoring and monitoring of safe clearance to traffic and terrain. The amount of information available has become too large for the crew to handle in high workload situations and prioritised presentation has been used in a varying degree.

In the specific research 20 pilots were interviewed regarding the warning system in the aircraft they were flying. The interviews were made with pilots flying aircraft with different technology, e.g. DC 9, F28, called 'Classic' by the pilots, MD 80 as the 'Hybrid' and Saab 2000, Airbus A320/340 and Boeing B767 and B777 as 'Glass Cockpit' aircraft.

The pilot interview results can be summarised in short that existing modern designs still have the potential to surprise the pilots in critical situations. According to the majority of the subjects information is difficult to understand or is causing overload in difficult situations when an immediate action is required.

The interviews showed some interesting results that can be summarised as follows:

- All pilots were pleased with the way the present warning systems handled single failures.
- For double failures most pilots stated that the warning system did not identify the primary fault and presented too many secondary faults.
- For multiple failures all pilots using electronic warning displays claimed that the system couldn't cope in a satisfactory manner.
- All pilots found the ALERT function of the warning systems necessary. Inhibit functions during critical flight phases were considered satisfactory.
- The REPORT function received different opinions from the pilots mainly depending on aircraft type. Most pilots stated that electronic displays present too much information and with no logical order.
- The pilots rejected the GUIDE function in case of malfunction. The diagnosis and corrective action was not to be automated according to the pilots.

As the final part of the project, some of the conclusions derived out of the pilot interviews were implemented in a simple simulation tool. This tool was to show a Proof of Concept for further research with improved display formats.

Based on the interview results above a hypothesis was made: *pilots in the multiple fault situations perform better when making their own decision based on all relevant system information displayed compared with when presented with system guidance.* This hypothesis was tested using an empirical method described in the paper *Warning Systems in Commercial Systems – Perceptual and Cognitive Problems* (Mårtensson and Singer, 1999).

The tool chosen for this simulation was a Virtual Prototyping tool developed by Virtual Prototypes Inc. This tool addresses three basic functions; rapid prototyping of operator interfaces, real time simulation and software generation for real systems. A virtual prototype is a functional equivalent of a control and display system. Implemented in real-time on a graphic workstation, it completely represents the target system in the man-machine interface.

The software tool for this Rapid Prototyping is called Visual Application Builder (VAPS) and is useful for the programming of interactive systems.

The VAPS software was applied on a Silicon-Graphics workstation in order to build a Rapid Prototyping tool for the SAAB 2000 EICAS displays. The application was developed by SAAB AB design office for future development of the aircraft and for other research projects. The full statistical analysis is published in the paper *Pilot performance during multiple failures: An empirical study of different warning systems* (Singer and Dekker, 2000).

Today's systems range from contributing almost nothing to doing almost everything in terms of failure management. In between, systems typically try to support the pilot by sorting through the multiple failures and prioritising them (which can reveal the nature of interdependencies, for example by recognising root causes), and by guiding the pilot on what to do next.

Training for complex systems

One way of improving the ability of pilots to cope with advanced warning systems is by training. It is definitely not the most efficient method, but in view of the long process of system design, this method is inevitable to address urgent safety issues.

In the article *Coping with Complex Alarms* (Gibson, et al, 1996) the authors discuss sophisticated alarm systems in aircraft. They have some recommendations for changing the training strategies. The foundation of advanced training is that crews need to know more than merely how to work the system in order to diagnose problems. They must have sufficient knowledge about the system functional levels down to the level where they can have an effect on the outcome. This will help their mental model and reduce the risk of commission errors.

The general goal of training is to improve response reliability and robustness of failure management and increase anticipation of alarm situations to the point of creating ideal alarmless environment. There seems to be a gap between designers and training pilots when it comes to the level of system understanding required. Addressing the training issues early in the design process and publishing a clear system philosophy to the users will help eliminate such gaps.

Conclusions

The two first two methods showed the utilising of flight test techniques in combination with other test vehicles. The first resulted in a late discovery of serious deficiencies, which were difficult to fix. The second showed a successful flight test method when used as a validation tool after a thorough simulation using high fidelity simulation tools.

The third and forth cases showed alternative methods for evaluating and setting design philosophy objectives. By interviewing the end user and validating the recommendations by simple simulation tools, early design inputs can eliminate weaknesses that would otherwise be discovered only later during flight test or in service.

Flight-testing versus other methods for improving flight deck design

When reviewing the methods for evaluating a flight deck design, it becomes clear that test pilots and test engineers have a critical role in the determination of the final design. They affect system interface, function and usability of each flight deck control and display formats and logic. It is therefore an important link in the determination of the aircraft future usability and total safety record throughout its life in service. The process of the design and evaluation of a flight deck must be done methodically, always returning to the requirements and the role of the system, avoiding the temptation of adding features just because they are available.

This role as a critical reviewer and evaluator allow the test pilot to improve upon the initial design and optimise the flight deck for the dynamic situation in which it will be used. The main value of a test team is to evaluate the flight deck as a user of the system in extreme conditions and at the limits of its operating envelope. Most of the test pilot's effort is put into using the system and abusing it until it fails or until it indicates to the pilot that an abnormality has been identified. Since systems today are highly integrated, this requires a very methodical approach in order to evaluate the flight deck system as a whole.

The question still asked is whether this is an efficient process and whether it can be applied in all parts of flight deck design evaluation. There might be better and more cost effective methods but how could their results be validated without increasing product risk and liability?

From the discussion it becomes clear that flight test remarks in many cases come too late for making an effective change. Using simulation at different levels of fidelity early on could probably result in better and less costly solutions. Flight test methods are needed even during simulation runs but should not be used as the main method for developing flight deck interface and system characteristics other than as validation methods of the developed design.

Objective criteria for measuring crew performance

The different test cases show that in the development of flight control systems, engine controls, evaluation of simulators and warning system logic a subjective pilot review is essential. Even in other projects such as initial ergonomic evaluation of controls and HUD development, subjective test pilot evaluation methods are required.

The structured method of HUD evaluation described in *Filling the Gaps in the Human Factors Certification Net* (Singer, 1999, pp. 87-107) shows the approach based on an objective criteria and a more representative population of users. Based on the predictable performance and good safety record of such systems it becomes clear that such a method should be used even when evaluating other complex systems. Areas such as warning systems, navigation systems and other integrated systems should be considered. By using an objective criterion in a structured experimental evaluation, the results can be generalised and predictions as to future system use made. In addition, a quantitative value of system misuse probabilities, crew errors and the effectiveness of system safety nets could be given and added to the general safety assessment analysis. In order for such a method to be effective, it must be structured to cover all the critical combinations and will still require expert inputs with the test pilot experience.

Lack of certification requirements

In order for new methods to be used by all, in a standardised way, a rule or advisory to a rule must be set by the certification authorities. Since such an effort will require additional investments in funds and resources, the manufacturers need an incentive. In order not to give the impression that this method will be just another difficulty in the path of new product, it is important to state that the focus will be on features with a high error probability or with such a error/failure effect that might result in hazardous or catastrophic outcome.

In a recent initiative of the FAA and JAA, a new Harmonisation Group has been formed with the mandate to recommend new design certification rules and advisories to improve the Human Factors issues that have been known to cause incidents and accidents. This *Human Factors Harmonisation Working Group* was formed in 1999 and is expected to deliver its recommendations by 2002. Being a member of the group I hope to be able to contribute with my experience to this process.

References

AIA/AECMA Project Report, (1998). *Propulsion System Malfunction plus Inappropriate Crew Response (PSM+ICR)*, volume 1.

Billings, C.E. (1997). *Aviation automation – the search for a human-centered approach*. Lawrence Erlbaum Associates, Publishers, Mahwah, New Jersey.

Boucek, G. (1996). *Crew Alerting – Then and Now.* Boeing internal document by the Senior Principle Scientist, Flight Deck Human Factors, Boeing, Seattle.

Cook, T.D. and Campbell, D.T. (1989). *Quasi-Experimentation.* Boston: Houghton Mifflin.

FAA (1995). *Advisory Circular 25-7-x, Flight Test Guide.* Washington, DC: Federal Aviation Administration.

FAA (1996). *Human Factors study team report on the interface between flight crews and modern flight deck systems.* Washington, D.C. FAA.

FAA (1997). *Advisory Circular 120-28D, Criteria for approval of CAT III weather minima takeoff, landing and rollout*, Draft 13, Washington, DC: Federal Aviation Administration.

FAA (1998). *Code of Federal Regulations (CFR 14), Parts 1-59 and 60-139, Draft 13*, Washington, DC: Federal Aviation Administration.

Gilson, R., Deaton, J. and Mouloua, M. (1996). Coping With Complex Alarms, *Ergonomics in Design*, (October).

Hicks, M. and Brito, G. (1998). *Civil aircraft warning, who calls the shots?* HCI International conference on HF in Aeronautics, Montreal.

Howard, R. (1997). Analysing pilot error. *Aerospace International, 24*, 28-30.

Mårtensson, L. (1995). The aircraft crash at Gottröra: Experience of cockpit crew. *International Journal of Aviation Psychology, 5*, 305-326.

Mårtensson, L. and Singer, G. (1998). *Warning Systems in Commercial Aircraft – an Analysis of Existing Systems.* Royal Inst of Technology, Dept of Industrial Economics and Management, TRITA-IEO-1998:01, ISSN 1100-7982, ISRN KTH/IEO/R-98-SE.

Mårtensson, L. and Singer, G, (1999). Warning Systems in Commercial Aircraft – Perceptual and Cognitive Problems. In, R. Jensen (Ed) *Proceedings of 10th International Symposium on Aviation Psychology*. Columbus, OH. Ohio State University Press.

Newman, T. (1997). Safety – The global challenge. CAA policy paper. *Proceedings of the Flight Safety Foundation's 9th annual European Aviation Safety Seminar*. Amsterdam.

Noyes, J., Starr, A. and Frankish, C. (1996). User involvement in the early stages of the development of aircraft warning systems. *Behaviour and Information Technology, 15*, 67-75.

Rogers, W. and Abbott, K. (1996). Presenting Information for Fault Management. *Journal of the Washington Academy of Science, 84*, 13-38.

Rogers, W., Schutte, P. and Latorella, K. (1996). *Fault Management in Aviation Systems*, (Draft, Chapter 14 pp. 281-317) NASA Langley Research Center, Virginia, USA.

Singer, G. (1992). The SAAB 2000 – Initial flight test status report. Proceedings of Society of Experimental Test Pilots (SETP) Conference. Beverly Hills, CA: September 1992.

Singer, G. (1999). Filling the Gaps in the Human Factors Certification Net. In, S. Dekker and E. Hollnagel (Eds) *Coping with Computers in the Cockpit*. Aldershot: Ashgate, pp. 87-107.

Singer, G. (2000). *Towards a Safer Cockpit – improving cockpit interface through flight test,* Licentiate Thesis 2000-8, Royal Institute of Technology, Sweden, ISSN 0280-4646.

Singer, G. and Dekker, S. (2000). Pilot performance during multiple failures: An empirical study of different warning systems. *Transportation Human Factors, 2*, 63-76.

Singer, G. and Persson, U., (1996). Fly-by-Wire for the SAAB 2000 – Concept, Development, and Testing. *Proceedings of 20th ICAS Congress*. Sorrento, Italy.

Wickens, C.D. (1992). *Engineering Psychology and Human Performance (2nd Edition)*. New York: Harper Collins Publishers.

Wilson, J. and Corlett, N. (Eds) (1995). *Evaluation of Human Work.* London: Taylor and Francis.

Woods, D. and Sarter, N. (1998). *Learning from Automation Surprises and Going Sour Accidents.* Institute for Ergonomics, Report ERGO-CSEL-98-02, prepared for NASA Ames, Calif, USA.

Woods, D.D. (1995). The alarm problem and directed attention in dynamic fault management. *Ergonomics, 38,* 2371-2393.

Acknowledgements

The photograph in figure 1 is reproduced courtesy of Saab Aircraft AB.

13 Assessing the human hazard

Hazel Courteney

Introduction

The Civil Aviation Authority (CAA), and parallel bodies overseas, exists to ensure that civil aviation maintains an acceptable level of safety. They do this by checking that all of the elements in the overall civil aviation system meet basic requirements, for example the standards to which pilots must be trained, aircraft are operated and air traffic managed. One important element that they assess is the design of new or modified aircraft types. This must meet the appropriate requirements (Joint Aviation Requirement [JAR] 25 for Large Aeroplanes) in order to gain the Type Certificate that will permit them to be operated by airlines in that country. JAR 25 is largely focussed on the *airworthiness* of the aeroplane, and contains requirements for strength, reliability and performance. It also contains some references to the way that the design accommodates the pilot, and requires that the projected pilot workload and skill levels are not excessive. Regulations concerning these 'Human Factors' issues tend to be rather general with little guiding detail about what is and is not to be considered acceptable. They were written at a time when aircraft systems were simpler and less sophisticated, integrated and automated. The certification team, specifically the test pilots, has to make a judgement and interpret the requirements for themselves and some improvement is needed to address modern aircraft flight deck design (FAA, 1996).

It has long been recognised that 'crew error' is a causal factor in three-quarters of all fatal aircraft accidents (e.g. CAP 681). It is also known that the design of a human machine interface (HMI) such as the flight deck can have a significant effect on the likelihood of the human user making an error, and the subsequent possibility of it being detected and rectified, effect. For these reasons the UK CAA and their equivalents in Europe and North America are investing considerable effort in improving the certification requirements for Human Factors aspects of flight deck design. This chapter will outline some of the central issues

301

in the debate, current activities and questions that remain to be solved. These will be the views of the author at one particular point in time and may not feature in the final outcome. However it is hoped that it will give readers a small insight into the workings of the regulatory world and a slightly different perspective on 'Human Factors' issues in design.

What are regulatory requirements like?

Minimum standards

The first thing that is important to know about regulatory requirements is that they are a minimum standard. That is something that many Human Factors specialists find perplexing. Most courses in engineering psychology, ergonomics and related disciplines teach students to compare one design solution with another, to determine which will facilitate the best human performance, such as least errors or fastest operation. This may be unwise because it is not necessarily the form in which industry design teams actually need the information Courteney (2000). Thus the institutions that confine themselves to this method could be held guilty of not doing the very thing that they are trying to persuade other design engineers to do – presenting information in a format that is appropriate to the users needs! However, whatever its usefulness to industry, it certainly is not suited to the minimum standards of regulatory requirements. That is not how the system works.

For a member of a certification team, the manufacturer will approach them with a proposed design. They will not ask whether the team members think that the design is ideal, or whether there is some better way to do it, but whether it meets the certification requirements as set down in the relevant JAR. It is no use to say to them, it would be better if the design were like this or like that. In fact, it would be very unwise for a team member to ever give such advice, and they are strongly discouraged from doing so. They cannot accept responsibility for a design feature – or how it may be combined with other features or used in the future. It is the manufacturer's choice. Therefore it is not enough to know that in general round knobs are better than square ones, that grey is better than blue or that textured switch-tops are better than smooth. We need to know that round ones are acceptable but square ones are not, that either blue or grey can be tolerated and that critical functions must have textured switch-tops but the non critical functions can have either textured or smooth. It is impossible to overstate the importance of this concept.

Different kinds of requirements

There are many different potential kinds of requirements (Courteney, 1997 which will not be described in detail here. They could be prescriptive ('warnings must be red'), process related (e.g. 'testing must be conducted at each

stage...'), quantify performance ('achieve 1000 simulated landings using...').
Singer (1999) gives criteria that rely on judgement ('displays must be clear and
unambiguous'), require that a certain function exist ('the means for the pilot
to...'), philosophical ('quantitative assessments of the probabilities of crew error
are not considered feasible...' JAR 25 – AMJ 25.1309), and so on. Any of those
could be in abstract or concrete form. For example, abstract prescription might
say 'no single error by the crew should result directly in a hazardous situation
without compelling feedback to the crew'. A 'concrete' process would not only
require that some process is used to test a function but would specify the tasks,
iterations and measurement instrument. Some requirements are very general and
are often referred to as 'grandfather' clauses ('the equipment must fulfil its
intended function'). This is like a safety net for features that are clearly
unacceptable but are not covered by a specific regulatory clause. Of course they
could apply to almost anything but can also be subject to debate and
interpretation. Each of these regulatory styles has its own particular strengths
and weaknesses and there is a strong case for using a mixture of approaches. In
addition to the requirements for the aircraft design there are also requirements
for the approval of the design organisation as a company. These too may be
used to improve the likelihood that the product will be sound – this will be
discussed later on. To supplement the words of these mandatory requirements
there is often additional regulatory material giving further guidance on
interpretation, means of compliance or 'best practice'.

The need for a policy on error

It is worthwhile spending a little time on the issue of error specifically as distinct
from issues such as performance scatter, general ease of use and ergonomics.
Probably the clearest omission from today's requirements is a clear policy on
how design vulnerability to user error should be viewed. There is regulatory
guidance (e.g. JAR 25: Lloyd and Tye, 1992) for ascertaining the required
reliability of technical systems based upon the consequences of failure. Each
component of a system is assigned a numerical probability of failure and the
probability computed of the system function failing. The more severe the
consequence of the failure, the more rare the failure must be. These system
safety criteria are well established. However, if the human 'part' instead of a
mechanical or electrical 'part' does one of the functions within the system, then
the risk arising from that action being done incorrectly is removed from the
calculation. That may seem strange considering that a 'system' consists of all
the component parts needed to fulfil the overall function (which therefore
implies the human is included) and this is the 'part' that it is known to be the
highest risk in aviation.

Occasionally engineers encounter situations where it is difficult to proceed without designating some kind of quantity to the human action being incorrect. Some will assign to it a probability of less than 10^{-9} and thus be able to dismiss it as 'negligible'. This kind of approach is equally difficult to defend. Whilst the problems in accurately assigning numerical probabilities to human error are discussed elsewhere (e.g. International Electronics Council – Dependability Management Part 3 Application Guide; ACSNI, 1991; Courteney, 1997) there are few if any estimates that place the probability so low as to be less than one in a billion. In fact, one reason for automating functions on aircraft – or any other safety critical technology – is to remove the risk of human error from the situation. This would suggest that it is already recognised that the likelihood of a human error is far higher than for a technical failure. Since the technical failures in question are typically assigned probabilities in the order of 10^{-3} or 10^{-5}, it makes little sense to then assume that a human failure would be much less frequent. Yet the risks from that technology failing are carefully assessed and the risks from human error rated much less likely ($p<10^{-9}$) or excluded.

It would be very easy to hold our hands up in horror and say that this is a clear omission by the regulators, but it is not so simple as that.

There are many good reasons why this has not yet been conquered. For one thing the responsibility for crew error is not entirely in the province of the aircraft manufacturer. The recruitment, licensing standards and ongoing crew training will be relevant; the operational pressures and distractions, the air traffic management, aerodrome design and navigation aids will all play a part. There is no established, accepted method by which the possibility of error should be incorporated into the assessment. There have been proponents of quantitative, probability based methods but most of those have reconsidered once they come to actually apply it to real certification issues. The probability data is notoriously unreliable. It is terribly difficult to define the nature of an error and the probability number can vary wildly depending on the exact design details tested and the circumstances of the data collection exercise (Courteney, 1997). This is further complicated by the fact that although accidents have been known to result from a single crew error, it is more usual to find a number of errors or combining circumstances (such as technical failures and poor weather) that combine to cause the disaster. Are all of these events independent, related, or some combination of the two? How should we incorporate the safety factor of monitoring and checks by the second crewmember? Do some errors resemble the 'common cause' or 'common mode' failures of the avionic environment? Finally, (and this is probably the central challenge for aviation psychology in this area) there is the question of what kind of errors a trained pilot should be expected to make. We know that even the most highly trained, skilled people spill their coffee, transpose digits and occasionally misread instruments or fail to hear warnings. We know however that they do not usually make arbitrary wild inputs to the flying controls for no reason, misjudge the steering so that they just roll off the runway, become suddenly baffled by the workings of the ailerons or forget where it is they are going. Indeed it would not be fair (or feasible) to insist that manufacturers designed aircraft such that they would still remain safe no matter what the crew might do. However we *are* now discussing the prospect that manufacturers should make aircraft safe if the crew actions are imperfect within the bounds of normal trained human performance – that is, including a certain amount of foreseeable error. The difficult question is what kinds of error should be classed as 'foreseeable' and how often should we assume they will happen? Should we accept 'extra training' as a proposed solution? What kinds of error can be successfully addressed by training? The examples above are simple and fall clearly into each side of the dichotomy, but when assessing real designs and complex functions the possibility of error becomes much more difficult to discriminate. Will the pilot ever fail to read altitude correctly in a complex format? What about if it is presented in an ergonomically ideal format – could there ever be an error? How often will it happen in each format? How big could the error potentially be? How likely is it that it will be noticed by the second crewmember, immediately, later, or too late!

At the present time 'foreseeable error' is regarded as 'slips and lapses' (as described in Reason, 1996) plus any cases where similar errors have been previously reported in service. We know that this is a conservative set, but await the time when the definition can be realistically developed. Of course, in many cases we know how to make the interface the best we can, or that it would be a 'good thing' to provide extra training, more feedback, bigger fonts. At this point it is worth returning to the point about 'minimum standards' that was made earlier. Certification requirements are not in the business of suggesting 'good things', but of accepting or rejecting a specific proposal. More feedback may be 'a good thing' but is it sufficiently critical to be enforced, make the aircraft late, uncompetitively expensive and, as a side effect of the additional information, the display more cluttered and thus potentially more error prone?

As a personal view, the use of probability numbers is best avoided where this can be achieved. Where the safety assessment system makes this impracticable, it may be plausible to use 'broad brush' statistics for a estimate that we can expect human performance to be 'no better than' a certain level. This is coarse but still an improvement on the current situation. Thus we may wish to say that if the safety assessment of the design must assume that the probability of the pilot making a 'slip' is less than 10^{-3}, then it is very optimistic. (Of course the probability of error may be far greater, but it still falls into the category labelled 'probable' by avionic engineers and as such demands a certain level of caution.) In these cases it either needs to be improved in terms of reduced criticality, or the Human-Machine Interface (HMI) aspects of that task need to receive particular attention to ensure the crew performance is supported as much as possible.

Box 1 – Human Error and Certification

Considerations of human error are inextricably linked to certification requirements for technical systems. How reliable should we require the EICAS to be in order to avoid presentation of false warnings? It is only one of many indicators, so there is redundancy of information. A manufacturer may argue that pilots are quite capable of checking their other instruments, all of which are perfectly legible. If the decision were made to insist upon a high level of required reliability for the EICAS such that the standard could not be achieved, should the considerable safety benefits of EICAS be removed from the flight deck to avoid the (very low) possibility of false warnings?

It would be useful to generate a method that will encourage systematic consideration of the potential risks arising from human error in a new system. In order to do that it seems sensible to begin with the methods that are already used in engineering safety assessment. These might be augmented to incorporate human error considerations or else 'mirrored' by similar techniques for addressing 'human error' in place of 'technical failure'. This would arguably have the best chance of fitting into the safety assessment process and also of acceptance by the engineering community.

Common methods in use include the Functional Hazard Assessment (FHA) where the top level hazard is systematically decomposed into possible contributors or routes by which this might occur. Using the basic layout of the FHA, it is immediately apparent that unsafe conditions associated with the human part of the system are not adequately addressed.

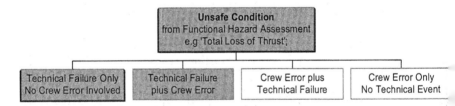

Figure 1   Possible routes to an unsafe condition

Figure 1 shows how some routes to an unsafe condition are already represented in the requirements (shaded areas) whilst others are not (un-shaded).

The following is a very crude example offered to illustrate the point for 'loss of thrust':

- A purely *technical failure* of both engines during flight. The existing requirements address these events in a systematic and comprehensive fashion.

- A *technical failure* + *crew error* in responding to it (on a two engine aircraft, one engine fails and the pilot closes down the wrong one). The requirements state that if pilot action is expected to contain the effects of the failure, then the design should 'minimise' the likelihood of error in that action. However, there is no guidance to ensure an acceptable degree of safety is achieved despite the residual level of error present in all human performance. Thus if a single 'slip' in the pilots intervention could be directly catastrophic, the design is permissible as long as the likelihood of that slip is minimised.

- A *crew error* + *a technical failure* in the aircraft protection system (human inappropriately places thrust reverser levers in 'deploy' position in flight, and then protection systems fails, and so does not prevent them deploying). Currently there is no consistent policy for reliability requirements on such protection systems as it is assumed that the crew will not make this error. This again is a questionable assumption given that the existence of a protection system inherently assumes the error *will* happen.

- A *crew error with no associated technical failure* (crew switching off both engines, or not carrying enough fuel) are not adequately addressed in JAR 25. If a single pilot action / error could directly hazard the aircraft there is no requirement for the system design to provide a secondary source of information or pause to challenge them with an *'are you sure?'* if they were to – for example – attempt to close off the last remaining source of propulsion.

- *Related and Independent combinations* are also not addressed. These would be identified by studying the 'latent consequences' through dormancy of an error (what other error or technical failure are now more likely or more serious? (Doherty, 1999).

There are two immediately obvious problems with this from the Human Factors point of view. First, the risk conditions considered are purely aircraft related (e.g. 'total loss of thrust'). Crew related conditions that are also unsafe (e.g. 'loss of position awareness') and in fact more frequently precipitate accidents. Such crew related situations could equally be decomposed into causal routes that are technical, human, or some combination of the two. In addition only the aircraft related proportion of the causes are systematically addressed. The requirements also ignore the safety risk from error in systems that are *not flight critical* (i.e., it is possible to fly without them), but may be *safety critical* if they are used in error. For example, the FMS is not flight critical because it is possible to fly without it *but* through human error in navigation inputs it could be on a direct 'fault tree' path to 'loss of position awareness'. There is an argument to prohibit information presented on the flight deck that is compelling and could precipitate an unsafe action – but is potentially less reliable than if it were crucial to technical airworthiness.

Fault trees use a similar logic and explore in more detail the various failures and combinations of failures that could potentially lead to the unsafe condition, and whether they are acceptably unlikely. These can be augmented to include additional 'human error' branches within a single analysis (Courteney, 2001). This would seem to be a good policy where it can be achieved for the practical reason that it is more likely to gain acceptance within the existing project infrastructure. Certification of avionic systems tends to use the numerical probability analyses as described in Singer (1999). Other engineering disciplines do not rely on numerical failure probabilities because they believe that the failure statistics are not sufficiently reliable, and so tend to use inductive, qualitative techniques to demonstrate safety such as the Failure Modes and Effects Criticality Analysis (FMECA). This is a tabular format that leads the user through a series of questions to consider 'what if' certain failures were to occur. These kind of techniques are more usual in the propulsion and structural areas of certification and may prove to be a good model for the Human Factors considerations to follow.

For this purpose a technique known as 'Human Hazard Analysis' (HHA) is under development (Courteney, 1999; Courteney, 2000; Courteney, 2001). It has been experimentally applied in various areas of research and it there are plans for validation trials on full aircraft systems under design in industry. This begins with the 'FHA' style breakdown in figure 1, proceeds to greater levels of detail with an augmented fault tree approach that should identify the important areas for further investigation using an FMEA style tabulation (Courteney, 2001).

Ultimately it may be found that the analysis of design for vulnerability to error during maintenance or production lends itself more readily to these techniques. That in itself would be a benefit. However, on the flight deck it may at least provide clear direction for the acceptability or otherwise of some design features, identify those functions that must be ergonomically optimised and those that can be the subject of some compromise, and in some cases indicate whether design change or training would be the appropriate solution. A side benefit – but not to be ignored – would be that the requirement to use such methods will prompt design engineers to include 'Human Factors' considerations in their everyday thinking. The HHA emphasises the need to:

1. *Identify the critical risk* areas where human error/human performance limitations can impact safety, and
2. *Evaluate the HMI* for that area to ensure error likelihood is minimised and detection/recovery maximised.
3. *Mitigation hierarchy* The most preferred solution should be to design out the risk (i.e. make the task less critical). The next most preferred should be

design to prevent/reduce impact of error. Where risks are high, a 'hard' fix should be preferred (i.e. prevention of the error). The next most preferred would be excellent ergonomic design and only at the last stage should training or procedural 'fixes' be considered.

The HHA is philosophically similar to the HAZOP technique that is popular in the petrochemical industries but is more adapted to the application. This tabular analysis begins by considering the task and systematically works through questions such as:

- What does the human operator have to do?
- Are there any vulnerable features of the design?
- What alternative/incorrect actions are plausible?
- What would the immediate/direct consequences of the error be?
- What are the indications/how would the error be detected?
- Could anything else produce the same indication?
- What opportunity would there be for reversal/correction?
- What could be the latent/indirect consequences through dormancy?
- Comments (e.g. what is known about similar risks in service?)
- Mitigation – is the risk acceptable given the ability to detect/reverse a potential error, and if not what mitigation is required (e.g. mitigation hierarchy)?

The effects of quite simple errors are not always supported by flight deck system design. For example, if there is no basic 'undo' function then a small error may be difficult or time consuming to reverse. Singer (1999) writes of this subject: 'Any user of a PC software expects an *UNDO* function in order to recall inputs, whether they are due to errors or slips. This function is not a standard feature in CDU software ... (it) may be lacking even in the flight critical parameters such as *Direct-To* and *Delete*. In some cases the selection of *Delete* to the wrong line select key cancels the whole flight plan without any *Review* or *UNDO* options'.

Other Human Factors aspects of the flight deck design

Vulnerability to error is not the only 'Human Factors' aspect of flight deck design that should receive attention. If an item of equipment is designed such that it is not easy to use, demands excessive 'head-down' attention and takes a long time to achieve a particular task, then it may not be vulnerable to error itself but may cause the pilot to make errors elsewhere. If it occupies too much mental and temporal space then it will create time pressure, distract the crew from general checks and awareness, or cause other tasks to be rushed and perhaps conducted without the necessary care and attention. This kind of issue is very difficult to detect from accident or incident data, because the guilty item per se is not necessarily 'involved' in the result. Such difficulty can arise in all sorts of ways, from inconsistent or deep menu structures to ambiguous presentation of information giving poor or unhelpful feedback. Or, it may be very complex and demand a level of comprehension that the standard training does not provide or sustain. The distribution of the task across time or between crew may be affected as technology changes. In integrated systems where multiple functions are accessed through a single device the ability to interrupt one task to activate another function and then return to the original task may be affected. The first task would perhaps have to be closed down, the second function located, opened and operated, then the users would have to withdraw from that function and re-establish themselves in their original task. This may also cause difficulties in cross crew monitoring. For example, in conventional systems it may have been clearly visible that the other crewmember was operating a mechanical switch in the overhead console. However, it could be more difficult to stay aware of data entry by small finger movements through integrated electronic media. Further, the use of menu systems for some functions and the requirement for others to be readily available for quick access may potentially cause functional groups to be split up between the two locations. Of course it is easy to point out that there are established ergonomic principles that could be applied here. The problem, as any design practitioner will tell you, is that the devil is often in the detail and sometimes there are conflicting principles and concerns about a single design feature, such that it can never be 'right' on all counts. If a warning siren is loud and continuous enough to ensure that it is not ignored will it then be so intrusive it interferes with the cognitive performance of the crew? If a function is made easy to access because it may be needed in an emergency will it then be *so* easy to access that it is operated inadvertently and actually creates an emergency instead? Suppose retrofit of new safety equipment is only possible in a less than optimal location such that in addition to the benefits, it may introduce some new risks. Should installation be prohibited and the crew subjected to the (much greater) risks of *not* having it? At present there are established procedures for considering the potential risks introduced by a new system. How to balance the any risks against the potential benefits is less clear.

The many faces of Aviation Human Factors

Direct Human Factors

The term 'Human Factors' is used to describe a range of very different subjects. Major areas of aviation (design, licensing, operations, maintenance) have very different ideas about what 'Human Factors' entails. Those concerned with the design of aircraft flight decks will assume it to mean ergonomics and related disciplines, error resistant features, anthropometry, colour coding and the need to design for realistic pilot performance levels. (This style of thinking is gradually spreading if those who design other parts of the aircraft in the 'design for maintenance' philosophies). However, pilots and others in the light operations area will assume Human Factors to mean Crew Resource Management (CRM). This is a subject in which all UK pilots receive mandatory training, to learn how to interact with the other crewmember and manage their working time to best effect. They may also consider it to apply to other parts of their training such as Line Oriented Flight Training (LOFT), or even the usability of checklists and manuals. If pressed they would probably also include the Flight Time Limitations (FTL) that are imposed to avoid undue fatigue, and pilot physiology issues such as hypoxia and disorientation. In contrast the Licensing area would think of the Human Performance and Limitations (HPandL) Examinations that all student pilots and more recently maintenance engineers have to take as part of their training. They might also mention considerations involved in pilots transfer between aircraft Types, medical and age limitations. In yet another area, maintenance practitioners might consider 'Human Factors' as the management of engineer errors in the hangar. They would probably think first of error reporting programs and tools such as the Maintenance Error Decision Aid (MEDA) that assists management in deciding upon the culpability – or otherwise – of individual engineers who make an error during maintenance work. They might talk about the use of duplicate inspections, the accessibility and quality of instructions available in the maintenance manuals and the likelihood of the data being correct; the long hours worked by maintenance engineers and their vulnerability to fatigue on the job; the conditions in hangars such as heating and lighting that make it conducive to effective working, and the necessity for good shift handover practices to avoid discontinuities in a long task procedure. So, it is clear in all it is a pretty risky thing to start a conversation about 'Human Factors' and it is to first determine the perspective of the person you are talking to first. However, until now it has been treated as if these are all almost the same thing and clearly that is not the case.

All of the examples of 'direct' Human Factors have one thing in common – they are issues arising from a single area of aviation interacting with the human element. Elsewhere (Courteney, 1999) I have discussed at length that the main risks to aviation safety come, not from any of the areas outlined above (although they are all important) but from the relationship between them.

'Meta' Human Factors

As we have said, 'Human Factors' is a term used for all of those issues that arise from the interaction between the human operator – such as pilots and engineers – and other elements of the system, such as flight deck design, training regimes or hangar lighting levels. Since there is little prospect of significantly changing the nature of the human being, then 'Human Factors' refers to the ways in which these other elements should be adjusted to ensure that their interaction with the human is successful. This is complicated by the fact that in aviation, the human interacts with not one element at a time but several. For example, the pilot interacts with the training regime, the duty roster, the flight deck design and the operations manual. These interactions are not independent; the extent to which the pilot will successfully interact with a complex flight deck design may be a direct result of the merit, depth and presentation of the training regime. The same could be said of the effect that the merits of the operations manual (for clarity) or the duty roster (for fatigue) will have upon them and their ability to safely use a highly demanding aircraft system. For the aviation system overall to exhibit 'good Human Factors', not only must each individual element of it be endowed with 'user friendly' characteristics, but it must be appropriately matched with other elements of the system as a whole. The training regime must provide instruction that is effectively structured *but must also be appropriate to the demands of the flight deck design.* The operations manual must be clear and readable *but must also contain procedures that are compatible with the design assumptions of the aircraft systems.* The flight deck systems must of course have 'good ergonomics' *but should also be compatible with the air traffic environment within which it will operate.* This can be extremely difficult to address during development because in addition to the awesome scale of the issue, the elements may be developed concurrently.

In previous work (Courteney, 1999) the author has presented research that recorded FMS operations in more than 2000 sectors of commercial passenger flights by UK operators. The results showed that whilst the issues predicted by the conventional 'Human Factors' wisdom were indeed present – inadequate feedback, not understanding the system behaviour, crew errors and so on – their incidence in real field operations was relatively low. They were far outnumbered by crew efforts to overcome the mismatch of the FMS system design with the air traffic management system, the need for pilots to 'workaround' the system design in order to achieve their goals, and reports of incorrect data in the system, specifically from the Navigation Database and also fuel calculations. This shows that whilst the design of an individual flight deck or piece of equipment is important, its compatibility with other systems outside the flight deck is also likely to affect pilot workload and ease of use. The interface between aircraft design and air traffic systems probably falls between areas of responsibility in all organisations connected with the overall aviation system and so the 'links' between them are not good.

The reason for these links being so important to the overall system 'Human Factors' is that where there is any mismatch between elements, it creates a new level of Human Factors issue that could be termed 'meta Human Factors'. It is a new level beyond the simple interaction between the human and single element of the system such as the flight deck. It is the strain created by the (imperfect) interaction of all aviation elements with each other through the mediation of the humans involved – notably pilots (Courteney, 1999). In any large and complex sociotechnical system (such as aviation) the human beings are the only system element that is sufficiently flexible and adaptable to compensate for gaps between other elements of the system. Unfortunately this flexibility is not limitless. If the gap is too wide it may stretch the human beyond their comfortable capacity and create performance failure. This may put us in mind of that famous catchphrase from the London Underground – *'Mind the Gap'* – because it is the gap between elements that causes the problem and we must watch out for it. Additional effort on the individual elements in isolation – even the 'Human Factors' aspects – will not entirely solve it. Hence 'Human Factors' as an issue may appear to be elusive, everywhere and nowhere, and that is why.

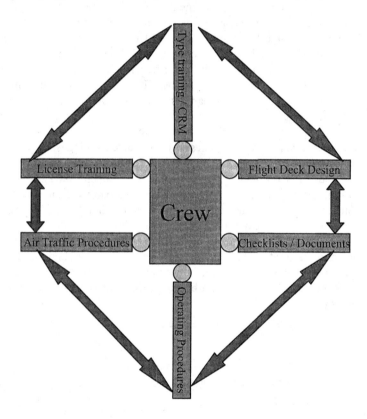

Figure 2   The relationship between conventional Human Factors and Meta Human Factors

---

Box 2 – Gap between flight deck design and crew training

Until fairly recently it was normal for civil aeroplanes to fly with three flight crew: two pilots [a captain and a first officer] and a flight engineer. The flight engineer has to know what the aircraft systems were doing and inform the pilots as necessary. To help fulfil these duties, part of the flight engineers training syllabus was the recognition of propulsion system malfunctions.

Later aircraft were designed with sufficient automation to be flown by two crew on the flight deck – both of them pilots. The flight test engineer was no longer required. The Design department within both the manufacturer and the regulator assessed the workload that would be placed upon the two flight crew and it was agreed that it was not excessive. However, those parts of the flight engineer task that would now be conducted by the pilots [e.g. recognition of propulsion system malfunction] were not transferred from the flight engineer licensing syllabus to the pilots' syllabus. It is easy to see how this could happen because the Design department has no jurisdiction over training. Recently a large international working party on Propulsion System Malfunction plus Inappropriate Crew Response was formed by the manufacturer organisations to address crew actions, the biggest single factor in propulsion system accidents. They highlighted [Propulsion Systems Working Group Report, 1998] this licensing issue and many others, such as the fact that most flight simulators represent engine failure so badly that it not only does not train crews correctly, but actually provides negative training, giving them false information and experience. However, despite the two years elapsed since the report, no action has been taken; the report is written by, and circulated to, persons working in the area of aircraft design, and those who can influence areas such as licensing and simulator approvals rarely receive it. Those who do, tend to disregard it because propulsion system malfunction is a design issue.

In figure 2 a schematic shows the existence or conventional areas of Human Factors and the 'meta' Human Factors that tend to be invisible in the system and consequently overlooked. The blocks are examples of different areas of the overall aviation system. The circles at the interface between each area and the pilot represent the conventional areas of Human Factors discussed above, such as ergonomics and CRM. The arrows represent the interfaces that are important in 'meta' Human Factors. They are not the interfaces between the conventional 'Human Factors' aspects of each area, but actually the interfaces between the areas themselves where a poor interface can cause a mismatch for which the flexible human pilot has to (try to) compensate. If the crew are not fully able to compensate then the result is likely to be a 'failure' apparently attributable to them – known in the accident reports as 'pilot error'. The interfaces shown in the schematic are arbitrary and could have been presented in any order. For example there are known mismatches in the interface between flight deck design and Air Traffic procedures (Courteney, 1999) or Licensing Syllabus (Propulsion Systems Working Group Report, 1998). The point is that it is the interface between the fundamental content of the elements themselves that potentially disrupts the 'meta' Human Factors.

A crucial feature of this phenomenon is that the way in which the industry (indeed any industry) does business can be shown to actively encourage gaps between these elements such that they literally '*dis*-integrate' within the system (Courteney, 1999). The boxed examples below illustrate how a disparity between different areas of aviation can create a mismatch that creates a strain on pilot performance.

Box 3 – Gap between design assumptions and procedures

During a study of the FMS in service (Courteney, 2001) some pilots had complained that the speed of a particular FMS processor was too slow. This made it difficult for crew to reprogram quickly at low level following, for example, a late runway change. The engineers at the FMS supplier company said that the specification that they had from the airframe manufacturer stated that the FMS would never be used below 10,000 feet. Since the competition is on cost, and the company must make a profit, the system suppliers did not spend the extra money getting the performance speed up to rates that would be needed for the 'below 10,000 feet' case. However, the idea that it should not be used below that height had not reached the pilots normal working procedures and caused a distraction at a critical flight phase.

Approval of design organisations

The organisations that design flight decks and associated equipment have themselves to undergo assessment for approval from the aviation authorities. These Design Organisation Approvals (DOA) ensure that the manufacturer companies comply with another set of Requirements contained in JAR 21. In the future, it may be that these too incorporate Human Factors concerns. There are at least two separate aspects to address. First, it may be that there should be some evaluation of their competence to incorporate 'good Human Factors' into their products. How do they liase with users, do they have facilities for iterative testing, time and money identified in their schedules for that purpose and people responsible for doing it? Do they systematically identify Human Factors risks for users and minimise their vulnerability? How do they make sure that the training is appropriate to the design? Do they validate maintenance procedures and data? Do they collect and learn from in-service feedback – not just incidents, but how their designs really perform in the field? The second perspective on DOA would be to evaluate how well the company protects itself from the effects of staff error and the frailties of human performance in its day to day business. If a design engineer were to make an error, how and when would it be detected? How do they ensure that management initiatives to improve on some selected performance measures (e.g. faster time to complete a task, more units produced) has not been achieved at the expense of product quality that is more difficult to measure but ultimately more important.

Box 4 – Gap between flight deck design and Air Traffic procedures

The following are example pilot quotes collected during the FMS study (Courteney, 1999)
- 'Lack of appreciation of relationship between [company briefing] profile and L*EGS* set up.'
- 'During set up, the scratch pad often gives prompts at the wrong time.'
- '... in busy ATC environments, especially in the USA, the anticipated arrival/descent routing is very often changed. This results in several reprogramming operations, often at a time of high crew workload which can distract from the main task of flying the aircraft safely'
- 'If a height restriction is programmed in for a descent and the aircraft is subsequently cleared to a more distant waypoint, even if abeam waypoint is selected, the height restriction falls out. This is incredibly irritating and very time consuming. It also destroys the VNAV profile as a whole load of power comes on as the aircraft thinks it is now low and by the time the restriction is re-programmed the VNAV profile is irrecoverable'.

At the time of writing ...

There is a great deal happening in the Aviation Authorities to address these issues. In the UK and France, Engineers and Test Pilots are taking training in Human Factors. The Joint Aviation Authorities (JAA) of Europe and FAA have established a joint Harmonisation Working Group (HWG) to investigate whether new design requirements on Human Factors are needed. For the first time ever there are positions for 'Human Factors' assistants on some Type Certification teams. These projects are already using some regulatory material generated through the JAA Human Factors Steering Group (HFStG) as a temporary measure that has now been incorporated into a formal JAA Interim Policy INT/POL/25/14. This requires that the novel features of flight deck design should have addressed the foreseeable performance of the crew and specifically the effects of error, ease of use, task distribution and adequacy of feedback. Most importantly, it requires the manufacturer to produce a plan showing how they are going to address those issues during development.

This is all good progress but it should not be assumed that the problems are therefore solved. In fact, it could be said that more and more issues are coming to light. However, the long standing division between Human Factors and the more traditional disciplines in aviation is being bridged and there is positive movement toward an integrated solution.

References

ACSNI (1991). *Human Reliability Assessment – a critical overview.* ACSNI Study Group on Human Factors. London: Health and Safety Commission.

Civil Aviation Authority (1998). *Global Fatal Accident Review 1980-96 (CAP 681).* London: UK CAA.

Courteney H.Y. (1997). The Silent Dictators. In, Proceedings of the Conference on Function Allocation. Galway: University of Galway.

Courteney, H.Y. (1999). Human Factors in Automation. In, S. Dekker and E. Hollnagel (Eds) Coping with Computers in the Cockpit. Aldershot: Ashgate.

Courteney H.Y. (2000). New Frontier Issues for Cognition Technology. *Cognition, Technology and Work, 2,*142-153.

Courteney, H.Y. (2001). Human Centred Design for Maintenance. In, Proceedings *of the Human Factors in Maintenance Conference.* CAA/FAA/ Transport Canada.

Doherty, S.M. (1999). *Development of a Human Hazard Analysis Method for Crossed Connection Incidents.* In, Proceedings of Symposium on Aircraft Maintenance. Bournemouth University 1999.

Federal Aviation Administration (1996). *Human Factors study team report on the interface between flight crews and modern flight deck systems.* Washington, D.C: FAA.

International Electrotechnical Commission (1991). *Dependability Management Part 3 Application Guide – Section 8 Human Reliability (56/455/CD).* Geneva: International Electrotechnical Commission.

Joint Aviation Authorities (2000). *Joint Airworthiness Requirements (Change 15): Part 25 – Large Aeroplanes.* Hoofdorp: Joint Aviation Authorities.

Joint Aviation Authorities (2000). *Joint Aviation Requirements (JAR) 25 Large Aeroplanes.* Hoofdorp, NL: Joint Aviation Authorities.

Lloyd, E., and Tye, W., (1992). *Systematic Safety.* London: Civil Aviation Authority.

Propulsion System Malfunctions plus Inappropriate Crew Response, Working Group Report (1998).

Reason, J. (1996). *Human Error.* Cambridge: Cambridge University Press.

Singer, G. (1999). Filling the Gaps in the Human Factors Certification Net. In, S. Dekker and E. Hollnagel (Eds.) *Coping with Computers in the Cockpit.* Aldershot: Ashgate.

Index

320

Printed in the United States
by Baker & Taylor Publisher Services